Anglicizing America

EARLY AMERICAN STUDIES

Series editors:
Daniel K. Richter, Kathleen M. Brown,
Max Cavitch, and David Waldstreicher

Exploring neglected aspects of our colonial, revolutionary, and early national
history and culture, Early American Studies reinterprets familiar themes and
events in fresh ways. Interdisciplinary in character, and with a special emphasis
on the period from about 1600 to 1850, the series is published in partnership
with the McNeil Center for Early American Studies.

ANGLICIZING AMERICA

Empire, Revolution, Republic

EDITED BY

Ignacio Gallup-Diaz, Andrew Shankman
and David J. Silverman

PENN

UNIVERSITY OF PENNSYLVANIA PRESS

PHILADELPHIA

Published by
University of Pennsylvania Press
Philadelphia, Pennsylvania 19104-4112
www.upenn.edu/pennpress

Printed in the United States of America
on acid-free paper
1 3 5 7 9 10 8 6 4 2

Library of Congress Cataloging-in-Publication Data

Anglicizing America : empire, revolution, republic / edited by Ignacio Gallup-Diaz,
Andrew Shankman, and David J. Silverman. — 1st ed.
    p. cm. — (Early American studies)
  Includes bibliographical references and index.
  ISBN 978-0-8122-4698-8 (alk. paper)
    1. United States—History—Colonial period, ca. 1600–1775.   2. United States—
History—Colonial period, ca. 1600–1775—Historiography.   3. United States—
History—Revolution, 1775–1783.   4. United States—History—Revolution, 1775–
1783—Historiography.   5. United States—Civilization—English influences.
6. United States—Civilization—To 1783.   7. United States—Civilization—1783–1865.
8. United States—Ethnic relations—History—17th century.   9. United States—Ethnic
relations—History—18th century.   10. United States—Relations—Great Britain—
History.   11. Great Britain—Relations—United States—History.   12. Racism—United
States—History.   13. Slavery—United States—History.   I. Gallup-Diaz, Ignacio,
1963–   II. Shankman, Andrew, 1970–   III. Silverman, David J., 1971–   Series: Early
American studies.
E188.A59   2015
973.2—dc23

                                                                      2014029115

CONTENTS

Introduction   1
Ignacio Gallup-Diaz, Andrew Shankman, and David J. Silverman

PART I. ANGLICIZATION

Chapter 1. England and Colonial America: A Novel Theory
of the American Revolution   9
John M. Murrin

Chapter 2. A Synthesis Useful and Compelling: Anglicization and
the Achievement of John M. Murrin   20
Andrew Shankman

PART II. EMPIRE

Chapter 3. "In Great Slavery and Bondage": White Labor and
the Development of Plantation Slavery in British America   59
Simon P. Newman

Chapter 4. Anglicizing the League: The Writing of Cadwallader
Colden's *History of the Five Indian Nations*   83
William Howard Carter

Chapter 5. A Medieval Response to a Wilderness Need:
Anglicizing Warfare in Colonial America   109
Geoffrey Plank

PART III. REVOLUTION

Chapter 6. Anglicanism, Dissent, and Toleration in Eighteenth-Century British Colonies   125
Nancy L. Rhoden

Chapter 7. Anglicization Against the Empire: Revolutionary Ideas and Identity in Townshend Crisis Massachusetts   153
Jeremy A. Stern

PART IV. REPUBLIC

Chapter 8. Racial Walls: Race and the Emergence of American White Nationalism   181
David J. Silverman

Chapter 9. De-Anglicization: The Jeffersonian Attack on an American Naval Establishment   205
Denver Brunsman

Chapter 10. Anglicization and the American Taxpayer, c. 1763–1815   226
Anthony M. Joseph

Conclusion. Anglicization Reconsidered   239
Ignacio Gallup-Diaz

Notes   249

List of Contributors   297

Index   299

Acknowledgments   311

Introduction

Ignacio Gallup-Diaz, Andrew Shankman, and David J. Silverman

Anglicizing America reevaluates the idea of Anglicization, a seminal theoretical model for the study of early American history. Anglicization explains the process through which the English colonies of the Americas emerged from their diverse beginnings to become increasingly more alike, expressing a shared Britishness in their political and judicial systems, material culture, economies, religious systems, and engagements with the empire. Anglicization hinges on two powerful ironies: first, that the thirteen mainland colonies had never been more British than they were on the eve of their War of Independence from Britain; and, second, that this shared Britishness, rather than a sense of American distinctiveness, enabled those colonies to make common cause in the Revolution and the creation of the early Republic.

This compelling, synthetic idea first appeared in the scholarship of John Murrin in the 1960s and has since inspired a host of the most important books in the early American field, including Richard Bushman's *King and People in Provincial Massachusetts*, Richard R. Johnson's *Adjustment to Empire*, T. H. Breen's *Marketplace of Revolution*, Frank Lambert's *Inventing the Great Awakening*, and Brendan McConville's *The King's Three Faces*. It has also drawn retorts from those who have argued that the colonies were becoming more particularly American on the eve of the Revolution, a claim recently articulated by Jon Butler in his *Becoming America*. Regardless of where one stands in the debate, any scholar interested in the early modern empire and the American Revolution must contend with the concept of Anglicization.

The early twenty-first century is an opportune time to revisit the idea of Anglicization. For the past thirty years, early American historians have been drifting away from the traditional centerpiece of the field—the thirteen mainland British colonies and their advance to revolution and nationhood—toward topics that their predecessors usually treated only tangentially. These themes include the British Caribbean, Native Americans, slavery, transatlantic migrations, and other European colonies. Recent scholarship sees colonial America not as the prologue to the United States but instead as a convergence and clash of many peoples and imperial powers across the hemisphere over the course of three centuries. New analytical frameworks have arisen in turn. One framework posits the existence of an early modern Atlantic world connecting the peoples of Western Europe, West Africa, the Caribbean, and the eastern coasts of North, Central, and South America. Another model calls for a continental history of North America centered on Indian country and contests between the various European powers for Indian alliances and resources. These approaches have immeasurably enriched the field by expanding its geographical and thematic range, but the multiplication of topics has led many scholars and students to wonder if Early America remains a coherent field of study.

This quandary is a primary reason for renewed discussion of the Anglicization concept. There is pent-up scholarly demand to restore attention to the American Revolution's origins, events, and outcomes, as evidenced by the McNeil Center for Early American Studies conference, "The American Revolution Reborn," held in spring 2013, which drew a larger audience of scholars and the general public than any other event of its kind in recent memory. Concerns over fragmentation in early American studies make this a ripe moment to explore the applicability of the concept of Anglicization to current scholarly interests such as the Atlantic world and American Indian history. Bringing the concept of Anglicization to these areas of scholarly inquiry invites many new questions.

To what degree did Anglicization shape Britain's Caribbean colonies, and how did that process influence the Caribbean colonies' response to the American Revolution? Did the French and Spanish colonies also become more like their parent societies over time, and does the answer help to explain their independence movements in the late eighteenth and early nineteenth centuries? How did American Indian engagement with the British Empire, British material goods, the British market, and British missionaries shape their contests with British colonists? Might one refer to some Indians as Anglicizing too? For excellent reasons, there is no turning back to a time when early American history focused squarely on Anglo-American people and the colonies that became the United States. This volume does not take such a reactionary position, nor does it contend that the process of Anglicization applies to the colonial histories of other imperial powers. Yet highlighting Anglicization will refocus scholarly attention on issues that promise to bring greater coherence to the field. These issues include how the British mainland and Caribbean colonies fit together within a single British imperial system; the extent to which Anglo-American colonists, Indians, and African slaves shared experiences amid their profound differences; and how the early republican United States managed to endure in the absence of a well-developed national identity and in the face of staggering social and political divisions.

Anglicizing America is divided into four parts designed to introduce readers to the theme of Anglicization and then explore its applicability to the colonial, revolutionary, and early U.S. national periods. Part I, "Anglicization," opens with a concise 1974 essay by John M. Murrin that defines the idea and shows how it can be used to explain the development of the British colonies, the coming of the American Revolution, and the consolidation of the early Republic around the federal Constitution. The subsequent essay by Andrew Shankman traces how Murrin developed the Anglicization concept over the course of forty years of scholarship in conversation with the emergent trends of the field. Shankman argues that Anglicization was a vital process intimately connected to the momentous changes that England (and then Britain) experienced between the Exclusion Crisis and the Hanoverian succession. The long process of establishing a Glorious Revolution settlement that addressed the religious, constitutional, and financial conflicts of the fractured English seventeenth century allowed eighteenth-century Britain to impose a new degree of imperial order that dramatically shaped its colonial possessions. England/Britain itself underwent Anglicization during the formative years of its "long eighteenth century," and its North American colonies, in diverse ways, followed suit.

Part II, "Empire," explores how Anglicization illuminates the histories of African slaves, Native Americans, and military affairs, which have been of peripheral interest to most subsequent Anglicization scholars, although not to Murrin. Simon P. Newman's essay situates the development of plantation slavery in both the Caribbean and the mainland colonies within English labor practices, suggesting that American slavery was not such a sharp break with English methods of labor coercion. In doing so, Newman shows how uncovering the transmission of English influence can stretch and, to some extent, redefine the idea of Anglicization. For Murrin, Anglicization was a process of the eighteenth century, and at its core it remains so in this volume. Yet Newman shows that being English mattered a great deal in the initial decades of the empire, well before the most intense period of Anglicization.

The English enslaved others in English ways, providing a way for what, at first glance, appears to have been a very un-English institution to play a central role as the slave societies of British North America began aggressively to imitate variants of English politics and culture during the eighteenth century.

William Howard Carter's essay discusses how English expectations shaped imperial relations with the Iroquois League. Carter considers the implications when a quintessential early modern state found its ability to influence a nonstate people to be quite limited. Geoffrey Plank's essay closes Part II by discussing how colonial British societies increasingly relied on Anglicizing ideas regarding military preparedness and action to deal with adversaries, especially Native peoples, who would not yield to British aspirations.

In Part III, "Revolution," Nancy L. Rhoden and Jeremy A. Stern examine Anglicization and the movement toward independence in the South and New England. Rhoden traces the conflicts between Anglicans and dissenting Protestants in Virginia and shows how Anglicization could function both as a unifier and as a divider within the empire. Stern provides a careful examination of the eight election sermons delivered in Massachusetts during the Townshend Acts crisis and explores how a thorough embrace of British ideals produced a revolutionary political culture and sensibility in conflict with the British state.

In Part IV, "Republic," David J. Silverman discusses how a shared commitment to white American racism was essential to the thirteen colonies' decision to revolt against Great Britain and band together to form a new nation, a development that he characterizes as a distinct Americanizing trend overlapping with and sometimes reinforcing the process of Anglicization. Essays by Denver Brunsman and Anthony M. Joseph explore the lingering effects of Anglicization in the early Republic. Anglicization merged with an intense postrevolutionary preoccupation with Britain. This preoccupation ranged from revulsion to qualified embrace as Britain began to stand as a bulwark against the violence of revolutionary France. The complex attitudes toward Britain, so stimulated by Anglicization and revolution, influenced central policy questions in the early Republic such as the proper way, if indeed there was one, to build a navy and how, whether, and when to tax the nation's citizens.

In the "Conclusion," Ignacio Gallup-Diaz follows the insight of the concept of Anglicization and contextualizes the various local events and phenomena addressed by the authors by placing them in conversation with larger structural frameworks. While it cannot provide a single explanatory path, model, or route, Anglicization does help us look at a hemisphere over a long span of time and understand and explain the complex processes at work—those that enhanced systemic coherence and those that drove the system to disorder and disintegration. Anglicization focuses on local communities while also exploring their embeddedness within larger structural systems. Gallup-Diaz examines one of Anglicization's core insights: that by the eighteenth century the British Atlantic world had become a complex multinodal network. In addition he underscores the connections between Anglicization and certain interpretive tendencies present in other scholarly disciplines.

Anglicizing America owes a special debt to John Murrin. The editors and authors, all students of Murrin, have long understood his seminal role in shaping the field of early American history. Murrin is both a brilliant historian and the consummate historians' historian. It is our hope that *Anglicizing America* will allow our friends, colleagues, and fellow laborers in the field to appreciate, as we have long done, the profound impact and achievement of our friend and mentor John M. Murrin.

PART I

——————

ANGLICIZATION

CHAPTER ONE

England and Colonial America:
A Novel Theory of the American Revolution

John M. Murrin

The American people, everyone now agrees, are a nation. But we are more than a little perplexed about how and when it happened. Although about 170,000 Englishmen crossed the Atlantic to the mainland colonies before 1700, nowhere did they create a society that can accurately be described as just "an English world in America." Traversing the ocean did generate startling changes almost immediately. But if the wilderness itself had been the major active agent in these transformations, we would expect all the intruders to have been affected in similar ways. They were not. A more significant force was the sheer absence of people which made replication of England's sophisticated social structure quite impossible. Drastic changes had to occur, but the settlers did have choices of what to transplant and what to leave behind. Because distinct bodies of colonists selected different options, they created equally distinct societies in their wilderness environment. Not one America but several appeared in the seventeenth century.

Chesapeake society rapidly organized itself around the production of tobacco for sale on the world market. It might be called an agrarian capitalist fragment of England that could in the permissive environment of the New World explore the logic of its own social imperatives with a freedom from restraint never found in the Old World. Its central difficulty remained the quest for an adequate labor force, a need that sustained an astonishing influx of white servants almost until the century's close. Almost 60 percent of all Englishmen who came to mainland North America before 1700 sailed to Virginia, and possibly over 70 percent went to one of the tobacco colonies. Yet as of 1700 Maryland, Virginia, and North Carolina could claim barely more residents than New England, which attracted roughly fifteen thousand people (9 percent of the total), nearly all of whom arrived before 1640. Women provided part of the difference, for only they can bear children. In addition, life expectancy fell in the tobacco colonies while it rose phenomenally in New England. Thus in terms of England's social spectrum, Puritans seem to have been badly underrepresented in the exodus itself, but by 1700 natural increase had inflated their relative importance in North America far beyond English norms.

As we now realize, Chesapeake society was frighteningly turbulent, racked at times by ugly tensions between large and small planters, masters and servants. The lack of women rendered most of the newcomers demographically useless and condemned most young males to sexual frustrations whose impacts we can barely attempt to imagine. In addition, positions of leadership fell to a small minority of free immigrants at the expense of natives and, of course, the swelling mass of white servants and ex-servants. Instability derived as well from acute poverty and a severe expression of English deference stimulated by the absence of family life. Without families, men do not easily acquire a stake in the future—their own or the community's—upon which deference ultimately rests. Englishmen had managed to create a society remarkably different from the one they left behind.

By contrast, in erecting their wilderness Zion, English Puritans created the most stable English-speaking polity of the century, but they also cut themselves off from the dynamic of change that eroded Puritan beliefs at home. One basic decision made in the 1630s would absorb most of the region's intellectual energies for the next century and also intensify New England's insularity. This was the determination to build a territorial church (embracing the entire populations) while confining full church membership to visible saints (those with "proof" of election). In other respects, Yankee stability rested upon a family pattern of settlement, ethnic homogeneity, the cohesive powers of village life, and the imperatives of common religious commitment. The wilderness never disproved the dreams of the Old World. Rather it offered the only environment in which they could actually be implemented with a minimum of outside interference. Their eventual failure owed much less to the frontier than inner contradictions present in the attempt itself.

Like New England, the middle colonies were settled largely in family units, but no colony from New York to Delaware ever attained the same

degree of cohesion. Religious and ethnic diversity diluted provincial loyalties and seriously weakened local institutions. It injected into political life a
persistent bitterness difficult to match in other mainland societies. In New
York, East Jersey, and Delaware, settlement patterns became hopelessly inter-
mixed through the Dutch conquest of New Sweden and the English conquest
of New Netherland. Instead of coherent fragment of an Old World society,
these colonies contained random chips from several European countries. The
middle colonies faced the unpromising task of trying to amalgamate antago-
nistic elements that, for the most part, showed no interest in amalgamation.

As the Glorious Revolution revealed, nothing resembling a coherent
American society had taken shape in the wilderness before 1690. The Crown,
not the settlers, tried to unite the colonies through the Dominion of New
England. Multiple Americas had appeared in the English New World, and the
passage of time threatened to drive them farther apart, not closer together, if
only by intensifying the initial transformations by which each had become
distinct. All had retained portions of their English heritage, but not the same
portions. New England greatly strengthened the village while weakening the
county and the gentry, and eliminating the vestry. Virginia expanded the role
of the gentry, county, and vestry while eliminating the village. Village, county,
and gentry were each severely weakened in Pennsylvania, while South Carolina all but eliminated every form of local government except the parish. Economic patterns were equally distinct, especially in the contrast between the
staple colonies and the more diversified societies to the north. In a word, the
colonies differed from one another about as drastically as they had deviated
from English norms.

Yet already the Virginia elite had begun to imitate the English gentry in
a way that sharpened loyalties to England despite the simultaneous intensi-
fication of the more basic differences that separated the two societies. New
England, by contrast, retained far more institutional structure of the Old
World, but Puritan convictions reinforced a painful sense of isolation and
separateness. Only on occasion did realization of what happened in other
colonies force upon a New Englander an awareness of how truly English he
had remained.

How then did the colonies ever begin to acquire a common identity? To
an overwhelming degree they developed similar features and beliefs, not by
copying one another (for apart from interactions within specific regions they
remained generally isolated from each other) but by imitating the mother
country. The colonies had to grow consciously more English before they

would ever recognize themselves as Americans. I call this process Anglicization, a word that carries some danger if used too loosely. That is, it can become a catch phrase through which things are joined together that ought to be kept analytically apart. Yet it does describe a process of real change that overtook all the colonies before the middle of the eighteenth century, even though it assumed quite distinct forms in different regions.

New England Anglicized at the core while remaining stubbornly unique (or "American" by seventeenth-century criteria) on the fringes. The staple colonies Anglicized on the fringes but retained their unique "American" core (quite different from New England's) whose formative influence continued to expand in major new directions. The middle colonies present special problems. Anglicization occurred there too and generally along New England lines. But it was much more likely to follow ethnic and class demarcations.

The real social revolution engulfing the staple colonies after 1680 was the rise of a slave economy which became well entrenched by 1720. It, along with a balancing of the sex ratio and the opening of a vast French market for tobacco, finally brought social stability to the Chesapeake. Indeed at some point in the eighteenth century, Virginia displaced Massachusetts and Connecticut as the most stable society in the empire. South Carolina followed a similar path about a generation after Virginia. At their deepest social and economic roots, in other words, the staple colonies continued to diverge from English norms. Britain had no counterpart to the slave plantation, a fact that suggests the disturbing possibility that slavery rather than democracy may have been the most truly "American" creation of the colonial period. At the very least, it was something Europeans adopted overseas, not at home. From this perspective, Virginia was simply following, rather belatedly, a social pattern that had taken hold in most earlier staple colonies—Mediterranean islands in the fourteenth century, Portugal's Atlantic islands in the fifteenth, Brazil in the late sixteenth, and the West Indies in the seventeenth.

By giving whites a new common interest against blacks, the growth of slavery muted class tensions that had frequently erupted in the seventeenth century. Simultaneously, the county court developed in the Chesapeake as a kind of participatory oligarchy. Great planters retained a tight monopoly on justiceships, but to lesser county offices they appointed a remarkably high percentage of the small planters, especially the voters, who thus became more deeply involved in local affairs.

In brief, both seventeenth-century New England and eighteenth-century Virginia achieved almost incredible stability, but their formulas were quite different. Where New England had combined family settlement, village cohesion, some vertical mobility, and ethnic homogeneity with intense religious conviction, Virginia finally did improve general life expectancy and spread family life downward through the social order, but blended both with the isolated plantation, a highly visible line separating great from small planters, an almost deliberate dilution of religious belief, and an ethnic diversity so extreme that it united one race against the other, through a master-slave relationship that kept blacks divided. Only in the eighteenth century did the Chesapeake elite tend strongly to become hereditary in particular families.

In the southern colonies, economic growth meant expansion rather than diversification. Institutional life did become more sophisticated, and, at a superficial level, it did seem to duplicate Old World patterns as merchants, lawyers, physicians, clergymen, and teachers began to appear. But their functions, even their existence, remained subordinate to the imperatives of a staple-crop economy. Just as planters imported finished goods from Britain in exchange for the crops they exported, so they imported professional services and personnel as well. South Carolina's entire bar was trained at the English Inns of Court. Virginia was just starting to shake off its dependence on the Inns as independence approached. Of over three hundred Anglican clergy in Virginia between 1723 and 1776, only seventy-three had been born in the colony and only forty-five had attended William and Mary. The same pattern probably held for dissenting clergy (even Baptists), physicians, and tutors.

No matter how sincerely it may have been experienced by particular individuals, planter imitation of England remained a surface phenomenon—fringe Anglicization. To alter the perspective slightly, the tobacco and rice provinces remained preeminently colonial societies, hopelessly and continuously dependent on the outside world for goods and services that Old World communities provided for themselves. From this perspective, if the American Revolution was indeed the first outburst of anticolonialism in the modern world, it was conspicuously premature south of Pennsylvania, which, however, may be what colonial revolutions are all about.

New England also retained a visible dependence on Britain, especially for manufactured goods and credit. But the area was what we today might call a *modernizing* rather than a colonial society. That is, it had begun to create within itself a capacity to meet its own diversified needs. The pressure of population upon land began to stimulate new extremes of wealth and poverty, pushing toward European standards without ever reaching them. Family structure and even sexual behavior began to approximate Old World norms.

New England built its own ships, its merchants traded increasingly on their own risk, and through its own colleges it met the local need for professional services.

But in terms of surface behavior—the kind of thing that might overwhelm a casual visitor—the region appeared to have changed much less than it really had. Ministers droned interminable jeremiads, the Puritan Sabbath inhibited amusement, election sermons remained important public occasions, and most settlers evidently still believed in the New England way, despite the nasty buffeting it took during the Great Awakening of the 1740s. Thus where Virginia's House of Burgesses and South Carolina's Commons House of Assembly minutely copied details of British parliamentary procedure, the Massachusetts General Court happily continued its bizarre customs which, among several oddities, gave personal seniority almost no weight in making committee assignments. Despite the persistence of such behavior, New Englanders did generally shed their extreme distrust of Great Britain, preferring to believe that the area was a kind of junior partner with Britain in a common enterprise. They often expressed this relationship in their own religious idiom including their millennial expectations which, incidentally, focused strongly on the empire, not on America.

Ethnic and religious pluralism somewhat altered this process in the middle colonies. Apart, perhaps, from the New York City Dutch, pressures for Anglicization tended to pit non-English ethnic groups against the Anglicizers. "[W]hy should the Palatine Boors be suffered to swarm into our Settlements, and by herding together establish their Language and Manners to the Exclusion of ours?" exclaimed Benjamin Franklin. "Why should Pennsylvania, founded by the English, become a Colony of Aliens, who will shortly be so numerous as to Germanize us instead of our Anglifying them?" Within the Quaker community, Philadelphia friends were more tempted by English ways than were country Quakers. In other words, Anglicizers were more likely to be a self-conscious minority throughout the middle colonies where weak educational institutions continued to reinforce dependence on the Old World until the 1750s. Similarly the churches of the region acquired self-sustaining powers only after mid-century. But as in New England, the economy was diversifying and modernizing.

These different varieties of Anglicization began to converge in the realm of politics, where they laid a basis for a common identity—first British, later American. After the upheavals of the seventeenth century, Britain discovered its own form of political stability by the 1720s, resting in essence upon

the court's ability to discipline factions through its control of a vast patronage network and its influence in elections. The same era saw the establishment, indeed the institutionalization, of a permanent minority opposition in
Parliament that appealed to the political nation in the language of "country
ideology." It affirmed the liberty, virtue, and independence of the Commons
against the encroachments and corruption of the court. Although the opposition could almost never deprive the ministry of its parliamentary majority,
its rhetoric did dominate the London press. From there it passed across the
ocean to the colonies.

Colonial practices increasingly imitated English ones as the settlers interpreted their own struggles in terms of a continuing tension between "court"
and "country"—governor versus assembly, or power versus liberty. But once
again, New England and the staple colonies borrowed somewhat different
elements of a common tradition. In New Hampshire, Massachusetts, and
New York, stable government came to depend upon a powerful executive
who used patronage to control the assembly. Those left out of the system,
nearly always a minority before 1760, fought back in the language of English
"country ideology." Northern colonies, in other words, tended to replicate
the totality of the English experience. But in Virginia and South Carolina,
governor and assembly learned to cooperate voluntarily as conflicting economic interests became absorbed in the increasingly homogeneous world
of the great planters. Each respected the other while retaining its traditional
powers and independence. Because the system approximated the ideals of
the English opposition, "country ideology" merged as a consensual position
in the colonies—a device not for opposing the governor but for idealizing the
status quo.

The colonists by 1760 inhabited a world that offered them three targets of
political loyalty: their province; the continent, or "America"; and the empire.
Province and empire outweighed America in every respect. Loyalty to either
mobilized a cluster of expectations about revered, traditional institutions—
expectations that had been sorting themselves out in the century or more
since the founding. As of 1760, colonists experienced two levels—and the
loyalties each evoked—as mutually reinforcing. Loyalty to province strengthened loyalty to empire, and vice versa. In other words, intense attachment to
place, to a particular colony, did not lead inevitably to American nationalism
and the Revolution, even though some scholars do make this assumption. In
fact, practically every settler who loved his province enough to write a history
about it in the years after 1750 emerged as a Loyalist, not a Patriot, in 1776.

Compared with loyalty to province or empire, a sense of an American identity was unfocused, vague, weak. American loyalties had nothing specific to attach themselves to, and certain intercolonial events did not significantly alter this situation before 1760. The Great Awakening did leap over colonial boundaries, but it made little impression south of Pennsylvania until the 1760s except in the Virginia backcountry. By the time it took hold in the staple colonies, it had largely burned itself out elsewhere. Yet the small wave of college founding that it stimulated did involve visible intercolonial—and imperial—efforts. More important were the French wars, which may have brought over ten thousand New England and New Jersey soldiers into New York, over a thousand Virginians into Pennsylvania, and hundreds of North Carolinians into Virginia. Military service must have broadened provincial attitudes, but it may at the same time have intensified some intercolonial tensions, especially in rent-riot areas of New York and in the upper Susquehanna Valley of Pennsylvania. The wars did create stronger bonds of mutual dependence among the merchant communities of Boston, Newport, New York, and Philadelphia. The cities were also beginning to develop a common style of radical politics, but this phenomenon apparently had no significant intercolonial component before the 1760s.

The very idea of an American as against a Massachusetts or Virginia loyalty occurred more readily to Englishmen than to the settlers themselves. From their distant perspective the British were, in part, merely homogenizing provincial differences that few of them understood. But the French wars, especially after 1755, did make them treat America as a unit of policy to an extent never attempted before. In the process Britain rekindled her sputtering fears that one day the colonies would unite against her, and to an extent difficult to measure, this concern influenced postwar policy. Although London's new measures always involved other and initially more powerful interests and motives, Britain did find herself trapped in a self-fulfilling prophecy. She accomplished what she most wanted to prevent. In this sense, America was originally Britain's idea. Only with great reluctance did the colonies finally accept it for themselves.

For our purposes, colonial resistance became revolution by 1775 because British policy had managed to polarize for most settlers what had once seemed harmonious: loyalty to province and loyalty to empire. Why this happened remains debatable; that it happened is not. Ideology, clearly an essential element to the story, is nevertheless an insufficient explanation. In the Stamp Act pamphlets, the dread of power became a central theme only after modes of redress were closed. Corruption remained a peripheral issue and was applied mostly to the stamp masters, not Crown and Parliament. In other words, colonial attitudes did harden into an unyielding country mentality in the decade after 1765, but this uniformity was as much a product of colonial resistance as its cause. Moreover, Loyalists viewed the world in much the same terms.

Hard interests were at stake as well as beliefs. Tobacco planters felt grossly exploited by the old colonial system and fiercely resented the suggestion that they had not carried a fair share of the imperial burden. On this question the magic of Americanization has mesmerized even the sophisticated disciples of the new economic history who have taken great pains to compute the "cost of empire" in per capita terms for all Americans in the 1760s. As their own statistics show, Americans did not pay for the system. Tobacco and rice planters did—perhaps 70 percent of the whole. Thus while the benefits of empire were spread fairly evenly, its burdens fell most heavily upon tobacco planters in particular, a group already worried about it precarious profit margin.

But the argument from economic interests also has its limits. It works best for the planters, who did use the Revolution to liquidate the mercantilist economics that they resented, but it does not easily account for the high incidence of loyalism among northern merchants. In fact, as Arthur Schlesinger Sr. pointed out long ago, independence implied a choice of disasters for most merchants—either way. If they sided with the British, they faced confiscation from the patriots. If they embraced the Revolution, they would very likely be plundered by the Royal Navy. In a world organized solely by merchants, the Revolution could never have happened.

This article offers no final answers to these difficulties, only a few suggestions relevant to the origins of American national identity. The prerevolutionary crisis was fundamentally one of integration or centralization. Issues became so inflamed not because Britain and the colonies had been drifting apart for a century or more but because economics, politics, ideology, and London's administrative machinery had been drawing the empire closer together at an accelerating pace throughout the century. The Currency Act was so troublesome, after all, because by 1760 the separate colonial economies had linked themselves much more tightly with Britain's. They were more vulnerable than ever before to such dislocations as the credit contractions of 1762 and 1772. Most important of all, perhaps, this process of integration had not occurred the way London thought it should. That is, it did not adhere very closely to the expected norms of colonial behavior that had crystallized around the Board of Trade in the 1690s and that received new emphasis in imperial administrative circles after 1748. Many difficulties of the 1760s arose from Britain's attempt to apply outdated solutions to problems that were themselves anachronistic.

Without quite realizing what it was doing, London applied to the colonies an intensity of pressure that the ministry would not have dared to impose at home against the will of the community. Colonial recognition of this discrepancy is, at bottom, what the settlers meant when they demanded the rights of Englishmen. The colonies did not rebel because they were inherently less stable than Britain. Some were. A few were not. New Hampshire, Virginia, and lowland South Carolina were considerably less turbulent than Britain by the 1760s, a decade of extremely fragile ministries for the home islands. One difference deserves more attention than it has received. British politicians instinctively appreciated the boundaries to their effective power at home, no matter how genuinely they reverenced parliamentary sovereignty. Their sense of restraint did not characterize imperial relations from the time that Charles Townshend took charge. Beginning in 1767 Parliament never relented in its determination to force or trick the colonies into acknowledging its sovereignty. As the colonists recognized that their interests might indefinitely be sacrificed to Britain's, they expressed their anxiety in strident political terms. For legally the colonists had no place to hide from an angry Parliament and no other way to justify their resistance. Royal government, which had shown definite signs of resurgence after the repeal of the Stamp Act, finally shattered in the wake of the Townshend crisis. Virginia's gentry, fantastically loyal from 1720 to 1763, became almost unanimously disloyal by 1775, especially when Governor Lord Dunmore tried to raise their slaves against them. Country ideology, a tool once used to bolster the empire, became instead a shovel for burying it. In the northern colonies it became for the first time a majority opposition creed. By 1774 no imperial institution still retained the unthinking trust of the settlers that had been universal before 1763.

The crisis of imperial integration inevitably spawned a crisis of identity, rendered more acute by Anglicization. As the colonies had closed the social distance between themselves and Britain, the remaining gap between them had seemed ever more painful, an awkward measure of their provinciality. And because the Stamp Act exploded at the height of this process, colonial spokesmen had responded by claiming to be more English, not more American. They demanded the full rights of Englishmen. These emotions grew ever more strained as the imperial crisis intensified. Britain's most trenchant argument throughout the period reminded the settlers that, in the last analysis, the rights of Englishmen had always been defined by Parliament and could not provide an exemption from its authority. Not surprisingly, as colonists began to chafe against the parent-child metaphor that had once seemed a natural description of the imperial bond, their own perception of the relationship also changed. The colonies had thought of themselves as rude and incomplete Britons. Now the gulf between them became a measure not of their provincialism but of Britain's corruption and their own virtue. Britain became a corrupt and degenerate version of what America could still avoid.

The focus of colonial loyalties finally shifted. Loyalty to province may well have remained a constant among Patriots and Loyalists. Tories were a sizable minority, perhaps 20 percent of the whole. Even those who chose exile, apart from a small core of British placemen, expected to return triumphantly to their native province one day. But for those who embraced the Revolution, which included an effective majority in all thirteen colonies, loyalty to the empire became increasingly irreconcilable with loyalty to Crown and Parliament. Somehow they would have to make do with America instead.

CHAPTER TWO

A Synthesis Useful and Compelling: Anglicization and the Achievement of John M. Murrin

Andrew Shankman

In his biography of Ezra Stiles, president of Yale College from 1778 to 1795, John Murrin's Ph.D. adviser Edmund S. Morgan wrote that "one often gets the impression . . . that he was a monstrous warehouse of knowledge, spreading his interests . . . widely . . . and dissipat[ing] so much energy in the sheer joy of learning that there was little left for . . . reshaping . . . into something larger for the world to read. Stiles, in short, was one of those scholars who never cease to gather materials for a book but cannot bring themselves to write it." Of course what Stiles should have done was write essays. John Murrin, who has avoided monographs, has written nearly sixty at last count. Like Stiles's, "his reputation for learning remain[s] enormous during his lifetime," though only Stiles can claim the status of having "a pitifully small number of publications."[1]

And what essays they are, scattered throughout book collections and journals ranging from the truly obscure to the internationally acclaimed. Murrin's tremendous output from staggering amounts of research provides a coherent synthesis of the dizzyingly complex world of colonial British North America. The essays also suggest the close connections between the colonial period and what we, as we specialize, too often view as the distinct and separate world produced by the American Revolution. The coherence depends on Murrin's central organizing insight: Anglicization; and the synthesis stems from what Murrin shows Anglicization can explain and what it cannot. This essay, then, draws on most of the essays published by John Murrin. It provides a definition of the concept Anglicization and explores how Anglicization illuminates broad developments and themes that span early American history from the seventeenth through the nineteenth centuries. In particular, the essay discusses how the thirteen colonies became more, not less, English over time; explores the imperial origins of American federalism; and shows how the idea of Anglicization can help us to synthesize many of the different historiographical approaches that have often been viewed as competing to explain the causes and impact of the American Revolution. The essay closes by pointing to how the lingering effects of Anglicization and resistance to it contributed to shaping the political culture of the early American Republic.

The Seventeenth-Century Era of Experimentation

Colonial British North America has long daunted graduate students and interested citizens alike: so many different societies, seemingly growing more distinct, not less, over time. One of the many virtues of Murrin's career is that his essays treating the period before the Revolution allow us to discuss colonial America as a whole, and to see these distinct societies experiencing similar patterns of change that connect them to the developments that shaped the early modern Anglophone world.

To bring intellectual order to the colonial period, Murrin began by explaining the English colonial seventeenth century as largely an age of utopian religious and social experimentation. All of the significant colonies of English North America, with the exception of Virginia, were founded or conquered between 1629 and 1681, and all of them were meant to show England how good and decent people ought to live. Each of these colonies, in their very different ways, ended up failing spectacularly, and nearly simultaneously, to establish their utopian and improved societies. Their failures at the end of the seventeenth century and the beginning of the eighteenth brought each of them into crisis and chaos. Though Virginia could never be mistaken for a utopian experiment, Murrin's synthetic description of the seventeenth-century colonies failing to sustain the social orders they sought to create, and almost destroying themselves, also fits Virginia well.

The New England colonies are the most obvious examples of the colonial enterprise for the sake of social experiment. Those who participated in the "Great Migration" were "by comparison with the colonizing patterns of the European empires, from Columbus through the 1630s . . . the strangest group that had ever crossed the ocean." They fit no preexisting pattern or reason to emigrate for "nearly everyone else came to America to produce or acquire material goods they could not obtain in Europe. A huge majority . . . were . . . unmarried young adult men." Yet John Winthrop and his followers "liquidated extraordinary amounts of property in England and then sailed to America as family units." Such an odd decision could be explained only by their utopian vision: "[t]he whole enterprise made no sense at all apart from the religious impulse that gave it purpose and coherence."[2]

The start of the "Great Migration" coincided with the onset of Charles I's personal rule, and as it ran its course during the 1630s, angrier Puritans arrived with ever more separatist and perfectionist inclinations. In the name of preserving the English Puritan ideals of a priesthood of all believers, this angry first generation flirted with making nonseparating Congregationalism a hereditary tribal cult, a development codified in the Cambridge Platform of 1648.[3] The migration was in part an effort to alter English Protestantism radically, to lecture and to lead by example. It is not surprising that a group so critical of the mainstream English Calvinist tradition came very close to introducing an "American" innovation that threatened to equate grace with heredity or, if not quite that, which assumed much from the status of one's parents. Though Massachusetts ended up doing neither, it came quite close.

Such an innovation could be called "American" because it arose in North America, not England. A simple yet effective definition of "American" could be "not English" or, more precisely, something that departs from, dissents from, rejects, or insists on improving whatever the dominant practices of the English mainstream happened to be at any particular time. The very existence of Massachusetts, and indeed the rest of New England, in the seventeenth century was "American" by this definition. "Only when sinners obtained more leverage in New England," Murrin has argued in an essay investigating legal practices, standards of punishment, and the use of trial by jury, "would traditional English procedures become viable."[4]

Puritan efforts to be "American" in the seventeenth century are the best known. But Murrin has described how the spectrum of seventeenth-century English colonial settlement yielded example after example of "American" experimentation. Colonizers introduced into America every variety of experience that was marginal in England due to having failed to find the adherents its proponents felt it deserved. The English colonies founded in the seventeenth century "witnessed a startling range of social and political experimentation, as various promoters and religious groups tried to achieve in America what they could not do in England."[5] The Puritans were consciously and actively not being mainstream English in America, but so in the seventeenth century was almost everybody else.

Traveling south from New England, the Restoration colonies New York, Pennsylvania, and Carolina fit well the pattern of colonial experimentation as a way to show England how to improve itself. Those seeking to govern the Restoration colonies all hoped to show Charles II how to improve a Restoration settlement that depended on shrewd personalities determined not to revive silenced but hardly settled questions. The Restoration committed to High Church Anglicanism without comprehension, minimal allowance of Protestant dissent, and divine-right political theory, while hoping that English monarchs would remain self-censoring and not act in ways that provoked the conflicts that had produced civil war.

New York was the Duke of York's answer to what he viewed as an imperfect Restoration settlement. It was a bold, unabashed declaration of absolutism, which the duke viewed as a bracing antidote to the more anemic version practiced by his brother.[6] For as long as he could, the future James II denied New York an assembly and a charter of liberties. He foreshadowed his practice as king of seeking to restore Catholicism to the English mainstream by putting Catholics in prominent positions in New York's military and government. His treatment of New York rendered concrete the more speculative and theoretical fears that produced the Popish Plot and the Exclusion Crisis. The values of James, Duke of York, were far from John Winthrop's. Yet both engaged in "American" enterprises as they articulated a serious critique of the English mainstream and used their American colonies to provide an example that they hoped would redirect that mainstream so that it flowed through them.

Pennsylvania was an effort to keep alive some version of the egalitarian possibilities of the English republican period. In England, at the time of Pennsylvania's founding, the proposition that "[a]ll oaths are unlawful and contrary to the word of God" had been declared by the leadership of Oxford University, speaking in ways calculated to please the king: "false, sedition, and impious; and . . . heretical and blasphemous, infamous to Christian religion, and destructive of all government in church and state." Refusing to take an oath or to doff one's hat were acts so terrifying that they could cause one nobleman to call for his troops rather than consider the possibility of allowing someone to keep his head covered.[7] William Penn, instead, thought greater egalitarianism had something to do with toleration, being kinder and gentler to one another, and living life more comfortably and equitably.

Here was another way to be "not English" and so yet another utopian, that is "American," social experiment.[8]

Carolina was still another example of social experimentation using ideas that were no longer respectable in England. Proponents of Carolina, such as Anthony Ashley Cooper (who became the first Earl of Shaftesbury) and his secretary John Locke, relied "on the very latest in English social thought" as they planned yet another project to show Restoration England what it ought to be doing.[9] Like Penn, they drew on pre-Restoration radical ideas, though theirs came from a different ideological place than the religious and social subversiveness of Quakerism. Locke did know Levelers, though the Carolina constitution was not influenced by that tradition. It was shaped by the values that would soon influence the Country Whig opposition and by Cooper's and Locke's reading of the Commonwealth political theorist James Harrington.[10]

Carolina was meant to show Charles that a true mixed and balanced constitution was possible. With a constitution written by Locke, a sensible distribution of land would create stable political and social relations that could sustain the authority of monarchy while mitigating the dangers to liberty and property posed by absolutism. The Carolina constitution called for placing land in the hands of ordinary subjects, thus providing them the material independence to prevent their oppression. It also preserved enough land and authority in the hands of a hierarchically arranged governing class to maintain deference and obedience. A proper melding of Harringtonian ideas with the sober stability of a virtuous aristocracy would mean "that the government of this province may be made most agreeable unto the monarchy under which we live, and of which this province is a part, and that we may avoid erecting a numerous democracy."[11]

New England, the Middle Atlantic, and the South each produced utopian social experiments built on ideas that were marginal in seventeenth-century England, and that had already been rejected and stigmatized by the time they became the basis for colonial enterprises. Interestingly, when they were tried even mainstream English institutions proved dysfunctional in seventeenth-century America. After 1624 Virginia had royal government: a governor and a council that functioned as an upper house appointed directly and indirectly by the king respectively; and a lower house elected by enfranchised subjects living in Virginia. Virginia's would eventually become the most common model for colonial government. In the seventeenth century, among a series of colonies that grew unstable and almost collapsed, Virginia was probably the most divided and socially untenable. Even mainstream English institutions, though they were rarely tried in the seventeenth-century colonies, did not fare well in America.[12]

The common denominator for all the multifarious "American" (that is, not mainstream English) social experimentation was that each social experiment experienced acute crisis in the final decades of the seventeenth century, or in the case of Carolina, in the early eighteenth. In every case the way toward greater stability and social, political, and cultural cohesiveness was to abandon social experimentation. These colonies left behind "not English," "American" ideals and moved much closer to an English/British mainstream emerging from the Glorious Revolution settlement. This development in each region of British North America was the process of Anglicization.

The years beginning in the 1670s in New England brought King Philip's War and subsequent intense conflict with native peoples, the anxiety that produced the Jeremiad sermon, and the outbreak of witchcraft accusations.[13] In New York conflicts between ducal absolutism and the more Whiggish sentiments of English colonists merged with Anglo-Dutch conflicts to produce the bitter and violent divisions of Leisler's Rebellion. Once the Duke of York as James II had his chance, he spread his social experiment far beyond New York by creating the Dominion of New England, a super-colony that combined much of the Middle Atlantic except Pennsylvania and all of New England under an absolutist model. Spreading absolutism proved no more popular in the Dominion than it had been in New York. Meanwhile, in Pennsylvania early Quaker dreams of harmony gave way to economic and social conflict and the religious animosity of the Keithian schism. In Carolina the intricate neo-Harringtonian constitution collapsed under its own weight, while white settlers' lust for profits from deer skins and for Indian slaves produced Anglo-Indian and inter-Indian conflicts that eventually provoked the Yamasee War, which almost engulfed the colony.[14]

The final quarter of the seventeenth century, then, was a period of acute crisis in almost every Anglophone colony, including royal Virginia with its violent Indian wars and destructive servant rebellions. But by descending into crisis, the colonies simply reinforced a general crisis in the English-speaking world that was just as prevalent in England. From the late 1670s rising tensions over the specter of a future James II (tensions given concreteness by his treatment of New York) produced the Popish Plot, the Whig Party and the Exclusion Crisis, the Rye House Plot with its attendant schemes to assassinate both Charles and James, and, soon after James's ascension, Monmouth's Rebellion. While the various social experiments in

colonial America were coming apart at the seams, the Restoration Settlement was as well.[15]

The Anglicizing Eighteenth Century

In Murrin's telling of these dramatic events (the most extensive discussion is
his survey in *Liberty, Equality, Power*) English colonial American and English
history cannot be understood apart from one another. All of these Anglophone societies experienced crisis nearly simultaneously. All grew ripe for
new ideas and new processes of organization at precisely the time when space
opened in England for Whig ideas of governance and political economy to
move from the margins and to make a new mainstream. Between the Exclusion Crisis and the Hanoverian succession and especially after the Glorious
Revolution, England itself became Anglicized: that is, the English laid the
foundation for limited, constitutional monarchy and the fiscal-military state
that would propel Britain to first-power status in the eighteenth century. An
Anglicized England—polite, commercial, prosperous, Protestant, self-confi-
dent to the point of smugness—could better enforce long-standing imperial
laws and regulations; it could do much more than imagine an empire and
hope for the best. From the early eighteenth century, Britain began to act
upon and demand more of its North American colonies. It did so as an Anglicized and increasingly unique society, one with a distinct form of monarchy
and a refined capacity to tax, borrow, spend, and project its will outward. It
mattered tremendously, therefore, that an Anglicizing metropole developed
the capacity to impose its values and demands at about the same time that the
various social experiments to which colonists had devoted themselves had all
been badly shaken or had collapsed. England (after 1707 Britain) developed a
body of new ideas and methods for organizing government and society that
proved quite successful. Those ideas arrived in the colonies at a time when
many colonists had little reason to be confident that their own colonial pasts
yielded models that could reliably guide them.

The years from the Hanoverian succession to the start of the French and
Indian War (a period heavily influenced by the ministry of Robert Walpole,
first minister from 1721 to 1742) constituted an era of profoundly transforma-
tive Anglicization in both Britain and its North American colonies.[16] Such
a claim seems absurd on its face: surely England, by definition, was and
always is Anglicized. Anglicization, though, was the cluster of social, cultural,

political, economic, and religious practices, ideas, and values that gave definition to eighteenth-century Britain and to Britons. Anglicization can be viewed as a shorthand term for the complex constellation of developments that allowed eighteenth-century Britain to resolve the central conflicts that had shaped the English seventeenth century. Fundamentally the Stuart age had struggled with how to structure Crown/Parliament relations and how to manage often bitter conflicts among the varieties of English Protestantism. These two sets of problems overlapped and reinforced each other and were also exacerbated by chronic royal fiscal crisis and by the multiple-kingdoms problem of governance.[17]

Yet decisively and especially after 1688, the English resolved these issues. They did so by relying on a Whig-Lockean political settlement of limited constitutional monarchy. This settlement allowed for an established church that could peacefully exist within a broad pan-Protestantism that focused on commonalities among Protestants while insisting on fundamental differences between the monarchies of Britain and France and between Protestantism and Catholicism.[18] In addition, unexpected developments resulting from the Glorious Revolution were just as crucial for resolving the problems of the seventeenth century. In 1689 the English clearly intended to create a limited constitutional monarchy based on the contract theory of government. They did not intend to produce a vast fiscal-military state. But the War of the League of Augsburg began a "long eighteenth century" of warfare. Over the next 126 years Britain was at war for almost half that period and never stopped, during the years of nominal peace, maintaining the debts and taxes that helped fund the fighting.[19] The government of limited constitutional monarchy, in which the House of Commons was as representative of Britain's property-owning taxpayers as any eighteenth-century institution could be, proved a highly effective taxing state. Growing and reliable tax revenue became the source for substantial public debt since reliable taxation made funding the debt certain. Funding the debt, since it necessitated annual taxation, required summoning Parliament every year, which further consolidated the transformation of Parliament from an event into a permanent, sovereign governing institution.[20]

Robert Walpole sat at the center of this nexus of postrevolutionary developments and perfected the methods for managing a growing state bureaucracy, a complex fiscal-military state, and an imperial society that was increasingly spreading its wealth and its will throughout the Atlantic world. Walpole's governance depended on mobilizing and shrewdly and strategically

distributing the wealth generated by a fiscal-military state at or always prepared to be at war. By distributing patronage, the stuff of the fiscal-military
state, throughout the Commons, Walpole added a practical and self-interested dimension to the support for an imperial state. Feathering one's nest
could fit neatly with devotion to the Glorious Revolution legacy of preserving
liberty, property, and Protestantism. In the middle decades of the eighteenth
century, Walpole's centralizing Court Whigs argued that the rising debt, the
growth of the state, and the expansion of taxes all served to strengthen the
state and society produced by the Glorious Revolution, all while enabling
Britons to protect their legacy from its nemesis: France. Liberty, property,
and Protestantism stood against tyranny, poverty, and popery as surely as
limited constitutional monarchy opposed absolutism.

Those critical of Walpole had to separate him and the Court Whigs from
their claim of ownership over the Revolution of 1688, and the critique that
emerged produced an inversion of ideological commitment that had tremendous influence throughout the eighteenth-century Anglophone world.[21]
Leading critics of Walpole such as the Tory Viscount Bolingbroke, after failing to prevent the Hanoverian succession, shifted their arguments to claim
that they, and not Walpole's Court Whigs, supported the true spirit and
intention of the Glorious Revolution. To make this claim, Walpole's critics
had to revive the Country language that was associated with the early Whigs
of the Exclusion Crisis and prior to that with the Commonwealth radicalism
of Harrington.

The eighteenth-century Country critics argued that Walpole and the
Court, through crafty use of patronage, slowly and stealthily seduced and
corrupted the House of Commons, which over time ceased to function as
an institution separate from the monarchy. By blurring the lines between
the court executive and the Commons legislature, Walpole and his epigones
undermined limited constitutional monarchy and the Glorious Revolution
legacy by once again allowing the monarchy to overawe and control Parliament. This new version of absolutism, charged Country critics, was even more
insidious than the earlier Stuart variety. It cynically preserved the appearance of liberty and property while gradually eroding the independence of
the House of Commons, the institution empowered by the Glorious Revolution to limit the monarchy and protect the liberties of the subject.[22] The solution was drastically to scale back the fiscal-military state and to restore the
landed, independent squires of England to their former prominence in the
Commons. Such gentlemen, in control of the resources that sustained their

estates, would virtuously eschew Walpole's patronage and maintain the Commons as an institution separate from the king's will, as the Glorious Revolution had intended. With this ideological inversion, former prominent Tories denounced a strong central government, using the language of the Country ideology to do so, while Walpolean Whigs defended the fiscal-military state and argued that commerce, finance, taxation, and a centralized powerful government were the best preservers of the Glorious Revolution legacy.

In Britain the Country critique had little influence. Britain by circa 1740 was the archetype of Anglicization—an increasingly self-satisfied society confident that it had a unique form of limited constitutional monarchy in which liberty, property, and all forms of Protestantism were protected. It was an increasingly complex and sophisticated society with a mixed economy of commerce, agriculture, and manufacturing shaped by monetized and often waged social relations and economic growth fueled by an active state servicing a rapidly growing public debt. This society also produced a robust public sphere capable of publicizing through print both extensive self-congratulation and genuine criticism of these mainstream developments.[23]

The spectrum of political thought, ranging from Walpolean Court Whiggery to Country critique, shaped the official political culture of the eighteenth-century colonies and particularly the relations between colonial and imperial political institutions. These ideas replaced the varieties of seventeenth-century "American" utopian experimentation. They also replaced the version of royal government present in seventeenth-century Virginia that had also been shaken by internal chaos and the overthrow of the Stuart monarchy As the British North American colonies became more willing to receive alternatives to the ideas that had shaped their respective pasts, they also came into closer and closer contact with an eighteenth-century Britain that was producing, and proving capable of disseminating, attractive ideas about how best to structure state and society.[24]

The principal colonies cohered around ideas that celebrated what they understood to be the legacy of the Revolution of 1688. Thus Anglicization shaped the eighteenth-century British North American colonies, but it did so in ways that reinforced a diverse spectrum of settlement. Going from north to south, Massachusetts and New Hampshire (the two royal colonies of New England) were the most Anglicized societies in the eighteenth century other than England itself and lowland Scotland. In 1691 William and Mary replaced the Dominion of New England not with the original 1629 Charter, as Massachusetts had hoped, but with a new one that required the colony to conform

to the Glorious Revolution settlement. The 1691 Charter, most critically, separated voting rights and office-holding from congregational church membership and connected them more conventionally to landownership. In addition
the Charter created a royal governor for Massachusetts, though it allowed the
legislature to choose the upper house rather than have the governor appoint
it, as was the case in all other royal colonies. In 1691 Massachusetts, still overwhelmingly Congregationalist, cried out for the 1629 Charter. Yet by the late
1760s one of the colony's chief criticisms of more authoritarian parliamentary
policies was that they violated the colony's charter, which the people of Massachusetts had come to cherish.

The changing attitude toward the 1691 Charter was one result of the process of Anglicization in Massachusetts. From 1691 through 1760 the colony's
population grew from under 50,000 to just over 220,000. As the colony grew,
it began to embody the 1691 Charter. While Congregationalists still predom-
inated, by the mid-eighteenth century virtually every variety of Protestant
could be found in Massachusetts, in part because there was no longer any
formal danger or penalty for living there. Within a generation or so, few
could remember a time when non-Congregationalist Protestants were prevented from voting or holding office. It had become a new normal to accept
all forms of Protestantism, just as in Britain.

In addition, as the British fiscal-military state became more capable of
mobilizing resources and administering war and empire, it began to draw
on the labor and materials of colonies such as Massachusetts. Eighteenth-
century colonists were much more familiar with imperial expectations than
seventeenth-century colonists had been. Wars for empire against France,
and often Spain as well, almost always involved Massachusetts in conflicts
with New France, and the British identity of liberty, property, and Protestantism made a good deal of sense and was quite appealing in the colony. Most
critically, as Murrin has shown brilliantly in a 1972 review essay, population
growth, the proliferation of towns, and the increasing incidence of commercial transactions and legal business that could no longer be confined within
the boundaries of one town led to the rising importance of government at the
county level. At the county level, significantly, judges and court officers such
as justices of the peace were royal appointees.[25]

The rising significance of county government meant that it became
important to have stature at the county level and to have connections to
decision-makers beyond one's locality. Murrin has charted a clear progression between success in business and the professions, local prominence, the

capacity to get elected to the legislature, and receiving an office by the royal governor's gift, such as appointment as a JP, that allowed one to participate in county-level decision-making. From 1710 to the early 1760s the number of legislators who were also JPs (who had, in other words, accepted patronage from the royal governor) rose until it peaked in 1763 at an astonishing 71 percent. Seven out of ten members of the people's legislature accepting patronage from the Crown's governing agent were figures that even Walpole could envy, which shows that Massachusetts had fully embraced the Walpolean politics of Court Whiggery.

Massachusetts had come to resemble Britain closely: a mixed economy of free and wage labor that emphasized the unending conflict between Protestantism and popery while deemphasizing intra-Protestant differences. Massachusetts had begun to replicate British politics and culture and could even produce its own lawyers trained in British common law. Indeed by 1760 there was one such lawyer for every four Congregationalist ministers, though as recently as the 1720s the older Congregationalist view that the law was an unsavory profession had still held sway.[26]

Massachusetts showed that a provincial society that began, albeit on a much smaller scale, to re-create the economic, social, and cultural practices of mainstream Anglicized eighteenth-century Britain was also likely to develop the pattern of political culture and the tactics of political management conceived by Walpole. The same result developed in New Hampshire. There the royal governors Benning Wentworth and John Wentworth managed to turn the British fiscal-military state and its navy's insatiable need for timber, especially white pines, into a source of patronage that assisted the growth of Walpolean political culture.[27] The White Pines Act, passed by Parliament in 1711 and then reenacted in 1722 and 1729, demonstrated both the ambitions and the real limitations of British imperial power and policy-making. The act obligated colonists to provide white pines to the navy before all other buyers, and this requirement was especially frustrating in New Hampshire, where the trees and their prospective buyers were plentiful. The frustrations surrounding the White Pines Act provided Murrin a way to discuss and assess the nature of the British Empire and the practical impact of Anglicization, for from this obscure act many lessons could be drawn.

Initially the act proved most unpopular and was impossible to enforce.[28] The failure of enforcement helps to illustrate the contours, features, and limits of British imperial power. By the mid-1720s Britain could essentially assume enforcement of the Navigation Acts due to its navy. Yet the realities of the eighteenth century, the vast distance from Britain, and the large and sparsely populated North American landmass (even with a rapidly growing population) meant that British power was largely limited to the oceans and the colonial coastline. The empire functioned best when it oversaw island colonies that primarily produced what they did not consume and consumed what they did not produce. No colony in British North America fit that description as well as the British West Indies did, and so they were never as easily governed as the West Indian colonies. Where British North America most closely approximated the conditions of the islands, along the coasts and when subjects entered or left the colonies on oceangoing ships, the empire governed effectively. The Navigation Acts, which were the chief instruments for governing behavior along the coasts and on the oceans, then, were both the highest policy priority and the most readily enforceable one. But the farther into the interior one traveled, the more anemic British power became.

The empire produced an organic and de facto "imperial federalism."[29] Britain could, for the most part, do what it needed on the oceans, where it had the power to enforce its claims to authority. In the interior Britain needed, to use Murrin's phrase, the voluntary cooperation of the colonies in order to carry out imperial objectives. To a degree unprecedented in the eighteenth century, the North American colonies were societies of property-owning independent households that were also isolated and distant from the governing institutions that claimed final authority over them. In the interior if people wanted to ignore British policies, they usually could.

The White Pines Act had to be enforced in the interior, in the dense southern New Hampshire forest. There those holding the title "surveyor of the king's woods" were supposed to mark desired pines to be set aside for the navy's use. Unless the colonists voluntarily cooperated, however, they could ignore the law with little reason to fear punishment. Yet between the 1720s and the 1760s imperial federalism and the need for voluntary cooperation were merged successfully by the complex process of Anglicization. The royal governors of New Hampshire, Benning and John Wentworth, folded the White Pines Act into their increasingly successful Walpolean Court Whig methods of governance. They quietly began to make the navy the top bidder for pines, causing the surveyors of the king's woods to become welcome sights to New Hampshire property owners. Indeed the surveyors became popular enough that the office became a desirable form of patronage that the Wentworths doled out to members of the New Hampshire legislature in exchange for their support and loyalty.

There was much more at work here than simple self-interest. By the 1720s a great many New England colonists had come to accept the mainstream imperial narrative that France was the tyrannical popish enemy of British liberty and that imperial institutions such as the navy were essential for protecting Protestantism, liberty, and property. The culture of Anglicization, in other words, was producing a deep reservoir of colonial goodwill. Thus it took just a bit of tweaking to make the White Pines Act work. By spending a comparatively small amount, the fiscal-military state could get compliance and voluntary cooperation thousands of miles away in the middle of a forest, and from people freer than just about anyone else in the eighteenth century.

Imperial federalism offered a lesson for those who could see it. Anglicizing, Anglophone societies were growing ever more complex and sophisticated during the eighteenth century. Increasing social and economic complexity meant a diversity of interests, needs, and viewpoints. Management of this complexity was easiest on the oceans and along the coastlines, where King-in-Parliament's claim to authority and its actual power were rather closely correlated. As one proceeded into the interior, a gulf widened between the claim to authority and actual power. This gulf could be bridged only by securing voluntary cooperation from societies of independent households that collectively possessed the capacity to determine what happened in the interior. Yet the development of Walpoleon-inspired political culture in Anglicizing Massachusetts and New Hampshire showed that Britain could also govern effectively inside the colonies. However, to do so, British imperial managers needed to use different methods and approaches than those they employed on the oceans.

Concepts such as imperial federalism and the need to secure voluntary cooperation in the interior were difficult to express, though various people did try to theorize an imperial constitutional framework.[30] Still, the reality was simple; Britain could do what it needed to, for the most part, on the oceans because it had both the power to do so and because its actions were part of a compelling narrative concerning British liberty, the Glorious Revolution settlement, and the threat posed by France. In addition the Navigation Acts were becoming the spine of a commercial, oceanic empire that generally met the needs of the various metropolitan and colonial interests that comprised it. Britain could also govern effectively inside the British North American colonies that naturally produced Walpolean political culture, but Walpolean tactics still had to be tempered with an approach to colonists that would elicit their voluntary cooperation.

In the spectrum of eighteenth-century settlement, New England was the most thoroughly Anglicized region since it developed by replicating the political, social, economic, and cultural practices of the eighteenth-century British mainstream. The Middle Atlantic also became quite Anglicized, but less so than New England. The Middle Atlantic was more ethnically and religiously diverse, and slavery was more prevalent there than in New England. In addition the two most prominent colonies, New York and Pennsylvania, did not achieve the degree of political stability and harmony between the colonial political elites and their British imperial governing agents that Massachusetts and New Hampshire did. Yet Anglicization is essential for understanding the Middle Atlantic. In New York the economy and culture produced an Anglicizing political and social elite that during the 1750s brought greater political stability to the colony. New Yorkers such as James DeLancey, who was perhaps the most well-connected colonist in the British Empire, were able to create a much more harmonious relationship between the colony's political elites and the royal governor and British imperial structure (it helped DeLancey that he became governor). Men such as DeLancey were able to foster political harmony in part because they made themselves into highly accomplished British gentlemen and empire men.[31] The decade before the Stamp Act crisis was the most politically peaceful in New York in a generation.

The sources of Pennsylvania's problems were complex. But contemporaries such as Benjamin Franklin and Joseph Galloway blamed them primarily on Pennsylvania's remaining a proprietary colony, outside the emerging British mainstream of "royalization" of colonial government and Walpolean political culture. Pennsylvania's Quaker political elites, led by non-Quakers such as Franklin and Galloway, believed the solution to their problems was a royal takeover, a much faster and more extensive Anglicization of political culture.[32] Like DeLancey's New York City, Philadelphia was becoming a vibrant imperial city with the cultural and social capital to produce men such as Franklin, who could realistically model their aspirations on a provincial version of British polite, commercial gentility.[33] On the whole, both New York and Pennsylvania in the eighteenth century were moving in the direction of the Anglicizing mainstream, a process desired and facilitated by the elites in both colonies.

Recalling the working definition of "American," that is, unlike things English, the southern colonies, especially South Carolina, were the most

American colonies in British North America. Slave labor was essential starting in Maryland in ways that it was not north of Delaware, and slavery became more critical the farther south along the spectrum of settlement one traveled.[34] Southern colonies were slave societies, not societies with slaves. Enslaved people of African descent or taken directly from Africa were sizable minorities in every southern colony except South Carolina, where they were the majority, and Georgia, which was recently settled and sparsely populated. Unlike Britain and the northern colonies, the southern colonies depended on staple monoculture, primarily tobacco or rice. They did not produce the mixed economies or concentrations of white populations that were increasingly features of life in Britain and the northern colonies (though Maryland was beginning to produce both by the 1760s).[35] In many critical ways, the South stayed "American" while the North became much more fully and fundamentally Anglicized.

Yet crucially, that observation is much truer when the eighteenth-century southern colonies are compared to the eighteenth-century northern colonies rather than to their own seventeenth-century pasts. In important ways, as Murrin has shown, the South produced its own unique version of Anglicization. The South, significantly, became the only Anglophone region where the Country ideology became the dominant political idiom. If ever there were societies where that body of ideas, marginal just about everywhere else in the Anglophone world, could become central, they were Virginia and South Carolina. The elites of those colonies could see themselves as the independent squires Bolingbroke placed at the center of his vision. The central economic and social relationships in those colonies were organized around unfree labor and plantations that functioned as nearly self-contained productive enterprises, which saw the market sail up rivers to their private docks. These societies did not produce the commercially interactive, pluralistic, competitive connections that were such a fertile ground to grow the institutions, places, and patronage necessary for the development of Walpolean political culture.[36]

Though southern colonies did not develop those conditions, they did produce powerful, wealthy planters steeped in the Country opposition literature and committed to self-fashioning as English country gentlemen. Thus southern royal governors could never hope to use the methods of Benning Wentworth. Seemingly, then, the southern colonies best fit Bernard Bailyn's argument regarding the origins of American politics. Bailyn argued that the incendiary Country ideology was ubiquitous in the American colonies. Yet it combined with royal executives who had far more power on paper than the British monarchy but in reality far fewer sources of patronage. The disparity between perceived and actual power produced a structure of politics in which highly suspect and feared executives were also uniquely weak and vulnerable. The result, Bailyn concluded, was a brittle and combustible political culture that was chronically volatile and always on the verge of collapse.[37]

As Murrin has argued, that synthesis did not fit New England, where there were ample sources of patronage and where relations between legislatures and royal governors grew much more harmonious between 1715 and 1763. In those colonies Country ideology, while present, functioned as it did in Britain, as a marginal language taken seriously only by a minority that was on the political outs. Bailyn's synthesis did not work so well for the Middle Atlantic either, where Pennsylvanians longed for a royal executive and where New York was forging better relations with its royal governors after 1753 than it had had in the previous twenty-five years.[38]

It would seem that the South best fit Bailyn's argument. And yet Murrin's discussion of the South's peculiar Anglicization has shown that Bailyn's synthesis did not really explain southern colonial politics either. The South Carolina planter political elites developed harmonious relations with the colony's royal governors. Virginia produced the most harmonious political relationship between legislature and executive in the Anglophone world. In the politically stable southern colonies proud, consciously English country gentlemen increasingly functioned as an oligarchy owning most of the land and slaves and monopolizing political office. They demanded that they be treated like the virtuous, substantial, consequential country gentlemen they were certain they were. Royal governors learned to take them at their word, and to eschew the Walpolean tactics in favor of a political culture of mutual respect and flattery. Colonial legislatures grew in power and influence during the eighteenth century. Yet in the largest and wealthiest southern colonies, royal governors began to secure the legislators' voluntary cooperation. "Where the system did take hold," Murrin explains, "the politics of harmony involved government by persuasion, not through place and patronage, and it worked. Its spokesmen believed that their colonies really had achieved the ideas enunciated by the English opposition writers, that their constitutions were stable, and that their political practices were fully compatible with loyalty to the crown and empire. Indeed, one might carry this argument another step. Contrary to Bailyn's expectations, Walpolean tactics were actually dysfunctional in this environment."[39]

The southern colonies produced the most "American" economies and societies in British North America. But their development from the seventeenth century to the eighteenth century was clearly moving in an Anglicizing direction. The oligarchs of Virginia and South Carolina took their social and political cues from English writers and structured their lives and attitudes around the ideal of the English country gentleman and squire. The emergence of Country ideology as the dominant political idiom did not lead to Bailyn's brittle, combustible politics but rather, in the largest southern colonies, to a functioning and harmonious system predicated on voluntary cooperation. The beliefs that produced voluntary consent were strengthened every time planters found their self-images reinforced by imperial statesmen and functionaries, which further legitimated the general narrative Britons told themselves about their empire: that it was an essential protector and guarantor of liberty, property, and Protestantism in a world where the empire faced implacable enemies.

Taking so seriously a language that was marginal in eighteenth-century Britain bore only a superficial similarity to the earlier age of utopian experiment. The politics of Country harmony celebrated mainstream British institutions—King-in-Parliament and the Anglican Church—and fully embraced the Glorious Revolution and the Hanoverian succession. Southern elites did not think Britain needed to be radically altered; instead they felt that the nearly perfect achievement of 1688 simply had to be preserved. The political culture of Virginia and South Carolina suggested to their planter oligarchies that the very best political values were respected within the British Empire.[40]

Anglicization, then, produced greater political harmony among colonial elites and royal governors and other imperial officials in all of the principal royal colonies, and a longing for royalization in Pennsylvania. But it is crucial to see that Anglicization also meant creating something of the complex economic and social relations found in Britain. The eighteenth-century colonies experienced a rising concentration of wealth, inequality, conflict, and often social division. To a great extent colonial elites could find greater harmony with imperial officials because they were beginning to forge a transatlantic governing and ruling class that monopolized political office and was clearly wealthier than their fellow British colonials.[41]

The concentration of wealth and power, encouraged by the complex coterie of processes that was Anglicization, was obvious in every colonial region by the mid-eighteenth century. If compared directly to that in Britain, Anglicization in colonial America was far less extensive. The colonies were, in Gordon S. Wood's phrase, "truncated societies" producing within their white populations a more compressed social order.[42] But when compared to their own colonial pasts, the trend toward greater concentration of wealth and power within societies shaped by British identities and values was striking and obvious. In the mid-eighteenth century the wealthiest 5 percent in England controlled over 70 percent of the land, while in the colonies the top 5 percent controlled 30 percent. Yet this concentration was relatively recent and growing. As a result, in Virginia "few could doubt that those who governed . . . had become an easily recognizable group of planter dynasties." In Massachusetts those holding provincial office were becoming an ever more closed circle and "[t]he new secular elite had grown accustomed to exercising considerable power," with an ever closer relationship to the royal governor. Even in the more turbulent Middle Atlantic, colonial elites were beginning to dominate the polity and economy. "[N]o colony had an upper class as secure as Britain's, but in every detail the men of power by 1760 had more convincing credentials for becoming a traditional ruling class than had been true in 1690. Wealth, power, and status were converging in ways that might eventually have created one or more ruling classes in North America."[43]

This development produced some of the greatest landed fortunes and incidences of inequality found in the eighteenth century. Indeed in certain places in British North America concentration of wealth and power amounted to a veritable "feudal revival."[44] Many colonies, particularly New York, Pennsylvania, Maryland, Virginia, and North Carolina, had long-standing seventeenth-century land patents granting vast acreage to privileged families. In the "American" seventeenth century these patents had been largely irrelevant. "Feudal projects collapsed in the seventeenth century," Murrin has argued in an essay coauthored with Rowland Berthoff, "not because America was too progressive to endure them, but because it was too primitive to sustain them."[45] At its most "American," the thinly populated English colonies produced few tenants. English colonial society was too simple and too undifferentiated to sustain the complex social arrangements and relationships of manors, a rentier class, and stable, hierarchical, and reciprocating obligations. But after circa 1730 each colonial region was moving toward producing just such societies. Growing demographic pressure due to rising population, increasingly social complexity, and concentration of wealth led to rising incidences of tenancy, which made the old feudal patents immensely valuable.

In the early 1720s Lord Fairfax netted about one hundred pounds per annum from his colonial land patents in Virginia; in 1768 he received four thousand pounds in quitrents in addition to other manor rents. By 1745 the Earl of Granville owned over half of North Carolina and about two-thirds of the colony's population lived on his lands. The great manor lords of the Hudson River Valley were not quite as spectacular, but estates such as Livingston Manor, Courtland, and Rensselaerswyck brought their owners between one thousand and two thousand pounds per annum in rents. All in all, "exploitation of legal privilege became the greatest source of personal wealth in the colonies in the generation before independence. By the 1760s the largest proprietors—and no one else in all of English America—were receiving colonial revenues comparable to the incomes of the greatest English noblemen and larger than those of the richest London merchants." The Anglican Thomas Penn, Pennsylvania's proprietor and the descendant of William Penn, owned land in Pennsylvania that "was rapidly becoming the most valuable single holding in the western world."[46]

Not surprisingly, some of the most acute examples of internal conflict in colonial British North America prior to the Revolution—the Hudson Valley tenant riots, the political turmoil in Pennsylvania (which was connected to the march of the Paxton Boys), and the North Carolina Regulator movement—all overlapped with the feudal revival.[47] Anglicization meant a growing, shared sense of mission, an elite "clubbyness," at the top of increasingly divided societies—though of course nothing was more English than that.[48] The social order that in many places produced a "feudal revival," while truncated when compared to that in Britain, was becoming more complex, divided, and characterized by social conflict. The argument for a "feudal revival," then, fits well with the descriptions of eighteenth-century British North America provided by new-left inspired social history and the scholarship that follows in that tradition.[49]

Anglicization both produced and was intensified by growing inequality and social conflict. Anglicization also encouraged colonial elites, who increasingly were members of a transatlantic class of imperial officeholders and functionaries, to embrace a pan-British identity whose values were shaped by a shared narrative of Britain and the empire that celebrated liberty, property, Protestantism, King-in-Parliament, and the claim of a unique, superior post-1688 British constitution. That narrative was also attractive to many other colonial property owners and their families below the elite level. Thus Murrin's Anglicization thesis produces an arresting conclusion, one always fascinating to students. Between 1700 and 1760 the colonies became more British than they had been before, and

[b]y almost any measurable standard we try to impose, imperial rule was more effective at mid century than ever before. Compliance with the basic navigation acts had been minimal in the seventeenth century, but by the eighteenth century colonial trade sailed on British vessels, colonial staples went to England and Scotland and most European and Asian imports reached America through England. Similarly, if one cared to trace the pattern of inter-colonial cooperation in each war from the Anglo-Dutch conflict of 1652 to the fall of Canada in 1760, the pattern would undoubtedly show a marked increase over time in colonial response to imperial war needs, culminating in mass mobilization in most colonies by the 1750s. Finally, a comparable catalog of strong or successful royal governors, colony by colony, would find them concentrated quite disproportionately in this period.[50]

When compared to the seventeenth century, the eighteenth century was a period of imperial integration, an epoch in which the colonies looked to British cultural examples, sought to replicate British political forms, became increasingly enmeshed in an Atlantic world economy managed by the empire and protected by its navy, and developed a reverence for, and sacrificed much on behalf of, King-in-Parliament. As Murrin has suggested, this multifaceted process of Anglicization was clearest during wartime. Indeed the cooperative achievements of the colonies (especially Massachusetts) and Britain during the French and Indian War was the zenith of imperial accomplishment.[51]

Acute tensions characterized the war's early phase, and the Massachusetts General Court refused to supply any troops during the spring campaign of 1758.[52] Yet the final years of the war were a spectacular triumph primarily because the ministry of William Pitt recognized the reality of imperial federalism and the necessity of securing voluntary cooperation inside the colonies. The colonial theaters of imperial wars were the ultimate examples of internal legislation, the White Pines Act on a massive and bloody scale. During the French and Indian War the empire had three priorities: first, that colonial legislatures help pay for troops; second, that the legislatures provide funds to quarter troops adequately; and third, that provincial officers and men fit within an imperial military structure and obey a chain of command dominated by British officers. These goals were constant from 1756 to 1761; what changed after 1758 were the imperial methods for achieving them. Prior to Pitt, British policy-makers had coercively demanded colonial obedience. Yet the realities of their relative internal weakness were apparent. The voluntary cooperative societies the colonies had become had the power to withhold their cooperation, which Massachusetts made both clear and official in spring 1758. No doubt there were serious implications to concern good subjects of the king in colonial British America. War-time needs were leading to demands by unaccountable authority figures who claimed a right to seize subjects' property without representation, an action that besmirched the Glorious Revolution legacy and seriously threatened British notions of how best to protect liberty and property.

Yet Pitt dramatically turned the situation around. Upon taking office he instituted a "subsidy policy in which Parliament used specie grants to reimburse particular colonies in direct ratio to their military efforts. By offering valuable rewards to specie-poor colonies, it actually stimulated competition among them in support for imperial goals. Its achievements far surpassed anything that requisitions [the previous, coercive method] had ever accomplished."[53] Pitt set aside £133,000 in specie and reimbursed 33 percent of all expenses colonial legislatures voluntarily undertook, and paid with their own paper currencies, until the full amount of the fund had been used. He did the same thing with expenses that colonies incurred to quarter troops.

Pitt solved the chain-of-command issue with a master stroke. Prior to Pitt, all colonial officers, even those who had achieved the highest rank of colonel, were expected to obey even the most junior British officers. The usually older and more veteran senior provincial officers found this expectation frustrating and humiliating. Pitt, therefore, recommissioned every commanding British officer (that is, every highest ranking British officer who dealt with provincials) with the new rank "Colonel-in-America-Only." Provincial officers were willing to obey the orders of British officers of equal or greater rank, and now the lowest ranking British officers giving the orders were at least of equal rank to the highest ranking provincial officers. But the rank also disappeared as soon as the Colonel-in-America-Only left the colonies, thereby preserving the integrity of the British officer corps more generally. It was practical and inexpensive policies such as these (the £133,000 amounted to one-tenth of 1 percent of the total British public debt in 1763), policies that accepted imperial federalism and the resulting need for voluntary cooperation, that helped produce the empire's spectacular successes of 1759–62: the conquest of Canada and the occupation of virtually all of the French and Spanish West Indies.

Imperial federalism and voluntary cooperation resulted from Anglicization. Self-conscious British colonials believed in the mantra liberty, prosperity, Protestantism, 1688, and King-in-Parliament. The Glorious Revolution settlement had bequeathed to them an expectation that British officialdom would respect their property rights and representative institutions, and distance and demography reinforced that they could not be coerced within their colonies. Only voluntary cooperation could produce internal enforcement of imperial objectives. But the colonists' expectations, so heavily influenced by Anglicization, led to a convergence of values, needs, priorities, and ideals throughout the Anglophone Atlantic world. There was, then, a deep reservoir of goodwill and British identity on which Pitt and other policy-makers could draw. They could do so as long as they understood the right approach and practiced the methods of governance appropriate to the federal sphere of the empire in which they were acting. White subjects in colonial British America fully embraced the achievements of the empire led by Pitt. As the historian John Shy writes, in a paragraph profoundly shaped by the concept of Anglicization,

> Americans, delighted by the dream finally realized of French and Spanish removal, heartened by Britain's wartime generosity, and proud of their own considerable contribution to final victory, looked forward to a golden age in which an enlightened mother country would gently guide the growth of her colonial children. An ever more numerous people, secure in their British liberty, would carry the empire westward to the glory and profit of all Imperial subjects, British and American. In a word, Americans were never more British than in 1763.[54]

Anglicization and the Revolutionary Republic

Thus the onset of imperial conflict, and eventually the American Revolution, "was a countercyclical event. It ran against the prevailing integrative tendencies of the century."[55] Yet this countercyclical event emerged from what began as a very British conflict and, initially, a very British revolution. Between 1764 and 1776 all of the thirteen British North American colonies grew frustrated by the post-1763 imperial attempts to reorganize and more forcefully integrate and govern the colonies. But the most "American" colonies (that is, those least shaped by Anglicization), the British West Indies, did not try to join the independence movement. On the one hand, the West Indian colonies, with much smaller populations of white Anglophone subjects deeply jealous of their British liberties, much less differentiated social relations among whites, and less diverse economies (economies the least like Britain's), fit closest the classic colonial model of producing what they did not consume and consuming what they did not produce. They did not seek to leave the empire.[56] The North American colonies, on the other hand, replicated or imitated British culture, politics, social relations, and values and had growing local populations that increasingly identified as British. They went from frustrated to furious as they discovered that Britain did not view them as the British subjects they believed they were.[57]

The concept of Anglicization, then, allows the new and the newest cultural history to be incorporated into an explanation of the American Revolution while still taking quite seriously the conscious and fully self-aware words and deeds of the budding revolutionaries.[58] The idea of Anglicization draws at once upon cultural history, the new and the newest social history of "neo-Beardians" such as Alfred Young and Woody Holton, imperial histories new and old, and the Whig and "ideological school" tradition led by Morgan and Bailyn.[59] The concept of Anglicization helps to make traditional "neo-Whig" and "ideological school" stories of the coming of the Revolution relevant while also obligating them to become more complex. The synthesis that the concept of Anglicization offers also depends on developing the classic skill of being able to distinguish between the Stamp, Townshend, and Coercive Acts crises. Anglicization also helps to explain the outbreak of revolution by acting in service to "the oldest tool available to historians for explaining anything: narrative. We have to tell the story," Murrin insists, "of the three imperial crises that undermined the British Empire despite all the advantages it had won by 1763." That narrative can be told only by drawing on the insights of all the historiographical traditions that have long competed to explain the American Revolution. Murrin has said on more than one occasion that his views have become those of a "radical, imperial, Whig."[60]

Essentially, between 1763 and 1765 the ministry of George Grenville refused to learn the lesson of imperial federalism and voluntary cooperation put to such impressive use by William Pitt in 1759 and 1760. In the decade after 1763 the empire would break apart over the colonists' refusal to fund imperial projects in North America, quarter British troops, and respect and follow British military commanders. In the previous decade Pitt had shown that they could be convinced to do each of those things, and during far more trying circumstances than those of the postwar period. Under Grenville subsidy and voluntary cooperation were replaced by the Sugar and Stamp

Acts. A policy that had brought specie to the colonies, stabilizing colonial currencies, was replaced by the Currency Act. Grenville subscribed to a narrative of the war that ignored Pitt's achievements. Any who wished to point to problems of governance within the empire over the course of the eighteenth century certainly could. Colonists had initially disobeyed the White Pines Act; Massachusetts had refused to fund troops during wartime; and certain colonial governors (who did not learn the appropriate methods for governing their colonies) could and did report horror stories. Indeed there was a small industry of deep thinkers producing a stream of pamphlets focusing on all that was wrong with the empire and suggesting the reforms that were necessary to keep it intact.[61]

Yet virtually none of those involved in these discussions was a colonial, and many had never set foot in the colonies. Would-be imperial reformers, as Murrin has argued, seemed always to be seeking to correct problems that had already been solved and were incessantly fighting the last war. On this issue Murrin is well worth quoting at length. He describes "a startling pattern about British policy formation in the 1760s." A fine example was

> [t]he Quartering Act . . . of 1765[,] . . . a useless, ill-conceived irritant in imperial relations. The quartering of British soldiers had raised serious tensions early in the war, but colonists had resolved them by erecting public barracks for the redcoats in major provincial cities, while the assemblies had regularly voted supplies. Yet after the war General Sir Thomas Gage began to worry about his lack of power to quarter soldiers in smaller communities . . . [and] asked London to · obtain legislation enabling him when necessary to quarter troops in private homes. Eventually the ministry, nervous over this challenge to traditional English liberties, gave the problem to [Thomas] Pownall, who claimed expertise on the subject because he had been governor of Massachusetts during its quartering dispute of 1758. Accordingly, Pownall's statute addressed the problems of 1758, which had already taken care of themselves, rather than the new theoretical issue of 1765. The Quartering Act met no real needs. It did create real problems by compelling colonial legislatures to do what so far they had all done voluntarily. Thus it gratuitously antagonized assemblies that were proud of their record of cooperation with the army, while, ironically, it also denied Gage the one power he had requested—to quarter soldiers in private homes.

Murrin argues that "this bizarre sequence of events" became "the norm rather than the silly exception" for postwar imperial policy-makers. The "Sugar and Currency Acts of 1764, and in a looser way even the Stamp Act[,] all had similar origins." The Sugar Act was an

> attack on smuggling. . . . Alarmed by colonial trading with the enemy early in the war, the Board of Trade began to collect data from which the customs commissioners compiled a full report in 1759. Significantly, the most recent item in the report dated only from 1757. In fact, the smuggling problem was also taking care of itself, for as British forces overran Canada and the Caribbean, hardly any place remained worth smuggling to by 1760. Yet after the war the Board of Customs and the Treasury both used this report to help draft the Sugar Act. London's response was again anachronistic. The Sugar Act was more germane to the difficulties of 1757 than to the changed realities of 1764. . . . The Stamp Act can also be traced to the gloomy years of French victory, 1754–1757, when the traditional requisition system had revealed its inability to provide badly needed revenues. All royal (and some nonroyal) governors pleaded with London to obtain general parliamentary tax upon the colonies. Instead Parliament found a different answer by 1758—William Pitt's subsidy policy.

Britain, Murrin argues, "possessed . . . two sets of imperial precedents after 1763. To govern her colonies she could extend the lessons of victory by continuing to do what had won the war. Or she could revert to earlier more strident suggestions stimulated by fear of defeat." One option was the example of

> Parliament's subsidy policy. . . . With reasonable efficiency it provided provincial troops in large numbers, probably stimulated a dramatic rise in colonial importations of British goods, helped to stabilize paper currencies, and encouraged hearty cooperation with the mother country—all of this while respecting traditional colonial liberties. Yet after the war London regressed, almost without reflection or debate, to the attitudes of 1754–57. . . . Thus with amazing consistency Britain's imperial policies of 1764–66 carefully addressed the specific problems of 1754–57, most of which were well on the way toward resolving themselves through various informal mechanisms.

But if London was running only a decade behind the times during the Stamp Act controversy, the gap tended to widen, not narrow, as imperial relations worsened. The second colonial crisis (1767–70) found Charles Townshend unearthing the concerns of 1748–54, when the Board of Trade had identified the lack of an independent salary for the governor as the crucial weakness in several royal colonies, especially New York. Even more dramatically than the quartering problem, this issue had been dead for fifteen years, but Townshend's memory of his youthful experience at the Board of Trade after 1748 kept it alive for him. . . . His policy did not strengthen a single colonial governor. It did unravel informal accommodations that had worked reasonably well in most northern colonies for years. Then in the final crisis of 1774, Parliament reached back ever farther to the early years of the century. The Massachusetts Government Act resurrected the Board of Trade's ancient nostrum of depriving charter governments of special privileges by act of Parliament. This time the empire came apart with the charter, possibly a fitting response when a policy of 1701 had emerged as Britain's brightest idea for 1774.[62]

These quotations suggest what a complex, nuanced, contingent, but quite clear narrative of events from 1763 to the Battle of Lexington and Concord would look like. That narrative would reinforce the lessons of imperial federalism and Anglicization and connect them to the real, but less than insurmountable, complexities of governing the British Empire. The British, on the whole, lurched from what had worked to what did not, never really focusing on what they had achieved and why. As they grew more desperate to address problems, many of their own making, they revealed ever more clearly their inability to celebrate their achievement of 1763: "Britain may actually have lost her colonies because, in the last analysis, the English simply did not know how to think triumphantly."[63]

Instead they thought defensively. Taxation by an unrepresentative body provoked colonial fears for liberty and property, fears easily articulated by self-identified British subjects of King-in-Parliament. Yet, as Murrin points out, the colonists quite effectively nullified the internal Stamp Act, while the external Sugar Act, in its modified 1766 form, functioned as a revenue-maker. Parliament could impose its will on the oceans and could not govern internally without voluntary cooperation, a lesson both the Marquis of Rockingham (who had ultimately replaced George Grenville) and Benjamin Franklin understood.[64] The first imperial crisis exposed that Parliament's claim to sovereignty everywhere was not enforceable and also that the colonists' distinction between legislation and taxation, while it had enormous ideological significance for them, had far less practical impact than the axis of imperial federalism: the coastline. The tax on French West Indian molasses was equally ideologically obnoxious to colonists as was the tax on stamps, while the Stamp Act was equally within Parliament's claim to sovereignty. The difference was that oceanic measures did not require voluntary cooperation. Neither Parliament's nor the colonists' understanding of the distribution of power in the empire explained how the empire actually functioned.

In late 1765 and early 1766 there was real cooperation between Rockingham, the London merchants, and loyal empire men such as Franklin.[65] Before he heard a word about the colonial boycott, Rockingham had organized a merchants' campaign to portray the Stamp Act as disastrous to trade. The campaign gave Parliament a reason to repeal that did not have to acknowledge the colonists' ideological position. Franklin, in his lengthy public questioning before the House of Commons, made as cogent a presentation of imperial federalism as one could ask for. Stating to Parliament that "the oceans are yours," he conveyed clearly that Parliament alienated the colonists internally at its peril and that it should pursue potentially controversial policy needs on the oceans where its sovereignty was both theoretical and real.[66] Often lost in discussions of the Stamp Act Crisis is that when it ended in 1766, and with nearly universal rejoicing in the colonies and the voluntary disbanding of the Sons of Liberty, Parliament had in fact augmented its power.[67] Parliament was taxing the colonies with the amended and external Sugar Act, something it had never done before. Franklin's performance is an excellent illustration of the practical ways in which the shrewdest men could manage the empire and make it function, even in the aftermath of the Stamp Act riots. It is also an intimate depiction of the process of Anglicization and the mentality and identity it shaped in British North American empire men in the middle decades of the eighteenth century.

But in the decade after 1766 the perspective represented by Grenville won out over the lessons offered by the achievements of Pitt, Rockingham, and Franklin. Imperial policy-makers could look at thirteen separate polities, in at least three distinct and differentiated regions, and see one homogenous unit increasingly unwilling to be governed. At a distance they did not see a reality that was much more visible up close. Each of these regions was producing Anglicizing subjects who identified with many imperial goals. Imperial problems of the past had been resolved, were manageable, or were less significant than the empire's considerable achievements. During this decade of events, British imperial policy-makers identified one distinct "America" when few colonists did. They acted on this "America" simultaneously and in uniform ways guaranteed to terrify and infuriate colonial subjects who felt that British liberty applied to them. By doing so they provided a common enemy that could drive the different colonies together. British actions did more for nascent American nationalism than any of the naturally arising trends developing within the thirteen colonies.

As the colonists reacted to the Townshend and Coercive Acts crises, they relied on the process of Anglicization that had shaped their experience. Increasingly the Country ideology, which urged subjects to be highly suspicious of power and hypervigilant in protection of liberty, did seem to depict the British state accurately. A language that had been marginal in many colonies and manageable and conducive to a politics of harmony in many others rapidly began to function in the incendiary ways always possible with this bundle of assumptions and claims. Yet until very late in the process, the colonists clung to their idea of British liberty and the imperial constitution. The solution was to go back to the situation they thought had existed in 1763: an empire that honored the distinction between taxation and legislation.[68]

The Townshend Acts crisis severely escalated tensions and caused far more people to rely on the Country language of opposition to understand British actions.[69] The Coercive Acts crisis destroyed the colonists' sense of their place and liberties within the empire, for these acts were pieces of legislation, not taxes. Having always denied Parliament's right to tax them, the colonists came to the conclusion from the Coercive Acts that Parliament's legislation was an even greater threat to liberty than the right it claimed to tax. If Parliament could not tax or legislate, it could do nothing, making the colonists independent of Parliament. Yet that conclusion came only after a decade of escalating crisis and, from the colonial viewpoint, extreme provocation.

Murrin has often remarked that royal authority collapsed within weeks of a colony hearing about the overthrow of James II.[70] Between 1689 and 1764 Anglicization created conditions that gave imperial policy-makers a decade or so to come up with a solution to the empire's problems once they became manifest. The problems in the end were not solved. But considering how and why they might have been and with ideas, approaches, and policies that were available and that, at times, were actually in use, allows us to see the colonial period on its own terms. It was, among many other things, a period that produced provincial British societies in North America and an empire that achieved most of its key objectives, almost in spite of the men who ended up running it. Anglicization provided imperial policy-makers a real margin for error (over a decade's worth). But it was also Anglicization that provided the colonists the mentality, identity, and language that caused them to conclude that what was being done to them was wrong and to interpret what they believed were the reasons for British actions, and that gave them a program for how to respond.

The events of 1764 to 1776 produced a unique situation in the Anglophone world: in the thirteen colonies the Country ideology became the dominant political idiom, even for a time in those colonies where it made little organic sense for it to be so. But Country ideology was now mixed with the values produced by the radicalizing upheaval of prerevolutionary and revolutionary conflict. Internal social conflict did not necessarily unify the colonists or lead directly to the movement for independence (after all, social conflict was more likely to divide colonists than to unite them). But the external actions of the British did create a large political movement that swept up into it hundreds of thousands of people who were also quite interested in having revolutionary politics address internal social concerns.

Hence the radical, or "neo-Beardian," dimension of Murrin's "radical, imperial, Whig" synthesis. The Revolution was, in part, a movement for independence that resulted from the final contours of a long and complex process of Anglicization. It was also a sustained hegemonic breakdown and an assault on one form of authority that could quickly spread to assaults on other forms. As challenges to British authority, and ultimately demands for home rule, overawed existing structures of authority, space opened to articulate social and economic grievances. In this fluid and raucous context, the social and economic inequalities of colonial America (prime examples of Anglicization) encouraged further assaults on authority, which began to threaten colonial elites who would have liked to limit the challenge to the authority of British policy-makers.[71]

The Revolution made governance in the new Republic it created highly challenging, both in the short and long terms. Much of this challenge resulted from the remnant of political ideology that remained credible to the bulk of an Anglicized people who had turned against mainstream British political and cultural forms. What remained as the most dominant surviving example of Anglicization was a widespread belief in the Country ideology. But this belief was now expressed on a political terrain shaped by revolution, a terrain where virtually all examples of authority and hierarchy, both public and private, were being challenged and shaken.[72]

In many ways the revolutionary United States sought to make itself the anti-Britain. The Articles of Confederation government was about as complete a rejection of the fiscal-military state that a people could make and still claim to have a central government. This repudiation of the mainstream processes of eighteenth-century state formation fit with the general and more bottom-up rejections of authority. Those advocating the bottom-up rejections generally sought to place governance in much more local institutions. Potentially even more subversively, challenges to authority from revolutionary impulses could often develop within private spaces, within household walls, affecting the intimate relations of husbands and wives, parents and children, and masters, servants, and slaves. Revolutionary possibilities for change had real, profound, and deeply unfortunate limits. But those limits were measurable primarily because of the sharp challenge to authority that followed the repudiation of British authority and the Anglicizing mainstream.[73]

Many fissures and conflicts shaped the postrevolutionary United States and the early Republic. Some of the most critical resulted from the debates concerning how fully the Republic should repudiate the Anglicizing society, polity, culture, and economy from which it had declared independence in 1776. Murrin's ideas regarding Anglicization were never intended to be limiting or to cut off inquiry, and an effort to discuss them must not do so either. There are many fruitful ways to think about the post-Revolution period and the early Republic. One highly useful way is to assess how debates about the Anglicization legacy shaped attitudes toward state formation, the Constitution, and policy priorities in the early Republic. The countercyclical movement for independence and the revolutionary upheaval it engendered radically disrupted the steady and organic developments that had been producing social and economic hierarchy, political oligarchy, and, compared to the seventeenth century, unprecedented political stability. The 1780s came to be viewed by many elites as a "critical period," which led to real fear (especially among those elites) that the challenges to authority had gone too far. Those fearful of the revolutionary-era state constitutions, democratized state legislatures, and politics tinged with social leveling eventually sought to restore something of the social order of the world they had lost.[74] The nationalist impulses of the 1780s, which culminated with the Constitutional Convention, were, at least in part, an effort to establish through policy and a new political architecture the political and social forms that late colonial America had been producing organically.

Murrin has said in response to a question from me, "I never proclaimed myself a neo-Beardian, but I have no objection to that label."[75] The real anxiety felt by elites during the "critical period" helps to revive some of Beard's concerns, if not his explicit charges, regarding Federalists and the Constitution. As Murrin argues, "Without contending for a nationalist conspiracy or coup d'etat in 1787, let us nevertheless concede what Beard rather clumsily argued, that the United States Constitution was very much an elitist solution to the problems left by the Revolution and popular turbulence of the 1780s. . . . In a word, the federal Constitution shifted the entire spectrum of national politics several degrees to the right."[76]

Murrin's commitment to the synthesis of a "radical, imperial, Whig" led him to a deep appreciation of Gordon S. Wood's *Creation of the American Republic*, which has "done more than any other study in my professional lifetime to enrich our understanding of the origins of the United States Constitution." Indeed, Murrin's rubric Anglicization, which allowed him to draw on new-left, neo-Whig, and older imperial historiography, led him to perceive what "early critics were slow to grasp. . . . *Creation of the American Republic* was an intellectual approach to the Revolution that made social conflict more, not less, relevant to the larger story. The threat of aristocracy, the palpable reality of gentility, and the clash of interests all became central components of Wood's analysis. Wood made Charles Beard credible even if Beard's specific equation of personality and realty with Federalists and anti-Federalists respectively did not hold."[77]

This elitist solution centralized power in ways unimaginable in 1776. Yet crucially, the Constitution produced far less consolidation and centralized nation-state authority than did the very seriously considered Virginia Plan or the seriously respected, though never seriously considered, Hamilton Plan, both proposed at the Constitutional Convention. The Federalists of 1787, just like the imperial managers of the high colonial period, confronted the reality of an organic federal system. Their great achievement, and where they clearly departed from those who had managed the empire, was to articulate a political science and construct a political architecture that drew on expansive revolutionary language and that acknowledged the reality that the new Republic was federal in much the same way the empire had been. The central government would in general be able to govern citizens' behavior along the coastlines and when they sought to go onto or come in from the oceans.

It would see real limits to its authority in the interior unless it received the voluntary cooperation of those it ruled. Thus Federalists in 1787 gave up on a national veto of state laws and produced a constitution for a federal union that conceded significant areas of policy-making to the states.

The reality of the early Republic was that a national government in Philadelphia or Washington did not have much more practical power in the interior than Whitehall had possessed over the New Hampshire woods. The Congresses of the 1790s had an unambiguous right to lay and collect taxes (just as Parliament had claimed), a right that was not challenged by the citizenry in principle (unlike with Parliament). But in reality, the new nation-state could collect imposts highly effectively, while excises and direct internal taxes provoked armed rebellion. The new government could put down the rebellions, but it was not a legitimate taxing state in the interior. Taxation policy in the federal Republic stabilized only after the Jeffersonians arrived at the same settlement that the Rockingham ministry had conceived in 1766: repeal of all internal taxes and commitment to collecting external ones.[78]

The federal Republic's theoretical foundation emerged from the intellectual developments in political thought during the 1780s and the compromises at the convention that transformed the Virginia Plan into the document that was eventually ratified. These compromises were possible in part because nationalists in 1787 truly did participate in a "conceptual breakthrough." They declared the people sovereign and then allowed for practical, everyday governing power to be parceled out in ways that reflected the organic federal reality produced by a voluntary cooperative society of primarily independent households living on widely distributed land that they owned.[79] The remnant of Anglicization—the Country ideology—along with the organic federal reality and the revolutionary impact of the democratizing and bottom-up challenge to authority all combined to make a European-style fiscal-military state impossible in the United States. Murrin's synthesis, then, can easily accommodate the insight of the late, new-left, neo-Beardian scholar Alfred F. Young: that of all the compromises during the Constitutional Convention that made the document what it became, the most significant were between those who were there and those who were not, between those who participated in the convention and the revolutionary citizenry who had to be satisfied with their deliberations.[80]

The conflict of the 1790s can be understood, at least in part, as a protracted argument resulting from the efforts to explore the limits of the federal reality. The Washington administration tried to fit as much of a republican version of a fiscal-military state into the new constitutional order as it possibly could. Yet it kept running into the Revolution settlement that was shaped by the federal reality, that was profoundly Country and not Court, and that was increasingly legitimizing a democratized, localist conception of authority. Thus the meaning of American federalism was not determined solely (or even primarily) by the events of 1787–88. Rather it was defined by ongoing social and political conflict.[81] In shorthand, the nation-state could enforce wildly unpopular policies in the ports and upon American citizens on the oceans; it could not expect peaceful acquiescence or acceptance of the unpopular in the interior. A large and vocal group of Americans hated the Jay Treaty just as much as those who hated the whiskey tax of 1794 and the land tax of 1799. Yet the Jay Treaty was enforceable, while collection of the taxes was nullified by direct intervention. In the West, what it would have cost to enforce them in blood (literally) and treasure made the taxes an absurdity. The similarity of the differing fates of these external and internal policies to those of the enforceable external Sugar Act and the nullified and unenforceable internal Stamp Act is striking.

In one reading of it (as Alexander Hamilton understood) the Constitution created a potential framework for a consolidated and vigorous nation-state.[82] Yet the Constitution was, in Murrin's evocative aphorism, "a roof without walls."[83] Certain nationalists, especially those whose anxiety over revolutionary assaults on authority shaped their thinking more than their initial embrace of the Country critique of Britain, tried to take advantage of the centralizing possibilities that the Constitution seemed to provide. They could imagine a consolidated union and a vigorous nation-state, and so they could, in 1787, construct the roof. But the walls—reinforcing national institutions, a national market, and even such basic things as a uniform currency—did not exist. With Federalists making such extensive and weighty use of the nation-state during the 1790s, the roof, suspended in midair, threatened to collapse.[84]

The roof remained raised in the early Republic less because Americans built walls for it and more because the Jeffersonians accepted, even embraced, the fact that the walls were not there. The Jeffersonians reduced American taxation to imposts, in effect stripping the republican taxing state of all taxing power except that which many western European states had possessed unambiguously since the fifteenth century.[85] Jeffersonians consolidated their grip on national authority by confining their most vigorous uses of power visited upon citizens to the coastlines and to governing behavior when citizens entered or left the nation on ships. When they acted vigorously inside the nation, they did so almost exclusively to pursue policies popular with a majority of citizens, policies, in other words, that enjoyed voluntary cooperation. The Jeffersonian/Jacksonian coalition aggressively acquired western lands and mobilized national resources to terrorize Indians. Clearly these were examples of a vigorous nation-state. But the nation-state was usually vigorous only when it could fit that vigor within the postrevolutionary federal reality. In general the national government pursued policies internally only when those policies were highly popular and capable of receiving voluntary consent and support from the Republic's white male citizens (which usually meant carrying out policy in federal territories, not states).

As Murrin has explained, the Jeffersonian federal solution to the complex set of issues produced by eighteenth-century colonial development and the Revolution it spawned "had its soft and its hard side[s]."[86] White adult male heads of household might once have been victims of the social forces and concentration of power that produced the "feudal revival" and ruling oligarchies within most colonies. Under the Jeffersonians and Jacksonians during the first half of the nineteenth century, a politics of aggressive westward expansion, astonishingly light taxes, and, comparatively, virtually no interference from the nation-state meant genuine opportunities for social mobility and access to productive resources. For these citizens the nation-state was "a midget institution in a giant land." At the same time, "Indians, blacks, and Spaniards experienced the hard side of these formulations."[87]

Yet the "soft side" had fascinating, unintended consequences for those white male citizens it was meant to glorify. Convinced that inequality and abuse of power were the products of a corrupt, centralizing, Walpolean state, the Jeffersonians greatly reduced the state and unleashed its citizens. Compared to those residing in contemporary nations, full citizens of the early Republic had virtually no governing constraints in the internal realm coming from the national government. Yet the Jeffersonians had no real conception that the citizens themselves could create economic and social relations and forms that could produce as much, if not more, inequality and concentration of power as any Walpolean or Hamiltonian state. Social mobility could go in more than one direction, but the one common denominator was uncertainty. In breaking the special relationship to the state enjoyed by, say, holders of public funds after funding and assumption, indeed by dismantling the sort of state that could enact such policies, the Jeffersonians ended up not eradicating inequality but democratizing it. In the raucous world of rapid economic development without central direction, and with the sort of nation-state that might have provided it thoroughly discredited, boom and bust was the order of the day. Over the course of the nineteenth century the nation grew wealthier in the aggregate and living standards rose in general. But within the white population, while the highest of the high and the lowest of the low might still find their circumstances largely unchanging, for the vast 80 percent or so in the middle, who rose and fell was at once quite egalitarian and also often traumatically unpredictable.[88]

The Jeffersonians were able to govern as they wanted. They established policies expecting to produce a society that, in the end, bore very little relation to the intentions expressed in their political and policy triumph.[89] Dismantling the Federalists' nascent fiscal-military state, cheerful embrace of the organic federal reality, and the conviction that a Walpolean-like political culture was the sole source of dangerous concentrations of wealth and power produced a society in the early Republic where "Americans could compete ever more furiously . . . for the joy of outdoing their neighbors. So long as government remained all but irrelevant to society and the economy, the pursuit of equality was frustrating and often self-defeating."[90]

Economic and social inequality among white male citizens grew in the early Republic and over the course of the nineteenth century. Yet it was driven far more by the actions of private citizens than by the conscious intention of those governing the nation-state. Inequality increased within a federal Republic that protected the dominant social forms in the various regions that comprised it and that remained insulated from interference by the national government. For the sake of national political harmony, it was imperative that people in regions that could increasingly be differentiated as free and slave believed that their white rights to pursue life, liberty, and happiness were not being interfered with by fellow citizens from other regions. National harmony would become even more imperiled if citizens grew suspicious that fellow citizens in a different region had captured the nation-state and were using it to advance their interests at the expense of others. As long as those in all regions felt that they would be left alone and would not see the nation-state captured in this way, the Jeffersonian solution could keep the roof aloft with no worry about the walls. But over the course of the early Republic, the profound limits of the Jeffersonian solution to the complexities of Anglicization and revolution became manifest. The nation-state could accomplish in the interior only what was widely popular across regions. Essentially it could remove Indians and give away public land. With regard to land, by the 1850s it could no longer peacefully accomplish even that. There are many good reasons why historians specialize and the best of them, such as John Murrin, are as excited by what their ideas cannot explain as by what they can. Anglicization does not explain all of American history, and John Murrin, though he has profound thoughts about the subject, has never provided much discussion of the coming of the American Civil War. In this instance, as in so many others, I shall follow his example.[91]

PART II

EMPIRE

CHAPTER THREE

"In Great Slavery and Bondage": White Labor and the Development of Plantation Slavery in British America

Simon P. Newman

John Murrin's theory of Anglicization is nothing if not ambitious.[1] Between 1688 and 1763, Murrin suggests, England's disparate North American colonies became steadily more united in a newfound shared British identity, a process that had the unintended effect of creating the foundation for resistance to imperial reform during the 1760s and 1770s. Anglicization enabled Murrin to propose a grand narrative for American history, an explanatory link between the remarkably disparate seventeenth-century colonies and the intercolonial resistance and rebellion that created the American Republic, making sense of a long eighteenth century that had stymied historians unable to chart a coherent course from early Massachusetts and Virginia to Independence Hall.[2]

Other historians have built on Murrin's observations and his case study of Massachusetts, exploring how in the South, the great wealth of the planter elites enabled them to carry imitation of British style and culture further than other colonists did. Planters' great houses were filled with the consumer goods of Georgian Britain. T. H. Breen's exploration of consumption in colonial Virginia is aptly labeled "The Anglicization of Colonial Virginia," while Jack P. Greene has identified in the lower South "a demonstrably more anglicized socio-cultural life." The sons and daughters of the plantocracy spent far more time in Britain than had their parents and grandparents, learning, shopping and socializing. Robert Olwell concludes that Anglicization was so pervasive in South Carolina that even the enslaved began adopting British fashions.[3]

Murrin had noticed this trend in his original articulation of the Anglicization thesis: "Chesapeake planters carefully imitated the refinements and the vices of the English gentry, an impulse which assumed almost frantic proportions after 1740. Carolina planters showed more enthusiasm for the vices and extravagance of polite English society than for its refinements, but the basic trend was similar."[4] He had also, however, observed that Anglicization in the South was based on an archetypally American anomaly. Racial slavery was the exception to the Anglicization rule, one that would become stronger in the South during the very years that the colonies became identifiably more British. As Anglicization proceeded apace, slavery simultaneously nurtured an exceptionalist identity within the southern colonies and states, defining that region's antebellum sectional identity and eventually triggering the Civil War. On southern plantations a New World innovation, "the new and complex institution of Negro slavery[,] . . . overshadowed the more familiar labor system surviving from old England." For all that the Anglicization of the southern colonies was real, it was nonetheless based on that most American of institutions, plantations and racial slavery.[5]

Even when considering plantation slavery, however, Anglicization cannot easily be dismissed. The slavery that would spread from South Carolina across the antebellum cotton belt, the heartland of the future Confederacy, had originated in Barbados. For all that it developed into a uniquely American institution, this slavery had begun as a thoroughly English form of bound labor, in which planters from their British Isles deployed bound workers from the British Isles with singular brutality as they fashioned the most successful plantation economy the English Atlantic had yet seen. Thus the slavery identified as exceptional by Murrin had in fact originated as a modified English institution, more British in its precepts and personnel than historians have appreciated. The wealth that allowed South Carolina planters to emulate British society was made possible by a labor form rooted in early modern English agricultural society, a form that was arguably closer to these agrarian English roots than were the urban industrial work patterns already emerging in northern Britain. Based on the bound labor of Britons, the Barbadian diaspora had spread the practices and principles of enslaved labor to Jamaica, the Leeward Islands, and South Carolina, whence it would spread throughout the lower South, forming the backbone of the exceptionalist society of the future Confederacy.

The organization of labor and the compulsion to work were integral characteristics of early modern English society, as rulers and landowners sought to control a rapidly increasing mass of under- or unemployed people. During the later sixteenth and early seventeenth centuries the number of jobless people, vagrants, criminals, and prisoners of war grew rapidly as a result of significant population growth, consolidation of landownership, the disappearance of the traditional poor-relief systems of the pre-Reformation Catholic Church, and a series of rebellions and wars. Local and national authorities believed that the growing ranks of masterless men and women posed a threat to social order and good government. They passed laws and created new institutions to control the laboring poor and to force them to work, but such actions did little to reduce the ranks of men and women roaming the countryside in search of food, work, and shelter. During the early to mid-seventeenth century, English authorities were more than happy to ship tens of thousands of people to Barbados, many of them unemployed vagrants supplemented by criminals and prisoners of war or rebellion. English principles and precedents informed the earliest use of the bound labor of these people in England's wealthiest colony, but English authorities who were preoccupied with the domestic social and political situation paid little attention to the radical reformulation of domestic labor practices by Barbadian planters living beyond the pale.

The agricultural labor system that appeared to be in crisis in early modern England had taken shape in the wake of the catastrophic late fourteenth-century Black Death, following which the population of England had plummeted from some 3.5 million to 2.1 million. For generations there was more agricultural land than there were people to work it, and elsewhere in Europe the reduced population and the consequent scarcity of labor resulted in the institution of medieval forms of sharecropping, such as the *mezzadria* in Italy, which bound rural workers to large landholders. In England, however, the demographic decline led to the development of the institution of service-in-husbandry, annual labor contracts between employee and employer that advanced new ideas about the nature and practice of bound labor. The Ordinance of Laborers (1349) and the Statute of Laborers (1351) laid out the terms of such labor and were intended, at least in part, to check the potential increase in the power and independence of servants in this land-rich and labor-poor environment by mandating and protecting the rights of masters. These laws confirmed the deterioration of feudalism and its replacement by a wage-earning workforce. In place of the ancient rights of lords over tenants and serfs, this legislation established a new relationship between employers and employees.[6]

For generations service-in-husbandry benefited many in the rural population as a transitional stage between childhood and adulthood, providing preparation for an adult existence on the land as small farmers, cottagers, or laborers. At its best service-in-husbandry was beneficial to both employers and employees and thus could foster relatively equitable labor relations. On the one hand, those whose landholdings were too large to be farmed by family members hired servants; on the other hand, the children of those who had little or no land hired themselves out as servants. Perhaps as many as 60 percent of early modern English men and women between fifteen and twenty-four years of age worked as servants; in Coventry in 1523, two-fifths of households contained servants, who composed fully one-quarter of the population.[7]

While service-in-husbandry could function as a stepping-stone to independence, allowing poor, landless young men and women to gain experience and money sufficient to establish their own households, there was a price to pay. During the long years of service these men and women sacrificed their independence, and as dependent family members they were politically invisible. Unmarried and without property of their own, servants-in-husbandry were bound laborers subject to the authority of their masters. While a day laborer with his own home was subject to an employer only for the time that he was hired, the servant-in-husbandry lived in the home of his master and was subject to his master's authority and required to obey him twenty-four hours a day for the entire year of service. The power of the master over his servants was not absolute, however, and was mediated by a number of factors. The servant-in-husbandry retained certain rights while in service, such as the right to testify in court or to bring proceedings against a master who had breached the terms of the contract that bound them together, and the right to marry. The usually oral contract between farmer and servant was binding and protected both parties. Law and order depended in part on the respect of the governed for those with authority over them, and excessive and systematic abuse of power by masters over servants would have risked a breakdown of the entire system.[8]

Terms of service were carefully regulated, and in return for servants' labor, masters were bound to support servants during periods when there was little or no work to be done, when servants were injured or ill, and even when female servants fell pregnant; the servant could not use these or other events as an excuse to leave before the conclusion of the term of service, however. Under no circumstances could a master transfer a servant and his or her labor to another farmer. On smaller farms in particular, servants tended to share much the same standard of living as their masters and their families, eating the same food and working alongside their masters or mistresses. Masters who treated servants well could expect them to work hard and perhaps to renew their contracts, and an employer's good reputation might well make it easier to recruit other suitable servants. Such an idealized vision of the master-servant relationship was often difficult to achieve, however, and there were inevitable stresses and strains in the relationship. Servants were free to leave at the end of their year of service, and each year hundreds of thousands sought better terms and improved working conditions elsewhere. While not a full and formal apprenticeship, servitude trained the rural youths in the rural skills and crafts necessary for their own futures as farmers and laborers, as well as providing them with the financial means to begin independent adult lives.[9]

After two centuries of low population and plentiful food supplies, the situation changed dramatically in the sixteenth and early seventeenth centuries. English society and its labor system were challenged by rapidly increasing population levels, rising food prices, enclosure and engrossment of common lands, and increased rural unemployment and underemployment. Social and economic problems encouraged a hardening of attitudes toward laborers, and in the wake of the Reformation, English Puritans were simply the most zealous exponents of a creed in which labor was regarded as godly and was required of all. Regarding the rapidly increasing ranks of homeless and jobless vagrants with fear and loathing, political and religious authorities condemned as ungodly and criminal all who did not work and were not subject to the order imposed by a master. Throughout the sixteenth and seventeenth centuries the authorities were preoccupied with ensuring that the poor worked and were subject to proper authority.

Reduced access to land, an increasing shifting of resources from arable to pastoral agriculture, and rapidly rising population levels all contributed to a decline in wages and significant increases in the price of foodstuffs. Between 1500 and the 1650s food prices may have risen by as much as 550 percent, and periodic cycles of dearth and even famine compounded the problems faced by many. Poverty was nothing new, but during the sixteenth and early seventeenth centuries it was experienced by more people and on a larger scale than had been true for several centuries. Structural under- and unemployment became endemic. Towns and countryside alike seemed to be teeming with vagabonds, rootless and jobless men and women who were no longer employed on the land and who had no prospect of ever achieving the "sufficiency" that would enable them to establish households of their own. Perhaps one-sixth of the English population, from all corners of the country, spent some portion of their lives in London trudging desperately in search of work, telling evidence of a remarkably high degree of unemployment and mobility.[10]

This was a society in which wealth, commercial success, and independence appeared to those who enjoyed it as proof of personal merit and divine blessing, while joblessness, poverty, and homelessness were judged by the more fortunate as evidence of personal failings and immorality. One's economic condition, in short, appeared to be evidence of one's moral worth. "Man is borne to labour," proclaimed religious authorities, who were convinced that "poverty followeth idlenesse." All around England clerics warned their congregations: "We have to muche experience thereof (the thyng is the more to bee lamented) in this realme. For a great part of the beggery that is among the poore, can be imputed to nothing so muche, as to idlenes, and to the negligence of parentes, whiche do not bryng up theyr chyldren, eyther in good learning, honest labour, or some commendable occupation or trade, whereby when they come to age, they myght get theyr living."[11] Farmers and political authorities alike were deeply concerned by the unwillingness of potential servants and laborers to accept what these working people considered to be inadequate wages and inferior conditions. Moreover, the elites were terrified that the increase in the number of masterless men and women might incite crime, disorder, and rebellion. However bad the social and economic reality was, elites' fears perceived a situation that was even worse: the specter of hosts of undisciplined and mobile vagrants struck fear into the hearts of landowners and political authorities, transforming their attitudes toward the laboring poor.[12]

There were limitations on the ways in which the existing legal system could be used to force men, women, and children to labor, and the government responded by trying to refresh and strengthen existing labor practices, while also seeking new solutions to the problems they faced. The Ordinance of Laborers and the Statute of Laborers were confirmed and updated in 1563 by the Statute of Artificers, which redefined servants who broke the terms of their contracts as criminals; created mechanisms to ensure standardized wages, eroding the power of some laborers to negotiate more advantageous rates of pay; and laid out methods to require and enforce vagrants to work.

The new law accorded significant power to local authorities, and justices of the peace were empowered to enforce various provisions within local contexts. The Statute of Artificers articulated compulsion and control: all who were able were compelled to work, and their labor was subject to the legally mandated authority of their masters. Two decades later Sir Thomas Smith went so far as to assert that compelling vagrants and the under- and unemployed to work were among the "chief charges" of justices of the peace. This and related laws recognized the legal authority of heads of households, farmers, and landowners as agents of a larger society, enforcing social and religious discipline and ensuring peace and productivity within the realm. The head of each household ruled over a "little Commonwealth," a familial version of the state, and the government sought to confirm and strengthen this authority, placing all and sundry under householders' command.[13]

Pauper apprenticeship was a particularly stark form of Elizabethan and Stuart labor discipline, and it appears to have been more common than historians once assumed. Orphans and the children of the laboring poor were forcibly bound out as apprentices, usually but not always in husbandry, and required to work for their masters for lengthy periods, perhaps as long as a decade or more. Such an apprentice was required to "do all servile offices about the house, and be obedient to all his masters commandementes, and shall suffer such correction as his master shall thinke meete." Building on a range of Elizabethan poor laws and vagrancy statutes, authorities overrode reluctant parents and unwilling prospective masters, doing all they could to ensure that a new generation did not enter the growing ranks of unemployed and underemployed laborers. Enforcement was patchy. in 1617, for example, justices in Norfolk bound out over five hundred children, while those in neighboring Suffolk bound out virtually none. In 1624 the Hertfordshire bench apprenticed over fifteen hundred impoverished children, and eighteen certificates completed by justices drawn from five different counties in 1633 described the binding out of almost three thousand children. The impact on a single community might be enormous: in 1634 alone some forty boys and girls were forcibly apprenticed in the Sussex village of Cuckfield, a community of no more than twelve hundred people.[14]

Forced apprenticeship in husbandry and pauper apprenticeship were not the only ways in which the bodies and labor of men and women might be commandeered. Perhaps the most striking example of this was the Vagrancy Act of 1547, which instituted enslavement as a punishment for those who refused to work and subject themselves to the legitimate authority of a master. According to the law, any individual found "not applying them self to some honnest and allowed arte, Scyence, service or Labour" would be given three days to find work. Failure to do so, or entering service but then abandoning it before the end of the contracted term of labor, could result in the person being brought before two justices. If the charge was proved, the law mandated that the unfortunate man or woman be quite literally branded as a vagrant and made the slave of the person bringing suit for a period of two years. The master did not have to treat his slave with the care demanded by the law in the case of servants and was required by the law to do no more than feed the enslaved "breade and water or small drynke and such refuse of meate as he shall thincke mete." More tellingly, the master was free to "cawse the said Slave to worke by beating, cheyninge or otherwise in such worke and Labor how vyle so ever it be," and he was even empowered to place iron rings on the neck and the feet of the enslaved. Runaway slaves would be enslaved for life, and a second attempt to flee risked execution. Other provisions of the law extended existing practices. A vagabond child could be forced into apprenticeship without the permission of parents and forced to serve until the age of twenty-four if male and twenty if female. Should this apprentice flee, he or she would be returned and reduced to the status of slave for the remainder of the term.[15]

The Vagrancy Act lasted only two years in England. In the wake of Ket's Rebellion in 1549 the law was repealed, and there is little evidence to suggest that it had ever been enforced. Nevertheless the precedents for this law, its language and provisions, the survival of certain of its provisions long after its repeal, and the very fact of its passage in the first place all suggest that English authorities believed that in the right circumstances one individual could seize the body and labor of another, taking away liberty and independence and extracting work through violence. Such attitudes appeared in other legislation, including a poor law scheme in 1535 proposing that vagrants be forced to labor on various public works and with the provision that those who refused would be branded and even executed. Two different proclamations by Henry VIII had mandated that "ruffians, vagabonds, masterless men, common players and evil-disposed persons" could be sent to the galleys, "there to row as a slave" at His Majesty's pleasure. Slavery existed, at least in theory, in English common law, but the Vagrancy Act of 1547 represented a new way of thinking after other measures had failed. For those who would not work, enslavement was proposed both as a punishment and as the most radical means of forcing work. While this official policy of enslavement in England was short-lived, the overriding principle of forcibly binding out children and the unemployed remained a vital part of ideology, policy, and practice. Parish officials and justices of the peace employed bridewells, forced service and apprenticeship, and other institutions to extract labor from all homeless and jobless vagrants who were fit and able to work. Authorities sought not only to ensure a steady and affordable labor supply but also to keep the laboring population servile and compliant.[16]

In sixteenth- and seventeenth-century England there thus existed, both in theory and in practice, various forms of bound and even unfree labor. All who labored for others, whether laborers, servants-in-husbandry, apprentices-in-husbandry, or even apprentices, were bound by legal strictures that gave masters considerable power over them. Significant demographic and economic changes together with the expansion of commercial activity throughout the British Isles had encouraged the commodification of labor as a product to be sold and bought and, more significantly, to be owned. This enhanced the legal power of masters to ensure that they received compliance from those bound to serve them. The medieval right of a master to the good performance of a servant began developing into legal ownership of labor and a right of control over the body of the laborer. The rural poor could be made to work, some for no recompense other than the most basic food, clothing, and lodging. Their masters were entitled to use violence and the officers and instruments of state power in order to force obedience and to extract labor.[17]

Thus agricultural laborers and servants in early modern England lived and worked under conditions that in certain key ways prefigured free labor, bound labor, and even slavery as they would develop in England's New World colonies. Barbadian planters, many drawn from the middling ranks of English society, brought with them an understanding of how to compel and control labor, for it was at precisely the period between 1627 and 1660 that Barbadian planters seized their opportunity and drew tens of thousands of white laborers from the British Isles. Voluntary and involuntary indentured servants from the British Isles crossed the Atlantic in large numbers, and they were of far greater significance in England's colonies than in those of any other European nation. Christopher Tomlins estimates that 60 to 65 percent of those traveling from the British Isles to England's mainland colonies during the seventeenth century were bound servants, and those numbers declined to 40 to 42 percent in the eighteenth century.[18]

During the middle years of the seventeenth century Barbados drew more bound laborers from the British Isles than did any other English colony.

Between 1650 and 1659, for example, perhaps as many as 70 percent of the bound white laborers arriving in the Americas from Britain landed in Barbados. Upon arrival these bound workers faced an exhausting work regime and dwindling prospects. While courts, local communities, and popular and political opinion had forced some restraint on the part of employers in England, conditions in Barbados proved very different. English authorities were desperate to free themselves of as many vagrants, criminals, and military prisoners as possible. Thousands of miles away, a small group of Barbadian planters enjoyed a remarkable degree of control over government, the courts, and military power on their island, and they were effectively free of many of the legal and cultural restrictions that had restrained British landowners in their treatment of laborers. Bound white laborers were subject to the control of members of a small plantocracy who enjoyed a level of social and political power that would have been the envy of the English gentry and Stuart monarchs. By 1680 the 175 great planters on Barbados, representing less than 1 percent of the island's white population, controlled over 54 percent of the island's property, both real and human. From early in the colony's history the families of the great planters had dominated the Governor's Council or sat in the assembly, forming a cohesive and commanding ruling elite, and by 1680 virtually all of the highest political, military, and judicial offices were dominated by the elite planters. The great planters held the reins of political and judicial power on Barbados, and they shaped the island and its plantation labor system to suit their interests.[19]

The social, economic, and political situation of the British Isles aligned neatly with the needs of the developing Barbadian sugar economy, for conditions in the British Isles encouraged the migration of laborers to Barbados. Enclosure and engrossment, rising population and prices, and declining wages combined to leave many young Britons with limited or no employment, while vagrancy laws, rebellions, and wars created a surplus population of men who were a burden to the state. Yet conditions on the island had quickly made migration unattractive even for impoverished and unemployed English agricultural workers. Opportunities for the first few servants declined rapidly, and as conditions of labor deteriorated, the supply of voluntary servants diminished dramatically. By the mid-1650s many in the British Isles traveled to labor on the island only after they had been "Barbadosed," that is, kidnapped or "spirited" away, illegal practices that may have helped secure a few more bound workers but rendered Barbados an increasingly unattractive option for voluntary laborers. Desperate for workers, planters and their

English agents worked hard to secure state support for regular shipments of large numbers of unfree, bound laborers, and by the mid-1640s the largest market in bound white laborers in English America was in Barbados. The result was a telling difference in volition: a great many of the white servants sent to Barbados had not voluntarily entered a contract like that of servants-in-husbandry, exchanging their labor for passage and food. Instead they were more akin to pauper apprentices, vagrants, and even the slaves referred to in the notorious Elizabethan Vagrancy Act of 1547: men and women who did not control their labor or their bodies, people who were not free but bound. Many were prisoners, their lives forfeit in the British Isles. Labor in Barbados represented a reprieve from the gallows, and Barbadian planters did not hesitate to utilize and then expand the various forms of forced labor and labor discipline that had on occasion been implemented in early modern England. They regarded white servants on the island as people who had lost the right to life and were consequently undeserving of traditional English liberties. We have no idea how many people were sent from the British Isles to Barbados, but estimates of the number sent to the Americas from Ireland alone range between thirty thousand and one hundred thousand, and it is likely that a majority of these went to Barbados.[20]

With England preoccupied by the Wars of the Three Kingdoms, a Barbadian workforce composed of vagrants, criminals, and prisoners had few rights and protections, for imperial oversight was all but nonexistent. Thus, although it was grounded in the traditions of early modern English service and labor, indentured servitude in Barbados quickly developed into a radically different labor system. As Trevor Burnard has observed, "It took little time for the English coming to the islands to be caught up in a system that seemed internally logical and perfectly natural." Freed from the restrictions of English courts and customs, planters deployed and controlled bound laborers whom they judged to be vagrants, criminals, and prisoners rather than free-born English agricultural workers. Planters treated their bound laborers as chattel, "gathered upp . . . transported . . . [and then] Exchang'd for Commodities . . . at different rates & according to their condition or Trade by which they are rendered more usefull and beneficiall to their Masters." The growing power of large landholders on an island of only 166 square miles, and their absolute dependence on subservient cheap labor in order to make a profit from staple crops, resulted in very few servants being able to achieve the dream of landownership and a decent life. The names of only fifty-nine of the approximately two thousand servants who left Bristol for Barbados between 1654 and 1675 appear on the list of landholding freemen in the island's census of 1679, and even these most likely owned small, marginal plots.[21]

The large majority of bound laborers transported to Barbados were men. Most of the convicts and vagrants were male, as were all of the prisoners of war listed in various inventories, although it is clear that some women and children were included among those transported from Ireland by Oliver Cromwell. With many more men than women on the mid-seventeenth-century island, some bound female laborers were able to leverage their sexuality to improve their position. While skilled men were mere laborers, women were worth more "if they are handsome." In 1654 Henry Whistler wryly noted that "a Baud broght over puts one a demuor comportment, a whore if ansume makes a wife for some rich planter," and two decades later "Margarett Hamiltone, a pritty young girle" from Edinburgh's jail, had availed herself of just such an opportunity and was "about to be married to a doctor of phisick." But for every bound woman who became a planter's wife, others lived and died as bound laborers, or perhaps survived their long terms and married fellow sufferers. Margaret Burk was almost certainly one of the prisoners sent to Barbados from Ireland, and when her illiterate husband died in 1661, she inherited nothing more than an empty chest.[22]

Contemporaries were all too aware of the significance of the island's bound workforce, and in 1664 a committee of the Council of Foreign Plantations began a list of recommendations for the improvement of English colonies with the following observation: "It being universally agreed that people art the foundation and Improvement of all Plantations and that peopl. art increased principally by Sending of Servants thither, It is necessary that a Settled course be taken for the furnishing them with servants." The authors of these recommendations made no distinction along racial lines, simply noting, "Servants are either Blacks or Whites," for labor and class rather than race initially defined workers on the early Barbadian plantations. The committee went on to note that while merchants had traditionally depended on white servants, this had become a worryingly uncertain and insufficient source of labor as fewer and fewer Britons were willing to travel to Barbados. Suggesting that an act of Parliament might be necessary, the committee recommended various measures "for a more . . . orderly Supply," including the transportation of "all felons and such as are condemned to death" for a period of seven years' service, "all Sturdy beggars . . . and other incorrigible Rogues and Wanderers" for a period of five years, as well as the "poore and Idle" of English villages and parishes for an unspecified time. With magistrates and the Crown sharing the price paid for each of these felons and vagabonds, the task of ridding British society of undesirables was potentially a profitable one for the authorities. The committee relied on experience and common practice when drawing up these recommendations, for from the late 1640s on a majority of the white servants shipped to Barbados were convicts, rebels, or prisoners of war. Usually barred from returning to the British Isles on pain of death, and quite likely to die before completing their lengthy terms of service, many must justifiably have felt that they were bound laborers for life. As a result of the increasing number of involuntary bound white laborers in Barbados, visitors and planters alike were inclined to view the labor force of Scottish, Irish, and even English vagrants, criminals, and prisoners as being of low social and moral worth, dangerous, expendable, and in need of forceful control. Writing in 1654, Henry Whistler articulated this outlook perfectly: "This Island is the Dunghill wharone England doth cast forth its rubidg[.] Rodgs and hors and such like peopell are thos which are generally Broght hear: A rodge in England will hardly make a cheater heare."[23]

As plantation agriculture took hold of Barbados the rights and prospects of the laborers on whom the system depended dwindled, and there existed an unwillingness among planters to acknowledge the rights of current or even former bound servants who were nominally free men. What was perhaps of the greatest significance was planters' fast-developing sense of bound laborers as a new kind of workforce, inferior and contemptible, composed of commodities to be utilized rather than free-born individuals with rights. Richard Ligon acknowledged this commodification of labor in the most explicit terms when he alluded to laborers as property, writing that among the "Commodities these Ships bring to the Island; are, *Servants* and *Slaves*, both men and women," before going on to list less valuable imports such as livestock, tools, and so forth.[24]

Many of the moral imperatives that underlay traditional agrarian labor relationships in early modern England were abandoned on Barbados, and new attitudes and codes of practices sanctioned the brutal exploitation of bound workers. Servants were the largest expense for planters, and apart from sugar, servants constituted the most easily transferable embodiment of capital. Planters were free to buy and sell indentured servants, to bequeath them in wills, or to win or lose them in games of chance, and these servants could be used as collateral for loans and were taxed as property. In theory it was the labor of indentured servants that could be treated in this fashion, but in practice and most certainly in the experience of the servants they were commodified, body and soul. English servants-in-husbandry had annual contractual agreements with specific individuals, and in each case a contract died when either party did. In Barbados the contracts did not die with the planters, and indentured servants were disposed of as part of their estates. The "custom of the country" overrode the English common law in defining relations between planters and indentured servants, illuminating planters' attitudes toward their servants and these men and women's declining options and increasing hopelessness. Because they were institutionalized and given the full force of law by a servant and slave code in 1661, the promise of "freedom dues" for servants who survived had all but evaporated. While in England many workers enjoyed a relatively high degree of freedom outside of the time they labored for employers and masters, in Barbados all of workers' time was owned and controlled by masters who proved eager to exploit this advantage to the full.[25]

Contemporaries believed, whether correctly or not, that white servants were more susceptible to tropical diseases, including yellow fever, edema (dropsy), and yaws, than were the African slaves who eventually replaced them. Rather than concluding that white servants should be protected, however, masters generally preferred to extract as much labor as quickly as possible from them, for the smallest outlay of expenses, in order to maximize profits. Visitors to the island were awed by the sight of white servants, many without shoes and shirts, laboring in the fields alongside slaves. Writing in the mid-seventeenth century, Richard Ligon observed that slaves "are kept and preserv'd with greater care than the servants . . . [who] have the worser lives, for they are put to very hard labor, ill lodging, and their dyet very sleight." Without doubt, the systematic and brutal exploitation of white bound laborers eased the transition to slavery on Barbados, for planters became accustomed to treating their plantation workers as unfree, lacking in virtually all human rights, and expendable.[26]

Vagrants and convicts formed a substantial part of the bound white workforce in seventeenth-century Barbados. Typical were Francis Cherry, who had "neither family nor mother living," and George Fawre, who was "very poore and not able to maintain himself." Both were sent to Barbados by London magistrates in 1681. These boys were only eleven years old and bound to labor on sugar plantations for as long as a decade, although there was a good chance that neither would survive the term of service. Vagrants and convicts were also sent to Barbados from Scotland. Early in the seventeenth century Edinburgh magistrates petitioned the Privy Council of Scotland and complained that the city was "filled and pestred with a number of theives and whores," who ignored regular punishments and banishment and "remaine in the toune committing the greatest of villanies." The magistrates requested and subsequently received permission "to send all such men and women who shall be legallie found guiltie of whoredom or theift aff this kingdome with the first conveniency to Barbados," thus beginning the process of sending Scots prisoners to labor and die in the Caribbean. This involuntary migration did not lessen until the Navigation Acts of the 1660s excluded Scotland from England's colonial trade. Encouraged by various loopholes, however, Scottish merchants continued to present themselves as men who were working "to promote the Scottish and Inglish plantation ... for the honour of their countrey" and who were striving "to frie the kingdom of the burden of many strong and idle beggars, Egiptians, common and notorious whore and theives and other disolute and louse persons banished or stigmatized for gross crymes." While the process started as a way of ridding Scottish cities of more obdurate criminals, it was not long before young men and women who had done little wrong found themselves sent to Barbados in chains, most likely to an early death and with little hope of ever again seeing their homes. Thus when Edinburgh apprentices and "trades youthes" began carousing and upsetting the peace, an apprentice mason and an apprentice painter were seized as the ringleaders of "the said tumult" and were banished to Barbados; in all probability both were in their mid-teens.[27]

In addition to vagrants and criminals, the frequent wars and rebellions of the seventeenth and early eighteenth centuries provided the English and then the British state with large numbers of prisoners. European laws of war sanctioned extreme measures against soldiers and civilians alike: "With Pyrates, Rebels, Robbers, Traytors, and Revoltes," observed William Fulbecke in 1602, "the Law of Armes is not to be observed and kept." Expensive to maintain, imprisoned rebels and prisoners of war could usually expect to be executed or, if they were fortunate, pardoned and then released. The labor needs of England's New World colonies, especially Barbados and then later Jamaica, provided a convenient and indeed profitable alternative for officials who wanted neither to execute tens of thousands nor to release them without penalty. Instead capital sentences were commuted to banishment to the plantations with a fixed term of service, usually ten years. The single largest group of prisoners of war and rebellion to be sent to Barbados was dispatched during the period of the island's greatest need for laborers. The mid-seventeenth-century Wars of the Three Kingdoms resulted in Cromwell's army capturing soldiers and civilians in England, Wales, Scotland, and Ireland. Following the Battle of Worcester in 1651, for example, Oliver Cromwell's army captured some ten thousand prisoners. While some were conscripted into the New Model Army and sent to fight in Ireland, others joined thousands of Scottish prisoners who were sent to English colonies as bound laborers, with the greatest number going to Barbados. One survivor of this exodus recorded that he was among a group of thirteen hundred sent to Barbados, where each was sold for about eight hundred pounds of sugar. No seasoning period to adjust to the climate and conditions was allowed these new servants, and this prisoner recalled, "I had to sweep the plantation yard the first day; on another day I fed the pigs and thereafter I had to do the kind of work usually performed by the slaves. Our food was very bad and consisted only of roots." Of these thirteen hundred prisoners, "As far as I know no one returned except myself."[28]

To all intents and purposes many of these bound white laborers became virtual slaves in Barbados. In the coming years, more expensive enslaved Africans were commonly afforded a seasoning period. White servants were not valuable enough to warrant such treatment, and yet they had cost enough to make planters eager to extract as much labor as rapidly as possible, before the new arrivals died. Housed in inferior dwellings "almost like dog-houses" and denied virtually any meat as part of a decent diet, a great many did not survive the disease environment, the work regimen, and their decade-long period of service. Only a fortunate few of the prisoners from the Wars of the Three Kingdoms returned home from Barbados. Among these were Walter Lyon and Thomas Smith, who had been captured during Cromwell's subjection of Scotland and then "exyled to Barbadoes, where they continued in great slavery and bondag untill his Majestys happy restauration," after which they "returned to Scotland, their native countrey."[29]

A remarkable petition provides an indication of how victims of this process experienced transport, sale, and labor in Barbados. Having been taken prisoner in 1654, the two authors arrived in Barbados in May 1656 and were promptly sold to planters "according to their working faculties." Suffering the "most insupportable Captivity, they now generally grinding at the Mills, attending the Fornaces, or digging in this scorching island, having nothing to feed on (notwithstanding their hard labour,) but Potatoe Roots, not to drink but water." These men found themselves being "bought and sold still from one Planter to another," and any infraction led to their being "whipt at their whipping-posts, as Rogues, for their masters pleasure." Condemning those who "deal in slaves and souls of men," the authors complained bitterly at the "sale and slavery of your poor Petitioners." Their published petition to Parliament contained letters and pleas from others in similar situations, virtually all of whom referred to themselves as slaves, and who wrote not just on their own account but also on behalf of "fellow sufferers left behind" on Barbados. Yet despite such pleas by the fortunate few who returned to England, the practice of sending convicts, vagrants, and prisoners to Barbados would continue for almost a century.[30]

A great many prisoners came to Barbados from Ireland. Following the Irish uprising against English and Scottish planters in 1641, the Irish had recaptured all but Dublin and Derry. A decade later many Irish volunteers traveled to England to join the Royalist cause, and when captured these Irish Catholics were treated with singular brutality by the Protestant Parliamentarians: Sir William Bereton, for example, hanged every Irish prisoner he took. This set the scene for the English reconquest of Ireland and for actions against all who resisted. Oliver Cromwell and his armies regarded the Irish not simply as rebels but as almost savage, barbarous papists worthy of few, if any, of the rights accorded English and Scottish convicts and prisoners. In September 1649 the defenders of Drogheda refused to surrender, and Cromwell instructed his conquering army to give no quarter. Thousands of men, women, and children were massacred, and Cromwell wrote with enthusiasm that this was "a righteous judgement of God upon these barbarous wretches." He considered it a mercy that many of the survivors were to be "shipped for the Barbadoes." With savage and bloody efficiency, the English armies set about the reconquest of Ireland, and many of those not killed were dispatched to Barbados, Jamaica, and other colonies. One contemporary estimated that some thirty-four thousand men were sent to the Americas, close to one-sixth of Ireland's adult male population, and more of these went to Barbados than to any other colony. In the Clonmacnoise Decrees in December 1649, Ireland's Catholic hierarchy condemned the English attempt to destroy Catholicism, uproot "the common people" and dispatch them to "the Tobacco Island" (Barbados), and then replace them in Ireland with English soldiers and settlers. English merchants seized their opportunity and petitioned Cromwell for permission to transport Irish prisoners "out of Ireland for planting in the Caribbee Islands," after which these merchants would return to England with cargoes of tobacco, sugar, and other crops.[31]

These Irish prisoners arrived in Barbados at what was, for them, a particularly inopportune time. The rapid development of sugar led to a trebling of land value between 1645 and 1655, effectively excluding virtually all who might survive their lengthy term of bound labor from any prospect of eventual landownership. Imprisoned in Ireland by English invaders, forced to labor in Barbados for planters who did not want them ever to enjoy meaningful freedom and economic sufficiency, despised for their Catholicism, and with their condition countenanced by English authorities, Irish bound laborers had little hope and nothing to lose.[32]

As late as the start of the eighteenth century John Oldmixon compared the diet of white servants in Barbados unfavorably with the food enjoyed by English servants-in-husbandry, concluding, "Their Diet is not so good, as those who have been us'd to Rich Farmers Tables in *England*." Twenty years earlier Sir Thomas Montgomery, shocked by what he saw in Barbados, had gone much further in his appeal to the Lords of Trade and Plantations: "I beg . . . care for the poor white servants here, who are used with more barbarous cruelty than in Algiers. Their bodies and souls are used as if hell commenced here and only continued in the world to come. They want the merest necessities of food and raiment, and many die daily in consequence." In the late 1660s an observer recorded that he had "inspected many [of] their plantations and have seen 30, sometimes 40, Christians—English, Scotch, and Irish—at work in the parching sun without shirt, shoe, or stocking . . . [while] their Negroes have been at work at their respective trades in a good condition." Not only were most if not all white servants convicts or prisoners, working alongside slaves in plantation fields, but their shoes and clothing were often inferior to those allowed the more valuable enslaved Africans.[33]

The "Act for the good Governing of Servants" was passed by the Barbados Assembly in September 1661, and it said as much about the "custom of the country" over the preceding three decades as it did about plantation owners' desire to retain mastery over newly arrived white servants. Consolidating several previous laws, this new act moved beyond previous legislation in order to "prevent the bold extravagancy and wandering of servants" through "the good regulating and governing of Servants in all things concerning their Masters and themselves." Any servant jailed for a criminal offense would have his or her service extended for double the length of time served in jail. Not just servants but any ships' captains or others who might harbor runaways were targeted by this law, which detailed fines and punishments for any who dared to deprive masters of their property as well as fines for constables who neglected their duty in pursuing and apprehending runaways. The would-be runaway servant could expect to serve an additional term of three years for the offense. Similarly, any free man who made a planter's female servant pregnant would be liable to serve that planter for three years, while the unfortunate female servant would have her term extended by two years. The sheer brutal, violent power exercised by masters became clear in a provision of this new law designed to protect servants against murder by their masters. Admitting that some masters "have exercised great violence and great oppression, to, and upon their Servants, through which some of them have been murdered and destroyed," the law specified that no servant who died during his or her term of service could be buried before the body was examined by a justice of the peace or a constable "and two Neighbours of the Parish." Failure to comply would result in a penalty of "twenty thousand pounds of *Muscovado* Sugar": in short, a token fine was all that would be imposed on a planter who killed a servant and buried the body before it could be examined by outsiders. Moreover there is little evidence to suggest that this law was invoked and used against murderous planters.[34]

Planters enjoyed enormous control over white bound laborers, and Ligon admitted that "if the Master be Cruell, the Servants have very wearisome and miserable lives." Verbal and physical resistance was brutally punished, and even the most minor offenses could result in physical punishment and an extension of the already long period of servitude. Thus Edmond Hollingsteade complained in September 1657 that his servants George Dumohan and Walter Welsh had "rebelliously and mutinously behaved themselves towards him their said master and mistress," and the two Irish servants—prisoners of war sent by Cromwell—received thirty-one lashes apiece. Masters could deal with "impudent, saucy and provoking" servants by reporting them to a local justice of the peace, who was required by law "to inflict such corporal punishment as he shall judge the crime to deserve."[35]

Perhaps of more general significance was the almost total control planters enjoyed over servants and their lives. Even more than English farmers whose households included servants-in-husbandry, Barbados planters enjoyed ownership of all of their servants' time, not just the hours of labor or the work for which they were contracted. This enabled planters to restrict and control all aspects of servants' lives. It was white men and women from the British Isles, not African slaves, who first experienced such a dramatic reduction of personal freedom. Laborers were the most expensive commodities purchased by planters, and local laws and the "custom of the country" allowed planters to exploit their investments fully. Consequently, and because of the lengthy terms that many served, these servants more fully resembled pauper or vagrant apprentices, bound to serve masters for as long as a decade.

Hilary Beckles has estimated that during the pivotal years between 1650 and 1690 at least 40 percent and as much as 50 percent of the island's servant population was Irish, and it was common for Irish servants to be worked alongside early African slaves. The Irish prisoners were treated with singular brutality by Barbadian planters, who disdained them as illiterate Catholic savages who they feared were likely to join with African slaves in bloody rebellion. Given the nature of their treatment, such fears may have been well founded; it seems likely that one of the first maroon groups on the island was a multiracial mixture of about thirty Irish and African slaves and servants who took shelter in the remaining forested land in St. Philip Parish during the mid-1650s.[36]

Rebellion by these bound servants was a constant threat. Richard Ligon observed that "cruell Masters will provoke their Servants so, by extream ill usage, and often and cruell beating them, as they grow desperate, and so joyne together to revenge themselves upon them." In 1649 Ligon witnessed the results. The bound laborers' "sufferings being grown to a great height . . . some amongst them, whose spirits were not able to endure such slavery, resolved to break through it, or die in the act." Convinced that a majority of the island's bound white workforce were sympathetic to the planned rebellion, Ligon recorded with relief that it had been betrayed and that eighteen of their leaders had been executed. As the number of enslaved African laborers grew, the fear of servant rebellion expanded and planters dreaded the forging of an alliance between the Irish and the Africans. Militia groups during the latter decades of the seventeenth century appear to have been composed primarily of English and Scotsmen, differentiating them not just from runaway enslaved Africans but also from Irish bound laborers. Planters were so terrified of potential alliances between Irish Catholics and black slaves that in March 1689 the island's council ordered free blacks believed to be Catholic to be "sold or transported and sent of[f] this Island to be sold accordingly." For Barbados planters in the mid- to late seventeenth century, the years when the plantation system and racial slavery solidified, a rebellious combination of slaves, Irishmen, and Catholics was the stuff of nightmares. A rebellion in 1692 featuring Irish Catholics and African slaves saw the nightmare taking a horrifyingly real form, with Irishmen alleged to have been prepared to get soldiers on the island drunk and incapacitated.[37]

In the mid-seventeenth century planters began shifting from white servants to black slaves as the latter became a more cost-effective investment, for just as white bound laborers became more scarcer and thus more expensive, the price of West African slaves fell and their numbers increased. Richard Dunn posits a rapid change, while Hilary Beckles describes a more gradual transition. The supply of voluntary indentured servants diminished at the very time that expanding sugar agriculture and production required large numbers of laborers, and it is clear that demand for labor far exceeded the regular supply of bound workers from the British Isles. The criminals, vagrants, and prisoners of war, who from the early 1640s on constituted the bulk of bound white laborers arriving in Barbados, were by definition an occasional and irregular source of bound workers, and planters depended on the government and merchants for a supply of these unfree laborers. England, and then Britain, would continue to transport political and civil prisoners out of the British Isles for another two centuries, and the rising number of unemployed and homeless vagrants appeared to promise a seemingly limitless supply of workers who could be used and regulated with singular brutality in Barbados. However, the very success of the integrated plantation system developed on Barbados signaled the end of white servitude. By 1680 white servants in Barbados had been all but completely displaced by slaves on most plantations and in related activities; only fishing, dock work, boating, militia service, and plantation management remained exclusively white activities. The process was uneven, and demand for white servants remained strong throughout the seventeenth century, perhaps in part because many of these servants were prisoners of war and rebels with few rights, and planters could expect to benefit from their labor for as long as a decade, placing them in skilled and supervisory positions over the growing enslaved workforce, all at little cost. In 1686 the Barbados Assembly passed a law detailing the conditions of service of political and military prisoners: their decade-long indentures could not be sold off the island, they were prohibited from marrying white servants, they could not be freed before their terms had expired, and those who attempted to escape would be whipped and branded "FT" to mark them as fugitive traitors. The transition from white servitude to black slavery was eased by the existence of thousands of such servants, who could be worked longer and harder than voluntary white servants elsewhere in the British Americas. Thus as late as the 1680s at least 107 planters purchased the captured rebels from the Monmouth Rebellion, even though the transition from white servitude to black slavery was well under way. However, for all of the hardships faced by the Monmouth rebels, few were worked as harshly as the Irish prisoners of a generation earlier, and instead of working alongside slaves in the sugarcane fields, most were employed in managerial and more skilled occupations.[38]

It was on Barbados that an integrated plantation system and an accompanying labor system were created, to say nothing of the new attitudes toward labor fostered by this new system. These were then exported to the rest of the British Caribbean and the Deep South of the American mainland. Many of the "white slaves" of Barbados, along with their descendants, were placed outside of English traditions of servitude and North American adaptations of this model, as described by Christopher Tomlins. The result was that on this one island, the absolute differences between white servitude and African slavery posited by Tomlins were far less apparent: the laws that he describes regulating African slaves and their labor were on Barbados initially applied to white servants.[39]

What is perhaps most remarkable about Barbados is that the small planter elites maintained their disdain for the descendants of the bound white laborers who had created the plantation economy. Poor and unable to improve their lot, they inhabited small patches of marginal land, and they traded food and stolen commodities with slaves, earning the hostility of planters. The descendants of the maligned and marginalized poor of Scotland, Ireland, and England were held in the same disregard as their ancestors. By the end of the eighteenth century racial slavery had completely supplanted white servitude, and few of the original white servants survived. However, some of the impoverished descendants of indentured servants, including the prisoners from British jails and the captives from wars and rebellions, can be found on Barbados to this day, many with the Irish and Scottish surnames of their ancestors.

In 1643, with relatively few Africans on the island and most planters still growing tobacco, cotton, or indigo, James Holdip had twenty-nine bound white laborers working his 200-acre plantation. Like many of his contemporaries, he owned no slaves. Within a few years sugar became the island's great cash crop, and bound whites and enslaved Africans labored together on Barbadian plantations, including those growing sugarcane. The transformation was evident on Sir Anthony Ashley Cooper's similarly sized plantation, which in 1646 was worked by twenty-one bound whites and nine enslaved Africans. By the mid-1650s, and despite the influx of bound whites from the war-torn British Isles, enslaved Africans formed a majority of the unfree workforce. In 1654 Robert Hooper's 200 acres were worked by thirty-five white servants and sixty-six slaves, and by 1656 George Martin had no white servants and sixty African slaves at work on his 259 acres.[40]

By the end of the seventeenth century enslaved Africans dominated the Barbadian plantation workforce. However, although their bound labor had been shaped by the earlier exploitation of bound Britons, changes in the land worsened the work and living conditions of the enslaved newcomers. Deforestation and overplanting had exhausted the Barbadian soil, while declining sugar prices made it increasingly difficult for planters to make money. Once again Barbadian planters led the way, pioneering integrated plantations, the gang system, cane-holing, and manuring—all part of a back-breaking regimen of work that kept plantations productive and profitable.[41]

In early to mid-seventeenth-century Barbados chattel slavery had yet to cohere, and it was bound labor—not yet race or slavery—that defined the condition of those who shaped the island's early plantations. It was their labor and experience that in turn shaped the development of racial slavery. This suggests that some modification is required of Winthrop Jordan's observation that English ideas about color, Christianity, and sexual mores informed an "unthinking decision" to engage in the transatlantic slave trade and develop plantations powered by chattel slaves. Jordan's remarkably sophisticated and subtle analysis of the symbiotic emergence of prejudice and slavery did not allow for the unique situation in Barbados and its influence on the development of plantation slavery elsewhere. On this island planters' attitudes toward and treatment of bound white laborers informed the later development of ideas and practices of plantation slavery, and the evolution of a belief that only enslaved Africans were fit for such work, ideas and practices that were then exported in developed form to other English colonies. It was a class-based system of labor, shaped by ethnic and religious prejudices, that provided the foundation for slavery in Barbados and for the more fully formed racialized plantation slavery system that spread to Jamaica, the Carolinas, and beyond. A time of particularly intense social and political dislocation in the British Isles had provided the preconditions that encouraged large landowners in Barbados to treat English, Scottish, and Irish convicts, vagrants, rebels, and prisoners of war as persons whose lives were forfeit, and who could be treated as a disposable labor force. English authorities were preoccupied with domestic strife and a conflict over authority in the home islands throughout the second and third quarters of the seventeenth century, minimizing imperial oversight. This enabled planters to adapt English ideas and practices as well as the treatment of English bound laborers, in the process developing important foundations for the subsequent system of racialized plantation slavery. Generations of enslaved Africans and their descendants were destined to toil on the plantations of British America, facing unspeakable cruelty and the most arduous labor. This should not blind us, however, to the significance of class rather than race at the inception of this system in Barbados, as the island's plantation elites developed an exaggerated form of English agricultural labor. In its origins, at least, plantation slavery was rather more English and less exceptionally American than we have imagined.[42]

Anglicizing the League: The Writing of Cadwallader Colden's *History of the Five Indian Nations*

William Howard Carter

Cadwallader Colden's *History of the Five Indian Nations* was first published in 1727, fifty years after the creation of the Covenant Chain alliance that bound the British colonies to the Haudenosaunee, or Five Nations of the Iroquois League. The Haudenosaunee were strategically located between the British and French Empires in North America but beyond the control of either. Both of these rival empires had alliances with the Haudenosaunee, but neither had the promise of allegiance in case of war. Only when war was a reality could one see whether relationships soothed over the intervening years had paid off by who mobilized with you and who against, or by who came to aid in times of need. Everybody was gambling and the stakes were the fate of Native nations and Euro-American empires in North America.[1]

Intruding Europeans did not much like living in the midst of such uncertainty, but it was an inescapable condition of the life they or their ancestors had chosen when they came to North America. An invasive New Yorker observed of the Haudenosaunee, "To preserve the Ballance between us and the French, is the great ruling Principle of the modern Indian Politics." As much as he might wish to know for certain how the Haudenosaunee would act, the interests of the Haudenosaunee lay in keeping everyone guessing, which was good because they did not and could not know themselves what their men of war would do. The New Yorker believed that "their Affections are in our Favour" but thought that their fear of the French was increasing while their affection for the British declined by virtue of British neglect.[2] It was in this setting of fear, anxiety, and above all unsettling uncertainty that Colden sat down to write his *History*. He hoped to repair the Covenant Chain by convincing his fellow colonists to take measures to secure better "the Affections" of the Haudenosaunee. Alarmed by how the British made the same mistakes again and again, which "weakened" these affections, Colden wrote a didactic history that would provide lessons for the successful management of this crucial relationship, a sort of primer for the colonists and imperial officials involved in Haudenosaunee affairs. Colden tried to relieve the oppressive uncertainty of living among and depending on nonstate peoples such as the Haudenosaunee by bringing things vaguely and hazily understood out of the shadows and into the more precise clarity of Enlightenment knowledge.

As Colden well knew, Enlightenment knowledge was not innocent or disinterested but instead was produced to further the interests of the empires that made such knowledge both possible and necessary. It is in this imperial sense that John M. Murrin's concept of Anglicization helps illuminate Colden's *History*. In his famous frontier thesis, Frederick Jackson Turner argued that the societies that developed in new settlements underwent a "reversion" toward savagery that democratized and equalized society. Anglicization described the subsequent, countervailing processes toward increasing inequality and replication of English norms and institutions. Yet Murrin has also described how, after the English conquered Dutch New Netherland, they attempted to Anglicize the colony and its Dutch inhabitants. The Covenant Chain was an Anglicized version of the previous Dutch "Iron Chain" alliance with the Haudenosaunee, and the story of its initial period of Anglicization from 1677 to 1689 was precisely the subject of the first volume of Colden's *History*.[3]

Yet his book was also an effort to Anglicize knowledge *about* the Haudenosaunee by reducing English dependence on the Albany Dutch and Canadian French for such knowledge. In other words, Colden's *History* furthered the interests of the British Empire by engaging with Anglicization in two ways: first, by Anglicizing knowledge, narratives, and discourse *about* the Haudenosaunee and, second, by explaining why previous efforts to Anglicize the Haudenosaunee had failed, Colden hoped to guide future officials in making more effective decisions about how to manage the Covenant Chain. Colden was forced to develop new methods of narration for writing the history of a nonstate society and its foreign relations, and the work he produced should therefore be considered to be the first "ethnohistory" written in English. Colden's history revealed subjection to be a dangerous fantasy that produced alienation rather than affection. Colden advocated the emulation of the more successful techniques developed by the French that used mediation as a source of power—the same techniques later described by the ethnohistorian Richard White in his seminal book *The Middle Ground*. The Covenant Chain was also a "middle ground" forged between nonstate Native societies and the state-based empires of the invasive Europeans, and a better understanding of how power actually worked in it was essential for advancing the interests of the British Empire against those of the French.[4]

Colden's first encounter with the Haudenosaunee, the circumstances that led him to write the *History,* and the various ways in which it Anglicized knowledge about the Haudenosaunee are explored in this essay. I then turn to how Colden narrated in the first volume of the *History* the failed English attempt to Anglicize the Haudenosaunee in the early years of the Covenant Chain. Colden's *History* is not a neatly bound text—it sprawled and grew over the years with new volumes and materials added—but in this essay, I have confined myself largely to the first volume as published in 1727, only occasionally drawing on his later additions to the text.

The First Encounter

In 1721, at the age of thirty-two and with new appointments to the provincial council and as surveyor-general for New York, Colden made his way to Albany with the governor of New York to witness a meeting between the Haudenosaunee and the new governor of New York, William Burnet. Colden had grown up in Scotland and attended university in Edinburgh. He practiced as a physician for a short while, but after immigrating to the colonies, his interests spread to natural history, botany, physics, and increasingly politics and government. His gifts as an Enlightenment intellectual made him quite useful to Governor Burnet and propelled his rapid rise in provincial New York politics. The 1721 trip to Albany was the first real event of this trajectory, and it would set Colden on the path to writing the *History.*

In his unpublished papers, Colden wrote that the first meeting took place in a "Large boarded house" that had been specifically built for the purpose of housing the Haudenosaunee when they came to Albany on business. The inside walls were decorated with "a great many animals tolerably well delineated with coal" by the Haudenosaunee. Colden's interest in natural history drew him to these depictions of North American fauna. Drawings of "beefs" in different postures were proof to Colden that the artist "was not without a genius for Painting." He asked through the interpreter where they had seen such animals, and they pointed west in response, which suggests that the "beefs" in question were American bison rather than European cattle. Yet the "most remarkable" of the drawings was a "very well designed" "Crocodile." He again asked where they had seen such an animal, and this time they pointed southwest, which Colden took as evidence that the Haudenosaunee had traveled "very far to the southward's perhaps near to the mouth of the river Misasipi." The interpreter further informed him that they had the "dried skin of one of them att one of their Castles," or towns, which further piqued Colden's interest.[5]

Colden's curiosity was not limited to items of scientific interest, for he also recorded in detail the treaty scene and the speeches that followed. Colden noted that at the initial meeting, the governor kept his hat on and sat in an "elbow chair," or armchair. He was flanked by a seated gentleman on each side, with the rest of the gentlemen (including Colden) standing. Teganissorens, the great Onondaga orator famous for the policy of Haudenosaunee neutrality in wars between the English and the French in North America, likewise sat in an armchair with the rest of the Haudenosaunee men of peace seated on the floor. The two stars of the proceedings—Governor Burnet and Teganissorens—sat opposite each other on a footing of apparent equality while enjoying glasses of wine together.

Yet this public display of comity did not reflect the governor's true feelings. After the Haudenosaunee left, the governor sent word that Teganissorens was not "acceptable to him, he keeping a Correspondence with the French," and requested that the Haudenosaunee select another for the position of speaker. Teganissorens, as Colden reported, was "famous" among both the French and the English for "having been long a great Capt[ain] or Leader among the five Nations & generally their speaker at all treaties a very cunning suttle fellow." The next day Colden noted that while all the men of peace—some seventy or eighty of them—were "seated upon boards Laid in the street," Teganissorens "stood among the young Indians who made a cem-circle round the Sachems & lookt very much dejected."[6]

Governor Burnet's refusal to deal with Teganissorens stemmed from the very source of Teganissorens's success as a diplomat: his advocacy of a neutralist diplomacy that kept both the English and the French at arm's length. When Colden asked why the famous orator had been dismissed, he was told that when the previous governor had tried to get the Haudenosaunee to fight the French during Queen Anne's War, Teganissorens had "rais'd himself upon a barril to harrangue to his people & to disswade them from engadgeing in that Expedition." Teganissorens "said that they ought not to join either . . . butt to keep the ballance betwixt the two," for if either empire were to prevail, the victor would "enslave" the Haudenosaunee. Yet "if the five Nations would now observe an exact Newtrality they would be courted & fear'd by both sides." In a real demonstration of the limits of Teganissorens's power, many Haudeno-saunee ignored him and joined the embarrassing attempts to invade Canada in 1709 and 1711. Even though the previous governor had continued to treat with Teganissorens for the intervening decade, Burnet resurrected this past grievance and used it to justify Teganissorens's dismissal.[7] The final irony came a few years later when Burnet was forced to recognize the limits of *his* power and had to ask that Teganissorens be reappointed in order to get permission to build a new fort at Oswego. Sufficiently chastened, Teganissorens promised he would "promote the British Interest"—a significant departure from the neu-tralist position he had been advocating for nearly thirty years.[8]

Twenty years later, as Colden wrote the second part of his *History*, he reflected on the occasion he met Teganissorens. "He was grown old when I saw him, and heard him speak," Colden recalled. "He had a great Fluency in speaking, and a graceful Elocution, that would have pleased in any Part of the World." He quoted Teganissorens's speeches in order "to give the Reader as perfect a Notion as I can of the Indian Genius." Tellingly, the example Colden chose was one in which he defended his policy of neutrality before a hostile English audience. Colden chose this moment because it revealed the "Art he [Teganissorens] had, to make an Account of the Affair less disagreeable to English Ears, which had been undertaken against their Advice, and contrary to their Interest."[9]

As he wrote these words of praise, Colden could not have forgotten that this first meeting was also the time of Teganissorens's disgrace. The dramatic dismissal of Teganissorens, the greatest advocate of neutrality, could have been portrayed as a grand triumph of Anglicization and imposition of Eng-lish will, as it seemed to curtail Haudenosaunee sovereignty both internally in their ability to choose speakers and externally in their ability to conduct diplomacy with rival empires. Colden's intervening years of experience led him to see Burnet's imperious treatment as a mistake, a classic example of the boorish and counterproductive behavior that was typical of new governors eager to impose their will on the Haudenosaunee. Including this episode would have sent precisely the *wrong* message to ambitious new governors eager to make their mark. Colden went on to write his *History* to prevent future governors from repeating the mistakes of the past, in which high-handed efforts to Anglicize the Haudenosaunee had served only to alienate them further, damaging English interests and giving ground to the French.

Colden's initial encounter with the Haudenosaunee in Albany introduced concerns that would haunt the Covenant Chain for years to come: the rivalry between the French and British Empires; the importance of intelligence and knowledge; the limits of everyone's power; and the impossibility of reconciling the interests and needs of state-based empires and nonstate societies. Colden would be tasked with making some sense of this confusing situation, a task he was well positioned for as surveyor-general. As he surveyed Haudenosaunee lands and engaged in the scientific and legal alchemy that commodified those lands and made them available to British colonialism, he needed to come to acquire intelligence and knowledge about the lands and peoples he colonized. The various difficulties he and other officials faced all stemmed from the nonstate organization of the Haudenosaunee, as did the difficulties he faced in writing the *History,* so it is there that we must begin.

Nonstates, States, and Empires

Before immigrating to the colonies, Colden's ideas about the indigenous peoples he might encounter were shaped while he studied in Edinburgh. Thomas Hobbes and other European intellectuals imagined Native Americans as living in a "state of nature," a crude, earlier stage of human development. Life in the "state of nature" was, in Hobbes's estimation, "nasty, brutish, and short." Native Americans were imagined to be living relics of this primordial existence outside of historical time, without order, government, or rules. It was in this intellectual framework that John Locke could write, without appearing ridiculous, "In the beginning, all the world was America." Locke theorized that states eventually came into existence to enforce laws that could protect private property. Colden would later echo these sentiments in his *History,* but by that time his empirical knowledge of actual Native Americans had revealed the shortcomings of such philosophical models.[10]

Yet Locke's model had nonetheless captured some important truths about the differences between states and nonstates. For the vast majority of human history, humans lived in relatively small, egalitarian, nonstate societies organized primarily by kinship. In such nonstate societies, the anthropologist Pierre Clastres writes, "the chief has no authority at his disposal, no power of coercion, no means of giving an order." In some places, however, the domestication of a few key species allowed societies to grow in size and density to the point where persuasion became inadequate for keeping order, creating the conditions that favored the development of states that could impose laws and punish those who broke them. The difference, Clastres argues, "is the power to compel; it is the power of coercion; it is political power." States claimed a monopoly on the legitimate use of violence, both externally against enemies and internally to maintain order and compel obedience. In Locke's view, the absence of a coercive state resulted in a "state of nature" in which the legitimate use of violence was distributed throughout society, resulting in chaos and anarchy.[11]

While Colden agreed that Native Americans were living examples of life without the state, his experiences with real Native Americans led him to reject the ways Hobbes and Locke had theorized the state of nature. In the introduction to his *History*, Colden wrote, "As I am fond to think, that the present state of the Indian Nations exactly shows the most Ancient and Original Condition of almost every Nation; so I believe we may with more certainty see the Original Form of all Government, than the most curious Speculations of the Learned." In good Enlightenment form, Colden used empirical evidence to dismiss these speculations that were "no better than Hypotheses in Philosophy" and "prejudicial to real Knowledge."[12] Colden's description of the actual "government" of the Haudenosaunee conforms much more closely to modern anthropological understandings of nonstates than did the "curious Speculations" of philosophers like Locke.

Colden emphasized, above all, the absence of coercive government among the Haudenosaunee and the powerlessness of leaders. "Each Nation is an absolute Republick by its self, govern'd in all Publick Affairs by the Sachems, or Old Men, whose Authority and Power is gain'd by and consists wholly in the Opinion the rest of the Nation has of their Wisdom and Integrity," Colden wrote. "They never execute their Resolutions by Compulsion or Force upon any of their People." While the analogy with republics may have helped his readers imagine a nonmonarchical form of government, republics are, after all, still states, so the analogy falls flat. The absence of the power of coercion meant that people did as they wished. Older men of peace cultivated diplomatic relations that maintained peace through gift exchange, but these men of peace could not control the younger men who went to war, for these were largely separate and autonomous realms of power and authority among the Haudenosaunee. Much of the older men's diplomacy involved smoothing over relations upset by the violent actions of the men of war. The constant, small-scale violence that characterized Haudenosaunee interactions with other peoples frequently erupted into war, requiring renewed diplomatic efforts to restore peace.

Colden observed that cultural mechanisms among the Haudenosaunee prevented the accumulation of wealth and thereby suppressed the ability of leaders to rise in power. "Their Great Men," he wrote, "are generally poorer than the common People." Leaders gave everything away that they gained through treaties or war, "so as to leave nothing to themselves." Further, keeping any of these items—attempting to hoard or accumulate riches—would lead not to power but rather to its loss. If leaders were even suspected of selfishness, they would appear "mean in the opinion of their Country-men" and consequently "lose their Authority." While the power of the elites in states stemmed from their greater share of resources and accumulation of goods, in nonstates power lay in giving things away.[13] Not only were leaders unable to punish those who did not do as they were told, but the few sanctions that did exist in society served to punish and constrain the power of would-be leaders rather than to force commoners to do their leaders' bidding.

Colden's description of the ways that chiefly power operated is entirely consistent with the observations of political anthropologists today. "The chief is there to serve society," Clastres writes; "it is society as such—the real locus of power—that exercises its authority over the chief." Gift economies were the norm in nonstates—basic resources such as food, shelter, and clothing were shared without question—which meant that accumulation, hoarding, or a refusal to give were profoundly antisocial activities. At the same time that giving made leaders the poorest members of the community, however, it also enhanced their power. Gifts created debts that could never be repaid; reciprocated gifts created new debt relationships that ran in the opposite direction without canceling out the first. As Colden wrote, the poverty of leaders stemmed from their constant giving, and it was this giving that created their "Authority" and influence, even as it served as a check on their power.[14]

However impotent Haudenosaunee leaders and "government" may have seemed to British readers, Colden made it clear that the Haudenosaunee were no "meer Barbarians" living in a disorganized state of nature but were instead a major power that must be taken seriously. The Five Nations of the Haudenosaunee were "joyn'd together by a League or Confederacy, like the United Provinces [of the Netherlands], without any Superiority of any one over the other." Just as leaders could not punish members of society, the

League had no power to enforce its policies or decisions. Reciprocal gift exchanges condoled the dead and thereby prevented the escalation of violence within the League. The League channeled violence outward, toward other nations, and while the men of peace could not control the men of war, nonetheless they had influence and authority. To bolster his claim about the power of the League, Colden quoted a French authority who wrote that the Haudenosaunee were "the Fiercest and Most Formidable People in North America, and at the same time as Politick and Judicious as well can be conceiv'd." Their diplomatic gift relationships included not only "the French and English, but [also] . . . almost all the Indian Nations of this vast Continent." The webs of influence these men of peace spun did not result in the ability to command troops or enforce peace, but depending on how the relationships were nurtured, they could yield allies when war came. At that point, allies would weigh their different relationships and make their own decisions, but the extensiveness of Haudenosaunee gift-exchange networks meant that a great number of Native nations would give their proposals serious consideration.[15]

Anglicizing Knowledge of the League

As the quote from the French authority above demonstrated, influence over these Haudenosaunee networks was of critical importance in the imperial rivalry taking shape in northeastern North America. Colden feared that the British were at a severe disadvantage by virtue of their reliance on French texts for their knowledge of these networks. Colden's stated purpose in writing the first edition of the *History* was to Anglicize knowledge about the Haudenosaunee to free it from French bias. As Colden observed in the preface, "Though every one that is in the least acquainted with the Affairs of North-America, knows of what Consequence the . . . Five Nations are both in Peace and War, I know of no Accounts of them Published in English, but what are meer Translations of French Authors." Colden thought this reflected poorly "on the Inhabitants of this Province, as if we wanted Curiosity to enquire into our own Affairs." Consequently British officials had been forced to rely on French accounts that were written "in a different Interest, and sometimes in open Hostility with us."[16] The British were losing the war of words and consequently of the intelligence that the British needed to enlarge their empire. Colden implied that knowledge was power, and that the power that such knowledge gave was crucial to colonialism; yet he also recognized, however implicitly, that such knowledge was always interested.

In order to advance British imperial interests, knowledge about the Haudenosaunee needed to be Anglicized. Colden revealed as much when he expressed the hope that his *History* would "be of great use to all the British Colonies in North-America." Reliable English knowledge would be a sounder basis for the development of British imperial policy, and it would help governors and other officials make better-informed decisions to manage the Haudenosaunee in the British interest. Knowledge could do so by revealing how power worked both among the Haudenosaunee and through their diplomatic networks, and it revealed that some approaches were more effective than others. To make this argument—and to Anglicize knowledge about the Haudenosaunee—Colden had to forge new methodological and narrative ground by writing first ethnohistory in the English language. Colden's innovations were a necessary consequence of the nonstate organization of the Haudenosaunee and the challenges of writing a history that revealed the way power operated in their domestic and foreign relations. Because of the particular circumstances of his writing, Anglicization and methodological innovation had to go hand in hand.[17]

The first and most important way that such knowledge was Anglicized was by reducing British reliance on French books. The first of these was Louis Armand de Lom de l'Arce Baron de Lahontan's *New Voyages to North America,* translated and published in London in 1703. Lahontan's account was a memoir of firsthand experiences written down long after the fact and of questionable reliability; still, it contained important source material on Haudenosaunee negotiations with the French, which Colden used. The second was Claude-Charles Le Roy de Bacqueville de la Potherie's *Histoire de l'Amérique Septentrionale* (or "The History of North America"), which was published in Paris in 1722 but was never translated into English. Like Lahontan, La Potherie grounded his authority to claim knowledge in firsthand experience, though he also made use of official documents. Both of these works were heavily indebted to earlier French and Spanish "histories" of the New World, which tended to be either document-based histories of European colonies or experience-based memoirs, ethnographies, or works of comparative ethnology.[18] Colden's *History* broke away from these French accounts not only by virtue of being written in English but also in terms of genre. Colden grounded his authority as an author not in firsthand experience but rather in his own "Perusal of the Minutes of the Commissioners for Indian Affairs"—what we would today call historical research in primary documents. Colden has been credited with cocreating, along with Benjamin Franklin, the printed treaty as a new genre of literature, but this was not his only innovation.[19]

Colden used the documentary record of colonialism to write a history of a nonstate people. Writing a history of such "different People and different Ages," Colden reflected, required "different Rules, and often different Abilities to write it." Colden asked that his readers make "more than usually Favourable Allowances" for what was the "first Attempt of the kind, in this Country." He included a brief ethnography to orient readers to unfamiliar Haudenosaunee cultural patterns, but his treatment of the Haudenosaunee was fundamentally and deeply historical, unlike most of the other "histories" of the New World that coupled Native ethnography or ethnology with a history of Euro-American colonization. This made it a pathbreaking ethnohistory: it combined anthropological understandings of a Native culture with historical research in primary documents generated by Euro-American colonialism to write a history of that Native people. His history focused on the Haudenosaunee as a group of autonomous, nonstate indigenous nations, and he tried to convey some understanding of the different logic that stemmed from their nonstate organization and underpinned their actions and strategies. The freedom from coercion in Haudenosaunee society was at the root of these methodological and narrative innovations, and this also formed the central problem Colden faced in attempting to explain Haudenosaunee "government" to his readers. Colden viewed this as a mandatory first step, for he held that it "was necessary to know something of the Form of Government of the People whose History one reads." Colden thereby oriented readers to the culture he wrote about by combining ethnographic explication with historical narrative in true ethnohistorical fashion.[20]

In addition to these methodological innovations, Colden asked his readers' allowance for innovations he had to make in his narration. First, without a clearly bounded state to serve as the central actor, Colden faced the problem of decentralization. He was forced to fill up a "great part of the Work with the Adventures of small Parties" and could not make sense of their "Publick Treaties . . . without taking Notice of several minute Circumstances." In other words, Colden found it necessary to trace the divergent, uncoordinated, and at times mutually contradictory efforts of various parties who pursued different courses of action. Second, he apologized for including "so many Speeches at length," for he found it impossible "to show the Wit, and Judgment, and

Art, and Simplicity, and Ignorance of the several Parties, managing a Treaty, in other Words than their own." To describe the "genius" of the Indians required extensive quotation because they "use many Metaphors in their Discourse, which . . . may strongly move our Passions by their lively Images." One could not hope to understand these metaphors without being immersed in the speeches in which they appeared.[21]

Colden's use of these records, however innovative, also created problems for his *History*. Haudenosaunee speeches went from an oral Iroquoian language into Dutch and only then into written English, producing multiple layers of distortion along the way. The Albany interpreters did not do "Justice to the Indian Eloquence" and often reduced lengthy speeches to a single sentence. The material he borrowed from French authors had a more pleasing style but was therefore also less reliable. Perhaps out of necessity, Colden declared his preference for "Truth" with a "rough Stile" to "Eloquence without it." He further mused, "I have sometimes thought that the Histories wrote with all the Delicacy of a fine Romance, are like French Dishes, more agreeable to the Pallat than the Stomach, and less wholsom than a more common and coarser Dyet." In this simile histories were meals for the body politic. Colden's history, like English cuisine, would better nourish the British Empire.[22] Yet Colden's positioning of his English narrative against those of the French was only the most obvious kind of Anglicization it effected, for it was also an Anglicization of Dutch records and knowledge about the Haudenosaunee.

Colden Anglicized this knowledge to reduce English dependence on the Dutch in Albany, who likewise could not be trusted to further British imperial interests. Three years before writing the *History*, Colden had written, at Burnet's request, a memorial on the fur trade that described how Mohawks smuggled English cloth between Dutch merchants in Albany and French traders in Montreal. In the preface to part two of his *History*, Colden revealed that shortly after becoming governor, Burnet read the minutes of the Albany commissioners and determined that the illicit Albany-Montreal trade was damaging imperial interests. The French not only reaped the profits of carrying English goods to Native consumers but also thereby enhanced their standing—and ability to recruit military allies—among Native nations to the west. Burnet proposed to end this illicit trade and build a "fortified trading House at Oswego" on Lake Ontario, which would allow British merchants to sell directly to western Native nations. This would cut the Albany Dutch merchants out of two lucrative markets, as well as Mohawk middlemen, and

Anglicize this trade by taking it away from the French, Dutch, and Mohawks in one fell swoop. The need to secure Haudenosaunee permission to build this fort at Oswego forced Burnet to reconcile with Teganissorens, and it was the latter's consent to this imperial project that was the true triumph of Anglicization—not Burnet's earlier, imperious dismissal of him.

While Colden had stated that the purpose of his history was to Anglicize French knowledge, the Anglicization of Dutch-controlled economic and diplomatic relations was also a key underlying motive. Once they caught wind of Burnet's plan, Dutch merchants raised "a Clamour" and petitioned the king to repeal it. This public outcry led Burnet to give Colden the minutes of the Albany commissioners and to tell him that "the Publication of the History of the Five Indian Nations might be of use at that Time." Colden's *History* was a political weapon in the ongoing effort to Anglicize Dutch control of trade and diplomacy with the Haudenosaunee. In a private letter, Colden blamed the Dutch for the "mismanagement of the Indian Affairs of this province" and accused them of abusing and cheating their Native customers, all while allowing an "Indian to turn into bed to their wives" to secure their business. In the 1750s Colden continued the effort to Anglicize these relations by advocating for the creation of a superintendency of Indian affairs and thereby placing them under royal British, and not local Dutch, control.[23]

The Anglicization of knowledge about the Haudenosaunee was also a form of intellectual colonialism that sought to make Haudenosaunee history intelligible to English readers. While Colden's *History* by no means displaced Haudenosaunee understandings of their own history, it nonetheless translated their oral expressions into printed words through multiple levels of distortion and refraction, with the ultimate purpose of enabling greater British power over them. Colden's innovations in writing ethnohistory, however unappreciated, must be seen in terms of the power relations of colonialism that Enlightenment knowledge both depended on and enabled.

Anglicizing the League

In addition to Anglicizing knowledge about the Haudenosaunee, Colden's *History* was a narrative of seventeenth-century attempts to Anglicize the Haudenosaunee and their foreign relations. New Yorkers Anglicized the Dutch "Iron Chain" alliance with the Haudenosaunee into an English "Silver" Covenant Chain, but in doing so they tried to define the Haudenosaunee as

"subjects" to the English Crown. Internally the English hoped that the Haudenosaunee leaders they met with in council would be able to enforce an English
idea of what "peace" meant—that intercultural violence would cease and that
any violations of the peace would result in the punishment of those responsible. Externally they hoped that the Haudenosaunee would relinquish their
sovereignty and autonomy, break off all communication with the French, and
declare full allegiance to the English in case of war. Both external and internal
Anglicization failed for the same reason: as nonstate societies, Haudenosaunee
leaders had no power to compel the obedience of their people, as Colden
argued. When their efforts to persuade others failed, it was the responsibility
of Haudenosaunee leaders to try to mitigate damages and mend offended relations. Colden saw these same mistakes unfolding time and again, both in the
seventeenth-century history he related and in the ongoing eighteenth-century
efforts to secure the allegiance and enforce British ideas of peace and subjection. English governors of both centuries failed to understand the limits of
power among nonstate peoples and repeatedly bungled relations as a result.
This was the fundamental problem of managing relations between state-based
empires and nonstate societies in North America.

Colden began the body of his history by arguing that the French had
ruined their relationship with the Haudenosaunee by trying to use coercion
and intimidation. Their first mistake had been to ally with the enemies of the
Haudenosaunee upon first arriving on the St. Lawrence, which led to "a War
and Hatred between the French and Five nations, which cost the French much
Blood, and more than once had like to have occasioned the entire Destruction of the Colony."[24] Relations between the Iroquois League and the French
were poisoned for decades. The second French mistake was to antagonize the
Haudenosaunee during their attempts to make peace. The league sent Agariata on a mission of peace to the French in 1667, but the French commander
"resolved to make an Example" of the leader of the embassy, in vengeance for
the deaths of some Frenchmen. The French ordered Agariata "to be Hang'd,
in the Presence of his Country-Men, which kind of Death they having never
seen before, it struck them with Terror."[25] The French technique of using state-
sanctioned violence against one's own people was horrific enough to those
free from such a terrible power, but it made absolutely no sense in Haudenosaunee cultural terms to try to make peace by killing a peace ambassador. That
was how you started a war, not how you brought one to an end.

As much as the French had damaged relations with the Haudenosaunee,
Colden praised the French for their success with other Native nations. By

"making themselves the Arbitrators in all differences between the Indian Nations," Colden argued that the French had managed to "take Possession of all that Country"—what the French called the *pays d'en haut,* or upper country of Canada. The historian Richard White has argued that French colonists and Native Americans built a "middle ground" between European-style states and empires and the Native "nonstate world of villages." Colden described this relationship as an "Alliance agreed to with the French" in which "(ev'n by the French Books) no Subjection was Promised."[26] By serving as mediators in disputes between different Native nations, the governors of New France had managed to create a powerful alliance, but, as White has shown, not an "empire" as that term is usually understood. The French could not command their allies or claim them as subjects, but they nonetheless wielded a great deal of influence as mediators and, especially, as gift givers. Placing this account immediately after the discussion of the disastrous French attempt to use force to subject the Haudenosaunee was intended to lead readers to conclude that the mediation and alliance approach the French took with other nations was the better model to follow. The alienation of the Haudenosaunee by French coercion created an opportunity for the English, but only if the English emulated the more successful French use of gift giving, mediation, and alliance the French had used with other Native nations.

The problem was that this was not a message English governors and other imperialists wanted to hear: they wanted a Haudenosaunee subjection that promised not only strict allegiance to the English Crown but also the use of force to maintain an English peace through Haudenosaunee coercion of their own peoples. The instructive moral of Colden's history was that the direct pursuit of these goals was counterproductive and would result in alienation and war instead of subjection and peace. Colden suggested that these goals were better pursued indirectly. Colden thought that the English could succeed with the Haudenosaunee where the French had failed by "using the Indians well." Moreover, the better the English used them would make "the Indians . . . proportionably more Useful to us."[27] This less-is-more approach was counterintuitive, but the *History* demonstrated its greater efficacy. Colden, however, had the benefit of fifty years of hindsight; the early English governors of New York faced a steep learning curve in the years that followed the creation of the Covenant Chain in 1677. The first volume of Colden's *History* related the story of the failure of two different efforts to Anglicize the Haudenosaunee and bring them into conformity with English, state-based ways of managing affairs.

Peace and the Internal Anglicization of the League

The first area in which these early efforts to Anglicize the Haudenosaunee failed was the attempt to impose English, statist understandings of peace on the nonstate Haudenosaunee, which would have required the League to develop internal coercion within Haudenosaunee society. Colden explained that the "War-like Expeditions" of the Haudenosaunee had proved "Troublesom" to Virginia and Maryland, leading those colonies to send a representative to Albany to "make a League of Friendship" with the Haudenosaunee. The series of treaties that resulted in 1677 formed the basis of the Covenant Chain alliance between the Haudenosaunee and their Native allies on one hand and the governor of New York and the other English colonies on the other. As the complaints of Virginia and Maryland illustrate, a primary motive for the various English colonies involved was preventing the war-like expeditions of the Haudenosaunee. What the English failed to understand was that without the power of coercion, no one in the League had the power to enforce the statist English idea of peace.

While the Covenant Chain treaties were under way, several Haudenosaunee war parties were out that did, in fact, prove troublesome. One party fought and captured some Susquehannocks, who were allies of Maryland. The Senecas released their Susquehannock prisoners and sent them back with presents, but the Oneidas had adopted one of theirs. Another Haudenosaunee party was attacked by mounted soldiers from Virginia and, in retaliation, killed four and took six captives. Colden gave these concrete examples of the continuing "trouble" that had prompted Maryland and Virginia to enter the alliance in the first place. English colonists expected peace to bring an end to these troubles, while for the Haudenosaunee, peace did not mean that such troubles would, or could, stop. Peace meant instead that future violence would be handled through diplomacy, gift exchange, and ritual rather than lead to an escalation of violence.[28]

At the Covenant Chain treaties, Haudenosaunee leaders had warned the English that violence would continue after the conclusion of peace and explained how it was to be handled. Mohawk leaders said that "if any difference should aryse betwixt you [or] your Indians, and our Indians wee desyr that thar may not Immediatly a Warre aryse upon the Same bot that the matter may be moderat & composed betwixt us, and wee doe Ingage for our parts to give Satisfaction to you for any Eveill that our Indians might happen to doe." All of the other League nations made similar statements, repeatedly explaining the Haudenosaunee understanding of peace and means of keeping it.[29] When allying with another Native nation a few years later, the Haudenosaunee similarly proclaimed, "If any Mischief happened between us, we are to meet, and compose differences."[30] With such statements, Haudenosaunee leaders tried to make their expectations clear, but the message did not get through to the English, conditioned as they were to thinking of the world in very different ways.

Meeting regularly to compose differences and "give Satisfaction" for violence done was the Haudenosaunee method for maintaining peace. For nonstates, peace between different nations could not mean that violence ceased or was even supposed to cease, for there was no mechanism to force obedience or punish those who acted differently. The Haudenosaunee condolence ceremony resolved these differences and was the central ritual of the League. In this ritual, a number of strings of wampum were given to the bereaved. With the first string, the giver told the mourner that it would wipe the "tears off your weeping eyes, So that you may see clearly." Other strings removed the "sorrowness and sadness" that filled the mourners' throats, unplugged their ears, and restored both their bodies and their perceptions of the world to health and balance.[31] Once restored, the mourners would no longer feel the need to exact revenge. The Peacemaker, who created the ceremony, set the price of a human life at twenty strings of wampum. The killer's kin gave the wampum to the bereaved, an act that ritually "gathered up and bound" the bones of the deceased, muting the mourners' calls to further violence.[32] By contrast, European and Euro-American states of the period dealt with murder by punishing the individual who did the deed, often with death. This use of violence coercion was meant to deter would-be killers and was supposed to satisfy the desire for vengence of the bereaved. States tried to control the actions of individuals through coercive punishment, while nonstates developed mechanisms for coping with the consequences of individual freedom.[33]

The Haudenosaunee parties that had been out in 1677 caused a new round of trouble the following year. The Oneidas had warned Maryland and Virginia that a party was still out and requested that "if they should happen to do any harm, let it be passed by." A few months later the Oneidas reported that English soldiers had attacked this party, even though the Haudenosaunee had kept a careful distance from the "English Plantations." The Haudenosaunee fought back, killing two English colonists. Violence continued to escalate, with the English colonies demanding that the Haudenosaunee conform to an English peace. At a meeting the following year, a

Virginia emissary accused the Oneida of "having entred our Houses, taken away and destroy'd our Goods and People, and brought some of our Women and Children Captives into your Castles." Virginia did not adopt the "moderate and composed" attitude expected of allies reconciling differences; instead, they were prepared to escalate the violence to coerce and punish the Oneidas. The Virginia emissary threatened that the Oneidas' actions were "sufficient Reasons to induce us to a violent War against you." In the end, Virginia offered to forgive the Oneidas provided they promised not to "molest our People or Indians" in the future.[34] The impossibility of keeping such a promise was lost on the Virginians.

Virginia's frustration with the Oneidas' inability to coerce their warriors came to a head in 1684, when the governor of Virginia, Lord Howard of Effingham, made the long and difficult voyage to Albany in hopes of putting an end to the ongoing violence. "You have willfully broake the Covenant chaine," Howard told the Haudenosaunee. "Wee were willing to forgett," he continued, "but you not at all mindeing the Covenants then made, have Every yeare since com into our Country, in a warrlike manner."[35] He admitted to trying to convince the governor of New York, Thomas Dongan, to join him in "Warring against you, to Revenge the Christian Blood you have shed." Howard put on a great show of threats and menace, but in the end had to accept that both Euro-American and Haudenosaunee leaders were powerless to do much of anything about it. Only the mediation of the New York governor maintained the peace. In a move similar to the French "middle ground," Howard tried to appeal to Haudenosaunee cultural premises but misunderstood them. In a rare attempt to reify an Iroquoian metaphor, Howard proposed that they actually dig a pit and bury two hatchets, one for Virginia and one for the Haudenosaunee, "so that the Peace now concluded, may be lasting."[36] Howard vainly hoped that staging a bit of political theater with Haudenosaunee metaphors would somehow Anglicize Haudenosaunee ideas of peace.

The Mohawks responded with their own equally powerful performance of political theater designed to placate the English colonists, but one that fell short of giving up their definition of peace. The Mohawk speaker publicly berated the other nations of the League as "stupid," "brutish," and "void of Understanding," and alternately likened them to "children" and "deaf people" whose senses were "cover'd with Dirt and Filth." The Mohawks tried to "Stamp Understanding" into the other four nations so that they would be "obedient," and they "took the Hatchet" out of their hands. Having chastised the League—which carried absolutely no force—the speaker then obsequiously flattered Howard, telling him that he was "a Man of great Knowledge and Understanding, thus to keep the Covenant Chain bright as silver."[37] The Mohawks flattered Howard for behaving in accordance with Haudenosaunee understandings of peace by meeting to compose differences and troubles. Such theatrics also attempted to shame the warriors of the other four nations into avoiding future provocations to Virginia, to influence them through the power of persuasion. No one knew just how long the game could keep going without breaking down into violence, but for the moment no one had the power to coerce anyone to act differently. Instead of an Anglicization of Haudenosaunee peace, English peace practices were Haudenosauneeized.

Colden argued that Governor Dongan had achieved his influence among the Haudenosaunee through the mediation of disputes instead of turning to violence or coercion. He related how the Five Nations all thanked Dongan for intervening on their behalf and thereby won their "Esteem" and "Affections." Implicitly, Colden suggested that the English were learning for themselves that mediation and accommodation were more effective than attempts at coercion, much as the French had. Yet such influence stopped short of the more thorough Anglicization that remained the English ideal but which would have required deep and fundamental changes to Haudenosaunee society that were impossible to achieve for the time being.

Subjection, Allegiance, and the External Anglicization of the League

The absence of coercive authority among the Haudenosaunee caused immediate problems for their English neighbors by disrupting English ideas of peace, which would have required the development of coercive means of enforcing obedience within Haudenosaunee society, but, from an imperial perspective, the more serious problem was that of their subjection to the English Crown and of securing their allegiance in wars with the French. This Angliczation of the external or foreign affairs of the League through subjection to the English Crown and exclusive allegiance would fail for the same reasons that internal Anglicization did: Haudenosaunee compliance would require the development of coercive means of controlling Haudenosaunee people. The impossibility of such compliance is, in part, what made Teganissorens's strategy of neutrality effective: it let diverse parties pursue different ends. Burnet saw Teganissorens's neutrality and dealings with the French as a betrayal and so dismissed him, but his predecessors had faced this problem since the 1680s and 1690s.[38]

At the conclusion of the solemn burial of the hatchets with Lord Howard, Colden noted that the Haudenosaunee asked Governor Dongan to put the Duke of York's coat of arms "upon their Castles." Colden believed that they had been told that the duke's arms "would save them from the French." Dongan, however, saw this as an act of political subordination and ordered the Haudenosaunee to "Make no Covenant or Agreement with the French, or any other Nation, without my Knowledge or Consent."[39] Like the attempt to Anglicize peace, the attempt to Anglicize the League by abnegating Haudenosaunee sovereignty and ability to treat with other nations ended in failure.

At the core of the disagreements over the issue of allegiance was the status of the Haudenosaunee as nations. Were they free and equal allies of the English, as the Haudenosaunee insisted, or were they subjects of the English Crown? In a famous speech, the Onondaga leader Otreouti expressed this issue clearly. He told Dongan, "You say we are Subjects to the King of England and the Duke of York, but we say, we are Brethren . . . Those Arms fixed upon the Post without the Gate, cannot defend us against the Arms of La Barre," a reference to the French governor-general of Canada, Joseph-Antoine Le Febvre de la Barre. Otreouti defied English demands for allegiance and openly declared his intent to "bind a Covenant Chain to our Arm and to" La Barre's. This violated English understandings of subjection and of what they thought they had achieved with the Covenant Chain treaties and the nailing of wooden plaques painted with heraldry.[40]

When Otreouti subsequently met La Barre on the southern shore of Lake Ontario at La Famine, he found not a peace party but an army. In council, La Barre echoed English complaints about how the Haudenosaunee had "often infring'd the Peace" and violated French claims to dominion by bringing "English into the Lakes, which belong to the [French] King." La Barre threatened that if his demands were not met, he would have no choice but "to begin a War, which must be fatal to them. He would be sorry that this Fort [Frontenac], which was the Work of Peace, should become the Prison of your Warriors." La Barre's threats included not only further violence and war but also an imposition of French ideas of justice upon the Haudenosaunee. It might have been an intimidating performance—one designed, in Colden's words, to "strike Terror into the Indians"—had not his army been entirely incapacitated by sickness.[41] Colden based his account of this meeting on Lahontan, who had been an eyewitness. In his *New Voyages to North*

America, Lahontan related that the French were "dangerously ill of a Feaver" that produced "convulsive Motions, Tremblings, and frequency of the Pulse" that were "so violent, that most of our sick Men dy'd in the second or third Fit." Despite La Barre's attempt to hide the condition of his forces, Otreouti's spies learned the truth and turned it to advantage.[42]

In one of the most vivid passages of his *History*—albeit one borrowed from Lahontan—Colden described Otreouti's brilliant retort to La Barre's threats. The whole time La Barre had been speaking, Otreouti had "kept his Eyes fixed upon the end of his Pipe." Once La Barre finished, Otreouti arose and "walked five or six times round the Circle" and then stood while addressing La Barre, who sat in his "Elbow Chair," which Lahontan referred to as his "Chair of State." Otreouti said that La Barre spoke "as if he were Dreaming. He says he only came to the Lake to smoke on the great Calumet [peace pipe] with the Onnondagas. But [Otreouti] says, that he sees the Contrary, that it was to knock them on the head, if Sickness had not weakened the Arms of the French." He went on to mock La Barre as "Raving in a Camp of sick men." Otreouti defended the right of the Haudenosaunee to take the English into "*our*" lakes—not the king of France's lakes. He told the French in no uncertain terms, "We are born free. . . . We may go where we please, and carry with us whom we please, and buy and sell what we please. If your Allies be your Slaves, use them as such, Command them to receive no other but your People."[43] To Otreouti, subjection, exclusive loyalty, and allegiance were nothing short of "slavery," a complete abnegation of Haudenosaunee sovereignty. Otreouti rejected both French and English attempts to define the Haudenosaunee as "subjects." He further leveled a critique of both French and English colonialism in response to French complaints about how the Haudenosaunee had treated some of the Native allies of the French. "We have done less," Otreouti declared, "than either the English or French, that have usurp'd the Lands of so many Indian Nations, and chased them from their own Country."[44] Colden repeated this episode from Lahontan to drive home this point to his English readers: once again, French use of coercion with the Haudenosaunee was counterproductive, and the Haudenosaunee deeply resented European forms of colonialism that would deprive them of their lands or sovereignty.

Some of the differences between the text of Lahontan and that of Colden reveal the ways in which Colden Anglicized his narrative. Colden did not just repeat Lahontan verbatim; he selected, edited, and rephrased Lahontan in ways that constructed a new and different meaning from this episode. While

Lahontan was primarily concerned to clear La Barre's name, Colden omitted that issue entirely. Instead he related that when the Haudenosaunee next came to Albany, the governor chastised them for meeting with La Barre. In response, the Onondaga speaker, Garakontié, told Dongan, "We are sorry and ashamed; for now we understand that the Governor of Canada is not so great a Man as the English King that lives on the other side of the great Water; and we are vexed for having given the Governor of Canada so many fine Wampum Belts." Colden's ending to this episode constructs an entirely different meaning from that of Lahontan: La Barre's use of intimidation and coercion had backfired, just as Dongan's earlier attempt to forbid the Haudenosaunee from treating with the French had served only to alienate them. Instead, recognizing the reality of Haudenosaunee freedom of action allowed them to come to their own conclusions about the French. If the English resisted the temptation to use force and intimidation, the Haudenosaunee would see for themselves that their interests were better served by the English.[45]

While this lesson was clear to Colden in 1727, it was not clear to the seventeenth-century English governors who doggedly persisted in trying to subject the Haudenosaunee to the English Crown. One front of this battle was fought over the terms of address to be used in council, such as when Otreouti had forcefully told Dongan that they were "brethren," not "subjects." Yet the actual terms of address mattered less than the expectations that those terms entailed. As Colden reported in part two of his *History*, the Haudenosaunee later told another governor, "These Names signify nothing."[46] Without any sense of subjection within their own society, disagreements over the meaning of the term persisted. In 1684, the Onondagas and Cayugas asserted that they had put themselves "under the Protection of the Great Duke of York," that they would "not joyn our selves or our Lands to any other Government but this," and yet simultaneously maintained that they were "a Free People, tho' united to the English," who could give their lands and "be joyn'd to the Sachem we like best."[47] Colden offered no explanation for what would have seemed contradictions to English ears—one could not be subjects of the Duke of York and yet remain a "Free People." For the Haudenosaunee, however, there was a clear expectation that they were allies, not subjects as Europeans understood the term. Such an understanding is revealed in a speech that Colden did not include in his *History*. A Seneca leader explained to Dongan that they were "the King of Englands Subjects tough ourselves not obliged to harken to him."[48] For Europeans, such a statement was entirely nonsensical. Being "obliged to harken" was the very meaning of subjection.

That Natives possessed a clear understanding of these European attempts to subject them—and debated the best strategies of resistance—was revealed in a story Colden retold from La Potherie about some enemies of the Haudenosaunee. While the French were trying to rally some of their Native allies to attack the Haudenosaunee, a group of Ottawas secretly tried to talk the Potawatomies out of it. "The French invite us to War against the Five Nations, with design to make us Slaves, and that we should make ourselves the Tools to effect it," the Ottawas warned. "As soon as they shall have destroyed the Five Nations, they will no longer observe any Measures with us, but use us like those Beasts that they tye to their Plows."[49] Likening European subjection to their use of domesticated animals was perceptive and reveals a firm grasp of European subjection and strategies of colonialism. Colden argued that the French feared that the Potawatomies would be made "ungovernable" if they drank English rum. Colden's version imagined new possibilities for Anglicization arising out of the alienation of French allies. Once again, the moral was that attempting to coercively subject Native nations would backfire, while gifts of English goods could secure the desired Anglicization.

Colden's account of the ensuing French and Native attack on the Senecas in 1687 demonstrated how French coercion pushed the Haudenosaunee into welcoming English arms. The Senecas had located two of their towns near Fort Frontenac by the invitation of the French, but, in a treacherous move, the French launched a surprise attack on these settlements, burning them to the ground. Seneca captives were marched "in cold Blood to the Fort, and tyed to Stakes to be tormented by the French Indians." The Senecas died while singing of the "Perfidy and Ungratitude" of the French, who had grossly abused their trust.[50] Colden told how the other Seneca towns rallied in a counterattack that drove the French into "such a Fright" that, in their disorderly retreat, they ran around in the woods firing on themselves. The Senecas later abandoned one of their largest towns and burned it before they fled, leaving behind only two old men, who were captured and "cut into Pieces to make Soop for the French Allies." Colden ended his account by noting that the French sent thirteen captives back to Europe as "Trophies of their Victory, where they were put into the Galleys, as Rebels to their King."[51] Between the soup made of old men and the galley slaves made of young men, French coercion made few subjects but many enemies among the Haudenosaunee.

The final chapter of the first part of Colden's *History* sought to demonstrate the successful Anglicization of the Haudenosaunee, but a careful reading reveals significant reasons to doubt this hope. Colden opened the chapter with

Dongan telling the Haudenosaunee that if the governor of New France had "thought the Brethren were the King of England's Subjects," he would "dare not enter into the King of England's Territories." He told the Haudenosaunee that they had "brought this Trouble upon your selves" by making a "Covenant Chain with the French, contrary to my command . . . for as much as Subjects (as you are) ought not to treat with any Foreign Nation, it not lying in your Power."[52] Dongan offered twelve points of unwanted advice, but his main point was that they should never make treaties without his assistance. Colden did not record the Haudenosaunee response, but it was probably a good thing for the cause of Anglicization that Dongan was recalled shortly thereafter.[53]

Colden related how the Haudenosaunee ignored Dongan's "advice" and sued for peace with the French, but the treachery of a Huron effected what Dongan could not: their mobilization to fight New France. The Huron in question was none other than Lahontan's primary interlocutor, whom he called Adario, an anagram-pseudonym for the Huron chief Kondiaronk (also known as "Le Rat").[54] According to the story, Kondiaronk feared the imminent Haudenosaunee-French peace and laid a successful ambush for the Haudenosaunee ambassadors, capturing or killing the diplomats and an escort of forty warriors. Kondiaronk told the Haudenosaunee that he had been told by the governor of New France that fifty Haudenosaunee warriors would be coming that way to fight. Teganissorens, who was among the diplomats, told Kondiaronk that they were a peace embassy, and all blamed French treachery for the misunderstanding. Kondiaronk played his part by seeming to grow "Mad and Furious" and reviled the French governor for "making a Tool of him to commit such horrid Treachery." Kondiaronk released the Haudenosaunees he had captured and even gave them ammunition, keeping only one captive to replace the single loss in his ranks. He took this captive to Michilimackinac, where the captive was executed by the French commander in front of a crowd that included a Haudenosaunee prisoner. Kondiaronk engineered the escape of the Haudenosaunee prisoner, who would return to Iroquoia "to give an Account of the French Cruelty, from which it was not in his [Kondiaronk's] Power to save a Prisoner he himself had taken."[55] Once again, French coercive authority and an execution demonstrated French cruelty, duplicity, and treachery. Colden concluded the *History* with an account of the Haudenosaunee response, in which twelve hundred warriors "laid Waste" to Montreal and the surrounding countryside. If only the Haudenosaunee had besieged the fort, it would "have put a Miserable End to that Colony," leaving North America open to English imperialism.[56]

Conclusion

Colden's history was a remarkable achievement: an eighteenth-century, primary-source-based history of a nonstate people, written to further the aims of empire but also to bring about an understanding of the radically different world of nonstate peoples that was grounded in "real Knowledge" and not just the "speculations of the learned." That the nonstate peoples of North America did not receive similar treatment for over two centuries only serves to heighten the magnitude of his achievement. Indeed this is also the reason for the relative obscurity of the text and its minimal impact on subsequent intellectual history. When Colden wrote, it was possible that nonstate peoples would be claimed by the discipline of history. The scholarly division of turf into history for states and anthropology for nonstates did not take place decisively until the middle of the nineteenth century, and it is at least conceivable that nonstates would end up the "people without history" or, more accurately, the people denied history. The greater impact enjoyed by his anthropological French rivals is testimony to this later scholarly division of labor, which left Colden's *History* at an intellectual dead end. When ethnohistory emerged in the middle of the twentieth century, Wilbur Jacobs, one of its early leaders, decried the *History* as "disappointingly dull," "difficult to read," and a "knotty tree of a book." "Not troubled in the least by mere facts," Francis Jennings seethed, "Colden revived the empire-of-conquest myth" and thereby "donated an empire to the Iroquois in order to claim it" for the British. This is not a fair reading of Colden's book, though it made for an excellent straw man for Jennings to position his work against.[57]

Despite his misreading of Colden, Jennings raised an important point: the book was deeply implicated in the colonization of North America. The first edition of Colden's *History* ended on what seemed to be a high point of Anglicization, with New France all but destroyed. Yet it was not what the English did that rallied the Haudenosaunee against the French, for they fought for reasons of their own, perhaps owing to Kondiaronk's elaborate ruse. The impossibility of subjecting the Haudenosaunee to state ways of managing affairs meant that the wiser course to power lay in aligning interests and pragmatically working within the realities and ways to power of nonstate societies. By learning how to work within those constraints, the British could effectively extend their influence, and they did so through Colden's advocacy for the superintendency of Indian Affairs under William Johnson. Colden's history showed why it was necessary, and wise, to accommodate the nonstate

ways of the Haudenosaunee and provided lessons for the successful management of the Covenant Chain. Colden succeeded in advocating for the Anglicization of the Haudenosaunee and of knowledge about them, even if, in the
end, like his surveys of Haudenosaunee lands, such knowledge served the
interests of empire and was ultimately a form of colonialism itself.

CHAPTER FIVE

A Medieval Response to a Wilderness Need: Anglicizing Warfare in Colonial America

Geoffrey Plank

In 1914, in his essay on the frontier of Massachusetts, Frederick Jackson Turner argued that the original colonists of New England arrived with bags of inappropriate military technology. They lumbered themselves with "corslets and head pieces, pikes, matchlocks, fourquettes and bandoleers." During the seventeenth century, and especially after King Philip's War in the mid-1670s, the colonists gave up all that baggage along with the stale customs of European warfare and began to mobilize local men to defend frontier towns. According to Turner, the results were dramatic: "The settler on the outskirts of Puritan civilization took up the task of bearing the brunt of attack and pushing forward the line of advance which year after year carried American settlement into the wilderness."[1] After 1675 the historical pattern that Turner had earlier outlined in "The Significance of the Frontier in American History" was in play: slowly the east began to revert to old European patterns of behavior, while the west (or the extreme east, in the case of Maine) was continuously inventive as it defended and expanded the zone of white settlement, in the process democratizing American society.[2]

In the mid-1960s, when John Murrin was at Yale working on his dissertation, "Anglicizing an American Colony: The Transformation of Provincial Massachusetts," it was still acceptable—indeed it was often necessary—to cite old scholars such as Turner and Francis Parkman not only for their historiographical significance but also for the information those men had unearthed in their research. In his chapter 3, "The Colonial Militia: A Medieval Response to a Wilderness Need," Murrin drew on data from Turner's essay on Massachusetts, but he used that material (and a great deal of other evidence) to construct a narrative that redirected the thrust of Turner's argument. Murrin pointed out that just when Massachusetts was developing the locally based frontier defenses that caught Turner's eye, the colony was also embarking on a long project to develop a more hierarchical, centrally led, disciplined military. Edmund Andros launched this effort in the 1680s when he was governor of the Dominion of New England, and William Shirley carried it to its logical conclusion during the Seven Years' War when he served simultaneously as governor of Massachusetts and acting commander of British forces in North America. By the early 1760s the people of Massachusetts had developed their own European-style regular army. They had done so because they believed that such forces were effective. They paid high taxes to support the army, allowed their men to be subjected to severe military discipline, and sent recruits into the army at a per capita rate unmatched by any country in Europe at the time, with the possible exception (Murrin was careful to note) of Prussia.[3]

As with many other elements of his Anglicization thesis, Murrin's analysis of colonial military history challenged prevailing assumptions. Murrin called on scholars to critically reexamine old claims that the colonies' course of development represented a radical departure from European patterns of thought and aspirations. With reference to the colonial experiments of the seventeenth century, he wrote, "The significance of early America is not that it disproved the ideals of the Old [World], but that it was the only place where those ideals could be tried at all."[4] For the eighteenth century, he argued that the historical reality of Anglicization requires scholars to place developments in colonial America in a transatlantic frame, keeping in mind the elaborate cultural and political ties that bound the colonists increasingly to England. As Murrin observed at the outset of his dissertation, in the mid-1960s colonial American history was still a field "in search of its context."[5] Anglicization gave it one. Contextualization may be nothing other than good historical practice, but Murrin's Anglicization model met resistance, particularly from historians of colonial America's wars.

Wars are events where flags wave. When the topic is war, even self-consciously dispassionate historians, examining conflicts long after the fighting has ended, are tempted to follow the lead of contemporary commentators and study engagements for signs of difference between the antagonists. Some, such as Turner, associate contrasting fighting styles with profoundly significant, distinctive cultural characteristics. Murrin's Anglicization hypothesis suggests that this is an impulse we sometimes need to resist, at least when discussing fights that pitted "Americans" against "the British." Murrin did not initially generalize further than that, but the point should be expanded: we need to do more to historicize and contextualize all of early America's wars, and we should recognize the commonalities, as well as the differences, between all of early America's combatants.[6] In the years since Murrin wrote his dissertation, the agenda of early American historians has expanded. Today we are paying attention to a wider range of cultural conflicts and wars. As we early Americanists study more closely the inhabitants of the French, Dutch, and Spanish Empires and Native Americans, the stakes involved in our analysis of military culture increases. If we fail to contextualize and historicize the experiences of all the soldiers and warriors we discuss, and if we fail to recognize the commonalities between them, we will continue to produce partisan histories whether we intend to or not. In the worst instances, tacitly and perhaps unconsciously, our narratives may serve to defend acts of extreme violence.

Nearly everything Murrin discovered about the provincial army of Massachusetts was confirmed, and for the period of the Seven Years' War was elucidated in greater detail, in Fred Anderson's A People's Army in 1984.[7] Nonetheless even after that date historians continued to argue stubbornly over whether the colonists were hostile to regular armies, and the British army in particular, in the years leading up to 1763.[8] Among military historians, Anglicization did not simply win the day. Indeed even now one can hear echoes of Murrin's original debate in the contestation between John Grenier and Guy Chet over the defense of the seventeenth-century colonial frontiers. Like Turner, Grenier claims that the New Englanders and other English colonists developed a new "way of war" in the seventeenth century with distinctive features appropriate for North America including ranging and "scalp hunting."[9] Chet, by contrast, argues that the colonists were most successful militarily when they employed European technology and tactics. A generation ago in his dissertation Murrin wrote, "If the Puritans learned any important lessons of their own about forest warfare, they buried their secret carefully in the wilderness."[10] Chet agrees. According to Chet, if the colonists enjoyed any military advantage over Native American adversaries, it stemmed from their ability to transport and deploy large numbers of soldiers while keeping the men clothed, fed, healthy, and well armed. He demonstrates that the New Englanders consistently sought to maintain fortified strongholds with reliable, defensible lines of supply.[11]

Murrin and Chet do not deny that militiamen and rangers were deployed in colonial New England's wars. Their argument is that those forces were not very effective, that their deficiencies were widely recognized, and that over time the deployment of regular troops garnered increasing political support. These assertions are supported by considerable research into the late seventeenth century and the subsequent colonial era, but they raise a question about the earlier period that we are better equipped to answer today than we were when Murrin submitted his dissertation in 1966. If it is true, as Murrin insisted at the outset of his chapter on the military, that every government needs an effective military force to survive, how did the New Englanders get through their early years without a competent army?

We now understand that the colonists were, in Murrin's memorable phrase from 1997, "beneficiaries of catastrophe."[12] Between 1616 and 1622 successive waves of contagion decimated the Indians across the region where the New England colonies were to be established. Everywhere disease weakened the Indians' military capacity in material terms. The epidemics also had important and variable psychological effects. They helped convince some indigenous groups to give up any thought of offering military resistance to colonization.[13] In his dissertation Murrin highlighted the military significance of health, but only in connection with the problem of sanitation in the New Englanders' camps and garrisons.[14] It was only after Murrin had completed his dissertation, with the publication of startling work by Philip D. Curtin, William H. McNeil, and Alfred Crosby, that early American historians began to pay serious attention to the impact of epidemics on Native Americans.[15]

The field of Native American history has grown enormously since the 1960s, and Murrin's dissertation was a product of its time. The Indians appeared in it only as a challenge to the New Englanders. They were not well differentiated, and their behavior was almost constant. In one unfortunate passage Murrin seemed to suggest that they were incapable of restraining themselves in order to respect and maintain any European-brokered peace. He explained the persistence of violence on the frontiers of Maine by observing that "no chieftain could adjust the passions of his warriors to the timetables of European monarchs."[16] Murrin has since commented that this was the "worst sentence" in the thesis.[17] As a scholar with expansive interests, and particularly as a Ph.D. adviser, he has contributed significantly to our understanding of seventeenth- and eighteenth-century Native American history and helped shift our perspective on the colonial era.[18]

Recent scholarship has demonstrated that Native Americans were among the great innovators in North American warfare in the seventeenth century. The ongoing debate over Indian warfare in this period echoes, to a surprising extent, earlier scholarly controversies involving the ways of the settlers. Patrick Malone made an important contribution by emphasizing that Native American tactics changed after the arrival on the continent of colonists from Europe and European technology. He emphasized the Indians' adoption and adaptation of the firelock and suggested that by the late seventeenth century this weapon had become an essential component in an unusually successful method of warfare, which he called the "skulking way of war."[19] Malone, however, assumed that many practices that we have grown accustomed to associating with Indian warfare—the reliance on small-scale raids and ambushes, for example—had deep roots in the pre-Columbian past. More recent works, relying on the archaeological record and European accounts from the sixteenth and early seventeenth centuries, have led to a recognition that the Iroquois and other groups had at one time massed their forces, killed large numbers in battle including noncombatants, and relied heavily on fortification for defense.[20] Military engagements in the sixteenth century often killed far more people than did the skirmishes of the seventeenth century. This latest scholarship seems to lend support, at least in the field of military history, to James Merrell's 1984 hypothesis that American Indians entered into something like a Turnerian "new world" after coming into contact with Europeans.[21] Like Turner's rugged colonists, some Indian groups abandoned the trappings of old-fashioned military "civilization" and developed a new way of fighting that turned out to be so successful that eventually nearly everyone in North America, colonists and Natives alike, came to see it as an intrinsically appropriate, "natural" way to fight in the American woods.

By emphasizing how American Indian societies were radically altered, reconstituted, or remade in the aftermath of the arrival of European explorers, traders, and colonists, Merrell and other historians of his generation gave new impetus to the study of Native American history. In the last thirty years historians have traced the transformations overtaking eastern Native American societies in the seventeenth and eighteenth centuries with increasing chronological precision.[22] Ironically, however, the recent scholarly focus on "postcontact" changes—the impact of imported diseases, plants, animals, consumer goods, technologies, spiritual systems, imperial structures, and settlers—may have made it more difficult for us to construct histories that cross the pre-Columbian/post-Columbian divide.[23] The idea that the Indians' "world" in the early modern period was "new" can give us a better appreciation of the complexity of Native American history in that era and in all subsequent periods, but it runs the risk of denying Native peoples a deeper relevant past.

Adopting a longer perspective might transform our understanding of Native American military history. At the very least, we could reexamine events such as the destruction in 1637 of the village at Mystic during the Pequot War. Narragansett joined with New Englanders in burning the settlement and killing the men, women, and children who tried to escape through the stockades, and several hundred died. There can be no doubt that New Englanders led this attack, and scholars from a variety of ideological perspectives, from Francis Jennings to Chet, have cited it as an illustration of what happened following the introduction of alien, European, and colonial aims and tactics into the North American environment.[24] Nonetheless, in light of what we are learning about warfare among the nearby Iroquois, surely we should be able to say more about the Narragansett allies of the New Englanders than that they were misguided and surprised by what they witnessed in the assault.[25]

In the 1630s the New England colonies operated within an extremely complex diplomatic and military environment.[26] They negotiated constantly with Indians and almost never fought without some Native American support. There was nothing aberrational in the behavior of the Narragansett, neither in the context of New England nor more generally during the global expansion of the European empires.[27] In nearly every overseas territory that Europeans successfully colonized in the early modern period, indigenous allies fought beside the colonizers.[28] In North America and around the world, a colony's military strength rarely if ever depended solely on the capital, labor, and resources of the colonists.

Giving due consideration to the Native American role in New England's wars undoubtedly complicates Murrin's Anglicization thesis, but it should not fundamentally undercut his assessment of the aspirations of the settlers. Especially in the late colonial period, the New Englanders took pride in those actions that most closely resembled European operations. They seized Louisbourg in 1745 without assistance from any local indigenous allies. Though it was always more vulnerable than it appeared, Louisbourg remained a monument to military sophistication, discipline, and strength. When the British established Halifax in 1749, again without local indigenous support, they designed their new settlement as an answer to Louisbourg, which had been restored to the French. Halifax was dominated by European-style military architecture to such an extent that it did not resemble anything in Europe.[29] A new American military formalism was taking hold. Though less well remembered than the New Englanders' victory in 1745, the British siege of Louisbourg in 1758 served as the culmination of a trend toward conventional military operations in eastern North America. Though there were some dramatic, irregular incidents on the margins of the action, overall the two sides performed a set-piece engagement conforming to eighteenth-century European norms.[30]

It is ironic, therefore, that the Canadian maritime provinces during this period were the scene for a self-conscious reinvention of a distinctly American way of war. Leading the charge (or perhaps one should say the skulk) was a unit called "Gorham's Rangers." The rangers had been formed in response to a desperate plea from the defenders of Annapolis Royal, the old capital of British Nova Scotia. They were modeled on units that had been operating out of Massachusetts since King Philip's War, with colonial officers commanding Native American troops. In its original form in 1744, Gorham's Rangers included eight white officers and sixty enlisted Indians, most of them Wampanoag. The rangers were expected to fight "like Indians," and they did so, or at least they operated in conformity with the customs that such ranger companies had developed since 1675. They served in the Maritimes and Canada almost continuously for the next eighteen years, but over that time the supply of Indian warriors dried up, so that by 1762, when the unit was disbanded, nearly all of its enlisted men were colonists or Scots.[31] The commanders of Gorham's Rangers, John Gorham and his brother Joseph, who took over after John's death in 1751, belonged to a specific tradition peculiar to New England. By contrast, later efforts to "Americanize" Anglo-American war-fighting in the Maritimes were often led by Britons. Secondhand reports of irregular frontier violence altered the perspective of high officers in the British army, men who came to America already convinced that military success in the colonies required a radical change in tactics.

Nova Scotia's governor Edward Cornwallis was freshly arrived from England in 1749 when he began to recruit men to fight in ways that conformed to the savage "custom of America." Cornwallis offered bounties for the scalps of Mi'kmaq men, women, and children.[32] After John Campbell, Earl of Loudon, was chosen to command in North America in 1756, he received unsolicited advice from a correspondent in London urging him to pay Iroquois warriors bounties for the scalps of the French. One advantage of the scalp-bounty system, the writer claimed, was that it allowed the Indians to retain their independence: "They must be left to themselves, to distress the enemy in their own way, and not [be] put under any command or military law, for this they will not bear."[33] Before James Wolfe left England for America two years later, he heard "horrible stories of the Mic-macks and other formidable tribes of Indians" who would attack in the night "to scalp half of us" and would "live entirely on the carcasses of English men."[34] After Wolfe's arrival in Halifax, the sitting English governor of Nova Scotia, Charles Lawrence, warned Wolfe and others that the "miserable lurking Mickmack" were likely to "scalp and mangle the poor sick soldiers and defenseless women," and that therefore it was necessary to "entertain" the Mi'kmaq "in their own way" in order to "preserve the women and children of the army from their unnatural barbarity."[35] Jeffery Amherst (also newly arrived from England) relayed these warnings verbatim to his troops prior to their first landing on Cape Breton Island.[36] On June 8, 1758, the day of the first landing on the island, the British scalped two Mi'kmaq men. At least one of those scalps was cut by a Scottish Highlander.[37] During the previous year, Halifax had become the first port of call for Fraser's Highlanders, the first formal battalion of Highland soldiers deployed in North America. Though the Highlanders did not in fact fight like Indians, they had their own violent methods that British officers associated with savagery, and their deployment reflected a widespread assumption that they were well adapted for combat in the American woods.[38]

Colonial America's scalp-bounty policies appear to lend support to those military historians who assert that violence against noncombatants has long been a distinguishing feature of American warfare. In 1971 John Shy argued that the peculiar circumstances of the colonies inspired them to pursue "incredibly barbaric warfare, often followed by migration or subjugation. . . . With great strength but weak defenses, the colonists experienced warfare less in terms of protection, of somehow insulating society against external violence (as was increasingly true of European warfare)[,] than in terms of retribution, of retaliating against violence already committed."[39] Two years later, analyzing U.S. military policy from the Revolution through the Vietnam War, Russell F. Weigley argued that the American military initially had favored a strategy of attrition but in the nineteenth century moved to one of annihilation, which he defined as the total destruction of the enemy's military capacity. The pursuit of such annihilation became, as Weigley famously described it, a defining characteristic of "the American Way of War."[40] Taking Weigley to task and concentrating on the colonial period, Grenier has suggested that the Anglo-Americans adopted a distinctive strategy of "extirpative" warfare in the seventeenth century.[41] When the colonists sought to annihilate their enemies, their thinking was fairly simple. According to Grenier, early American military historians do not need to add much nuance to the concept of annihilation.

Superficially, at least, these arguments seem to run counter to the Anglicization thesis by emphasizing how American military culture diverged from European norms. But it is important not to overstate this. Shy's argument is not that the colonists grew more violent after their arrival in America, but rather that they retained the kind of ferocity that was common in Europe at the time of New England's founding—the era of the Thirty Years' War. It was the Europeans, not the Americans, who changed. Even granting that, there was never a period in which rule-bound, restrained warfare was consistently practiced in Europe, nor would it be accurate to say that Americans ever adopted a simple "way" of fighting that required attacks on noncombatants. Wayne Lee has called on military historians to recognize that a tension between violence and restraint has always been a defining characteristic of warfare. An array of factors including communal animosity, self-righteous moral outrage, and fear can precipitate indiscriminate killing. There is nothing distinctly "American" about these dynamics.[42]

Despite the obvious horror attendant to scalp-bounty policies, it is difficult to assess their military effectiveness. John Reid has argued that the Mi'kmaq remained the dominant power in the Canadian maritime region through the 1750s and perhaps into the late 1770s.[43] If Reid is right, the bounties did not deter the Mi'kmaq. But even if paying for scalps failed to achieve concrete military objectives, it still had enormous political impact. When he became commander in chief, Shirley renewed the policy, and not just for Nova Scotia; he encouraged several colonial governments to follow suit. Under Shirley's influence, using formulaic language, official proclamations declared various Indian groups "rebels and traitors" and made graduated prizes available according to the sex and age of the individuals killed.[44] Pennsylvania issued a scalp-bounty proclamation for the collection of Delaware scalps, and this led directly to the killing of an Indian woman and child in New Jersey. Those killings, in turn, contributed to a growing sense of crisis in New Jersey and helped inspire the establishment of that colony's first Indian reservation.[45] In the starkest possible way, the story of the scalp bounties and their impact should remind us that voluntaristic, irregular warfare often serves a political purpose that cannot be measured in simple military terms. Concentrating on late colonial Pennsylvania, Peter Silver has argued that a morbid fascination with "savage" violence, subsumed within what he calls "the anti-Indian sublime," helped transform American politics as the colonies moved toward revolution.[46]

The revolutionary crisis added a new dimension to discussions of irregular warfare in North America, especially after the Battle of Lexington and Concord in April 1775, when a loosely organized body of Patriot militiamen forced a body of British regulars to retreat. According to T. H. Breen's recent history of the coming of the Revolution, the militiamen who gathered to confront the British army on the road to Concord were thoroughly "ordinary" people and virtually leaderless.[47] The British forces, by contrast, were "an army of occupation" that "murdered Americans at Lexington."[48] Though he is not quoting anyone specifically, Breen uses these words in an effort to reconstruct the Patriot mind-set, and he is careful to place that sensibility within its immediate historical context. Nonetheless his "us and them" rhetoric, and the juxtaposition he presents—pitting an alien, hostile regular military force against a humble armed citizenry—resonates within an old tradition that has invested deep historical and political significance in the early American militia. Such celebrations of the militia contributed to the development of the myth that Murrin sought to demolish in 1966.

In his dissertation Murrin emphasized the colonial militia's English antecedents and suggested that the militia system was maladapted not only for North America but also more generally for the modern world. On a schematic level, the militia served the same role for Murrin that "corslets and head pieces" did for Turner. It was an English relic that the colonists had to replace in order to survive. The twist, of course, is that the colonists never abandoned the militia, nor did they reform it (as Turner would have had it) in any pragmatic response to the challenges of the wilderness. Instead, it seems, they just retained the moribund English institution. This part of Murrin's argument invites us to consider the persistent cultural ties that bound the colonists to their empire in all things, including their local military establishments. To the extent that the colonists' support for the militia had an ideological component related to their distrust of peace-time standing armies, that aspect of their thinking is best understood in a British imperial context.[49]

In her analysis of the politics surrounding the militia in England, Joyce Lee Malcolm emphasizes the second half of the seventeenth century when the fraught and often violent political debates over the viability, power, and legitimacy of the Stuart dynasty helped transform militia service from an onerous burden into something claimed as a birthright.[50] In an ambiguous provision that has had much less long-term political resonance in England than in the United States, the English Bill of Rights in 1689 guaranteed that "subjects which are Protestants may have arms for their defence suitable to their conditions and as allowed by law."[51] Despite this clause provisionally protecting gun ownership, by the end of the seventeenth century the militia had lost its military significance in most of England. As Murrin noted in his dissertation, the institution survived the longest in the northern English borderlands. That geographical pattern mattered. During the Jacobite Rising of 1745, northern English militias joined in a wave of punitive policing that affected the entire British Empire.[52]

Reforms introduced in England following the 1745 rising transformed the militia from a local or county-based institution into a more centrally controlled arm of the Crown.[53] Something similar but much more dramatic occurred in Scotland. While the English militia received a temporary boost after 1745, Scotland's local military forces were dismantled and the northern country's elaborate homegrown military tradition was comprehensively co-opted by the centralizing British state. David Thomas Konig has argued that this Scottish precedent made the American Patriots wary, and indeed may have informed the adoption of the Second Amendment to the U.S. Constitution protecting the right of citizens within each state to form a militia.[54]

The Second Amendment looms ominously over all scholarly discussions of gun ownership and militia service in colonial and revolutionary America. At the turn of the twenty-first century Michael A. Bellesiles tried to wish away early America's "gun culture" by undercounting the extent of gun ownership in the colonies.[55] He faced withering criticism, some from those who recognized and opposed his implicit challenge to the premises behind the constitutional right to bear arms, and some from others who may have shared his political inclinations but sadly acknowledged the deficiencies in his scholarship.[56] The controversy made him briefly famous, but it nearly wrecked his academic career.[57] The attention Bellesiles received was unusual, but no one in this field can escape the political ramifications of the topic.

Murrin's characterization of the colonial militia as a medieval English institution resonates politically in at least two interrelated ways. First and most obviously, this historicized understanding of the militia undermines the jingoistic, nationalist story promoted by Turner and others associating militia service with peculiarly American virtues. More significantly, recognizing the English origins of the militia, along with acknowledging the colonists' readiness to embrace "European-style" regular military service, diminishes our sense of the cultural gap between the antagonists at engagements such as the Battle of Lexington and Concord. This can have profound implications for the ways in which we interpret and write about the Revolutionary War.

Breen's use of the word "murder" to describe the actions of the British soldiers on that day reflects a common pattern of thinking when belligerents face each other without sharing common standards concerning the legitimate use of force. When opponents surprise each other and fight in unexpected ways, it is often easy for observers on both sides to view the other as lawless, undisciplined, and culpable. Within British and Anglo-American frames of reference, violence may lose its ideological legitimacy and be defined instead as crime. The attribution of criminality to one side, the other, or both has destabilizing implications when armed engagements reach such a large scale that they swamp the capacity of ordinary law enforcement. Under such circumstances the ideological and institutional structures that commonly place limits on the application of force break down, potentially ushering in episodes of uninhibited slaughter.

British soldiers in Massachusetts had been accused of murder before, in the wake of the "Boston Massacre" in 1770. Paul Revere's famous print depicting that episode draws on other contemporary images and accounts, and in an iconic fashion it shows the imperial government exercising its power without the formal restraint of law.[58] In later, revolutionary and postrevolutionary contexts—in the United States in following years and decades, and in other places where similar images have been used as propaganda—the picture of soldiers in uniform firing in line at a thoroughly civilian crowd pleads with us to abandon our faith in established institutions. When the authorities act en masse as perpetrators, can there be any recourse to the law? Of course sometimes there can be, and the "Boston Massacre" was in fact followed by the unsuccessful prosecution of two of the soldiers. The result was something of an anticlimax, but it stemmed in part from a fear shared by almost all of the parties involved in the trial that the foundations of public order were collapsing.[59]

The Revolutionary War occasioned a succession of debates over the rules regulating violence, as Patriots and Loyalists accused each other of committing, or at least abetting, seditious, large-scale, criminally culpable depredations. In some local theaters where militia forces were involved, the fighting became unusually punitive.[60] Nonetheless in the more formal engagements between Redcoats and the Continental army, both sides reluctantly acknowledged the credentials of their opponents, and the European "rules of war" applied.[61] The rival commanders' show of restraint may have stemmed partly from a modicum of mutual respect, but it also reflected their mutual fear of reprisal. Calculations we now associate with game theory may have operated historically as forcefully as ideology in restraining belligerents.[62]

Various factors can constrain combatants or give way. Military victories can lead to massacres if the losing side seems permanently weakened or disabled and the victorious fighters lack respect for the vanquished. Unrestrained violence is still more likely to occur in places without established legal institutions or other customary dispute-resolution mechanisms that the victors recognize as legitimate. Religious, ethnic, or racial prejudice can make the situation worse and in extreme cases lead to genocide. For these reasons and others, historians need to be particularly cautious when they adopt a language or mode of analysis that blurs the distinction between military action and criminality in the context of wars between colonists and Native Americans.

It is time for us to move beyond the "collision of military cultures" explanation of colonial-era violence. Under that analysis, in the early colonial period when Native Americans fought colonists, combatants on both sides were shocked to discover that the other side did not respect their own customs of war fighting. This resulted in confusion, rage, and an escalation of violence.[63] This analysis has considerable explanatory power, and similar dynamics operated in many places around the world where Europeans established colonies.[64] Nonetheless if we let it stand alone, it overstates the novelty of "frontier" violence and overemphasizes the cultural distance separating "Native" peoples from Europeans. Though few historians ever intend to legitimate or excuse massive violence, the "collision of military cultures" story turns the combatants on both sides into innocents, at least in the sense that it presents fighting men entering conflict unacquainted with the kind of violence they are about to witness. Readers can empathize with the fighting men's surprise, fear, and outrage, and this can make the escalation of violence seem more "understandable," in the colloquial sense of the word. The model may be, in effect, too persuasive and too widely applicable. Fighting men get startled frequently, and sometimes they get confused and angry. This is never the full explanation for what ensues. In analyzing colonial-era warfare we need to be careful to remain historians and place events in context by relating them to the historical actors' lived experiences, cultural heritages, and collective past.

There was a deep history of mayhem and slaughter on both sides of the Atlantic before the seventeenth century. Recent works that acknowledge this, such as Daniel K. Richter's *Before the American Revolution*, are sometimes distressing to read, but they take us much further than the "collision of cultures" model in reconstructing the violence of the colonial encounter and assessing its results.[65] Decades ago Murrin convinced us that the "frontier" did not create colonial culture and that to understand the colonists' ways of war fighting (and other aspects of colonial life) we need to consider where the colonists came from. We need similarly to historicize our perspective on North America's other fighting men, including Native American warriors, the other empires' soldiers and militiamen, and Redcoats alike.

PART III

REVOLUTION

CHAPTER SIX

Anglicanism, Dissent, and Toleration in Eighteenth-Century British Colonies

Nancy L. Rhoden

Anglicization, the multifaceted process by which the mainland British colonies became more like England by the mid-eighteenth century, coincided with another process that we might label *Anglican*ization, the consolidation and expansion of the colonial Church of England. Although the Church of England was already long established in Virginia, in the early eighteenth century there were reinvigorated efforts to improve its standing throughout the British colonies, including regions legally and numerically dominated by other Protestant groups that Anglican churchmen continued to label collectively as dissenters. Anglicanization may be considered one aspect of Anglicization, in that the expansion of the king's church in the colonies promoted a dominant, state-church strand of English religious culture. Meanwhile the British North American colonies experienced increasing religious diversity and toleration throughout the eighteenth century. These two trends—a revival of the church-state tradition and an increase in religious pluralism—may seem contradictory or alternative visions of colonial Protestantism, but both trends intermingled and had a significant impact on both Anglicans and non-Anglicans. Toleration and intolerance coexisted in Protestant thought, a fusion of theology, religious practice, and local experience. Colonial Anglicans' views on toleration were forged through their relations with other Protestants in America but also through their understanding of English practices and beliefs in toleration.

"Anglicanization" was not a term used by contemporaries. It is not commonly used among early American historians or church historians, and so it is employed here with an acknowledgment of what it was and what it was not. It resulted from the efforts of British leaders in church and state as well as colonial laity and clergymen, but it does not refer to an explicit plan or set of policies; nor was it a popular lay movement in the eighteenth century. Although it may seem to focus on one denomination's religious expression, the English church was varied, incorporating Whig and Tory, High and Low Church, with assorted opinions on dissent and toleration, so that the term "Anglicanization" is not meant to suggest a single viewpoint. Additionally, Anglicanization (like Anglicization) intersects with a myriad of social and political realities. The pace of Anglican growth, or the advance of Anglicanization, varied noticeably from colony to colony. Nor does the term "Anglicanization" mean to suggest that the Church of England was at all successful in remaking colonial British North America in its image. If seen from the vantage point of 1800, the trend definitely had been reversed. By then Methodists, Baptists, and Presbyterians outnumbered Episcopalians, who had in the revolutionary years lost the privileges of their former colonial establishments and ultimately lost the demographic race. Consequently a consideration of Anglicanization may explain an early to mid-eighteenth-century phenomenon, one of considerable significance but not one that persisted into the new Republic.

As John M. Murrin has taught us, Anglicization was the eighteenth-century process by which British colonial societies remade themselves in emulation of English models, but the Atlantic served as a prism transporting each different thread of English culture and concentrating it in a particular region so that its influence was thereby intensified.[1] At the local level, this resulted in ethnic-religious enclaves. In addition, regional variations emerged from early settlement patterns: a Congregationalist establishment in New England; an Anglican establishment in Virginia and later through the South; and no official church in the middle colonies—a situation that fostered greater ethnic and religious diversity. Throughout the eighteenth century Anglicization, as well as other factors including state formation, bureaucratic centralization, population growth, and immigration, continued to reshape colonial religious culture. In varying degrees increased ethnic and religious pluralism affected all regions, and yet the toleration of rival groups varied depending on local circumstances and the policies of any established church of that colony. Meanwhile the English church-state tradition was reimported to the colonies, where it revived and expanded: the Congregationalist congregations multiplied, and the Church of England added new colonial establishments in the early eighteenth century. Between 1680 and 1760 the Church of England

and other Protestant churches in America showed signs of moving toward either establishmentarianism or more centralized ecclesiastical governance, in a manner that seemed to embrace their English origins. As Murrin has explained, "The key to the puzzle is the different kind of Anglicization which each region had experienced during the previous century."[2]

Anglicization can refer to the process of foreigners joining the English, as experienced by French Huguenots and some other non-English settlers, but it also might be useful to think of Anglicization as a process of reintroducing English culture, both traditional values and new strains of Englishness, to colonists of British background. In the case of Congregationalists in New England whose Puritan ancestors migrated largely in the early to mid-seventeenth century, this makes considerable sense. Since each colony differed, its experience of Anglicization varied, and meanwhile England itself was evolving. Colonial contemporaries had to decide for themselves what constituted Englishness, among the divergent, changing threads. When English policies or values shifted, colonists had to decide which different strands they would imitate and which ones they would reject. Anglicization could include a reeducation about what British culture had become, but Anglican churchmen in Virginia did not necessarily want their colonial society remade in the post-1689 image of a more religiously tolerant England if that meant they would lose political and religious power to local dissenters. In a variety of ways, Anglicization unleashed a contest over which English values were worthy of emulation.

Reigning Atlantic perspectives have expanded historians' understanding of American denominational histories within a British and European context, and yet recent works commenting on religious toleration in early America, to one degree or another, have emphasized an Americanization argument. Religious changes of the eighteenth century, including church construction and expanded religious pluralism, have been credited with giving colonial religion its "uniquely American" character.[3] Other recent works have focused, understandably, on the ideas and actions of those resilient dissenting groups who sought to improve their religious expression in America by wrestling power away from an Anglican establishment.[4] As much as we have learned from such studies, they give, intentionally or not, an impression of Anglicanism as constant, unbending, and intolerant, while toleration appears an American and/or dissenting innovation. The extent to which toleration, for Anglicans and other British Protestants, was at least partially an imported, Anglicized concept deserves exploration.

That Anglicans in America and English ecclesiastical authorities persisted in using the terms "dissent" and "dissenters" likely contributed to the animosity of non-Anglicans toward them. It may have even inspired them to work together, as in the campaign over episcopacy. Non-Anglican Protestants of various denominational stripes, the so-called dissenters, were not likely to see themselves as "dissenting" so much as following their own inspired path to salvation. The term "dissent" collapsed, or failed to acknowledge, many significant differences among English Protestants and seemed to posit the existence of a hegemonic, centralized Anglican establishment, against which other Protestants disagreed. Yet there was no such uniform, comprehensive Church of England establishment in early America, where the church-state relationship differed even in those colonies where the official church was Anglican. Continued use of the term "dissent" evoked not only Anglican unity but also power, both real and imagined. Colonial Church of England spokesmen often claimed a superior status relative to that of other denominations, even if they did not necessarily succeed in defending it. Such binary terminology as "churchmen" and "dissenters," when widely used by Anglicans, would also have seemed insensitive in not acknowledging the increased toleration in England for a variety of Protestant groups. Moreover it seemed insensible to new British legal realities: not only the Toleration Act, but also the legal fact that Britain had two established churches after 1707.[5] Despite, or maybe in part because of, Presbyterianism's place as one of the two British national churches, many colonial Anglican ministers did not warm to it as much as they did to other European national churches.

This examination of colonial Anglicanism sketches its convergence with and reaction to various strands of Anglicization in the eighteenth century. The reinvigoration of the church-state tradition, patterns of church construction and growth, the centralized reform of church governance, and controversies over revivalism and episcopacy are some of the major themes that were, arguably, brought from England and are helpful in illuminating connections between the Church of England and Anglicization. Next a consideration of colonial Anglican perspectives on the church-state model and on religious toleration in two regions, Pennsylvania and Virginia, explains how and to what extent colonial Anglicanism intertwined with other forces of Anglicization: religious pluralism and toleration. Colonial Anglican perspectives, in turn, shaped both their public image and their reaction to Anglo-American disagreements of the 1760s and 1770s. The campaign for a colonial Anglican episcopate in particular showed how divisive Anglicization could be. Those who urged closer institutional, ecclesiastical ties with England inadvertently endangered the position of the Church of England in the colonies by seeming to confirm their opponents' fears that colonial Anglicanism could attain, especially with Parliament-appointment bishops, a privileged status too similar to the English model.

Anglicanism and Anglicization

At the end of the seventeenth century and the beginning of the eighteenth, the colonial Church of England witnessed a period of ambitious expansion that benefited from a reinvigoration of the church-state tradition, the implementation of policies for a strong imperial administration, and the strengthening of royal government in the colonies. Institutionally and financially this growth would not have been possible without the formation of the Society for the Propagation of the Gospel in Foreign Parts (SPG) in 1701.[6] These factors, each an example of Anglicization, converged to promote significant growth of the Anglican Church. Anglicanization, in turn, was an early example of Anglicization, one that began before the expansion of consumer culture after the 1720s and other Anglicizing trends that were arguably more noticeable at mid-century. In this respect the increased presence of the Church of England contributed to broader social and cultural patterns of Anglicization, but it also provoked controversy and a decidedly anti-Anglican backlash. By mid-century a campaign by prominent church leaders in London and some colonial clergy for an American episcopate provoked a pamphlet war with American dissenters. The integration of the British Atlantic world was simultaneously unifying and divisive: colonial Anglicans saw their church's progress over the course of the eighteenth century as evidence of their presumed integration with the English church and empire, while opponents increasingly saw such growth as evidence of an insidious plot to extend Anglican-style corruption under the umbrella of imperialism.[7]

Anglicanization can be measured in this early period, 1675 to 1715, in terms of the number of its legal establishments, its progress in other colonies where it was not the official church, and its connectedness to imperial government. This is the critical era in which the bishop of London received responsibility for overseeing the colonial parishes, royal governors received commissions and instructions on how to be the king's representative, and the SPG was formed. Yet Anglicanization, like Anglicization, could not be imposed exclusively through the actions of distant imperial or ecclesiastical officials; it had to be accepted voluntarily. A series of legal opinions in the first decades of the eighteenth century confirmed that the Church of England was not established in North America unless specifically established by law in a particular colony. The Church of England had long been the established church in Virginia, by virtue of laws passed by the General Assembly in 1619 outlining the church's civil and religious functions, in 1632/33 detailing clerical duties and salaries, and in 1642/43 establishing a vestry system.[8] This early official foundation in Virginia expanded at the turn of the century when the colonial Church of England secured religious establishments in Maryland and South Carolina, and later in North Carolina.[9] Once in place in Maryland, the royal governor encouraged the assembly to pass legislation for the establishment of the church. This unmistakable timing gave the clear impression that the Church of England was intimately connected with royal officers and royal government. In Boston, Governor Edmund Andros's efforts to build King's Chapel made the church and royal government seem doubly objectionable to local Congregationalists. The Church of England's activities in New England and the middle colonies, as well as the new establishments, had resulted from strong leadership in London, including the work of Bishop of London Henry Compton, Archbishop of Canterbury Thomas Tenison, and Secretary of the Board of Trade William Blathwayt, as well as the efforts in the colonies of Edward Randolph, Edmund Andros, and Francis Nicholson. Colonial governors, who had some ecclesiastical duties and the ability to persuade colonial legislatures to act on religious matters, played a significant role in the promotion of the king's church, particularly before 1720.[10] Yet because an establishment required specific colonial legislation, the local elites and electorates had to favor the decision as well.

Since a religious establishment had to be negotiated at the local level of governance, related debates and discussion about toleration, pluralism, and ecclesiastical establishments reveal alternative visions. Consider the case of the lower four counties around New York City following the New York Assembly's passage of the Ministry Act of 1693. Anglicans claimed confidently that by its terms their church was established there, a point which many other local Protestants refused to concede, given the precedent of toleration in the Duke's Laws and the similar wording in the Ministry Act (all congregations were to be supplied with "good sufficient Protestant" ministers). Several royal governors, including Benjamin Fletcher and Edward Hyde, Lord Cornbury, attempted to impose Church of England clergy, in a manner that structured pluralism according to their own Anglican-English model. This seemed an unwelcome innovation to local Dutch Reformed and other Protestants who had enjoyed the right to an ordained minister for each parish supported by local residents, a situation which had resulted in de facto local establishments led by dissenters in areas outside of New York City. Toleration in New York, though partially based on the French model and owing much to the Dutch, also followed an English model based on the Toleration Act of 1689 that granted toleration to Trinitarian Protestants and in so doing diffused dissenter opposition.[11] The status of Anglicanism in the lower counties of New York was a constant contest that Anglicization, with its competing models of Englishness, did not solve.

The contributions of royal governors notwithstanding, no group did more for the colonial Anglican Church than the SPG in terms of financial aid and organizational support. As the branch of the English church responsible for missions, and founded by royal charter, the SPG sent 309 Church of England clergy to the British colonies between 1701 and 1783 to minister to colonial Anglicans and to evangelize among Native Americans and enslaved African Americans. The SPG was well connected to the highest officers of church and state. Its membership included all the bishops and higher clergy as well as ministers from every diocese in England and Wales.[12] It also consulted with the Board of Trade before initiating new programs. As the name of the society indirectly implied, SPG members aimed to spread the Gospel and in so doing make British colonial possessions less "foreign" and more English. To its few hundred members and the readers of its annual reports and sermons, the society expressed the contemporary Anglican belief that theirs was the true church, best suited to promote order in church and government. As Rowan Strong has argued, these publications also helped to express an official Anglican concern for empire.[13] Yet because it was initially an internal discussion among SPG members, perhaps that minimized, if only briefly, the provocation of other American Protestants, at least until they personally could witness the mushrooming of SPG parishes. SPG missionaries were agents of Anglicization in that they self-identified ecclesiologically with the Church of England, its beliefs, and its history; they tended to be of a High Church persuasion that emphasized church hierarchy and episcopacy; and they wanted to export their church's traditional beliefs to the British colonies. In the purchase and distribution of religious books the SPG also contributed to an Anglicization of colonial reading tastes. For SPG members and missionaries, imperial expansion was intertwined with the promotion of the institutions and beliefs of the Church of England.

Ideological support, when matched with practical aid, facilitated the burgeoning of colonial Anglican parishes from 1680 to 1715 and a second era of growth at mid-century that entailed additional church construction and gentrified renovations of some existing churches. Although the Church of England had a reputation for being the church of the affluent, since so many royal officeholders and aspiring colonial elites attended it, none of the parishes outside provincial capitals were financially self-sustaining in the colonial period.[14] The SPG financed much of the expansion of the Church of England in those colonies without an Anglican establishment and continued to pay clerical salaries. Meanwhile local initiatives by parishioners and colonial governments provided financing for parishes in those colonies where the Church of England was the established church. In all, Anglicans created approximately 90 new congregations between 1680 and 1710 and added almost 150 more between 1740 and 1770. Such Anglican growth may have appeared related to other Anglicizing trends, such as rising wealth and increased social-economic stratification in colonial urban areas. Yet by mid-century other denominations' rates of growth were even more impressive: an estimated 400 Baptist and Presbyterian congregations were formed between 1740 and 1770.[15] Anglican expansion tended to be an urban and eastern phenomenon in colonial America, and it neither kept pace with frontier expansion nor benefited as much from new immigration in the latter period as some other Protestant churches did.[16] By mid-century the Church of England had missions among Native Americans, such as the Mohawk, and expressed a continued interest in evangelizing among African American slaves, although the actual number of converts was always modest.[17] Overall, its efforts tended to focus mainly on English settlers in already settled communities and those who had been drawn already to the Church of England.

Beyond the number of new churches built, the colonial Church of England did take a prominent role from mid-century to the American Revolution in the redesign of church buildings and use of architecture and material culture to express Anglicized tastes. In this era colonists witnessed a rapid expansion of church buildings belonging to many denominations—a "sacralization of the landscape" that transformed both rural and urban communities.[18] Skylines of colonial towns appeared more like those of English cities when bell towers and steeples appeared. Where simple wooden churches already existed, by mid-century many of these older buildings had been replaced with stone structures and their interiors renovated to the greater glory of God and to conform to more gentrified tastes.[19] In Virginia the colonial elites constructed their homes in the style of Georgian mansions and transformed their houses of worship, to include elaborately decorated pew boxes for leading families, in a manner that displayed their good taste, wealth, and social standing. The study of material culture has, in many respects, confirmed the Anglicization argument: the expression of lay Anglicanism, especially among the elites, can be linked to its use of imported devotional tracts, sermons, and household objects.[20] The display of the royal arms on the west walls of colonial churches served also as a reminder of the church-state connection, as embodied in the king. The impressive buildings of Congregationalists in New England and Anglicans in the South not only seemed to confirm the growing wealth and style of their leading citizens but also provided physical evidence of the resurgence of the church-state tradition.

Anglican spirituality also promoted various aspects of Anglicization and imperialism as well as reinforcing the church-state model as normative and beneficial. Theologically offering a middle path between Roman Catholicism and extreme versions of Calvinism, the Church of England prided itself on its moderation. The regularity of its liturgy, set out in the Book of Common Prayer, provided a fixed script for community prayer and an opportunity to promote unity in church and state as well as offering a source of private, daily devotional readings. Hearing a minister's sermon and participating in the sacraments, particularly the Eucharist and other religious rites of passage, benefited the individual while it provided a common Anglican experience.[21] Since all members of the polity were defined as church members, all could be encouraged to accept salvation by living faithful lives. Their faith needed to be matched by actions, including repentance and performance of one's duty. Contemporary critics claimed consequently that Anglicans practiced moralism, or mere moralism, and yet Anglicans in early Virginia, it has been argued, "cooperated with God in order to ensure their prior election by Him."[22] Often described as the one true church by its leaders, the Church of England had members who often articulated the idea that loyalty in religion would produce political unity in the state. Its liturgy, ceremonies, and rational spirituality contributed to colonial Anglicans' sense of belonging and union with the English church and with England.

Established Anglican and Congregationalist churches in the colonies were not the only ones influenced by the reinvigorated church-state model and its hallmarks of centralized authority and hierarchical organization.

Other Protestant denominations too reformed their church governance along the lines of their British and European counterparts and in a manner that embraced centralization and hierarchy. Quakers, Presbyterians, Baptists, German Reformeds, and German Lutherans created their own versions of annual meetings that assumed authority over their memberships and supervised church matters. Quakers began attending Philadelphia Yearly Meeting, modeled after the London Yearly Meeting, in 1685. Presbyterians met at the Presbytery of Philadelphia in 1706 and by 1716 had created the Synod of Philadelphia to include additional new congregations; in so doing they imitated practices from Scotland and Northern Ireland. Baptists had long held informal meetings but formalized the practice with the formation of the Philadelphia Baptist Association in 1707. In the 1740s the German Reformed Church created its assembly of ministers, and the German Lutherans formed the Lutheran Ministerium of Pennsylvania.[23] This trend could be both unifying and divisive to church members, and so might provoke as well as settle controversies. Yet the creation of these bodies for the oversight of ministers and parishioners and for the supervision of various church matters strongly suggests the imitation of British and European models of church governance that were authoritative, hierarchical, and centralized.

Another English and European import to the British colonies by mid-century that fundamentally altered colonial religious life and religious institutions was revivalism. This trend, however, represented a thread of English religious culture that the colonial Church of England (Methodists excepted) largely did not care to imitate. Anglican faithfuls had long imagined themselves as fighting off presumed religious perversions, such as Roman Catholicism, and religious errors, including dissent and deism, but enthusiasm raised new alarms. That the message of new birth came most infamously, for the Anglican orthodox, from a turncoat minister of the Church of England, George Whitefield, was especially disturbing.[24] The hidden benefit of revivalism, the Anglican clergy claimed, was that other Protestants wearied by its excesses found refuge in their more rational, stable church. Yet the disadvantages were numerous for those who favored an English church-state model: revivalism undermined clerical authority and hierarchical governance, and it contributed to increased religious pluralism and fragmentation. This era of heightened interest in religion showed colonial contemporaries that the Church of England, in England and in the colonies, was stretched too thinly to serve everyone adequately, given population growth and migration patterns.[25] Revivalism also pointed out the privileged position of an established church such as the Church of England when its clergy denounced revivalists as mere itinerants without legitimate posts and when one of its commissaries, Alexander Garden, reacted in an authoritarian (and ineffective) manner in his dealings with Whitefield.[26] Even if contemporaries did not always believe the revivalist rhetoric that the Church of England was spiritually dead, its actions in revivalism contributed to a certain public image of the church as privileged, authoritative, and unbending.

Ironically, colonial Anglicanism did not Anglicize as effectively as did some other competing Protestant groups in America. In reforming their church governance and in embracing the messages of individualized Christianity from revivalism, many Protestant denominations adopted practices and beliefs from their British denominational counterparts and put themselves on a firm footing for success in America in the late colonial period, particularly given the rising importance of evangelicalism in the nineteenth century. By contrast, the hierarchical Church of England not only shied away from revivalism but also was unsuccessful over the course of the colonial period in replicating its institutions of church governance. Most notably, the colonial Church of England lacked a colonial bishop, a situation that meant candidates for orders had to travel to England and rites such as confirmation could not be performed. In the absence of a resident bishop, oversight of the colonial clergy and church matters fell instead to the bishop of London and his commissaries, with some ecclesiastical powers residing in the governor and considerable authority resting with parish vestries in colonies where the church was established.[27] This division of authority between ecclesiastical and civil officers deviated from the English church model while adapting to local circumstances. Whether that suggests Americanization or Anglicization, the root cause was the absence of colonial bishops.[28] Other innovations that may seem democratic, such as clerical conventions, may also be seen as expedient measures to cope with the lack of the traditional office of bishop.

In those areas of governance where the colonial Church of England had not replicated its mother church's institutions, particularly bishops and ecclesiastical courts, the solution was often more democratic, rather than hierarchical. This was not to suggest a preference for democratic forums, but in the absence of authoritative agencies colonial Anglicans had to rely on themselves, that is the clergy in convention or laity in vestry. Over time these patterns became routine, and especially in Virginia, with its long history of Anglicanism, the local church gained a measure of self-governance and connectedness to local politics and politicians, along with a corresponding distaste for colonial bishops. Such democratic adaptations might be seen as practical responses to incomplete or failed Anglicization. That the campaigns for a colonial bishop were unsuccessful vexed other Anglican contemporaries, in the colonies and in England, who focused on the proposed colonial episcopate as a vital point of victory or convergence with the Church of England. Yet Anglicization of the empire had provided the structure for a hierarchical innovation such as colonial episcopacy to be envisioned and attempted in the first place. What the Anglican establishments in the colonies were able to achieve via the SPG, royal governors' support, and local laws had also been made possible by the process of Anglicization, with state formation and bureaucratic centralization as key contributing elements. Individual colonies' divergence from the English church-state model was a key feature of this system, suggestive of the adaptability of both the colonial Church of England and the process of Anglicization.

That an episcopal church labored without a bishop would be a logical problem for any denomination, but the pique lay in the fact that this was the Church of England, the king's church. In addition, bishops were vital not for supervising and disciplining clergy but because this was an apostolic church: the authority to ordain ministers descended, it was believed, from the Apostles to the bishops in an unbroken succession. Despite the work of advocates for colonial episcopacy in the colonies and in the English church and administration, and many plans to correct this anomalous situation, none met the favor of the English government before the American Revolution. Instead the more colonial churchmen and clergy defended their church's claim to be a bulwark of monarchy and empire, and consequently called for closer ties with England and the completion of their church infrastructure, the more they endangered the position of the Church of England within the colonies.[29] The campaign for a colonial episcopate showed that many British colonists in America, including Congregationalists, Baptists, and Presbyterians but also some southern Anglicans who did not want bishops, saw distinct limits to Anglicization.[30] English goods and even royal government might be perfectly acceptable, even desirable, but for many English Protestants in the colonies the importation of English-style bishops was a highly objectionable idea.

Although discussion about a colonial bishop for the Church of England dated back to Archbishop Laud, a point not lost on New England Congregationalists, the reinvigoration of colonial Anglicanism after 1701 offered new hopes of (and concerns about) such an appointment. English leaders of the SPG had delivered anniversary sermons about the need for colonial bishops, and they had lobbied government; one such plan with SPG sponsorship fell through with the death of Queen Anne in 1714.[31] The growth of the Anglican parishes in the colonies both pointed to the need for a bishop and contributed to the fiercely negative, organized response among various New England and middle colony Protestants who feared a bishop would result in the curtailment of their own religious liberties. Growing numbers of Anglicans, if reinforced with a colonial bishop and the support of royal government already in place, might even overturn a Congregationalist establishment to erect an Anglican one. Antiepiscopal responses therefore consisted of a backlash against both Anglicanization and Anglicization. Anglicans appeared to be reintroducing arguments from old England of the seventeenth century and making them relevant in New England of the eighteenth, including episcopacy. The Congregationalist claim was that English bishops had chased their Puritan forefathers out of England in Archbishop Laud's day and now were attempting to follow them to New England to drive them out all over again.

The relative scarcity of local Anglicans with whom they could argue throughout most of the seventeenth century meant that New Englanders by the early eighteenth century had largely forgotten the specific theological arguments for and against episcopacy. This point was made evident at Yale when a donation of Anglican books, the first ones of Anglican divines that many of the Congregationalists there had seen, caused the rector and four tutors by 1722 to accept the reasonableness of episcopacy, resign their positions, and seek ordination in the Church of England. The reintroduction of Anglican ideas on episcopacy had both shaken and chipped away at the local foundation of Congregationalism. By 1727 both Massachusetts and Connecticut allowed Anglicans exemptions from paying taxes to support Congregationalist clergy so that their church taxes instead could support the local Anglican ministers.[32] Between 1720 and 1759 the largest number of American-born college graduates entering the Anglican ministry came from Yale and Harvard, a trend that demonstrated the Anglicization of New England.[33] These candidates for orders were further Anglicized by their journeys to London, where they met the bishop of London and SPG officers if they were destined for such posts in America. Samuel Johnson had been a particularly keen tourist: as well as sightseeing, he had met many people with whom he would carry on future correspondence, and he had attended Christopher Wren's funeral.[34] Since these would have been the young men's first and (for most) only trips to London, the ordination experience contributed to the forming of an Anglican identity, while it also helped them to identify personally with English culture.[35]

In the 1750s and 1760s transatlantic campaigns concerning colonial episcopacy intensified, and opponents of episcopacy from the colonies and the metropole worked together. Meanwhile, Anglican clergy and some laymen who favored the appointment of a colonial bishop continued to send petitions, not quite understanding why they were not allowed to complete their church structure when every other group could. The British government had permitted Moravians to bring bishops to America and quietly allowed Roman Catholic ones within British territories. The internal ecclesiastical and organizational reasons demonstrated the colonial church's need for bishops, but its advocates failed to persuade government of a political justification to outweigh its political concerns about the loss of dissenter support for government if they passed such a measure. Church and state interests did not coalesce on this issue.[36] In the colonial pamphlet warfare that ensued, Jonathan Mayhew in 1754 accused the SPG of failing to minister to Native Americans and instead using SPG funds intended for that purpose to proselytize among New Englanders already served by other Protestant churches. Mayhew and later Charles Chauncy articulated broad fears that prelates would, in essence, speed up the trend of Anglicanization and ensure its sinister ends: that bishops would convert more colonists to the Church of England than ever and that then Anglicans would dominate other groups and force an establishment with ecclesiastical courts and test acts, which in turn would rob non-Anglicans of their religious liberties. Contrary to this imagined future, the controversy over colonial episcopacy and Mayhew's criticisms actually seemed to slow and suspend Anglican progress in New England. Additionally, Mayhew reminded New Englanders that their ancestors had fled England because of bishops, a history lesson which fueled the fear of bishops and lent support to their antiepiscopal remarks.[37]

The eventual colonial Anglican response by Thomas Bradbury Chandler insisted that only spiritual bishops were intended and that fears of ecclesiastical courts were unfounded; he also tried to challenge Mayhew's beliefs, and by extension the attitudes of colonial Congregationalists and other Protestants, concerning English bishops. While he acknowledged that bishops had once misused their power, English Protestants no longer had anything to fear from English bishops, who "for a long course of years, exercised their authority with so much mildness, tenderness and moderation, as scarcely to have afforded an instance of reasonable complaint, especially to Dissenters."[38]

Whereas many New Englanders saw an Anglican plot to impose Parliament-appointed bishops, colonial Anglicans saw Mayhew's remarks as an attempt to prejudice colonists against the Church of England. Meanwhile response to Mayhew's pamphlet demonstrated that opposition to a colonial episcopate in America was fierce and politically coordinated with English Protestants, a situation that persuaded the English government not to act on the matter.

When Thomas Secker, as archbishop of Canterbury after 1758, and colonial Anglican spokesmen claimed that they were seeking colonial bishops with only spiritual authority over Anglicans, a situation which they claimed posed no threat to the rights of other Protestants, Mayhew and his followers greeted this argument with disbelief. Even if they accepted that these bishops initially would have only spiritual jurisdiction over Anglicans, they trusted that Anglicization would, probably sooner rather than later, reverse that situation, because colonial bishops would not be content without the civil powers of English prelates. Nor did it seem plausible that Anglicans actually wanted a colonial church infrastructure topped with a suffragan bishop when that would be a departure from the English church-state norms. In private writings there is evidence to suggest that many Anglican ministers in the colonies did hope for and perhaps preferred a bishop on the English model, although this may also reflect their impression of what SPG officers, to whom they were writing, envisioned.[39] That a colonial bishop could be approved and sent only by the English government[40] seemed to confirm the colonial dissenters' view that it would be inseparable from civil powers—in origin and so likely also in function. Objections to Anglican episcopacy, in turn, contributed to a rejection of Anglicanization and Anglicization, as imagined by Mayhew, as a plot of the English government to destroy New England liberties. This unflattering image of the English church resonated strongly, particularly for those who found, or were about to find, aspects of royal government corrupt, distant, or exclusionary.

The campaign for a colonial bishop served as an uncomfortable reminder for other Protestants that the colonial Church of England was a highly visible local branch of an English institution, and most disturbing of all was the prospect that it might be further strengthened with bishops appointed by Parliament. Already it had the support of royal governors as the king's representatives, and it was integrated into those colonial governments where it was established and tax supported. Its episcopal structure meant that it was dependent on the English church for the ordination and licensing of ministers. Outside of Virginia and Maryland, almost all Anglican clergy received salaries

from the SPG, the English church's missionary branch. The cultural Anglicization of colonial society in the eighteenth century had led to an increased
presence of the English church, especially in seaports and larger towns, and
this growth had contributed to the backlash against the church. By the eve of
the American Revolution almost half of the ministers of the colonial Church
of England had been born in America, but Anglicanism was nonetheless perceived as an English institution.[41] This public image ill-prepared the colonial
church for political disputes of the 1760s and 1770s, when traditional Anglican loyalty to the Crown and state would raise further suspicions. Meanwhile
critics of episcopacy feared that once a colonial bishop was actually in place,
the colonial Church of England would consolidate its gains, Anglicize new
regions, and further restrict the religious liberty of non-Anglicans.

Anglicanism, Religious Toleration, and Anglicization

Religious toleration was not only an American achievement in the British
colonies but also an English import. In England toleration and cooperation
became an official policy with the passage of the Act of Toleration of 1689, a
law that protected the right to public worship for Protestants (Catholics, athe-
ists, and anti-Trinitarians excluded) if they registered their meetings. Related
developments, such as increased ethnic pluralism as well as interest in rationalism and the reformation of manners, also supported toleration. Although
the three kingdoms of Britain supported an Episcopal establishment or protected Episcopalians and the church-state model rebounded in America,
simultaneously the Church of England found itself far less able to compel
people to accept it.[42] Anglican coercive powers declined, inspiring instead
voluntarism and the missionary impulse; likewise government was less interested in compelling conformity. In the colonies after the Glorious Revolution,
as before, conformity also was limited by widespread diversity and the lack of
coercive tools. The meaning of the Glorious Revolution's religious legacy for
England and the colonies, including what religious toleration meant, what
its limits were, and what its implications would be, had to be figured out in
the early eighteenth century. Typically toleration fell far short of full religious
acceptance or equality. Members of the dominant group in society usually
assumed the nonconformist to be wrong and imposed some legal disabilities in a manner that showed the limits of their toleration. For instance the
English Toleration Act protected the right of Trinitarian Protestants to public

worship, but the test and corporation acts were retained so that all were not accorded equal political rights. What did colonial Anglicanism understand religious toleration to mean in the early to mid-eighteenth century, within the context of a reinvigorated church-state tradition, and what efforts did Anglicans make to extend or limit its expression? Other colonial Protestants could interpret the forces of Anglicanization as contrary to their religious freedom, but to what extent did Anglican practitioners articulate any beliefs about either promoting or discouraging religious toleration?

Because the experience of religious toleration varied tremendously depending on whether one was asking for it or awarding it to others, it is helpful to examine its expression both in a colony where the Church of England competed with other denominations without an official establishment and conversely where it wielded power as the official church and, along with local government, attempted to decide the limits of toleration of other denominations. This section draws on evidence from Pennsylvania and Virginia: the first, a region with unusual provisions for religious liberty indicative of its post-Restoration founding and the antiestablishment attitudes of its Quaker founders; and the second, the colony with the longest and deepest tradition of an Anglican establishment. While the Church of England was consolidating and expanding in the early eighteenth century, it was at vastly different stages of development in Pennsylvania and Virginia. Likewise ethnic and religious pluralism affected both regions unequally: Pennsylvania was among the most diverse of the British colonies; and Virginia was among the least diverse, though even Virginia hosted Presbyterian and Quaker meetings early in the eighteenth century. Yet the purpose here is not to compare the two colonies but rather to examine Anglican expressions of tolerance and intolerance, distaste for or cooperation with non-Anglicans, in two very different colonial environments so as to understand what religious tolerance meant within an Anglican worldview that generally favored the unity of church and state.

Pennsylvania

Of religious diversity in Pennsylvania, the German Lutheran leader Henry Mühlenberg wrote that "[w]hatever is not tolerated in Europe finds its place here."[43] Such pluralism was unsettling for Anglicans more familiar with an English national church tradition, wherein all citizens were theoretically members of the Church of England and some of those who dissented practiced occasional conformity.[44] Instead SPG missionaries, who provide a glimpse into colonial Anglican thought in Pennsylvania, reported that they were vastly outnumbered by other Protestants whom they collectively labeled "Dissenters," even though Pennsylvania had no local establishment against which to dissent.[45] Despite its minority status and equal legal position relative to other denominations, the Church of England locally did enjoy the support of royal governors and proprietors. One of the Anglican clergymen in Pennsylvania, Richard Peters, served as proprietary secretary and provincial secretary and later was a council member. Yet the expansion of the Church of England was modest in Pennsylvania, where fewer than twenty Anglican ministers labored at any point during the colonial period.[46] Most SPG missionaries were High Church men inclined to be wary toward dissent, as their letters to their superiors suggest, and the experience of religious pluralism in Pennsylvania both confirmed and moderated this view. Anglican clergy expanded their notions of religious toleration to find common interests with the members of some other national churches while they distanced themselves from other Protestant groups presumed to be rivals. In so doing, they hoped to swell the numbers sitting in Anglican pews as well as spread the values of the Church of England and the English empire within the province.

In a number of ways, Anglicans promoted a spirit of cooperation with other denominations in colonial Pennsylvania. SPG instructions to its missionaries throughout the British colonies urged them not to offend the civil government and to cultivate amiable relations with "all Protestant Inhabitants" in their district.[47] It was also quite common for rural clergy to allow ministers of other denominations to preach at their churches, and Anglican missionaries likewise might preach in a non-Anglican church in the country. This practice could fill the church for a late Sunday evening service or provide a Sabbath service when the rector was away visiting an outlying chapel in his parish. While it offered a partial solution to the scarcity of ministers and buildings, Anglican ministers also pitched the idea to their SPG superiors that they could thereby convince nonchurchmen to abandon their previous and false notions of the Church of England, and in some cases they might even be brought over to Anglicanism by the regularity of its liturgy. Through such interdenominational cooperation and tolerance, the Church of England might thereby be strengthened. Cultivating good relations with other Protestants was not only a high-minded and Christian approach, but it could also contribute to a favorable public image for Anglicanism.

Religious toleration was consistent with other trends embraced by the Church of England in the eighteenth century, such as rationalism and latitudinarianism, but among Pennsylvanian Anglicans it also seemed to offer a practical solution to their numerical weakness relative to other groups and a possible road toward the Anglicization of foreign Protestants. SPG missionaries and Anglican spokesmen wrote optimistically about a potential union with other Protestant national groups—German, Dutch, and Swedish—that shared a similar theology and church-state tradition. Anglican clergy, including the well-connected Richard Peters and the frontier missionary Thomas Barton, were particularly hopeful that a union with the German Lutherans would increase Anglican numbers and improve their respectability. Barton described that because the Germans were generally "well affected to the Church of England," consequently they "might easily be brought to unite with the Church."[48] For his part, Henry Mühlenberg had written to his mentor in Halle in the late 1740s and early 1750s to explore the possibility of union.[49] Anglicans noted similarities in theology and rituals between their church and other national Protestant churches, but they also defended the idea of union with a balance-of-power argument about how strategic alliances could limit the progress provincially of less tolerable groups, especially Presbyterians and Roman Catholics.[50] For them, the progress of the Church of England could be measured both by Anglican gains, including its Anglicization of certain foreign Protestants, and by Presbyterian and Catholic losses.

Educational initiatives promised to promote Anglicanism and English values, while being at least somewhat tolerant of other denominations and ethnic groups. A formal Anglican-German Lutheran union never came to pass, although the creation of English charity schools did promise the Anglicization of German children in Pennsylvania. Anglicans tended to favor the legislation passed by the Pennsylvania Assembly. William Smith indicated that this was the surest way for "incorporating these foreigners with ourselves" and wrote that once English and German children were taught together their loyalty would be assured. The archbishop of Canterbury likewise approved of this plan, which he claimed was created "upon a Large and Generous plan of religious Liberty, consistent with the national Establishment of the Mother Country, to instill and propagate the notion that these Germans are to become one with us, and that it were best for both to have, in time, one common Language."[51] While some German Lutherans opposed it, Henry Mühlenberg favored the plan for English charity schools. He was fully aware of its assimilative purposes but noted that German children were already exchanging their language for English. Because this plan would allow for instruction in both German and English and did not impose a specific catechism, Mühlenberg likely felt that the education would not impinge on their religious liberty. The purpose of the English charity school, as his mentor in Halle saw it, was "less theological than political, and less directed toward the rescue of souls than aimed at securing [the loyalty of] the German inhabitants and melting them together with the English nation."[52] In his support of English-language instruction and in his pioneering of sermons in English, Mühlenberg saw the advantages that improved access to English society and commerce could offer his parishioners.

Although Anglicans seemed more comfortable discussing religious liberty as a gift they could bestow rather than receive, as a minority population Anglicans benefited from the provisions for religious liberty in Pennsylvania. At times they employed arguments of religious equality to assert their own rights, as in the campaign for episcopacy. More frequently, and in a manner revealing a partisan, even privileged worldview, they referred to the goals of the Church of England as synonymous with those of Protestantism or religion more generally. Such was the perspective especially of SPG missionaries raised in or converted to a national church. Their beliefs in the merits of a strong church-state establishment were largely confirmed by their local experiences with religious pluralism. An appreciation of religious toleration could, but did not necessarily, mean an acceptance of denominationalism. Perhaps that helps to explain why some Anglican ministers disagreed about the interdenominational foundation of the College of Philadelphia. Hugh Neill complained in 1763 that there were too few Anglicans among the college's staff and so it was becoming too Presbyterian; meanwhile Richard Peters more liberally and positively contended that the college plan was "not confined to this Church, but founded upon a coalition of all religious Societies." If the college showed the Church of England to be tolerant, then perhaps, as William Smith hoped, the religious diversity of the college would improve the church's reputation among other Protestants.[53] Beliefs such as religious toleration and establishmentarianism coexisted in the Anglican mind, and practitioners believed optimistically that expressions of toleration might serve partisan ends and benefit the Church of England.

Virginia

By the early eighteenth century the Church of England establishment in Virginia was firmly in place, owing to its longevity and the ethnic and religious homogeneity of the province. As John Nelson reminds us, all Protestant dissenters in Virginia were Anglican parishioners who paid parish levies to support the local Church of England.[54] Until the 1730s Virginian dissenters were relatively few in number, a situation not unlike that of England. Small numbers of Quaker migrants and pockets of German settlers in the seventeenth century had not threatened the hegemony of the establishment, though Quakers had faced persecution.[55] When imperial governance and the church-state model were reintroduced with new vigor at the turn of the eighteenth century, the early history of Virginia already seemed to offer abundant assurances of the health of its church-state connections. Yet Anglicization, in all its various incarnations, was not always welcome in Virginia or in Virginia's church. Leading gentry families, holding positions at all levels of government from the parish vestry to the House of Burgesses and the governor's council, opposed efforts to centralize church authority in a bishop.[56] Instead the local elites nurtured a Low Church view of Anglicanism that enhanced the local vestry's responsibilities and further confirmed their lay influence. Indicative of gentry power, after 1662 the parish vestries became self-selecting. James B. Bell has argued that the parish vestry was "the most Americanized element of the colonial King's church."[57] Even so, on the matter of clerical appointments, vestries did not escape the forces of centralization. The right to hire and dismiss clergymen was not exclusively a vestry duty; it overlapped with the bishop of London's powers to ordain and license and the governor's powers of preferment, and by 1748 governors had won the contest with the assemblies over who had the power to appoint ministers.[58] Curbed somewhat by centralizing forces, lay authority in Virginia remained strong without the traditional oversight of a resident bishop.

James Blair's appointment as first commissary in 1690 served to support the planting of Low Church Anglicanism as it was evolving in Virginia. A latitudinarian Scot, Blair founded the College of William and Mary and contributed to the strengthening of the colonial church. The college, his special project, promised to be a colonial Anglican source of educated men for the ministry. Blair's fiery personality, directed toward the defense and expansion of the prerogatives of his office and therefore the church's interests, was displayed in bitter disputes with three governors, even those who were ardent friends of the Church of England.[59] His role as deputy bishop may be seen as part of an effort to centralize Anglicanism. Blair initially had wanted ecclesiastical courts and the permanent induction of ministers, and his advocacy of both provoked lay fears about hierarchical and ecclesiastical power. Colonial Virginians shared a popular English concern about corruption linked to the operation of ecclesiastical courts.[60] Yet Blair recognized that a seminary, an ecclesiastical court, and his unique position as the bishop's representative all aimed to correct omissions in the church infrastructure, so that the colonial Church of England would be better able to serve its parishioners, conduct missions, and compete with other Protestant churches. In his initial efforts to set up ecclesiastical courts, Blair appeared to be overlooking the English Toleration Act.[61] The proposal, described to a convention of clergy, fit with his commission and English practice, but it would have allowed his new ecclesiastical courts to supersede existing civil ones upheld by Virginian laws. Blair wanted the ecclesiastical courts to be responsible for the discipline of clergymen and laity, and he implied that they would suppress dissenters, at least Quakers and enthusiasts.[62] The plan failed, but the attempt shows Blair's commitment to solving the church's structural challenges and his early willingness to disregard Virginian laws and even the bishop's instructions (that is, to focus on a review of the clergy and to avoid meddling with the laity). In his half-century in office, Blair witnessed and participated in the strengthening of the provincial Anglican establishment, to the point that other Protestants in Virginia later claimed that they were not accorded the same rights of worship as their English counterparts.

In England the Toleration Act's protection of the public worship of all Trinitarian Protestants meant that Anglican clergy quickly faced greater competition from rival denominations and their multiplying meetinghouses. Furthermore the Toleration Act was widely interpreted to mean that churchgoing was voluntary, despite the fact that attendance was still a statutory obligation for Anglicans.[63] In this context Anglican ministers either had to accept the new religious marketplace of voluntarism and persuade their listeners or campaign for the return of a more authoritative church-state regime. In the early eighteenth century Virginian ministers and politicians did not need to make such a difficult choice between uniformity and toleration: they continued to preserve their strong establishment. Blair's early efforts, elite control of local politics, and the relative absence of serious challengers until the middle of the eighteenth century had led to a firm church-state union. As a nod to the Toleration Act, Virginia's government set up regulations for local dissenters, requiring that their places of worship be licensed and that their ministers be examined and licensed and that each confine his activities to a specific meetinghouse. Faced with increasing populations and insufficient Anglican ministers, the provincial government tried to curb the growth and organization of dissenters with restrictions and fines, and it justified its actions, at least initially, with claims that the English Toleration Act did not apply in Virginia.[64] Whereas many High Church men in England had worried that the Toleration Act would lead to a huge expansion of dissent there, that fear had not come to pass by the 1730s. Consequently a spirit of moderation could prevail, a traditional Anglican quality of finding a middle path between extremes of Rome and Geneva or between enthusiasm and indifference.[65] The Virginia experience differed in scope and chronology: there churchmen firmly held on to the principles and practices of uniformity well past 1689, until the rise of rival Protestant populations after the 1730s and their resulting political demands required a reevaluation of how English policies of toleration fit in a Virginia-styled, authoritarian church-state establishment.

Ethnic and religious pluralism came later to Virginia than to many other British North American colonies. Beginning in the 1730s, the sustained migration of Scots-Irish, other north Britons, and Germans into the Shenandoah Valley and into the backcountry altered the religious landscape. In the 1710s the burgesses had been willing to grant multiyear exemptions from parish levies to encourage the migration of some German and French Protestants, in likely anticipation that they would soon be friends, if not converts, to Anglicanism.[66] However, the arrival of larger numbers of Presbyterians and evangelicals posed more of a threat. Their rapid growth meant serious competition for souls in an era of Anglican expansion. The number of Church of England ministers in Virginia rose in the second quarter of the eighteenth century, with a new focus on doctrine and catechizing youths. Yet Anglican efforts were still concentrated mainly in the Tidewater, allowing others, including Baptists, to expand in areas where the Church of England underserved the region and where they could upstage Anglicans and Presbyterians by mobilizing many preachers and quickly gaining converts.[67] Only when a critical mass of dissenters lived in Virginia and when they asserted their right to worship did Anglicans there have a pressing reason to express or even to formulate local policies of toleration or intolerance.

Enter Samuel Davies, a savvy Presbyterian minister, who successfully argued for his right to itinerate between Presbyterian congregations, despite an inhospitable reception from members of the governor's council, the House of Burgesses, and from Attorney General Peyton Randolph. In 1750 Randolph claimed that the Toleration Act's enforcement would only produce confusion. The implication was that Virginia's politicians felt their church-state establishment to be powerful enough, and local dissent politically weak enough, that they did not necessarily have to abide by this prominent English

law and that the local elite could consequently choose unanimity over toleration. The religious demography of Virginia made such assumptions possible:
in 1750 the Presbyterians and Baptists were too few in number and political
strength, a situation that changed by the 1760s and 1770s. For their part, the
bishop of London and some of the Anglican clergy in Virginia did not so
much argue in the mid-1750s that the Toleration Act did not apply in Virginia as they questioned the motives of Davies and others and the legitimacy
of itinerancy. The bishop of London asked,

> how is Mr. Davies's conduct to be justified, who under the colour of
> a Toleration to his own conscience is labouring to disturb the con-
> sciences of others, and the peace of a Church acknowledged to be a
> true Church of Christ? He came 300 Miles from home, not to serve
> people who had scruples, but to a Country where the Church of Eng-
> land had been Established from its first plantation, and where there
> were not above 4 or 5 dissenters within an 100 Miles, if not above six
> years ago. Mr. Davies says . . . "We claim no other liberties than those
> granted by the act of Toleration," so that the state of the question is
> admitted on both sides to be this: how far the act of Toleration will
> justify Mr. Davies in taking upon himself to be an itinerant preacher
> and travelling over many Counties to make Converts, in a Country
> too where till very lately there was not a Dissenter from the Church
> of England.[68]

The accusation was that Davies was poaching souls belonging to the
Church of England through illegitimate methods such as itinerancy. The
bishop of London also denied knowledge of any oppression or persecution
of dissenters, noting that if that were the case, it was the civil government
at fault.[69] Additionally he pointedly focused on what he saw as the hypocrisy of dissenters proclaiming their rights to toleration while obstructing
Anglican efforts to have colonial bishops. A petition from the clergy and
churchmen of Virginia to the burgesses similarly mentioned their concern
over itinerancy, noting that a license would not give a preacher permission
to preach throughout several counties. They suspected that "Lay Enthusiasts"
and "strolling pretended Ministers" reading "sundry fanatical Books" and
using extemporaneous prayers, as opposed to an educated, licensed ministry
using the fixed liturgy from the Book of Common Prayer, would gain converts among "ignorant and unwary People" and "under pretence of greater

Degrees of Piety among them, than can be found among the Members of the Established Church . . . seduce them from their lawful Teachers, and the Religion hitherto professed in this Dominion."[70] The Anglican complaint was a compilation of the presumed ill-effects of an uneducated ministry, itinerancy, and enthusiasm proselytizing among their parishioners under what they saw to be the false disguise of toleration.

Ironically, Presbyterians and later Baptists in Virginia engaged in a difficult campaign to convince Anglicans to Anglicize their laws, that is, to follow existing English law. As early as 1758 Presbyterians were mobilizing politically to support candidates who would protect their rights. While newly arrived Governor Francis Fauquier promised his help to secure Presbyterian religious rights under the Toleration Act, the House of Burgesses proved more intractable. Presbyterians and Baptists ultimately targeted and reformed Virginia's practice of toleration, but initial efforts sometimes included impolitic criticisms of the Church of England and its ministers that led to accusations of blasphemy or slander. The presence of uneducated New Side Presbyterian leaders with large crowds in the 1740s tended to convince Virginian authorities to persist in their limited interpretation of the Toleration Act. Samuel Davies's success can be attributed to his deference toward the Anglican ministry and the court, as well as his strategy of convincing the authorities that Presbyterians were willing to comply with all of the regulations of the Toleration Act, including Anglican oversight. He was not challenging the law or broadening its interpretation beyond the right to public worship, as Quakers and Baptists attempted. Rather, Davies tried to show that his sect already conformed to Virginia law and thereby argued that Presbyterianism did not present a threat to the establishment. In so doing, Davies and other licensed Presbyterian ministers complied with the requirements for toleration, and so tried to get Virginian authorities to recognize the English Toleration Act, a law that some members of the governor's council even in 1755 claimed was not in force in Virginia.[71] Instead of challenging the politicians' right to regulate other religious groups, these Presbyterians demonstrated their conformity with Virginia law, and so made it difficult for Virginian authorities to deny the English legal terms of toleration.

Separate Baptists, in contrast to Presbyterians, pressed for an expansion of the legal understanding of toleration, beyond freedom to worship.[72] Arriving in northern Virginia in the 1750s, Separate Baptists had radical practices that challenged prevailing social and cultural conventions. Anglicans found their evangelicalism objectionable enough, but their opposition to the civil regulation of religion posed a more fundamental, political problem. These Baptists refused to register their meetinghouses or allow their ministers to submit to Anglican examinations, and so they defied the authority of the local government. Prosecution and persecution seemed only to make the Separate Baptists more determined, and they shifted their demand from dissenters' rights to the disestablishment of Anglicanism. Recent work on Baptist and Presbyterian activism in late colonial Virginia has demonstrated how its advocates managed to secure greater religious freedom in exchange for their support of the Revolutionary War.[73] Dissenters had worked first to encourage the Virginian authorities to recognize and abide by the English Toleration Act and then to broaden its interpretation, and ultimately these challenges contributed to the destabilizing of Virginia's church-state bond.

A strong Anglican hegemony in church and state, relatively small dissenter populations, and the political impotence of dissent in Virginia until the last couple of decades before the American Revolution meant that Anglican authorities could largely avoid the matter of toleration—avoid it, that is, until war-time circumstances made that impossible. The pressures of the Revolutionary War made it necessary for the Anglican establishment to negotiate improved religious toleration in exchange for military mobilization. Pennsylvanian Anglicans, by contrast, operated within a religiously plural context, and their lack of power and privilege (relatively speaking) meant that the arguments for religious toleration could advance the cause of their own church. Yet SPG missionaries also believed in the merits of a church-state establishment and saw themselves as part of the national church, the Church of England; they did not expect to be treated merely as members of a minor denomination. The Anglican church-state model had especially thrived in Virginia, but the particular English establishmentarian seed that was planted there had grown more intolerant over time because of its relative isolation from dissenters of critical size and organization. By the time it met such challengers, political circumstances meant that the religious establishment did not have long to survive.

Anglicanization, or the strengthening of the colonial Church of England, coincided with and reinforced other Anglicizing trends in the eighteenth century. The creation of royal government, the administration of imperial policies, the importation of British culture and goods, and a reinvigorated church-state tradition all converged and, in turn, encouraged further colonial Anglican growth. SPG missionaries had a zeal for loyalty and building congregations indicative of the turn-of-the-century Anglican evangelizing spirit. Its clergy and sometimes its practitioners saw themselves as spokes-men for a church-state model, and in this respect they had taken a domi-nant strain of English culture and intensified it in the colonies. Church of England clergy and elites in Virginia defended vigorously their local version of a church establishment against those Baptist and Presbyterian challengers seeking to extend religious liberty and thereby reduce uniformity and also against potential threats from inside the English church and state to create ecclesiastical courts, bishops, or other hallmarks of centralizing ecclesiastical authority. Anglicanization caused divisions within the members and clergy of the Church of England over how best to promote the church's interests locally or imperially, and it had its detractors. In the first several decades of the eighteenth century, Anglicanism's presence had increased dramatically in regions dominated numerically and legally by other Protestants. This growth, as well as other Anglicizing trends, fueled a backlash against the church that proved detrimental to its public image. Meanwhile Protestant challengers were concerned that they were witnessing the reinvigoration of Anglican-ism in America, and they increasingly interpreted the church to be a local institution of a distant and corrupt English government. At the same time, migration, population growth, and the rise in religious and ethnic plural-ism contributed to the heightening of interdenominational competition over souls. The Church of England was less successful than its competition in reaching the backcountry, and other Protestant denominations had certain strategic and financial advantages in putting ministers into the field and set-ting up congregations.

Anglicanism and Its Limits

Colonial Anglicans believed that their church benefited from a post-1688 spirit of toleration and moderation, though many of its leaders were also so deeply convinced of the spiritual and political advantages of the church-state model, including its promotion of loyalty to government, that they could not easily embrace the merits of religious diversity and denominational-ism. Explicit toleration of other denominations posed numerous problems. In colonies where Anglicanism was not established, such as Pennsylvania, it suggested that Anglican progress would always fall short of achieving an official status commensurate with its missionaries' self-image as bear-ers of the national church. In Virginia broad religious toleration was risky at mid-century, when other Protestant groups were beginning to pose both demographic and political challenges. These were dangerous times to accept, let alone expand as some Baptists urged, the terms of the English Toleration Act. Anglicans not only found it difficult to let go of their church-state principles, but at mid-century they also saw little reason to do so. Events in 1760 seemed to support the hope of an Anglican triumph in America: the coronation of the new king and the recent translation of Thomas Secker, a longtime advocate of the colonial church and head of the SPG, to the position of archbishop of Canterbury seemed good omens. This was a confident moment. Colonial Anglicanism, like the recently victorious British Empire, might be a rising star. Even so, Anglican values could divide as well as unite. Anglicanization had provided a kind of religious and cultural integration for its members, and it had supported various other strands of Anglicization that promoted imperial unity, but in its intensified embrace of the church-state model, colonial Anglicanism had seemed to go against a prevailing tide of religious pluralism, toleration, and equality. Additionally its historic, ecclesiastical, and political ties to the English king meant that the Church of England and its followers would not only be seen as loyal to Britain in the American Revolution but also be interpreted as part of an old regime of privilege and intolerance.

CHAPTER SEVEN

Anglicization Against the Empire: Revolutionary Ideas and Identity in Townshend Crisis Massachusetts

Jeremy A. Stern

When John Winthrop and his followers landed in 1630 at the new colony of the Massachusetts Bay, it was far from clear how "English" they intended to remain. One hundred and thirty years later—though important religious and political ideas persisted from those early generations—Britishness lay at the core of the colonists' self-definition. Trade with Britain was central to economic life, and British culture and fashion were eagerly imbibed. Under its second, 1691 charter, Massachusetts accepted the substantial powers of the royally appointed governor (powers, albeit, more circumscribed than in most royal colonies). Parliament's right to regulate trade for the good of the empire was almost universally acknowledged, and more obeyed than not. The British constitution was venerated as the fount of the English liberties that British Americans enjoyed. The province's Anglicization—culturally, politically, and economically—was profound.

The 1765–66 Stamp Act crisis rattled this long-accreted structure but failed to undermine it. Contention over parliamentary taxation spurred high emotions and fresh examination of political ideas often taken for granted. Many Americans began to question the validity and safety of broad parliamentary authority over the colonies, even beyond taxation. Yet most aspects of the imperial system—the king's position as head of a unitary Anglo-American world, Parliament's "superintending" role, the basic trustworthiness of British officialdom—were staunchly defended. Even amid protests, colonists fiercely professed their loyalty. A sense of common British identity remained a core self-definition.[1] Yet ten years later the province was at war with its estranged mother country and ready to declare independence.

The colonists long and insistently presented themselves as true inheritors and defenders of Britain's traditional liberties. As the Townshend Acts crisis escalated after 1767, they accused British officials—and ultimately the British people—of betraying hard-won freedoms secured through centuries of struggle. But under the strain of evolving crisis, the colonists' own core ideas were inexorably shifting. Piece by slow piece, hardly realizing it themselves, they redefined their basic concepts of free government. Though Americans continued to build on many strands of English inheritance, Britain's political realities became increasingly unacceptable. Clinging to deep traditional attachments, Americans professed their imperial loyalties and appealed for a return to past harmony. But as Britain's rulers dismissed American claims—firmly, even contemptuously, demanding submission—the deep sense of common British identity was gradually ground away. Distant powers beyond the people's influence came to seem ever more suspect, even dangerous. British institutions, Americans became sure, had been corrupted, but was the once-vaunted British constitution on which those institutions rested safe even in its ideal form? In time even royal prerogative became irretrievably compromised, and with it monarchy itself. Britain, the onetime parent, became the enemy, not only of traditional British freedoms but also of a rising American identity.[2]

One of the province's oldest traditions, the prestigious annual "election sermon," offers a unique year-by-year window into this traumatic yet inexorable transformation.[3] Late each May, before the new House of Representatives and outgoing province council elected the new council for the coming year, a local preacher[4] (invited alternately by the old House or council earlier in the spring) would offer a treatise on the nature of good government—and as the crisis grew, on the state of the province's liberties.[5]

In April 1766, as news of Stamp Act repeal became firm, the province erupted with joyous declarations of imperial loyalty. All blame and guilt were thrust upon George Grenville's fallen ministry. Parliament and the wider British power structure were seen to have vindicated themselves, throwing off the lies of the conspirators. The Declaratory Act joined to repeal—asserting Parliament's right to legislate for America "in all cases whatsoever"—was dismissed as toothless face saving or ignored completely. Local affairs, as was often the case, were less harmonious. Loath to blame the British elites, the province was happy to blame local officials and their allies: Governor

Francis Bernard and his self-interested cabal had surely helped trick Britain into the Stamp Act in order to profit from the spoils. A "black list" targeted dozens of town representatives suspected of promoting or defending the act, defeating many.[6]

The 1766 election sermon was delivered as the new, more heavily antiadministration legislature convened. Its preacher, Edward Barnard of Haverhill, was the choice of the outgoing council, a divided but still largely conservative body dominated by prominent and wealthy men with a stake in the status quo. Haverhill was one of Essex County's safely proadministration commercial towns, and Barnard was cautiously conservative.[7] The heart of Barnard's political universe was Britain's celebrated mixed constitution: the people had a voice but were held in check by the prerogative powers of the Crown. Setting a tone of gratitude, optimism, and dutiful submission to legitimate authority, Barnard blandly invoked conventional Whig compact theory—congenial both to British sensibilities and to New England's powerfully rooted Protestant covenant doctrine. Government had formed when society surrendered its inherent power to "*wise men* for *pilots*," to guide the people and protect them from the dangers of man's fallen state. Barnard emphasized the king's paternal care and Parliament's wisdom and equity. The British world had been restored to harmony; the people's privileges were safe, their future secure. Such blissful fortunes were not to be squandered in petty faction and dispute, a pointed admonition to avoid factional local quarrels. Resistance was valid against true tyranny, for "unlimited submission . . . cannot be duty." But under a benevolent government concerned with the public welfare, "respect and subjection are due to those concerned in it." Such sentiments would have offended few listeners.[8]

Local conflict continued, nonetheless, to seethe. The sharply antiadministration majority forced five of the governor's stalwart supporters off the council, sharply shifting the board's political center, and the assembly battled fiercely over compensation for the victims of anti–Stamp Act riots. Yet local animosities stayed firmly local. The House assailed Bernard's high-handedness in pushing compensation, but the king's urging proved a potent spur amid outpourings of gratitude for repeal. Letters from royal ministers criticizing the province's 1765 disorders were determinedly read as friendly, with any incontrovertible rebuke blamed on Bernard's misrepresentations. Parliament's new Molasses Act—which explicitly listed revenue among its aims—was ignored, dismissed as a constitutional regulation of trade. Some fretted about future British conduct, but fears remained muted and hesitant.

Even as House members quarreled with the governor, they called Reverend Ebenezer Bridge, from generally proadministration Chelmsford, to deliver the 1767 sermon.[9] His tone was solidly supportive of established power structures. Parliament was honorable, "tho' liable to mistakes," the king wise and good, prerogative important and unassailable, and imperial crisis definitively over. Bridge warned rulers to admit their errors (as, he plainly implied, Parliament had done by repealing the Stamp Act). But he sternly warned the people against factious distrust of those in authority. Rulers must see the people as "of the same species with himself, as entitled to many great and special rights and privileges"—but not equality. In the state of nature, men were "all equal and upon a par," but natural equality was surrendered, by compact, to gain the protection that fallen man required. Though the particular form of government was the choice of a given people at its formation, "*The powers that be are ordained of God*"—particularly, of course, the British constitution, which Bridge singled out for special praise, noting approvingly that it could not be altered without the people's consent. But while rulers followed constitutional dictates and the fundamental laws of God, on which any sound constitution must rest, they remained inviolate. In a spirit of imperial confidence, Bridge thought that "the rights and privileges of the colonies are established, perhaps, upon a better basis than ever." He urged the public to respect the virtuous governors set over them by heaven and their British sovereign: "at this very time, perhaps we are more happy in these respects, than some are willing to allow." His ultimate message for the people was, "May *every one study to be quiet and to do his own business*." A happy state was one in which "the true honor of government is supported, and the people are submissive, quiet, free from uneasiness and tumult, peaceable and prosperous."[10] Bridge was surely more conciliatory to Bernard than many of the representatives who summoned him: the legislature continued to defy the governor, refusing to return his ousted allies to the council. But even local tensions began to ease as the session advanced.

Then, in the summer of 1767, disturbing rumors began to mount. Parliament, it was said, would again lay revenue taxes on the colonies, with funds used to pay the colonial governors, freeing them from dependence on the local assemblies. Many refused at first to believe it, but news of the new Townshend Acts soon became undeniable. Yet even amid shock and outrage, most colonists steadfastly refused to see deliberate malice. Britain had again been misled by a scheming cabal: a new customs board, to be based in Boston, was doubtless planned as an easy source of corrupt perquisites for the plotters.

The authority of the king was still firmly defended; many continued to see local charter rights as "granted" by the Crown. Yet nagging doubts percolated as the new acts took hold. The Declaratory Act, ignored in 1766, began to look more ominous. Most continued to acknowledge a poorly defined subordination to Parliament, and yet Parliament's elevated grandeur began to tarnish: were MPs not fellow subjects claiming to rule Americans as superiors? The colonists' root connection to Britain began to draw sporadic scrutiny: did colonial charters formalize inherent ties to Britain or form them outright— grant privileges or recognize rights? Proadministration writers scoffed that common people had no business meddling in such questions, further goading the opposition. Some began to speak of Americans and Britons as distinct peoples. Boycotts of British imports, mounted during the Stamp Act crisis, were swiftly renewed. All denied any thought of independence: leading liberty men bristled at the very suggestion. Yet there were rising invocations of a common pan-colonial Americanism and a fresh focus on the risk of future bad kings or ministers.

In this tense climate, the emboldened council invited Daniel Shute of Hingham to preach the 1768 election sermon. Shute was known for outspoken opposition to the Stamp Act and the governor's political circle. For the first time an election sermon would, however tentatively, challenge the imperial status quo.[11]

Shute's case rested on basic Whig compact theory.[12] Society was ordained by God to secure the natural rights of "life, liberty, and property"—the famed triad of Whig theorist John Locke. In the natural state any right to rule "must arise from the choice of whole," though for practical reasons authority must be vested in a few individuals. So far safely conventional: the governor's party, too, saw themselves as Whig sons of the 1688 revolution, agreeing that men possessed equality in the state of nature and established government by mutual compact to escape the evils of anarchy. But in accepting government, this version of the argument ran, men had *surrendered* their natural rights, accepting their subordination to a governing elite and *constitutionally* enjoying only those rights consistent with order. A right of resistance applied only if tyranny nullified the constitutional order, in which case the people resumed their power to establish a new government.

Shute, however, went further: "delegation" of power did not give away "the right the whole have to govern" but only "provid[ed] for the exercise of their power in the most effectual manner." Indeed, he argued, "natural and constitutional rights" should "be so nearly the same that there is no

interfering between them." Shute had begun to suggest that society's fundamental power *continued to reside in the body of the people* even after government was established.

Shute did not, indeed, carry this suggestion far. He in no way denied the
validity of monarchical and hereditary powers, which existed "by virtue of
the previous consent of society." He had conventional words of praise for
Governor Bernard. And, while emphatic about liberty and the right to resist
unjust rule, he was equally insistent on order. Much of his sermon dwelled on
the people's obligation to submit to the proper exercise of moral laws consistent with "the ends for which [rulers] were given authority." Rulers who did
their duty and promoted God's aims should be "considered as his vicegerents
executing his will . . . worthy of esteem and veneration." Disrespect equaled
destruction: "To pour contempt upon rulers is to weaken government itself,"
sowing "the seeds of libertinism." A balance must always be struck between
"anarchy and slavery."

Yet the colonies' precise relation to British power gave Shute pause. Due
to local circumstances, the colonists had "been indulged to form into little
distinct states under the same head, and to make laws and execute them."
This hinted, boldly, at a federal empire under a common king, but—like many
ideas in the politically unsettled province—the notion remained protean. The
colonies were "indulged," not *entitled* to "distinct states." Shute added that the
colonies remained "restricted . . . by the laws and dependent on the supreme
power of the nation," though only "as far as it is consistent with the essential
Rights of *British* Subjects and necessary to the well-being of the whole." The
colonists, Shute insisted, in no way resented such restrictions, seeing their
connection to the empire as essential to their happiness. Yet, paradoxically, it
was their British status—the need to preserve their essential British rights—
that had necessitated their "little distinct states."

On one key point Shute was firm, perhaps, in part, determined to convince himself: however dark the present hour, it could not "be thought that
Great-Britain would designedly enslave any of her free-born sons," thereby
undermining the constitution "on which her own safety depends." But even
if Britain did not *wish* them ill, Shute left no doubt that the Townshend Acts
endangered Americans' liberties. Their happiness, he repeatedly insisted,
rested on those liberties, which rested on their constitutional rights. Every
threat to those rights must be resisted. Dependence on Britain was their glory,
but dependence "on the supreme power of the nation" could not make it "unfit
to remonstrate under grievances"; rather it urged remonstrance, for "by the

constitution every subject has an equal claim to protection and security in the exercise of that very power." With the broader Massachusetts opposition, Shute retained full faith in ultimate redress: the province's loyalty to the best of kings "will always incline his gracious ear; and give weight to their petitions with his parliament." Enemies, he plainly insinuated, had tricked Parliament into unjust conduct. Surely they would yet come to their senses.

But the coming year instead brought a disastrous hardening of British policies, driving American positions and ideas to harden in response. In June the aggressive seizure of John Hancock's sloop *Liberty* sparked a short but angry anticustoms riot. Soon thereafter Whitehall stunned the province by ordering the House—on pain of dissolution—to rescind a February circular letter to other colonial legislatures. The letter had sought to coordinate petitions against the new taxes, but encouraged by Governor Bernard, the ministry denounced it as treasonous incitement. A strong majority refused to rescind, making them popular heroes. Long-conservative towns turned on their prorescinding representatives, and the council turned on the governor with newfound vehemence. Political writers were increasingly troubled by Britain's readiness to be misled. Patriotic sentiments still abounded, wishing union with Britain repaired and forever protected; however, many hinted that it was in peril if its foundations were not soon repaired.

In September the province learned that troops had been sent to Boston to "restore order." For most Americans, this was an illegal use of military power to force obedience to unconstitutional acts. As the occupation took hold, the press assailed the troops' conduct, the misrepresentations that had brought them, and increasingly the ministers who had sent them. Americans still spoke of themselves as Britain's brothers and sons, imploring their British fellow subjects to save their bonds from destruction. Yet as trust faltered, Americans' lack of checks on the empire's powers drew ever-greater attention. "Citizen" began to displace "subject" in newspaper pieces. Rights "as men" were invoked alongside rights "as Englishmen." Many were appalled by British claims that any act of Parliament at once became part of the Constitution, an argument that would destroy American claims of fixed constitutional principles and create utterly unfettered Parliamentary supremacy. A growing number of writers described the colonies as separate states under the British king.

A batch of Bernard's letters, leaked and published, confirmed the worst fears about his reports. Britain did not rebuke him but instead made him a baronet, an honor that in province eyes could only taint the king who gave it. More and more Massachusetts turned its hopes to the British people, demanding that they throw off their corrupted government, free the king from evil influences, save British liberty, and rescue the imperial bond. [13]

In 1769 it would have been the House's turn to choose the election preacher, but the General Court had been dissolved over the circular letter, and Bernard, citing ministerial instructions, had refused to call new elections. The council could sit only in its executive capacity as the governor's advisers, unable to take any step without his approval. A bare quorum asked Bernard to nominate a preacher. The final choice was Jason Haven of Dedham. From Bernard's perspective, it was a baffling selection: one can only assume that the governor knew little of the young minister or his views. [14]

Haven's fundamental ideas were in many respects similar to Shute's, emphasizing natural rights and the foundation of power in the people. But his confidence in the imperial power structure had been still further damaged. His emphasis fell more firmly on popular political rights and the boundaries government could not cross without nullifying the people's duty to obey. To protect the indispensable Lockean triad of natural rights—"life, liberty and property"—men formed government and society. In so doing, "men do indeed give up some of their natural rights," but only to guarantee "the better security of the rest" and those new rights founded in their constitutions. A society's specific government rested on "free choice and agreement": men had "a natural right to determine for themselves" how and by whom they would be governed. Claims of divine right in any person or family were as absurd as the papal claim of apostolic descent. Haven even inserted a quotation from an anonymous political writer: no man was in "any way superior or inferior to his fellow citizens" save by mutual agreement. Placement of power in a single family was a mere convenience, instantly cancelled if the good of the whole were infringed. [15]

It was the people's God-given duty "to submit to their political fathers in every thing lawful": so long as magistrates governed justly, they were entitled to respect and reward. Honest error should not be taken as ill intent or ground for opposition. But when a ruler abused his delegated power, blatantly encroaching on the subjects' "natural and constitutional rights," it was "impiety against God" and "injustice to themselves, and the community" to obey. Haven emphasized the point with a lengthy quotation from the "great Mr. LOCKE"—the traditional basis for an appeal to fundamental *right* over present *law*. The passage raised a crucial point that many still skirted: *who* was to judge when government was lawful and when it was not? Locke answered that the *people* would judge, for, he asked, who could judge the probity of a deputy but he who deputed him? Prerogative, in short, could not be exercised at the ruler's sole discretion: the people could judge the acts of those they had elevated to power.

God's Providence, Haven agreed, raised or destroyed rulers. He invoked the overthrow of Charles I—an event Edward Barnard in his 1766 sermon had clearly found discomfiting—as God's protection of his people. But accountability to God did not make rulers unaccountable to the people who had given them power. God worked through men. Divine allowance of wicked rulers did not excuse their conduct, and a just Providence would remove a tyrant through the *people's* action.

Haven retained the still-ubiquitous faith in the British constitution as the world's best. Yet his defense of a royally appointed governor strongly implied that even such a provision required popular sufferance: "in this we acquiesce," considering it "preferable to annual elections by the people" (as under the first charter). No one could doubt that the people's state was "difficult and perplexed," however they differed on "the immediate occasions of our troubles." He warned that "mutual confidence and affection between Great-Britain and these Colonies, I speak it with grief, seems to be in some measure lost." Certainly the colonists' loyalty to George III, the best of kings, was undiminished, and they would "yield obedience to the *due* exercise of the authority of Parliament"—the qualifying italics, of course, speaking volumes. But the people "generally apprehend some of their most important civil rights and privileges to be in great danger," particularly from certain recent acts of Parliament.

Haven claimed not to judge the merits of such fears or the best steps for redress, but he dropped unmistakable hints. Rehearsing the proper qualifications for councilors, he pointedly noted the vital importance of the province's elected council; his listeners knew well that Bernard, in his now-published letters, had demanded a Crown-appointed body. "This is a privilege secured to us by *royal charter*," and indeed was more than merely privilege: "What we enjoy by charter, is not to be looked upon barely as matter of grace; but, in a measure at least, of right." Yet such rights still rested on the colonists' very Britishness: they were "those of Englishmen, those of the British constitution," as the province's system "is an image in miniature of that of our nation." Haven would not accept that British actions were founded on evil intent. "If we suffer by being misrepresented to our most gracious Sovereign, or to his ministry," he told the assembled legislators, "'tis your part to remove the hurtful influence thereof . . . to set the temper and conduct of this people, in a just light

before the throne," carrying the people's "cries, and tears, and humble petitions thither . . . 'words of truth,' which must, which will prevail." Haven could
not more squarely have blamed the governor without naming him.

If the people avoided sin and practiced virtue, Haven promised, "mutual
harmony and affection" would surely "be restored between Great-Britain and
her colonies, and between all orders of men in them. The burdens we groan
under shall be removed," along with any suspicion that they lacked "loyalty to
our King" or had "the least disposition to refuse a constitutional subjection to
our parent country." Then their "rights and privileges shall be established on
a firmer basis than ever." Just two years earlier, Ebenezer Bridge had declared
in the same pulpit that their rights and privileges were *already* established
"perhaps, upon a better basis than ever."

In the months that followed, crisis only deepened. Bernard was recalled,
but with no mark of disfavor. Before he left, he responded to bitter House
complaints over the military presence by moving the assembly to Cambridge (freer, he hoped, of the Boston "faction," on which he and his allies
consistently blamed all opposition). The removal, ostensibly based on royal
instructions to the governor, sparked an increasingly open fight about the
boundaries of royal prerogative: the representatives began, as had Haven, to
edge toward a claim that the people themselves could judge whether prerogative's exercise was valid. In addition they began to accuse many in power—in
Britain as well as the province—of directly conspiring toward arbitrary rule.
Boston native Thomas Hutchinson took over as acting governor in August.
Many congratulated him, but most made it plain that approval was contingent on a change of measures. Political writers stressed America's rising
strength, warning Britain to avoid its own ruin.

Matters grew sharply worse in March 1770, when long-standing tensions
with the soldiers—illegal and abusive occupiers in the minds of most townspeople—culminated in the "Boston Massacre." Weeks later word reached the
seething province that the Townshend Acts had been partially repealed, but
on purely commercial grounds and leaving the tax on tea to preserve Parliament's purported powers. This was seen as no more than a low trick, an effort
to carry the real point by making the tax less burdensome. Political writers
and people through town meetings warned that the British constitution was
near collapse. Some, including the Boston meeting, urged the cultivation of
"martial virtues."[16]

That turbulent spring, members of the House invited Samuel Cooke of
Cambridge to give the election sermon.[17] Hutchinson had lately complained

that the province clergy were "slavishly subservient to the people and fol-low them in their prejudices." Cooke, surely, confirmed the acting governor's fears. His insistence on popular equality and the roots of all power in the peo-ple further undermined core concepts of imperial dominion, raised doubts about the British system, and encouraged a distinct and separate sense of American identity.[18]

Cooke's social compact doctrine was pointed. Men emerged from nature all equal. Rulers derived their "political existence" from the ruled and remained accountable thereto. The people had a right to require virtuous rule, "not as an act of grace, but as their unquestionable due." If governors kept the people's good in view, "the extent of prerogative and liberty, will be indisputable." The just ruler, God's minister for good, remembered that he ruled over men "of the same species with himself, and by nature equal," all made in God's image and of equal importance in God's eyes: a degree of natu-ral equality persisted even in society.[19]

Reason and experience demonstrated that the best form of government was a mixed polity, and the best such polity was surely the British constitu-tion, a system refined through repeated battles against arbitrary power. But here Cooke began to betray some doubts. Was the British constitution in fact as well framed as it could be? The elected Commons were, "while incorrupt . . . a check upon the highest offices in the state." But such a constitution was particularly susceptible to venality in the representatives. Whether Britain's infrequent septennial elections—a constant target of English reformists—tended to such corruption, "time may further show"; whether they were "an infraction of the national constitution, is not for me to determine."

Even the best constitution needed good rulers to have good effect. With a clear jab at Parliament, Cooke observed that the good ruler must have an eye to consequences, ready to repeal anything that mistakenly contravened God's laws or men's rights. Rulers had "mistaken apprehensions of true dignity" if they thought to gain credit "by persisting in wrong measures." Only God was above error. "Arrogant pretences to infalibility [sic] in . . . state or religion, represent human nature in the most contemptible light": thus Cooke likened Parliament's persistent claims of power to popish dogma. The good ruler must welcome public inspection of his conduct and encourage a decent free-dom of speech, a "liberty . . . essential to a free constitution, and the ruler's surest guide," which "the just ruler will consider not as his grant, but a right inherent in the people." It was true that this freedom could degenerate into licentiousness and weaken a just government. But experience showed "that the greatest dangers have arisen from lawless power," not licentious protest. If rulers forgot the ends for which the people had raised them, the people "have the most evident right, in every decent way, to represent to rulers their grievances, and seek redress." A people who forgot their equality with their ruler and the root of his power in their consent "forfeit the rank they hold in God's creation."

Cooke not only questioned the wisdom and good faith of British rule but also cast a skeptical eye on any intrinsic, unbreakable tie to the mother country. Most had long assumed that the first settlers, as subjects of the British Crown, had carried that allegiance with them, remaining—along with their descendants—inherently under British authority. At the very least, most had agreed, the colonists owed obedience in exchange for imperial aid and protection. But Cooke, in a lengthy historical discourse, took such notions to pieces. Their ancestors had been driven from England by religious oppression. Though it was doubtful that the lands they settled "were properly under English jurisdiction," the refugee settlers *voluntarily* maintained a tie with their homeland. In return they were strongly assured that they and their posterity would enjoy all privileges of free-born English subjects, a guarantee enshrined in their charters.

The original 1629 charter had thus created the link with Britain. It was not "an act of grace" but "a compact between the Sovereign and the first patentees." Here then was the province's own social compact, by which an unfettered people had granted power *to* the king. They had likewise submitted to the 1691 charter, trusting the wisdom and paternal regard of the sovereign to ensure "that in all appointments reserved to the Crown, a sacred regard would be maintained to the rights of British subjects;—and that the royal ear would always be open to every reasonable request and complaint."[20] American rights *were* thus British rights, but only by mutual agreement, not intrinsically. Colonists furthermore had "dearly purchased this land with their treasure," defending it "with unknown cost,—in continual jeopardy of their lives—and with their blood." They had struggled, fought, and expanded without help, all the while incalculably enriching Britain with their trade. They owed nothing for services rendered.

Both Shute and Haven had vaguely referred to Parliament's "due" authority over the colonies. For Cooke, that authority receded to a right to regulate imperial trade, to which the colonists "chearfully submit" for "the common interest," so that even this limited power rested on the colonists' consent. The colonies were not tributaries of England, Cooke pressed on, with inferior liberties. They were "sons, arrived to mature age—entitled to distinct property,—yet connected, by mutual ties of affection and interest, and united under the common supreme head," the king. Despite his carefully cool language, Cooke's implications were radical. Sons of "mature age" were entitled to move on, to form their own households, and—while maintaining familial ties—to move beyond parental authority.

Cooke declined to judge whether the province's own charter had been violated, but it was, he left no doubt, at best a close-run thing. He was thankful that efforts had failed to undermine the elected council and leave "this invaluable branch of our constitution, wholly dependent" on the royal governor—a glance at the departed Bernard and his letters. Should the scheme ever succeed, the province's constitution would be fatally unbalanced, and "Liberty here will cease."

Cooke remained respectful and carefully neutral toward the new acting governor. He expressed his gratitude to the king for elevating a local man of such distinction, stressing that such a man would clearly have the interests of his fellow countrymen at heart. But he reminded Hutchinson so pointedly of his obligations to serve the people that praise became implicit warning. Bernard, in his published letters, had notoriously insisted that Hutchinson could be relied on to follow his example. The people, Cooke hinted, would accept Hutchinson with joy, if he defied Bernard's expectations. Yet Cooke made it clear that Hutchinson's administration had not begun well. He pointedly noted that the assembly had again been convened, against "the general desire," in Cambridge. (Even as Cooke spoke, an unofficial election sermon was being delivered in Boston at the arrangement of local politicians, to keep the custom in its proper seat.) In addition he indirectly attacked the much-resented "pensioners and placemen" in the customs service: the just ruler would not "multiply lucrative offices on the community, which naturally tends to introduce idleness and oppression."

Cooke particularly assailed the use of "military aid" to back civil power. Such practices had "ever been deemed dangerous" to free states and "often" had been used to subvert them. When a people were subjected to men "detached from their fellow citizens,—under distinct laws and rules—supported in idleness and luxury—armed with the terrors of death—under the most absolute command—ready and obliged to execute the most daring orders—What must!—what has been the consequence!" Less than three months after the massacre, his words hit all too plainly. A happy people would find "their persons in safety—their liberties preserved—their property defended,—and their confidence in their rulers entire." Clearly, Cooke saw none of those conditions at that point fulfilled. He urged the House and the council to heed "our present distresses" and secure the people's liberties. (Troubled that those fighting for liberty would deny it to others, Cooke also implored the legislature to abolish slavery, or at least the slave trade.) [21]

Yet through it all, Cooke clung to the idea that Britain was merely misled. "From misinformations, only, we would conclude," their distresses had arisen. "They need not be mentioned—they are too well known—their voice is gone out thro' all the earth—and their sound to the end of the world"—blunt reference to Bernard's letters. America only "pleads her right to her possessions." The colonists' constitutional claims were not "novel, or wantonly made, but founded in nature—in compact—in their rights as men—and British subjects"—the same claims that had driven their ancestors to take refuge in the American wilderness. The empire's fate, clearly, was now in Britain's hands. Cooke did make the customary injunction to the people to yield proper subjection to good and lawful government—in one sentence, in the next to last paragraph.

Such ideas had already pressed further than imperial authorities could ever accept. Over the coming months, the gulf only widened. As the battle over the Cambridge removal grew more bitter, House members' challenge to royal prerogative grew more blunt. Increasingly they seemed reluctant to leave any power in royal hands without a popular check. There were rumbles, in the press and in the legislature, about the people's right to rebel, even if such extremities were not necessary—yet. Despite Boston's fierce efforts to sustain it, the intercolonial nonimportation agreement crumbled that fall. But even there, amid government-party jeers that opposition was collapsing, the end of nonimportation marked no ideological retreat: when it failed to obtain rapid results, the embargo simply became too burdensome to maintain. But the boycott on tea—still subject to the Townshend tax—remained in place throughout the colonies.

Hutchinson was formally appointed governor late in 1770. Like Cooke's, most congratulations made it very plain that he must break with Bernard's policies if he wished to hold local esteem. But it was also said that he would finally receive a royal salary. Hutchinson was convinced that this stipend, ending any local control over his pay, would deal the final blow to his enemies. Instead this new grievance gave the opposition even greater urgency. Government men scoffed at popular claims, insisting that the 1688 revolution had empowered only Parliament, not colonists, to balance the king. But liberty papers, with growing urgency, predicted the fall of British freedom to corruption and lust for power, stressing the right of resistance and the imminent danger to imperial union. The March 18 anniversary of Stamp Act repeal, once a highlight on the calendar, was by now totally ignored. Instead the province determinedly commemorated the March 5 massacre. A growing number explicitly rejected any parliamentary power over America, insisting that American legislatures were completely distinct and separate. For some, a lingering sense of shared British heritage was all that now held the empire together. While few if any urged independence, some at least insisted that it held no terrors.

In the spring of 1771 the council selected John Tucker of Newbury to deliver the next election sermon.[22] Tucker took as his text 1 Peter 2:13–16: "Submit yourselves to every ordinance of man for the Lord's sake: whether it be to the King as supreme; or unto the Governors who are sent by him . . . and not using your liberty for a cloak of maliciousness, but as the servants of God." In another place and time this could have grounded a paean to order and submission, even a call to Tory passive obedience. But not there, not then.[23]

Tucker's compact theory was familiar, but he rested more and more on its foundation. All rulers, all powers, every aspect of constitution and government having arisen from the people, "civil government, is called, and with great propriety, the *ordinance of man*,—an human institution." Thus the biblical text's "ordinance of man" became, for Tucker, the government established *by the people*, and submission to every such ordinance became submission to the *people's* fundamental law. He had turned the text's outwardly authoritarian message completely on its head.

Tucker offered just one example of a constitutional violation, one aimed squarely at Britain: "It is essential to a free state . . . that no man shall have his property taken from him, but by his own consent." If rulers violated "this fundamental principle" and "by such usurped authority, they can demand and take a penny," they could take "the whole substance of the subject, so as to make him wholly dependent on their pleasure, having nothing that he can call his own; and what is he then but a perfect slave?" (In the printed sermon, a long footnote quoted Locke on the right to property.) Good rulers must concede errors and redress injuries: like Cooke, Tucker saw no place for pretenses of infallibility in mortals.

A Christian people were, of course, bound to obey good magistrates. But faced with unconstitutional abuses, they must not yield their "just rights" from "courtly complaisance" or "a mean, timorous, and slavish temper": free men must "act as *free*." Even when prudence urged against violent resistance, it should never urge tame submission "to unlawful claims." Tucker quoted "the great and judicious Mr. LOCKE" on tyranny (the exercise of power beyond right) and echoed Locke on the people's "undeniable" right of resistance should petitions fail. On the still-vexed question of who would judge when government was unlawful, the answer was now unhesitating: "the people as well as their Rulers, are proper judges of the civil constitution . . . and of their own rights and privileges." Otherwise how would they know "when submission is due . . . and when not?"

Still, Tucker did not mean "to prove an Incendiary." He put heavy stress on the need to preserve order, swinging between exhortations for the defense of liberty and pleas to obey proper authorities. Though "ardently in love" with liberty, he decried the "querulous and factious" who raised tumults from ambition or love of conflict, magnifying government's small mistakes for their own ends. Such men "cry up liberty, and make a mighty stir to save the sinking state, when in no danger, but from themselves." Yet—whatever Hutchinson, as he listened, might momentarily have hoped—Tucker quickly made clear that he was not describing the present defenders of American rights. They showed no mere "spirit of faction and discontent"—words often repeated in Bernard's published letters—but rather "that spirit of liberty, which is . . . the *animating soul* of a free state." The line between "slavish subjection . . . and lawless license" clearly caused Tucker angst, but he had no doubt that this was "a time of peculiar difficulty" among the colonies, "and with this Province in particular." Competing claims of prerogative, liberties, and privileges "engross our conversation, and agitate our minds with hopes and fears."

Like his predecessors, Tucker lavished traditional praise on the wisdom, balance, and security of the British constitution. But his fervent prayers for its inviolate continuance betrayed an increasingly shaky confidence. Indeed, Tucker clearly had nagging doubts about prerogative. His faith in a royally appointed governor was clearly tattered: such a system, he noted with strikingly faint enthusiasm, "perhaps, all things considered, is not to our disadvantage." He hinted thankfulness that members of the assembly had not yet been deprived of their "important" constitutional right to elect the council: the return of election day should remind them of God's goodness "in still preserving to us our civil constitution,—the basis of our common freedom, and common happiness." He added his "thanks to indulgent heaven, that we are still, thus far, a free people"—hardly phrasing calculated to inspire confidence. Tucker longingly wished "that all distrustful jealousies, with the grounds of them, between Great-Britain and these Colonies were removed," all disputes amicably settled, confidence restored, and perpetual mutually happy connection ensured. Yet the colonies need not yield their freedom to that end. If they surrendered their rights and took "in exchange, the chains of slavery for ourselves and children,—could we forgive ourselves? Would our unhappy posterity forgive us?" Should they not feel "the guilt of assassins, for having stabbed the vitals of our country?"

To Hutchinson, now officially governor, Tucker offered veiled warning. He hoped Providence had favored them with a good ruler "in such an unhappy situation of affairs." The people had reason to expect tender regard from one born and educated among them. They had no wish, of course, for the governor to reject *proper* Crown prerogative: he must be "true and faithful to his Majesty." But he must also "be just to this people . . . ready, we hope, to use your influence" to defend "those rights and privileges to which they are intitled, as British Subjects, and by virtue of the Royal Charter." Of course, the only dangers against which a province governor could thus use "influence" were Britain's imperial policies.

In the coming legislative session, the new House continued to hammer the Cambridge removal and whittle away at the concept of royal prerogative. A chorus of progovernment writers gloated still at the absence of violence, proof, they said, that the province was at peace and the "faction's" power ended. But even as a lack of fresh British measures opened a period of cautious and watchful waiting, the tone of popular outrage only escalated. Just a few representatives from outlying towns still backed the governor and his circle of isolated allies. With the governor paid by the Crown, the legitimacy of his appointment was increasingly questioned. Liberty-party newspapers explained that government could commit treason against the people. America was invoked ever more firmly as savior of age-old liberties fast dying in Britain. Though most strenuously denied any desire for such a step, independence was discussed more openly as a realistic possibility: Britain, it was stressed, needed vigorous and growing America, not the other way around. The press warned harshly against popular apathy, the only true threat, it was said, to American liberty, for a free man could be enslaved only if he submitted.

That spring members of the House invited Moses Parsons of Byfield to deliver the election sermon.[24] Though lighter than his predecessors on constitutional theory, Parsons went further than any of them in his bleak view of the times. A firm Calvinist who had dabbled with New Light revivalism, he unleashed a true Jeremiad, an eruption of bleak despair at political oppression and moral decay. His text was Proverbs 21:1, "The King's heart is in the hand of the Lord, as the rivers of water: he turneth it whithersoever he will": political evils were instruments of God's purpose.[25]

Parsons briefly acknowledged standard compact theory: government was established to protect society from the anarchic evils of the natural state. But tyrannical government, he added, was worse than anarchy. The blessings of good government were, by contrast, beyond measure. "I have been ready," he said, "to look upon the British nation, as this happy people—That we had the best plan of civil government, of any nation or people under heaven.—That the King of kings had smiled upon us in a peculiar manner, in thus distinguishing of us." But Parsons invoked Britain's example only *in the past tense.*

The province charter had been granted by the great William III, but as no mere act of grace: it "contains our rights and privileges—which have been dearly bought by us—honestly paid for—which we have an undoubted claim to, and I hope in God shall never be deprived of them." Their present Majesty, George III, was a prince born and educated among his people, glorying in the name of Briton, uniquely placed to make his people happy. Or *so he had seemed.* "How could we wish," Parsons lamented, "that bright day had continued clear and serene!" Now "the scene is changed—Grievances are complain'd of" throughout the empire. "The day is become gloomy and dark, and the waters are troubled."

Even the best government could alter, just as a bounteous river could change its course and wreak destruction. "A King may be *misled* by evil counselors" or "*corrupted* by bad ministers." Were he persuaded that his subjects enjoyed excessive freedoms, despotism might "look fair—and a King under a limited monarchy may desire to become independent and absolute." Even well-meant policy could be distorted "by subordinate Rulers"—governors— or "bad ministers." Through "Bribery and corruption . . . a nation may be even sold, to satisfy the ambition and avarice of wicked men"—a net that encompassed the customs commissioners, their parasitic minions, and other plotters determined to profit from the people's oppression. Rivers, of course, might shift without injury, and government might change without harm. But the present flow had "become *bitter,—yea* . . . the waters are become *bloody.*"

These woes were known to all, making "a deep impression on our minds." The question, then, was not what they suffered, but *why.* Parsons dismissed any claim that the people had warranted such treatment through their political conduct. As virtuous "as any part of the king's dominions, or as any people upon the face of the earth," they had done nothing to forfeit what he still reflexively called their "Charter privileges." They had always been "loyal and dutiful subjects"; he doubted there was "a native of this Province, who does not bear unfeigned loyalty" to George III and his line. On the contrary, "It would require volumes to recount all that this people have done, to settle and support themselves ... without any charge to Great-Britain," and "to *secure defend* and *enlarge* the British dominions," supported only by God. If any people could deserve their sovereign's smiles, it would be these people.

But if God allowed oppression, the people must bear fault, and Parsons found it in their conduct toward God. It was an argument rooted deep in New England tradition: the people had declined from the piety and morality of their sanctified ancestors, succumbing to infidelity, deism, profanity, Sabbath breaking, intemperance, debauchery, murder, "and all kinds of wickedness." Their sufferings were God's punishment for such degeneracy. The colonists had "reason to complain of men, that they have been our enemies without cause ... that we have been misrepresented ... that our liberties have been invaded." But through it all, it was God's "hand which is lifted up and stretched out against us."

Parsons stressed, at length, the need for moral and religious reform, hoping that an appeased God would yet soften Britain's heart. But, he was careful to add, this did not preclude direct resistance. "'Tis but presumption" to trust in God and passively submit to ruin. They must use the "best *means*, the most vigorous persevering endeavors ... to help ourselves." Among these was the election of proper councilors, "a privilege which through the smiles of heaven we yet enjoy." Always they must preserve their political claim to their rights by paying due respect to *lawful* authority, upholding their side of the charter's contractual agreement. Nor did the hand of Providence excuse "the practice of wicked men." God "may suffer, or permit such things to be done, which are sinful and wicked, and yet be holy and righteous." The same did not apply to men, who would meet their "deserved punishment," even if they acted as God's tools. Only by winning back the smiles of God—who alone would bless or doom their efforts against the evil deeds of men—would they find salvation, temporal and spiritual. Parson's message, for all its Calvinist calls to repentance, was politically shocking: Britain's conduct was by now so resented, it could be invoked as a divine judgment.

In the assembly that followed this grim polemic, the House kept up a steady barrage against binding royal instructions to the governor, royally granted salaries, and the Cambridge removal. Hutchinson, exhausted, returned the legislature to Boston. London's hated and officious minister for the colonies, Lord Hillsborough, gave way to the more sympathetic Lord Dartmouth, but imperial policy hardly changed. Before word of Dartmouth's appointment even came, long-dreaded news arrived that province judges, already removable only by royal consent, would now receive Crown salaries. The judiciary was thereby made entirely independent of the people and wholly beholden to an uncontrollable external power. Watching and waiting no longer seemed an option. The liberty press stressed the growing skill of the militia; some hinted openly at a war for their freedom. Britain was increasingly referred to as an unfriendly foreign country.

In November 1772, with the press stridently warning that the people must act or be slaves forever, Boston's town meeting adopted a bold statement of rights as men, as Englishmen, and as Christians—in that order; a committee of correspondence would coordinate with the other province towns. Government men, ever certain that all opposition sprang only from a small set of Boston villains, jeered at the effort, waiting eagerly for the humiliating silence that would break the faction's hold. Instead townspeople flocked to respond, confirming Boston's radical sentiments with stunning unanimity and shattering at a blow any claims of a "lull" or retreat since 1770. In an ill-judged effort to stem the tide, Hutchinson delivered a lengthy lecture to the assembly, seeking to explain the true nature of the constitution. There was, he insisted, no middle ground between full subordination to Parliament and catastrophic independence. After recovering from blank astonishment, both houses dismantled his arguments in lengthy replies. If, members of the House of Representatives declared, there truly was no choice between full subordination and independence, then they were de facto independent. By the May 1773 House elections, even the province's conservative far west was turning. There were by now perhaps five reliable government votes among well over one hundred representatives.

In the midst of the heated exchange with Hutchinson, the council—now nearly as hostile to the governor as the House—chose Charles Turner of Duxbury, well known as a strong liberty man, for the 1773 election sermon, the first to be preached in Boston since 1769.[26] By Turner's own later account, his selection gave the governor and his supporters considerable unease, and their concern proved wholly justified.[27]

Turner's sermon was surely one of the most radical political statements yet heard in America. He preached from Romans 13:4: "He is the minister of

God to thee for good." The magistrate was thus required to do good for the people, and it was the right of the people to ensure that he did.[28]

Turner endorsed the conventional view that rulers were established through divine Providence. However, the people must nonetheless "have a voice in the elevation of those who are, in a civil sense, to rule them"; anything less was opposed "equally, to the will of God, and to the rights of mankind." Turner not only rejected the deferential faith in the ruling elite so evident just a few years before but also now evinced an almost contemptuous suspicion. Rulers were all too prone to be driven by "worldly interests, inconsistent with the publick welfare and the duty they owe to the community." It was thus the people's right and duty "to fix on certain regulations," in short "a *constitution*," determining both the powers "they will invest their rulers with" and the rights they would retain "in their own hands." The magistrate, in turn, should be "awed by that Sovereignty which God has been pleased to invest the people with," scrupulously obeying the constitution they had established: only "the public consent" could alter that fundamental law.

This was compact theory, but with a new thrust. There was little sense left of *mutual* compact between ruler and ruled: the people were the arbiters, and rulers their mere creation. As Turner's argument developed, it struck not merely at the imperial establishment but at monarchy itself. While "the People may, by a constitution, make an office hereditary in a Family," they retained "an unalienable right to alter [the] constitution at pleasure, and to interpose *immediately* in the election of their officers, whenever they judge it proper." The earlier election preachers had posited such a right only if the ruler failed in his trust and broke the compact. Now the people could oust rulers at will and elect replacements. "Rulers are at once, *ministers of God*, and *servants of society*. . . . And if God has given to the community a right to appoint its servants," they had a right to ensure those servants' behavior, dismissing them if necessary. "That servants of the publick, should not be responsible to the publick, is popery, either in religion, or politicks."

Turner acknowledged that "the misguiding arts of designing men, mistakes and freakish passions" could sometimes lead popular governments into disruptive measures, and that absolute monarchy might prevent such disturbances. But "the people are not under such temptations to thwart their own interests, as absolute government is under to abuse the people." Government thus succeeded best "where the people have, by the barrier of a constitution, retained power in a great degree in their own hands." The traditional notion of a mixed constitution balancing monarchical, aristocratic, and democratic elements was barely in evidence. Turner was edging close to outright republicanism.

Turner continued nonetheless to praise the British constitution, or rather its ideal form, which he saw as wholly consistent with his own ideas. But no constitution, however wisely framed, was immune to misinterpretation and wicked designs. Startlingly, Turner announced that the constitution had been subverted in Massachusetts as far back as 1684, when Charles II abrogated the 1629 charter. The "inestimable" rights and privileges of "the English constitution . . . were once enjoyed by this province" under that charter, "a charter that was inhumanly murdered, and over whose grave many of the people are now disposed to raise a fresh lamentation." Under that charter, as Turner's audience well knew—very much including governor and preeminent local historian Thomas Hutchinson—the governor had been elected.

Having constituted civil powers, the people were naturally bound to obey them. They too must keep the public good at heart and "yield all loyal subjection to well regulated government, in opposition to every thing of a factious nature and complexion." In addition good rulers, though not to be exalted excessively, should receive "a certain distinguishing respect and support." However, the people were always free to defend themselves "when constitutional boundaries are broken over, and so their rights are invaded." There was no longer any hesitancy in asserting popular oversight of prerogative: "*the People have a right to judge* of the conduct of government and its tendency; and this again supposes them capable of judging in things of such a nature"— an angry shaft at the government party's frequent and open derision of the people's capacities (one notorious such writer had smirked at "the peasants and their housewives" for presuming to hold political opinions).[29]

Turner would "not pretend to determine" whether those behind the present crisis had *knowingly* violated the constitution. But even if they believed their actions to be correct, might they not be respectfully reminded "of their liableness to be mistaken?" After all, he noted, continuing to deflate any pretense of special wisdom in those of rank and fortune, eminent men were as liable as others to "have the judgment unduly influenced by the affections." Well-treated communities were generally "contented." America, dramatically otherwise, should therefore give Britain pause, especially since Americans "have been trained up, from their cradles" to revere the royal family. They deeply respected what "they think to be constitutional government" and had at least as much knowledge as the enlightened parts of Europe, despite frequent sneers at supposed American backwardness.

Affairs had reached a critical point. If all appeals and petitions were ignored, "what may the consequences be!" "It is hard to say," Turner intoned, "whether this country ever has seen, or ever will see, a more important time than the present, when it *seems* as if the question, whether the people and all they enjoy shall be at the *absolute* disposal of a distant Legislature, is soon to be determined." He scoffed at the notion that the colonies, being only part of a larger whole, were inherently subject to Parliament or lacked the rights of separate societies. A hypothetical example could surely settle the matter: would the people of Great Britain, themselves only part of the larger whole, be content "if the Parliaments of the Colonies should lay taxes on *them*, and claim a right to make laws binding them in all cases whatsoever"? Any lingering sops to "due" parliamentary authority had vanished: Americans were bound by no law and no legislature save those to which they consented.

Turner reserved particular scorn for officials who betrayed their trusts through greed—the case, he strongly implied, with many present enemies. For civil or religious ministers to live in luxury "on the spoils violently extorted, or slily drained from the people, is altogether foreign to the design of God, in setting them up." It was equally contemptible that any should be "disengaged from *such* a cause as that of their countries [*sic*] freedom, by small private piques and prejudicing contentions" or "by little hopes and fears about worldly promotions and interests."

His eye fixed on such weakness and corruption, Turner—in a less strident echo of Parsons the previous year—warned that God allowed calamities for a reason, urging the clergy to lead the people in moral repentance and reformation. What was truly astonishing was the *source* he identified for his countrymen's venality and vice. Parsons, like generations of New England preachers before him, had pointed to the people's own moral decline from their forebears' piety. In Turner's eyes, the people's sins were "in a great measure borrowed (with unaccountably fond embraces) of the very people from whom our sufferings proceed"—from Britons.

Whatever respect he still had for an unspoiled British constitutional ideal, Turner had little for the British nation. Concerned that corruption had influenced the just-concluded election of Massachusetts representatives, he decried "the known prevalence of bribery and venality in the land from which our ancestors fled," sternly warning of "the facility wherewith we drink in the vices of that which we have been used to call by the endearing name of the *Parent State*." Despite the province's distance, he thought it "sorrowfully infected with the irreligion and vices, which are predominant in England."

He warned of Britain's dangerously soft treatment of Catholics in Canada and pointed out the efforts several years earlier to establish an Anglican episcopacy in America—a plot, in the eyes of non-Anglican Protestants, to impose a religious tyranny.

Turner—echoing Boston's instructions to its representatives in the aftermath of the massacre—even warned that enemies might be *deliberately* introducing England's sins to America knowing that a people weakened by luxury would be more easily subjugated.[30] Sin, in fact, reigned in Britain "to such a degree, that we can scarcely forebear applying, such language as that in the Revelation, *Come out of her, my people, that ye be not partakers of her sins, and that ye receive not of her plagues; for her sins have reached unto heaven, and God hath remembered her iniquities.*"[31] Britain, once called "by the endearing name of the *Parent State*" and now reduced to "the land from which our ancestors fled," had become Babylon.

In spite of these extraordinary arguments and this savagely bitter estrangement, Turner balked at actually renouncing British ties: residual loyalties were deeply ingrained. He still saw his political principles as the true, uncorrupted ideals of the 1688 revolution, unquestionable to any "who pretend the least regard to the continuation of our present Royal Family in the government." The promotion of any contrary idea "is a virtual, secret, and treasonable undermining of the present Chief Magistrate, in the British Dominions," among which Turner still placed the American colonies. Even as he argued that the people could, at pleasure, remove a royal family from power, he urged them not to forget the divine commandment to honor the king. Nor, in their travails, should they slip "into an [sic] habit of despising *all* government . . . because of the wrong steps of particular rulers," any more than corrupt clergymen should spur the people to reject religion. Yet, returning the final focus to abuses of power, he closed with a plea to God that government fulfill its end, "the general happiness," that "*judgment* (and not innocent blood) *may run down as waters, and righteousness as a mighty stream.*"

Hutchinson, inevitably, was enraged by Turner's radical declarations. According to Turner's later recollections, the governor sat flushed with anger and once came close to walking out. Afterward, as Turner remembered it, Hutchinson committed an extraordinary breach of traditional etiquette by neglecting to invite the preacher to the election dinner that followed the sermon; later, Turner said, Hutchinson changed his mind, but Turner could not be found, having already sat down to dine with a group of liberty-party supporters.[32]

Among liberty men the sermon was greatly admired. Thomas Cushing, the Speaker of the House, sent a copy to Benjamin Franklin, House agent in London; and Samuel Adams sent a copy to Arthur Lee, his regular correspondent and Franklin's deputy-agent.[33] John Adams hoped that the sermon, amid other fresh developments, reflected a resurging defiance of tyranny.[34] The recently established and staunchly liberty-party *Massachusetts Spy*, soon echoed verbatim by the venerable *Boston Gazette*, enthused that Turner preached "perhaps in as clear and close a manner, holding up the duties both of rulers and subjects, as was ever heard in this country." The proadministration *Boston News-Letter*, by contrast, omitted the usual formulaic description that the sermon was "suitable to the occasion."[35]

That this sermon could be so readily and unreservedly hailed starkly highlights the extent of alienation from Britain, and the degree to which radical interpretations of constitutional liberty had taken hold. Had Turner delivered the same sermon even in 1769, he would have been widely denounced. In 1766 he might well have been indicted for seditious libel.

The summer of 1773 offered a last glimmer of hope that Britain might be vindicated: the publication of several of Hutchinson's old letters—including a soon-notorious declaration that "there must be an abridgment of what are called English liberties"—seemed again to suggest a local plot to force Britain into dangerous measures. (It was apparently these letters that pushed Ebenezer Bridge, preacher of the cautious 1767 election sermon, into the liberty movement.)[36] But while the letters destroyed any remaining effectiveness Hutchinson had as governor, Britain's course did not change. London rejected a petition for his removal, branding it undutiful and improper. The most Lord Dartmouth would offer was a promise that if the colonies acknowledged Parliament's authority, it would be exercised as little as possible—or, as Samuel Adams bitterly rejoined, if "this Country" would "be thus submissive beyond the bounds of reason & Safety their Lordships will condescend to be familiar with us and treat us with Cakes & Sugar plumbs." The image of Americans as Britain's children had grown stale indeed.[37]

In October word came of Parliament's new Tea Act. Lowering tea's price and authorizing agents to monopolize its sale, the act seemed a mere trick to secure payment of the unrepealed Townshend tea duty, thereby dealing the final blow to American liberty. Boston's carefully orchestrated destruction of three tea ships' cargoes led, in 1774, to the harsh punitive measures that Governor Bernard had so long urged. But the province, rather than returning to meek obedience, joined with its consciously *American* fellow colonies against corrupted British authority—resistance that would quickly spiral into war and revolution.

The Anglo-American link was in collapse politically and emotionally. By 1770 America's evolving constitutional ideas were already all but incompatible with empire. By 1773 monarchy itself was in doubt. America's tie to Britain had become conditional on concessions Britain would never consider, concessions that would have meant in essence a separate American union sharing only its king with Great Britain. Americans still avowed their loyalty to Britain, but in truth, years of crisis had moved Britons and Americans down irrevocably divergent paths, creating a gulf neither was fully prepared to admit. A growing sense of joint American identity drew the colonies together in their increasingly urgent common cause.

Even after the Revolution, America would remain deeply Anglicized in language, law, institutions, material culture, and outlook. But political union with Britain had become impracticable by the early 1770s. Americans continued to insist that they were defending and saving true British freedoms in the face of Britain's own decline. However, as those traditional freedoms evolved in new and bolder directions, challenging key elements of British political practice, they were seen ever more as specifically *American* liberties, part of a distinctively American community. Anglicized though American culture was and would remain, being "British American" was by now a residual and habitual notion, even a wistful memory, more than an active and meaningful self-definition.

PART IV

REPUBLIC

CHAPTER EIGHT

Racial Walls: Race and the Emergence of American White Nationalism

David J. Silverman

White Americans' shared racism was basic to their decision to break away from Britain and unite as a new republican nation. Threats posed by George III to the American racial hierarchy in the critical year between the Battle of Lexington and Concord and the Declaration of Independence helped to convince reluctant patriots that independence was necessary for the preservation of their society. Thereafter white people's confidence that neighboring colonies would remain dedicated to pursuing their interests at the expense of Indians and blacks undergirded their support for the military campaign against Britain and then the effort to create a national framework to unite the states. Even as the northern states began phasing out slavery in the 1780s and 1790s, and even as regional divisions between North and South appeared at the Constitutional Convention, hardly anyone doubted that white superiority, black degradation, and Indian dispossession would remain basic features of life throughout the United States. That faith enabled the national experiment to proceed.

This argument amends more than challenges the premises of John Murrin's Anglicization thesis. Anglicization submits that the mainland British colonies revolted against the mother country not because they conceived of themselves as a separate American nation, but rather because they were determined to participate in the empire as coequals. By contrast, Parliament and eventually the king suddenly seemed intent on subordinating them after the Seven Years' War. In the decades preceding this break, American colonists had become more integrated into the empire politically, legally, economically, socially, and culturally, a trend in which they took enormous pride. They saw the British Empire as a guarantor of their liberties, not as a threat. Yet Parliament's attempts during the 1760s and 1770s to force colonists to pay taxes without the consent of their provincial legislatures turned what had been a remarkably successful trend of imperial integration into a rebellion.[1] One of the rebels' dilemmas, Murrin contends, was that they had little in common on which to base a new nation aside from their shared participation in the British Empire. The individual states, particularly those from different regions, were so unalike in terms of their economies, ethnic and religious makeup, and values, and white Americans were so conscious of these differences, that they struggled to conceive of themselves as a people. Ultimately a shared commitment to the Constitution substituted for this lack of national identity. Thus, Murrin likens the Constitution to a national roof without social or cultural walls to uphold it.[2]

Taking a page from Murrin and posing a counterfactual question to this thesis suggests how American racism constituted the walls, however fragile, for the early Republic. Imagine that citizens of revolutionary Massachusetts or Pennsylvania had decided not only to rid their states of slavery but also to raise free people of color to full social, political, and economic equality and oppose expansion of the national domain into Indian country. It is inconceivable that the other states would have continued to favor a union with such radical partners or that the Constitutional Convention would have ever taken place. The reason for this implausibility is that whites throughout the states, whatever their feelings about slavery or position on evangelizing Indians, generally agreed on the principle of white superiority. It would take until the 1850s for these racial walls to buckle under the constitutional roof with the added weight of the question of slavery's expansion.

Anglicization and the Americanizing trend of racialization took place contemporaneously during the colonial era and synthesized in the revolutionary movement. Murrin is convincing that Anglicization is the most powerful explanation for why the revolutionary crisis occurred and why white Americans struggled to unite in the war against Britain and the nation-building experiments that followed independence. Yet if "Anglicization," as Murrin argues, "is the story of the eighteenth century," so is racialization.[3] White racial ideology, and the social hierarchy from which it sprang and which it reinforced, became fundamental to all British colonies during those same years and one of the primary legacies of the colonial era. Indeed white racism became hegemonic in the colonies, so basic that it went almost unquestioned until the egalitarian principles and social upheaval of the Revolution ignited the debate, albeit temporarily. The thirteen colonies, for all their divisions, were able to rally together against Britain not only because they agreed that the mother country threatened their English rights or because they shared a single British consumer world; equally critical was that they shared an identity as white people and a vision of where they stood relative to blacks and Indians. That same consensus emboldened them to forge a republic once they were free of the British Empire. British colonists rebelled against the mother country largely because of what they shared as Britons. They united as Americans partially because of their shared racism.

If this argument complicates certain aspects of the Anglicization thesis, so too it challenges Murrin's critics in what might be called the Americanization school. Americanization scholars contend that the British colonies were becoming more distinctly American in the run-up to the Revolution in terms of antideference, religious and ethnic pluralism, a commitment to free markets, and even vernacular forms of architecture.[4] Independence was the capstone of this process. Yet the Americanization school fails to convince on a basic point: that revolutionary Americans themselves thought of these supposed characteristics as bases of national identity. Americanization scholars have neglected their best example in white racism. Though white racism was so ingrained in Anglo-American society that few contemporary whites probed its logic in writing, nevertheless they codified its principles over and over again, including in some of the nation's foundational documents. Their message was that the United States was to be a nation of, by, and for white people.

The Racial Spectrum

Racial ideas and social structures reveal the limits of Murrin's otherwise convincing thesis that ties to the mother country tended to unite the British colonies whereas their various American characteristics tended to divide them. By the early to mid-eighteenth century—at the latest—every mainland British colony was premised on dispossessing nearby Indians of their land through means fair and foul. This was the case regardless of the Indians' treaty status, regardless of the Indians' Christianity and civilized reforms, regardless even of the Indians' subjection to the king. For that same reason,

by the mid-eighteenth century every colony except Pennsylvania had a history of brutal wars with Native Americans, practically all colonists in what
the British called the backcountry lived in dread of Indian attack, and eastern
newspaper readers consumed a constant flow of stories dramatizing Native
atrocities in the west and northern New England. Likewise every colony held
blacks and a smaller number of Indians as slaves. Every colony had laws and
customs that conferred white privilege and enforced black and Indian subordination. Colonists everywhere referred to themselves as white, to Africans
as blacks or Negroes, and to indigenous people as Indians and savages. To be
sure, these characteristics varied in degree along the Atlantic seaboard, often
significantly, but they were basic in kind for all colonies in British North
America.

Defining the limits of colonial Christianity was one of the key constituents of whiteness and Indianness. Virginia and Massachusetts cited bringing Native Americans to Christianity and civility among their founding
purposes. In Virginia the best-known example of this principle in practice
is the John Rolfe–Pocahontas marriage and the lineage it spawned, but this
was just one of a handful of contemporary English-Indian couplings premised on the female Indian partner's adoption of Christianity.[5] Massachusetts expressed its utopianism in missionary work that reached thousands
of Native Americans from the 1640s to the 1670s, prompting a 1652 statute
that encouraged towns to allot land to Indians "brought to civilitie" so they
could live "amongst the English."[6] Yet in both colonies the people in general,
if not the religious and political elites, largely abandoned this commitment,
to whatever extent they had it earlier, amid the horrors of their respective
Indian wars.[7] Virginia never seriously pursued Indian evangelization after
the Powhatan Wars of the 1620s and 1640s.[8] Instead it relegated Indians to
reservations that in most cases soon fell to colonial encroachment.[9] During
King Philip's War in New England colonial vigilante bands treated Christian
Indians as wolves in sheep's clothing, interning some on the Boston harbor
islands and attacking others indiscriminately.[10] Evangelical work continued after the war, but with grudging popular support and sometimes over
opposition. Tellingly, New England colonists continued to refer to Christian
Native Americans as "praying Indians" even after the Natives had been practicing Christians for decades, as if a praying Indian were a hyphenated or
qualified Christian, akin to a trespasser. To be simply Christian was to be
European; a praying Indian was, by inference, someone in between savagery
and civility. Colonists thought of Christianity as passing naturally through

their own bloodlines, whereas heathenism was the Indians' inheritance. This belief, combined with the growing landlessness, poverty, and debt-peonage of southern New England Indians, encouraged the English to view even Christian Indians as a permanent, degraded caste. As Massachusetts governor Thomas Hutchinson acknowledged in 1764, "we are too apt to consider the Indians as a race being by nature inferior to us, and born to servitude."[11] The older notion that Christianity would unite English and Native societies was generally abandoned except among the most committed missionaries.[12]

Warring against Indians greatly influenced this shift and practically every facet of British colonial development. At its most basic, the colonies' victories over Native Americans enabled colonists to seize their lands, but these wars were also consequential in terms of race. For one, in warfare colonists singled out Indians for brutal treatment to which they never would have subjected fellow Europeans. It is still questionable whether the colonies' pattern of waging total war against Indian civilians and the Indian food supply was more inhumane than warfare in Europe.[13] Likewise it is debatable whether Virginia's and New England's enslavement of Native American prisoners of war was racially motivated, given that the English subjected Scots and Irish prisoners of war to indentured servitude and perhaps even lifetime slavery in the Caribbean during this same period.[14] However, slave raids by South Carolina and its Indian allies against the Florida missions in the late seventeenth and early eighteenth centuries, which netted between fifteen and thirty thousand people, made a clear distinction between Indians and Europeans as targets for enslavement. Europeans had a long-standing argument that only heathens captured in just wars should be subject to slavery.[15] Note also that a number of South Carolina's raids against the Florida missions were premised on the excuse that England and Spain were at war. Yet the raiders enslaved only Indians, not Spaniards. In many cases these Native Americans hailed from communities that had been practicing Christianity for as long as a century. As in New England, Christianity did not spare Indians from inhumane treatment at the hands of South Carolinians. Strikingly, there is no surviving evidence that South Carolinians thought of enslaving Catholic Indians as a challenge to the principle against enslaving fellow Christians, or that purchasers of these slaves elsewhere in the British Atlantic raised such an issue. Indianness had come to trump religion in determining a people's vulnerability to exploitation.[16]

As newspaper publishing expanded during the eighteenth century, so did stories about Indian raids that encouraged colonists far from the scene of action to identify with the Natives' European victims and to think of the Indians as a single group of savages.[17] Consider a twelve-month run of the *Boston News-Letter* between November 1711 and November 1712. An issue from November 26, 1711, contained two stories about the exploits of the "Savage Enemy" in North Carolina's Tuscarora War, including an attack on "127 of the Palatines" and another incident in which "the Cape Fear Indians had cut off about 20 Families of the Inhabitants, Men, women, & Children, and Scalpt them."[18] Then, with the spring thaw, grisly tales of war flowed in from another quarter, Maine. Nearly every issue that season contained graphic reports of skulking Indians falling upon unsuspecting farm and fishing families, whom they would leave "inhumanely stript, scalpt, and battered" amid butchered cattle and scorched homesteads. By fall this news included a panicked rumor that unidentified Indians "design to surprise Albany, and Murder all the English."[19] Such accounts made it possible for a reader safe in Boston to imagine bloodthirsty savages massacring fellow colonists—be they English, German, or Dutch—in all corners of the provinces.

Reports of Indian savagery became more graphic, hate filled, and melodramatic with every subsequent war, and more widely circulated. The flow of colonial blood, and racial bile, was especially strong during the Seven Years' War and Pontiac's War of the 1750s and 1760s, as Indian attacks took place up and down Appalachia and throughout Pennsylvania.[20] One Boston newspaper reported Shawnee Indians killing a Virginia family and then instructed its readers, "Think you to see the infant torn for the unavailing Struggles of the distracted Mother, the Daughters ravished before the eyes of their wretched Parents; and then, with Cruelty and Insult, butchered and scalped. Suppose the horrid Scene completed, and the whole Family, Man Wife, and Children, murdered and scalped by these relentless Savages, and then torn in Pieces, and in Part devoured by wild Beasts, for whom they were left a Prey by their more brutal enemies." Lest anyone miss the point, the piece closed by castigating Indians as "bloody villains" and "Vermin."[21] Similar racially loaded accounts of frontier warfare could be found in newspapers throughout the thirteen mainland colonies and, as such, in their common rooms and taverns.

Whiteness emerged as a salient colonial identity in counterpoint with colonial constructions of Indianness. Though the colonies' separate interests sometimes prevented them from springing to one another's defense in Indian wars, none of them could conceive of allying with the Indians against their countrymen. Within colonies, officials who obstructed indiscriminate attacks on Native Americans often found themselves the target of the mob, as in King Philip's War and Bacon's Rebellion. Virginia governor Alexander Spotswood captured the principle in 1720 when he wrote that a colonial governor had "to steer between Scylla and Charybdis, either an Indian or a civil war."[22] Pennsylvania proved him right again during the 1760s. Frustrated by the unwillingness of Philadelphia Quaker legislators to defend exposed western communities around Lancaster, Scots-Irish Presbyterians and German Lutherans rallied together as the Paxton Boys under a banner of white unity against savage Indians and treacherous Quakers. Their massacre of Conestoga Indians, who had long lived at peace with the colony, followed by a march on Philadelphia to lynch pacifist Moravian Indians who had taken refuge there were designed both to rid the colony of Indians and to humiliate Quaker authorities. Benjamin Franklin just barely managed to convince the Paxton Boys to halt in Germantown before they could complete their plans, but the mob action worked. The following year Pennsylvania placed a bounty on Indian scalps and Quakers began abandoning office rather than compromise their peace testimony. By the end of the Revolutionary War, white Pennsylvanians had effectively cleared Indians from their borders. In this, William Penn's colony was a latecomer, not a forerunner, of white identity emerging in the context of Indian hating and Indian wars.[23]

Colonists' enslavement of Africans also contributed to a shared white identity. During the late seventeenth and early eighteenth centuries, slavery—as a labor system, a legal regime, and a cultural system—solidified throughout the thirteen mainland colonies except for Georgia, which was soon to follow. Christopher Tomlin has offered a useful framework for thinking about this trend. He asserts that Ira Berlin's popular distinction between "slave societies" (that is, societies in which slavery rested at the core of the economy, social status, and law) and "societies with slaves" (which had slaves but were less dependent on them) should be amended to include "societies with slavery." His multifaceted definition of "societies with slavery" is worth quoting at length. By this term he means the following:

The colony no longer simply acknowledges that slaves have been brought within its precincts and deals with their presence with such resources as it has to hand, it consciously creates a distinct and highly consequential legal condition of being that has no prior existence within its institutional structure, qualitatively distinct from and absolutely subordinate to all other social and legal conditions of existence.

It endows that condition with dedicated institutions, practices, and cruelties, considered necessary to ensure its indefinite perpetuation: specialized jurisdictions, elaborated restraints, calibrated corporeal punishments and mutilations, deliberate sanctioned killings. All are peculiar to that one condition of existence, to which no one not of that order of being is subject. And it defines by preemptive ascriptive characterization the identity of the population that shall thenceforth be confined within that condition. In other words, the colony creates a regime.[24]

This appellation, "societies with slavery," fits not only the staple-crop southern colonies of South Carolina, Virginia, and Maryland but also the northern colonies of Pennsylvania, New Jersey, New York, and even Rhode Island, Connecticut, and Massachusetts.

Thinking in terms of "societies with slavery" reveals important similarities between the thirteen colonies' racial regimes instead of focusing too exclusively on the varying importance of slavery to regional economies. Even the New England and Mid-Atlantic colonies passed special statutes to protect slaveholders' property in slaves. They too restricted the condition of slavery to Africans and Indians, and increasingly to just Africans and their descendants, as traced through the female line. The northern colonies also passed restrictions against whites manumitting slaves, selling slaves liquor and arms, mustering slaves in the militia, and against slaves traveling the roads and gathering in groups. Like their southern counterparts, northern whites associated delicacy with white women alone, claiming that it was their naturally feminine characteristic, even as they prescribed raw sexuality and drudgery to black women, as if these qualities were natural to them.[25] In addition northerners defined white maleness in terms of mastery, including property holding, the exercise of political and economic judgment, and status as head of household and protector of wife and child dependents, while obstructing black men's access to those things.[26] All the British colonies deputized white colonists to police blacks. Whites throughout the colonies were expected to ask blacks on the road for their travel passes and respond to the runaway ads that increasingly filled the newspapers.[27] Without such support from nonslaveholders—the vast majority of the white population—the slave regime would have collapsed. Additionally, by the eighteenth century practically the only public episodes of human burning, mutilation, breaking on the wheel, and gibbeting involved judicial punishment of blacks. The black bodies or their severed parts that one could find on grisly display at the entrance to the harbors of New York or Charles Town, or at crossroads in Massachusetts or Virginia, testified to the legal terror that upheld slavery and to the white privilege and black degradation that characterized all British American colonies.[28]

Everywhere in British America, Christianity partnered with the law to reinforce the racial regime of slavery. In the mid-seventeenth century, Virginia's House of Burgesses acknowledged that "doubts have arisen" about whether baptizing a slave entitled him or her to freedom. It then passed legislation stating unequivocally that baptism conveyed no such worldly liberty.[29] Colonists in Virginia and elsewhere remained skeptical that it was right for them to hold other Christians (even black ones) in bondage, despite laws entitling them to do so, but a generation later no such doubts remained. Small numbers of blacks and Indians could be found in predominantly white churches throughout the northern colonies, in rural as well as urban settings, in Old Light as well as evangelical congregations. In all of these churches, colonists forced people of color to sit in the back benches, gallery, or stairwell, to symbolize their subordination. Whatever satisfaction blacks and Indians derived from this worship, the message whites wanted them to hear was that it was their Christian duty to abide by their earthly masters and wait patiently for relief in the afterlife.[30] Certainly some churches encouraged white masters to solemnize slave marriages and moderate their discipline, but no denomination aside from the Quakers expressed antislavery sentiments, never mind calls for racial equality.

Colonists, despite their heterogeneous origins, explicitly self-identified as "whites" against the black and Indian populations. The term "white" seems to have appeared first in Barbados during the mid- to late seventeenth century, right after the colony had transitioned from a labor force of European indentured servants to a slave regime.[31] The mainland colonies gradually followed suit.[32] By 1690 South Carolina's Act for the Better Ordering of Slaves distinguished between "Negro slaves" and "white persons."[33] A year later Virginia passed an act to prevent "that abominable mixture and spurious issue which hereafter may encrease in this dominion, as well by negroes, mulattoes, and Indians intermarrying with English, or other white women."[34] Massachusetts passed a similar measure using the same language in 1705.[35] Three years later Connecticut issued special penalties against any servant of color who "shall Offer to strike any White person," believing that "Indian, Negroe, and Molatto Sevants and Slaves are very apt to be Turbulent."[36] Judging from the language of the law, by the early eighteenth century the term "white," encompassing

Europeans of all types, had spread throughout the British colonies as part of the legal and social processes that granted those people privileges at the expense of darker-hued others.

These colonial racial patterns were barely evident in Britain proper. Obviously, Britons did not have a local American Indian population to use as a negative point of reference, though newspapers there sometimes ran accounts of Indian wars in America. The English notion that Irish Catholics and Highland Scots were violent savages in need of outside education in Christianity and civility, for all its similarities to Anglo-American constructions of Indian savagery, did not carry the same racial overtones, particularly in terms of promoting either a white identity among the English or the idea that these populations were beyond redemption.[37] On those rare occasions when Indians did show up in London, usually as part of political delegations, the English public tended to view them as exotic curiosities from the periphery of the empire rather than as bloodthirsty savages.[38] There was a noticeable population of black slaves and sailors in the ports of London, Liverpool, and Glasgow, but not enough to prompt a systematic legal and cultural response by the white majority. By the eve of the 1772 decision in the case of *Somerset v. Stewart*, which ruled that there was no legal basis for slavery in Britain proper, the nation had between three thousand and fifteen thousand black slaves (compared to nearly five hundred thousand in the Caribbean colonies, and another nearly five hundred thousand in the thirteen mainland colonies).[39] Certainly, *images* of exotic Africans and grateful black servants were widespread in portraiture, tavern signs, packaging labels, and map illustrations, but these works appear to have served less to reinforce white racial identity than to symbolize Britons' sense of themselves as opulent beneficiaries of a benevolent global empire.[40] Tellingly, Britons rarely referred to themselves as white until after the 1800s, well after most American colonists had adopted the term.[41] Racial identity in the colonies was of a different order than in Britain as part of the experience of warring against Indians, enslaving Africans, and qualifying Christian universalism with white superiority.

Racial Panic

We tend to think of colonial antipopery as an Anglicizing characteristic binding the colonies and Britain together as fellow Protestants in an age of Atlantic warfare against the Catholic empires of France and Spain. Yet in the colonies militant Protestantism and antipopery became fused with whites' fears of blacks and Indians. This development is best witnessed in the pan-colonial panics associated with the Glorious Revolution of 1688–89 and the War of Jenkins' Ear (segueing into King George's War) in the late 1730s and 1740s. British patriotism, religious tribalism, and race became mutually rein-forcing for American colonists during these transatlantic events, with lasting consequences for the colonial racial order.

Amid the tumult of the Glorious Revolution, colonists throughout New England, New York, and Maryland were convinced that broad coalitions of Indians and Catholics were conspiring to put English Protestants to the knife.[42] In New England the charge centered on Edmund Andros, who had been appointed governor of the Dominion of New England by the Catho-lic James II and granted autocratic powers. Earlier in his career Andros, as governor of New York, had raised colonial suspicion by brokering an alli-ance with the Mohawks at the same time that they had begun to host Jesuit missionaries as part of a peace with New France. By 1688 New England-ers feared that Andros was plotting with Catholic Wabenakis and perhaps New France and the Mohawks to butcher New Englanders if they dared to resist James II's supposed Romish designs. Unwilling to watch this horror unfold, militiamen streamed into Boston, unseated Andros, and sent him back to England with the explanation that he had been part of a "horrid Popish plot . . . to crush and break a country so entirely and signally made up of Reformed churches."[43] To believers in this conspiracy, the Glorious Revolution exposed the human and cosmic forces aligned against the puri-tan Israel in America. In human terms, New England seemed under attack from papists, ranging from James II to black-robed Jesuits in Indian country to the Catholic Indian allies of New France. In cosmic terms, New England Puritans believed that they were under siege by the devil. These anxieties, when combined with the local tensions of a place called Salem, would pour forth in a stunning series of witch trials and executions in which New Eng-land saints saw the devil in the guise of churchgoing matrons. These events were sparked in part by the visions of orphans living as servants in Salem homes after they had lost their parents and homes in Maine at the hands of Catholic Indians painted black for war. During the trials these same girls would say that the devil had appeared to them as a black Indian. In the colo-nies English antipopery and the associated dread of France had become of a piece with the dread of Indians. Religious and racial fears were a potent combination.[44]

Similar terror associating Indians and Catholics unraveled New York and Maryland. Militia captain Jacob Leisler, an arch-Calvinist of German and Huguenot background, was struggling to consolidate his authority over New York after the collapse of the dominion when disaster struck. On February 8, 1690, a force of Frenchmen and mission Indians surprised the New York frontier town of Schenectady, torching every house but one, putting every-one who resisted to the sword, and carrying off twenty-seven survivors. This calamity, in addition to the uncertainly of who sat on the English throne, encouraged Leisler to view anyone who questioned his increasingly auto-cratic rule as a papist conspirator. His inability to distinguish friend from foe ultimately cost him his office as well as his life when forces from England arrived to establish William and Mary's rule.[45] In Maryland, Protestants long opposed to the Catholic proprietor Lord Baltimore also entered a frenzy of conspiratorial thinking upon receiving news of William's invasion. The most repellent charge was that Baltimore's Catholic allies in the colony had hired the Senecas to butcher Protestant Marylanders. This fear galvanized a force of "Protestant Associators" under the leadership of John Coode to march on the capital at Saint Mary's City and lay siege to Baltimore's mansion. In the aftermath a new Protestant-dominated assembly established the Anglican Church as the colony's official religion and banned Catholics from public office on the grounds that they might support the French.[46]

Whereas during the seventeenth and early eighteenth century English colonists associated the threat of Catholicism with Indian savagery, after 1700 their fears of papists and slaves became mutually reinforcing. During this era the growing slave trade brought large numbers of Africans with military backgrounds into colonies, a danger of which white authorities were acutely aware. At the same time the War of Jenkins' Ear (beginning in 1739) and the War of Austrian Succession, or King George's War (1744–48) pit Britain against Catholic Spain and France, unleashing waves of militant Protestant patriotism and antipopery.[47] It was no coincidence that the anthems "God Save the King" and "Rule Britannia" appeared during this era, the latter con-taining the telling lines "Rule Britannia! Britannia rule the waves! / Britons never, never, never shall be slaves." Imperial subjects were increasingly sensi-tive that their liberty and African slavery rested on British military might, and nowhere was that lesson more poignant than in the colonies. In 1738 the governor of Spanish Florida declared freedom to slaves from the British colonies who managed to escape to his jurisdiction, and he gave them their own town with a former Carolina slave as its ruler. Colonists throughout the

British Atlantic saw this offer as a sign of a popish plot to unleash black slaves on white Protestants. That dread combined with very real incidents of African slave unrest threw the colonial world into panic.

The variety of real and suspected uprisings by slaves during this period, often in combination with Catholics, is remarkable. In 1736 authorities on Antigua believed that they had uncovered a massive slave plot to blow up the gentry while they were at a genteel ball. The parallels with Guy Fawkes's Gunpowder Plot of 1605 were too close to ignore, raising the question of whether foreign Catholic conspirators were involved. Within four months white Antiguans had executed eighty-eight slaves, with seventy-seven being burned at the stake. In 1734, 1738, and again in 1739 New Jersey experienced incidents in which slaves threatened revolt, fired barns, and attacked their masters, which appeared coordinated to some colonists. Then in 1740 whites in Prince George's County, Maryland, believed that they had foiled a massive slave uprising at the last minute. Clearly British colonists were living on edge.

The most serious incidents fed off the threat of Spanish Florida. The danger posed by the Spanish offer of freedom to British slaves became manifest in South Carolina's Stono Rebellion during the fall of 1739, in which up to ninety slaves killed twenty-five whites and burned several plantations while making an unsuccessful run for the Spanish border. Months later Georgia governor James Oglethorpe alerted the other colonies that the Spanish were sending undercover priests throughout British dominions to foment more slave uprisings. This burgeoning fear set the stage for the trials of the New York Slave Conspiracy of 1741, which Murrin rightly has dubbed the worst travesty of justice in colonial American history.[48] The crisis began when New York City officials busted an interracial theft ring comprised of slaves and a white family named the Hughsons, who ran a low-end tavern. Slaves would rob colonial homes and then repair to the Hughsons' to pawn their loot and spend the proceeds on food, drink, and sex. In this, the Hughsons' tavern gave palpable meaning to complaints by white authorities that the city had grown too lackadaisical in its policing of slaves, including interracial socializing and black freedom of movement. To make matters worse, one of the accused burglars, named Caesar (or John Gwin), had fathered a child with a young Irishwoman named Peggy Kerry, who lodged at the Hughsons'. Around the same time as the robberies, a series of fires broke out around the city, perhaps set by the burglars to provide cover for their illicit activities. Yet one local official, Chief Justice Daniel Horsmanden, believed that he had stumbled upon something even more menacing than a gang of arsonist thieves. He discovered a willing accomplice in an indentured servant of the Hughsons', Mary Burton, to whom he promised freedom and an ample reward if she told all she knew. Gradually the story ballooned from a supposed theft ring, to slave design to commit arson and theft, to a plot to have the slaves commit mass arson and murder, until in its penultimate incarnation it became part of a continentwide conspiracy hatched by the Spanish crown and brought to New York through the auspices of an undercover Jesuit, John Ury, posing as an innocent schoolteacher. A Spanish fleet would sail up the Hudson while the city's slaves murdered whites and burned their property to the ground. It was the British colonies' most fantastical nightmares come true—and yet there was more.

In its planning and execution, this supposed conspiracy was an inversion of the colonial racial order. Burton and then other witnesses charged that as the ringleaders of this plot met at the Hughsons' tavern, "black men feasted on veal and goose, as if they were gentlemen; they pledged themselves to a secret society, as if they were Freemasons; they plotted to appoint a new governor, as if they were party politicians; all while flirting with young white women who laid a tablecloth before them and served them meat and poured them drinks."[49] The goal of the plot was to make this transposition permanent. After looting and killing New York's elites, Hughson would sit as king of the whites and Caesar as governor of the blacks. The slaves would go free and take white women as their wives—the greatest of taboos in this racially biased society with slavery.

Unsurprisingly, the trials of this case sometimes resembled racial diatribes. One judge lectured Hughson that it was appalling for Christians "to be guilty not only of making negro slaves their equals, but even their superiors, by waiting upon, keeping with, and entertaining them with meat, drink and lodging."[50] The prosecutor William Smith railed that "no scheme more monstrous could have been invented; nor any thing be thought more foolish . . . that . . . Caesar, now in gibbets, a Governor! that the white men should all be killed, and the women become a prey to the rapacious lust of these villains!"[51] The supposed priest behind this conspiracy, John Ury, tried to prove his innocence by asserting his racist credentials, calling forth a witness to testify that he had said blacks "were not proper Objects of Salvation . . . [that] They are of a Slavish Nature, it is the Nature of them to be Slaves, give them Learning, do them all the Good you can, and put them beyond the Condition of Slaves, and in return, they will cut your Throats."[52] Yet Ury's suspected Catholicism associated him with the slaves. It took the jury just fifteen minutes to find him guilty.

By the conclusion of this business, white authorities had burned thirteen slaves at the stake for petty treason, hanged seventeen slaves and four whites (two males, two females) for arson, sold eighty-four slaves to the Caribbean, and banished seven white men from the colony. The carnage did prick some New Yorkers' consciences. A handful of people murmured that the trials had been a mistake, but no one stepped forward to contest the proceedings. Indeed most New Yorkers believed that they had barely averted disaster, for in 1742 Spain sent thirty-six ships and two thousand soldiers from Cuba with orders to devastate South Carolina and Georgia and free the slaves, only to be driven back by a force of just nine hundred men under Georgia's Oglethrope. New Yorkers also found confirmation of the executions as rumor began to spread that the bodies of Hughson and Caesar, which had been hung in chains to rot, began to change colors. As the newspaper reported it, "Hughson had turned negro, and Vararck's Caesar a white."[53]

This rumor was at once startling and funny because eighteenth-century colonists throughout the British Atlantic believed that such a phenomenon was impossible. They had come to view "black" and "white" as fixed, natural, physical categories that corresponded to equally natural social hierarchies such as free and slave, civilized and savage. Their associated fears of Catholicism, slaves, and savages, and the panics such thinking produced, helped make race salient in their lives. Yet white and black were defined not by nature but rather by colonial law and custom, each one mutually reinforcing the other. It was New York's jurisprudence that decided that only slaves convicted in the conspiracy, not their white co-conspirators, would be burned at the stake. It was custom in New York, as in every colonial society with slavery, that European men who owned female African slaves could exploit them sexually without penalty based on the notion that these women were property and had no reputations to defend. It was also law and custom that when white women had sex with black men, the consequences were severe. As such, Horsmanden, who had spent his wayward youth patronizing prostitutes in London, was sickened by the thought of the coupling between the Irishwoman Peggy Kerry and the African slave Caesar. It was both law and custom that defined the child of this relationship as black instead of white, based on the twisted logic that whiteness was a privilege to be defended against the threat of expanding, corrupting blackness. Of course, expanding blackness was precisely what the law did by defining people of almost any black descent as "black," with the aim of expanding the pool of servile black laborers. That law eventually became custom, which was why Mary Burton, the Hughsons' servant, was said to have refused to care for Kerry's mixed-race baby, though the child shared the same household with her; the customary revulsion at race mixing was also why the crowd at the trials was at once horrified and titillated by the suggestion that the slave rebels intended to make wives of New York's white women. The use of law and custom to determine who would be debased, servile, and subject to arbitrary justice, or, by contrast, privileged, free, and empowered at the bench, was what demarcated and defined the categories of white, black, and Indian that had become so fundamental to colonial American life.

Raising the Roof

The Revolution was a watershed not only in the establishment of American independence but also in the creation of a republic premised on defending white citizenship and equal protection under the law even as it degraded blacks and dispossessed Indians. Obviously such patterns were evident in the colonies before the Revolution. Yet until American independence, subject-hood, not citizenship, was a person's basic political identity. For all the political privileges of whiteness, blacks and Indians could be subjects of the king too and thus claim some protection from the Crown. After the Revolution this leverage, such as it was, disappeared. One state after another and then the nation took the white populace's formerly *im*plicit assumptions about who belonged to the body politic and who did not and made them *ex*plicit by codifying them. Whiteness became the basic quality of citizenship and blackness the basic symbol of subordination. Engrossing Indian land for the benefit of whites became the closest thing to a major political consensus that the partisan-riven Republic could claim.[54]

The Revolutionary War, not just white Americans' colonial heritage, contributed to this trend, for it was a racial upheaval as well as a colonial rebellion. Blacks everywhere clamored for their own rights by employing revolutionary slogans and volunteering to serve in the contending armies in exchange for freedom. Indians fought for their independence by striking up and down the trans-Appalachian region. After the war came the white backlash, magnified by new opportunities to engross Indian land and profit from slavery. In the South the sudden profitability of cotton and an upsurge in the size of the white population provided fresh motivation to force Indians off the land, put blacks to work on it, and quicken racial justifications for doing

so. In the North the white reaction against newly passed gradual emancipation laws and the growing free population of color took the form of segrega-
tionist laws and informal discrimination. In this context whiteness, defined
against blacks and Indians, became a building block of nationhood.

Racial tensions ran high throughout the imperial crisis, particularly
as it grew clear that nothing short of armed conflict or royal intervention
would resolve the dispute.[55] The startling appearance of slaves in the streets
of Charles Town cheering "Liberty" like their white neighbors augured that
throwing off the imperial yoke might prompt slaves to seek their own freedom. Whites throughout the colonies, especially in New England, began to
acknowledge the incompatibility of their own liberty talk with slaveholding. In the mid-1760s several town meetings in Massachusetts began to issue
denunciations of slavery, and in 1766 the colony saw the beginning of a series
of lawsuits stretching into the 1780s in which slaves and their white advocates
hired lawyers to sue for their freedom. Such litigation, combined with ebbing
popular support for slavery, effectively ended racial bondage in Massachusetts in the early 1780s. Massachusetts was not alone. In 1768 the College of
Philadelphia held a debate over the legality of slavery. Newspapers began to
publish articles excoriating white Americans for their hypocrisy on slavery.
These attacks appeared even in Virginia, where half of the slaves in the North
American colonies toiled and where practically every leading revolutionary
was a slaveholder. One such essay by Arthur Lee, scion of an elite planter family, castigated slaveholding as a violation of every individual's "birthright" to
liberty. Whites could not easily ignore, and slaves would not let them ignore,
that their egalitarian principles undermined the basic premises of slaveholding. Once the rationales for slavery were scrutinized in a context shaped by
Enlightenment principles of natural rights, they were at risk of crumbling
into dust.

In colonies dependent on slavery, such arguments were of little consequence. One of Lee's antislavery essays in the *Virginia Gazette* drew so much
controversy that the printer refused to publish the second part of the article.
When a junior member of the House of Burgesses, Thomas Jefferson, got his
senior cousin, Richard Bland, to propose a law that would eliminate colony
approval before a slave master could free his slaves, Bland, a veteran legisla-
tor, "was denounced as an enemy of his country, and treated with the grossest
indecorum."[56] Similar forces were at work in Newport, Rhode Island, even
though the city was a center of revolutionary agitation and Quaker antislavery sentiment. At the same time, Newport's merchant fleet included some

150 slave ships, and its thirty rum distilleries depended on slave-produced molasses. Thus when the Congregationalist minister Samuel Hopkins gave a stern abolitionist sermon in 1770, his parishioners warned him to tone down his rhetoric.[57] Slaveholding interests could see that their own liberty talk was becoming a Pandora's box of radical racial reform.

The danger sensed by Hopkins's parishioners came into stark view during the long year after the Battle of Lexington and Concord, as the Crown responded to the mounting rebellion by turning toward African slaves and Indians for help. In so doing, George III took over the role once held by Catholic kings and the pope as foreign incendiary of the colonies' racial enemies. The first ominous sign came in the summer and fall of 1775, when Virginia governor John Dunmore proclaimed freedom to all slaves who would fight against their former masters for the Union Jack. He made this decision not on his own but only after he and other royal governors received numerous hushed offers from slaves seeking liberty. Shortly after Dunmore's incendiary order, two hundred slaves rushed to join the British ranks, and they were eventually joined by some six hundred more. This group included twenty-seven slaves from the Williamsburg estate of none other than Peyton Randolph, Speaker of Virginia's House of Burgesses and a delegate to the Continental Congress. Not only had these escapees thrown off their chains, but in bearing British arms they also wielded the consummate symbol of English manhood and citizenship, and in donning sashes emblazoned with the saying "Liberty for Slaves," they threw the colonists' political slogans back in their faces. To rub salt in the wound, in December 1775 Dunmore employed his black forces in an attempted sweep of royal opponents in the area of Hampton Roads, which resulted in the near destruction of the town of Norfolk. Southern slaveholders could no longer imagine that they remained under the king's protection.[58]

Colonists everywhere feared that the Crown's next move would be to enlist Indians to attack the backcountry. Throughout 1775 Sir Guy Johnson, Britain's superintendent of northern Indian affairs, was known to be negotiating with the Iroquois to war against American rebels. In November of that year Johnson even sent the Mohawks' Joseph Brant to London to meet with the king and his ministers. Brant made his conditions clear: that the Iroquois would come to Britain's defense if and only if the Crown pledged to defend Iroquois lands. With the subsequent agreement, suddenly the colonies faced the prospect of having their frontier descend into bloody terror again. Indeed the Continental Congress's belief that the British and Indians would attempt to cut off New England from the north led it to launch a disastrous preemptive invasion of Canada in the winter of 1775–76. For the better part of a century, white colonists' fear of savages and slaves had fed off of their antipopery. Now Britain became the foreign enemy conspiring with domestic ones.[59]

The Declaration of Independence became the first official American statement that white nationalism, as defined against black slaves and Indians, would be a foundation of the United States. As Pauline Maier and Robert Parkinson have emphasized, the Declaration begins with specific, local, and seemingly minor grievances against the Crown and then builds gradually toward emotive charges of general concern to eliminate all doubt that George III is a tyrant.[60] The twenty-seventh and final charge is that "[h]e has excited domestic insurrections amongst us and has endeavoured to bring on the inhabitants of our frontiers the merciless savages, whose known rule of warfare is an undistinguished destruction of all ages, sexes, and conditions." The reference to domestic insurrectionists alluded not to white Tories but to black slaves. "Merciless savages," by comparison, was not meant as a euphemism. Nothing the king had ever done was more egregious than encouraging blacks and Indians to rise up against his white American subjects. The king's fatherly responsibility was to protect his white children in their liberties, including their liberty to hold blacks as property and seize Indian land. Though blacks and many Native Americans could claim to be the king's subjects, whites judged their subjecthood to be of a lesser sort, designed to protect them from the most excessive abuses of colonialism but not to set them on any kind of an equal footing. The king's actions threatened to turn slaves against their masters in the hope of attaining freedom and unleash Indians against the backcountry in the hope of reclaiming their land. It was a nightmarish vision of colonialism in reverse that, delegates to the Continental Congress assumed, would galvanize the white American public in all its varieties. They were right.

Whites' fears of the threats posed by blacks and Indians certainly materialized throughout the Revolutionary War. Sylvia Frey has aptly characterized the Revolution as the largest slave rising in American history, in reference to the thousands of slaves who escaped to British lines or otherwise managed to throw off their shackles while their masters fought for their own narrow liberty. Georgia lost two-thirds of its slave population during the war, and South Carolina lost a quarter.[61] The northern equivalent was black men negotiating their freedom in exchange for military service in the American cause. Their sacrifice, however reluctantly accepted by some northern whites, was yet another blow against the white public's support for slavery and thus to the slave system. Whites' response to Indian participation in the Revolution was much less conflicted. The white public tended to ignore support for the American cause by groups including the Catawbas, Oneidas, Mohicans, Mohegans, Pequots, and Narragansetts, despite communities such as the Mashpee Wampanoags of Cape Cod enlisting a larger percentage of their men than any neighboring white towns. Instead white Americans focused on the numerous Indian allies of Britain, who raided across what is now upstate New York, Pennsylvania's Susquehanna River valley, and the Smoky Mountains and absorbed American scorched-earth campaigns in turn. For white Americans, the consummate symbol of Native Americans' role in the war was the 1778 attack by Iroquois and white Loyalist forces on Cherry Valley, New York, marked by the slaughter of noncombatant civilians and desecration of many of their remains. For Indians, the equivalent was the 1782 massacre of pacifist, Moravian Mohicans and Delawares by white Ohio Country militia, who systematically hauled off Indian women, children, and the elderly while they were huddled together singing hymns and then executed them with blows from a cooper's mallet.[62] As Richard White has observed, this was the age that gave rise to the saying "the only good Indian is a dead one" and in which "murder gradually and inexorably became the dominant American Indian policy."[63] For both parties, this murderous treatment became their lasting memory of each other's role during the Revolution.

In terms of U.S.-Indian affairs, the Peace of Paris represented little more than a partial British withdrawal from an ongoing war for Indian country. Keeping the nation solvent, including paying off the nation's debts to Continental soldiers, hinged on the federal government selling and distributing that very land. The struggle for control of this acreage took the form of a series of wars that engulfed the Ohio Country and the southeastern interior throughout the mid-1780s and the 1790s, consuming nearly five-sixths of the government's operating budget during the Washington administration.[64] Not until the 1794 Treaty of Greenville and, in some senses, not until the end of the War of 1812 would the young Republic's wars with Indians east of the Mississippi come to a close. However much the egalitarian principles of the Revolution had inspired white Americans to reevaluate hierarchies of class and gender and even, in some sectors, the justice of racial slavery, hardly anyone was making serious proposals to respect Indians as autonomous authorities over their own land and people or of integrating them within white American society. To the extent that religious and political authorities encouraged Indians to make Christian and civilized reforms, it was in exchange for immediate Indian land cessions and in the expectation that more would follow. The time for bringing Christian, civilized Indians into the body politic was reserved for some vague, distant date. In any case, the holders of such a vision were far and few between, with most of them in positions of authority where frank talk of Indian extermination was considered impolite. Less visible white Americans were less circumspect. An Englishman who visited the United States during these years observed that "the white Americans have the most rancorous antipathy to the whole race of Indians, and nothing is more common [than] to hear them talk of extirpating them from the face of the earth, men, women, and children."[65]

On the face of it, there appears to have been less of a white consensus on blacks than on Indians. Following the Revolution, southern slaveholders quickly began to rebuild their slaveholdings with new purchases from international and domestic sources. Aside from some easily defeated proposals in Virginia to consider a gradual emancipation, voices challenging the slave regime were slight and easily drowned out. That was doubly true with the newfound profitability of cotton following the invention of the cotton gin in 1793, a development that, combined with the country's campaigns against Indians, thrust slaveholders westward into what would become the states of Alabama, Mississippi, and Louisiana following the War of 1812.[66] Things could hardly have been more different in the northern states. Vermont outlawed slavery in its constitution of 1777. Pennsylvania and Massachusetts began to phase out slavery before the Revolution was even over. In 1784 Connecticut and Rhode Island followed with their own gradual emancipation laws, to be joined much later by New York in 1799 and New Jersey in 1804. Most northern cities began to host abolitionist societies dedicated to ending the slave trade and even slavery itself. Though slavery would persist in small pockets of the North into the 1800s, the institution had all but collapsed well before that date as blacks began to negotiate early release and run away, and as nonslaveholding whites refused to turn in fugitives. Rather than qualifying this change as some kind of natural economic evolution in a region that never depended on slavery in the first place, we should see it as a triumph of human will and the power of revolutionary principles over a generations-long assumption that slavery was natural and right.[67]

Our retrospective that these developments were the first stages in the creation of the North and the South as distinct, rival regions can mask that whites in both places generally remained committed to white superiority, black degradation, and Indian dispossession.

Precious few northern whites argued that the end of slavery should be accompanied by blacks' political and social equality. Indeed many of the staunchest white opponents of slavery were among the greatest proponents of sending free blacks "back to Africa," so that northern whites would not have to deal with the problem of a free black population, and free blacks would not have to deal with the presumably intractable problem of white bigotry.[68] It is easy to see why contemporaries viewed whites' prejudice as permanent. Within a short number of years, practically every northern state had set up a Jim Crow system to relegate free blacks to the lowest ranks of society. There were separate and unequal schools, segregated seating on public transportation and in churches, bans on black suffrage or special poll taxes for black voters, bans on blacks bearing arms in state militias, antimiscegenation laws or at the very least antimiscegenation customs, and restrictions on free blacks entering from other states. White mobs filled whatever void was left by the law, keeping legal black voters from the polls, attacking black men for real and imagined romantic relationships with white women, and protecting white workers from black competitors. Northern whites' opposition to slavery was clearly not the same thing as support for racial equality. As for allowing Indians secure land and autonomy or an equal place in white society, those matters never came up for serious discussion. Rather, in the years following the Revolution, Connecticut, Rhode Island, and especially New York accelerated their efforts to force out their respective Native populations and largely, if not entirely, "succeeded." White northerners, like white southerners, generally remained committed to the colonial racial hierarchy in the era of the early Republic.[69]

This consensus formed a basis for statements of white nationalism at the federal level. Aware that they might be judged harshly by international opinion and posterity, the framers were at pains to avoid being explicit in the Constitution that "We the People" meant just white people. Take, for instance, Article I, Section 2, which specifies that "Representatives and direct Taxes shall be apportioned among the several States which may be included within this Union, according to their respective Numbers, which shall be determined by adding to the whole number of free Persons, including those bound to Service for a Term of Years, and excluding Indians not taxed, three fifths of all other Persons." This passage might be read to imply that free blacks and tax-paying Indians were included among "the People," given that they would be counted for purposes of state representation and taxes. Yet future statements by the federal government made it clear that this was not the case. The federal 1790 naturalization law limited naturalized citizenship to "free white persons," a term which went unquestioned during legislative debate. As Matthew Jacobson has observed, this language "demonstrates the republican convergence of race and 'fitness for self-government'; the law's wording denotes an unconflicted view of the presumed character and unambiguous boundaries of whiteness."[70] Two years later Congress passed a militia act that called on "each and every free able-bodied white male citizen of the respective states" to contribute to the common defense.[71] Despite invaluable black and Indian service during the war against Britain, the nation now denied even free blacks and tax-paying Indians (few as they were) a role in maintaining the nation they had helped to create. There were several reasons for this. For one, in the Anglo-American tradition bearing arms was a symbol of political equality, representing that the militiaman had a stake in the society and government he was defending. The Republic did not grant blacks and Indians such a claim. Moreover the purposes of the militia included defense against Indians and slave uprisings. The militia act suggested that free blacks and tax-paying Indians could not be relied on to perform that role because race made each loyal to people of a similar complexion, as was the case with whites.

John Murrin, like many other historians, has spent a career exploring J. Hector St. John de Crévecoeur's provocative question "What then is the American, this new man?" In one of his later publications, Murrin drew on a burst of recent scholarship, much of it by his own students, to conclude that this problem needed to take race into account. He submitted, "American citizens had to perceive themselves as white before they could define themselves as a people."[72] In classic Murrin style, these apparently straightforward words are packed with subtlety. The British American colonies were indeed distinctive from Britain proper in terms of race. Arguably the most characteristic features of the colonies as colonies were race consciousness and racial hierarchy. Yet, as Murrin's analysis suggests, white American colonists either were unaware of this difference or, more likely, saw no reason to comment on it. After all, they were Britons who took great pride in the Anglicization of their society. At the same time, white American racism powerfully shaped why and how the thirteen colonies banded together first to seek their collective independence from Great Britain and then to build a republic. For all of the innumerable divisions within the white ranks during these years, which have captured the bulk of scholarly attention, there remained a consensus racial worldview and support for white rule. That consensus, along with commitment to the Constitution, was the bedrock on which fractious national politics could play out without resort to secession and civil war—at least until 1860. All of the central players knew that "the American, this new man," was white.

CHAPTER NINE

De-Anglicization: The Jeffersonian Attack
on an American Naval Establishment

Denver Brunsman

In his 1999 presidential address at the annual meeting of the Society for Historians of the Early American Republic (SHEAR), John Murrin recounted a humorous story about his reading of Thomas Jefferson's military policy when he was an early graduate student. In an 1808 message to Congress, President Jefferson explained his administration's plan of employing "such moderate garrisons in time of peace as may merely take care of the post, and to a reliance on the neighboring militia for its support in the first moments of war." According to Henry Adams, Jefferson's program was "that the settlers should protect the army, not the army the settlers." Murrin shared Adams's disdain. "When I first read that comment," Murrin recalled, "I laughed heartily at the foolish notions of Jefferson, the philosopher statesman." Yet over time Murrin came to appreciate the sincerity of Jefferson's ambitions: "Now that I am much older, I realize that Jefferson meant exactly what he said, and on the whole the Jeffersonians were able to make these goals coherent and to implement them."[1]

Though certainly influential, Murrin's framing of the early national era—centered on the almost inconceivably nonstatist policies of the Jeffersonians—has never had the same impact on the early American field as has his treatment of the colonial period. One reason is that his ideas about the early Republic have not benefited from an organizing construct as powerful as "Anglicization." Yet Murrin's most prominent writings on the early national period present a consistent vision, if not a unifying term, for the early Republic. In the first years under the Constitution, the United States closely followed Britain's blueprint to national and imperial greatness after the revolution of 1688: a national bank, debt financing supported by taxes, an expanding executive, and an emerging army and naval establishment. But with the triumph of the Jeffersonians in 1800, the United States reversed course. As Murrin, ever the film aficionado, put it, "America's Revolution Settlement resembles the remake of an old movie classic, except the new producer has altered the ending to suit the changing tastes of his audience." That altered ending included dramatic reductions in federal taxes and spending, the lowering of the national debt, and the downsizing of the army and navy—a formula that, as Murrin's presidential address to SHEAR highlighted, resulted incredibly in continental and eventually hemispheric hegemony for the United States.[2]

In this essay, I suggest that what Murrin described, but was too modest to characterize in exactly these terms, is that the Jeffersonians pursued a concerted program of *de-Anglicization* after twelve years of Federalist rule under the Washington and Adams administrations. As a project, de-Anglicization was committed to reversing trends in American state building patterned after the British fiscal-military state, particularly a government dependent on ever-increasing tax revenue and debt financing to fund continuous war.[3] Although the Jeffersonians' antistatist views had numerous ideological underpinnings, we should not discount their visceral opposition to all things British. Jeffersonians interpreted such disparate events as British naval impressment and trade restrictions, northwestern Indian uprisings, Algerian piracy in the Mediterranean, and supposed domestic spy rings as a coordinated plot by Britain to destroy the American Republic.[4]

Murrin traces Jefferson's Anglophobia to the American Revolution. As governor of Virginia, Jefferson was humiliated and barely escaped capture as the British army ravaged his state in 1780 and 1781. In 1787 he acknowledged "that I considered the British as our natural enemies, and as the only nation on earth who wished us ill from the bottom of their souls. And I am satisfied that were our continent to be swallowed by the ocean, Great Britain would be in a bonfire from one end to the other."[5] Jefferson and his followers thus reacted with nothing short of horror to the Federalist program in the 1790s to recast America's weak state institutions in the British mold. In his infamous letter to the Florentine Philip Mazzei in April 1796, Jefferson implicated the Federalists, even George Washington, in a conspiracy to sell out America's republican experiment in favor of a return to British-style rule: "In place of that noble love of liberty and republican government which carried us triumphantly thro' the war, an Anglican, monarchical and aristocratical party has sprung up, whose avowed object is to draw over us the substance, as they have already done the forms, of the British government."[6] Such fears only intensified during the Adams administration and its march to war with revolutionary France. Of America's ongoing mimicking of British forms of government, Jefferson wrote to Thomas Pinckney in 1797, "I wish any events could induce us to cease to copy such a model, & to assume the dignity of being original."[7]

In few areas did Jefferson and other Democratic-Republicans prove more "original" than in their naval policy. Jefferson's vision for the U.S. Navy made his ideas for the army, which drew chuckles from Henry Adams and the young Murrin, seem militant and statist. The Republicans' approach to the navy was also more surprising. Whereas Jefferson's dismissal of a standing army was consistent with his other positions that derived from the British opposition, or Country Party, tradition, his views on the navy went against that pattern. Country Party writers such as John Trenchard, Thomas Gordon, and Henry St John, Viscount Bolingbroke, celebrated the Royal Navy for safeguarding liberty, and colonial Americans generally concurred. For this reason the early U.S. Navy provides a particularly compelling example and case study of de-Anglicization. Jefferson's support for a strong American navy, especially in the face of ongoing depredations at sea by the British navy, would have made perfect ideological sense. Few writers in the Anglo-American tradition feared that navies posed the same threat to domestic liberties as standing armies did. Put simply, the genius of a navy was that it was at sea. Yet aside from the Bank of England and the monarchy itself, no institution had a greater association with British state power, and hence tyranny, for Jeffersonians than the Royal Navy. As the leading recipient of British government revenue, the navy became the largest industrial organization in the western world in the eighteenth century. For many Jeffersonians, debt and taxes were merely symptoms of the root causes of British despotism: war and naval power. Moreover, in forcibly manning its navy through impressment, the British state directly violated the liberties of not only its own subjects but also American citizens. For Jeffersonians, then, the Federalist buildup of the U.S. Navy in the latter 1790s, on the heels of the founding of the Bank of the United States and the first national taxes, signaled nothing less than the final step in transforming the American Republic into a British-style war-making state.[8]

This is a story largely absent from early American historiography. In the past generation, popular accounts of the early U.S. Navy have proliferated amid general scholarly indifference. The problem, to paraphrase Isaac Land, is that naval history is too important to be left to naval and amateur historians. The curious evolution of the American navy makes sense only in light of Murrin's Anglicization thesis. The Jeffersonian experiment in naval downsizing, both in total tonnage and in size of vessels, was not simply a funny or ironic detour on the road to American greatness but a fundamental feature of the nation's founding.[9]

Revolutionary Aspirations

Before the political battles of the 1790s, Americans viewed the Royal Navy with mostly wonder and admiration. During the colonial era, Benjamin Franklin was not alone in boasting that "our Navy at present is the greatest and most formidable that the World ever saw."[10] Naval affairs represented one area in which Anglicization did not stop with American independence. Given the success of the British navy, Americans naturally sought to emulate the service. The process of imitation took place even while they began to establish a separate national identity during the American Revolution.

With the British model in mind, American revolutionaries had long believed in America's bright naval prospects. In 1755 John Adams, likely inspired by Franklin's recent demographic observations showing the colonial population doubling every twenty-five years, dared to imagine a future when America would be the capital of the British Empire. "Since we have (I may say) all the naval Stores of the Nation in our hands," Adams reflected, "it will be easy to obtain the mastery of the seas, and then the united force of all Europe, will not be able to subdue us." In *Common Sense* (1776), Thomas Paine found comfort in America's future because of its naval stores: "No country on the globe is so happily situated, or so internally capable of raising a fleet as America. Tar, timber, iron, and cordage are her natural produce. We need go abroad for nothing." In the long term, of course, Paine's argument had merit. For those American readers worried about confronting the world's naval superpower, however, his only consolation was that the North American continent had plentiful forests.[11]

Early Americans consistently underestimated the amount of time and resources needed to convert trees into warships. This basic miscalculation made the founding of a navy during the American Revolution an exercise in humility. Although Adams and other appointed members of the Marine Committee in Congress aspired to the British example, they had impossible ground to make up. During the Revolutionary War, the British navy consisted of several hundred vessels, including about one hundred ships of the line (though not all were operational), a ship of the line defined then as a two- or three-deck warship with more than sixty guns. The American Marine Committee pursued a two-track plan, purchasing and fitting out merchant vessels for war while following a modest shipbuilding program. The committee renamed the first merchant ship that it purchased *Alfred* in honor of the British navy's founder. In 1779 the five-member administrative head of the U.S. Navy became known as the Board of Admiralty, the same formal name used for Britain's Lords of Admiralty.[12]

The American "Lords" had no way to expedite the century-long process that had produced the Royal Navy. In 1775 Congress authorized the construction of thirteen light frigates. Not to be confused with America's larger and more famous frigates of the 1790s, such as the USS *Constitution*, the revolutionary-era frigates had single decks and between twenty-four and thirty-six guns each. In European navies such frigates were used as auxiliary and reconnaissance vessels for the main battle fleet. In the American service, with no other larger vessels to serve, the frigates were the primary fleet. None of the thirteen frigates saw service before 1777 or lasted until the Battle of Yorktown in 1781. More than half were surrendered to the British, and three others were destroyed to avoid capture. In 1776 Congress approved a plan for eleven seventy-four-gun ships of the line; three would be built in America, and eight would be purchased or chartered from the French. The French ships never materialized. Only one of the American warships was completed, but not until after the end of major hostilities in November 1782; ultimately it was made a gift to the French. The American navy's foremost highlight in the war, John Paul Jones's bold raiding operations and victories off the coast of Britain in 1778 and 1779, were accomplished in a converted French Indiaman, the forty-gun *Bonhomme Richard*.[13]

While early Americans struggled to duplicate the industrial power of the British navy, they Anglicized more easily in behavior and maritime customs. "The Rules and Regulations for the Government of the Navy," first drafted by Adams in 1775, closely resembled the British Articles of War. Into the nineteenth century, American naval officers modeled their command on the British service. One of President Jefferson's most successful naval officers,

Edward Preble, used a copy of standing orders that he received from a British captain to exercise command of his squadron. Preble also used the instructions for navy surgeons issued by the British commissioners for taking care of sick and wounded seamen. His personal library was filled with works on the Royal Navy, including histories, seamanship manuals, naval dictionaries, navigation guides, and volumes of *The Naval Chronicle*.[14]

Early U.S. Navy officers could benefit greatly from the example of their British counterparts, the world's most talented naval officer corps. Yet American officers also imitated British practice in a realm less beneficial to the national interest: recruiting. During the Revolutionary War, the Continental navy and eleven state navies (all the original thirteen states except Delaware and New Jersey) practiced a range of compulsory recruiting measures up to and including impressment.[15] To borrow Winthrop Jordan's famous phrase, resorting to compulsion was in many respects an "unthinking decision" for early national Americans. They had lived with impressment for so long in the British Empire—and practiced it themselves for ships armed to protect individual colonies—that it came as second nature. Impressment would eventually come to help define the differences between volitional, or voluntary, citizenship in the United States and involuntary subjecthood in Britain, but the break was still fresh during the Revolution.[16]

Congress never went so far as to establish impressment as an official policy for raising men for the Continental navy, but neither did it ever fully ban the practice. In November 1776 a committee in Congress proposed forcing British prisoners into service to retaliate against British impressments of American sailors: "By thus executing the great and necessary law of retaliation, our Enemies may be induced to put a stop to a practice so dishonourable to human nature, and first taught the world by the british nation." Although the proposal never became law, individual American commanders violated normal procedure by impressing British prisoners rather than delivering them to American jails.[17] At various times the Continental navy and state navies also impressed Loyalists and accepted captured army deserters into service as a form of punishment.[18]

The impressing of fellow Americans always incited the most controversy during the war. Individual Continental ship captains impressed American sailors as part of their responsibility for raising men for their own vessels. In fall 1779 Joseph Reed, president of the Pennsylvania Council, issued a grievance to Congress against the navy for "impressing Seamen & Landsmen with many Circumstances of Hardship & Cruelty." Reed warned Congress about the possible consequences if the American navy followed the British in embracing impressment: "We cannot help observing how similar this Conduct is to that of the British Officers during our Subjection to Great Brittain and are persuaded it will have the same unhappy effects viz., an estrangement of the Affections of the People from the Authority under which they act which by an easy Progression will proceed to open Opposition to the immediate Actors and Bloodshed." For Reed, impressment exemplified why America had declared its independence. He ended his grievance by identifying the navy's actions as "very derogatory to the Principles of the great Contest in which we have been engaged."[19]

Congress showed sympathy for Pennsylvania's position without completely renouncing impressment. It issued new directions that Continental commanders could not impress without the consent of the legislature or executive of the state where the impressment was being carried out.[20] The directive did not change the navy's behavior, as Reed repeated Pennsylvania's grievances to Congress in 1780. Early Americans struggled to escape some of the least desirable aspects of their Anglicized past.[21]

Federalist Navy

Following the Revolution, whatever consensus had existed in America about building a British-style naval establishment disappeared. The navy became part of the larger struggle between parties who sought to re-create elements of Britain's fiscal-military state in America (Hamiltonian Federalists) and those who adhered to a nonstatist governing philosophy (Jeffersonian Republicans). The two sides framed debates over the creation of a national bank, debt, tax structure, manufacturing program, and army and naval establishment as a question of Anglicization versus de-Anglicization. The navy took on particular prominence in the discourse because of its legacy costs. More than any other policy, a permanent naval establishment, as the British example taught, created the prospect of unending government spending, taxing, debt, and war making. Jeffersonians therefore favored a small, defensive navy or no navy at all.

In fact, for the decade between 1783 and 1793, the United States effectively had no navy. Events in the 1780s persuaded a broad cross section of American elites, including Jefferson, that the national government needed some type of naval force. In 1784 American shipping experienced interference in the Mediterranean by the Barbary States of North Africa. Previously America had come under Britain's protection, secured through a combination of might and payments to the states of Morocco, Tripoli, Algiers, and Tunis. By the summer of 1785, Algiers had declared war on the United States, which could neither offer naval protection for its shipping nor pay off the Barbary States. The United States escaped the episode only when Portugal enforced a blockade against the Algerines.[22]

In 1787 the Constitutional Convention concluded, apparently without much debate, that Congress needed the power "to provide and maintain a navy" and that "the President shall be Commander in Chief of the Army and Navy."[23] The provisions reflected the hopes of Alexander Hamilton and other leading American nationalists to model the country's new government more closely on the British example. Madison's notes from the convention leave no doubt of Hamilton's early intentions to forge the Anglicization of American state institutions: "In his private opinion he [Hamilton] had no scruple in declaring, supported as he was by the opinions of so many of the wise & good, that the British Govt was the best in the world: and that he doubted much whether any thing short of it would do in America."[24]

Anti-Federalists did not dwell on the navy in opposing the Constitution. In Virginia's ratifying convention in June 1788, William Grayson made a regional argument against the navy, which he believed would be mostly built and equipped in northern states.[25] Patrick Henry, in the same convention, most anticipated the Jeffersonian position. He warned that rather than a government committed to liberty, a permanent army and navy portended an American state "about to convert this country to a powerful and mighty empire." However repellent, the threat of the United States transforming into a British-style imperial power ranked below more immediate Anti-Federalist concerns with the Constitution, particularly its lack of a statement on rights.[26]

In the early 1790s the new government had no immediate need to create a navy as it focused on securing its northwestern borders against the confederated Indian groups of the Ohio River Valley and the Great Lakes. In early 1794, however, the navy reentered the national discourse as the United States came closer to war with Britain than at any other time between the Revolution and the War of 1812. Amid general frustration with Britain's trade restrictions, particularly in the Caribbean, and its ongoing occupation of American northwestern forts and alliance with Native Americans came the news in December 1793 and January 1794 that Algerian pirates had captured eleven American ships and were holding more than one hundred crew members as slaves. The depredations took place after Portugal, at the prompting of Britain, signed a peace treaty with Algiers and removed the blockade that had indirectly protected U.S. shipping.[27]

In the winter of 1794 Congress debated the size of a naval force adequate to protect American shipping against Algerine corsairs. A committee appointed to consider the question recommended in January that six vessels—four frigates of forty-four guns each and two smaller frigates of twenty-four guns each—would be sufficient. In eighteenth-century European navies, frigates usually rated no more than thirty-eight guns. The proposed American "super frigates" of forty-four guns showed awareness, absent during the heady days of the Revolution, that the young country was ill-equipped to build true ships of the line.[28] The proposal still garnered fierce opposition from the emerging Democratic-Republican coalition in Congress. Coming after Hamilton's economic program, a navy seemed the crowning piece of America's transformation in the image of Britain. William Branch Giles, even more Anglophobic than Jefferson or Madison, took the lead in arguing against the bill in Congress. Rather than a measured response to a short-term crisis, Giles argued that the bill provided for "the foundation of a permanent naval establishment." The problem was that "a navy is the most expensive of all means of defence, and the tyranny of Governments consists in the expensiveness of their machinery."[29]

Republicans did not have the votes to defeat the bill, and it became law in March 1794. But Republican opposition to a naval establishment produced an important concession. A clause in the bill called for a stop in the building of the warships in the event of peace with Algiers. As it turned out, the United States reached a treaty with the Algerines in early 1796, and Congress voted to continue with the construction of just two of the forty-fours and one thirty-six-gun frigate. Even these ships would remain unequipped and unmanned, so for the time being at least, the country would not have an active peacetime navy.

The 1794 debate also provided Republicans with an opportunity to rehearse arguments against a naval establishment that they would use up to the War of 1812. Adams claimed in his retirement correspondence with Jefferson that Jefferson had supported the original creation of a navy in 1794, Hamilton had opposed it (presumably out of fear of war with Britain), and President George Washington had been indifferent.[30] Actually, Jefferson, along with Madison and James Monroe, followed the developments in Congress with great concern. Although Jefferson had supported action against the Barbary States a decade earlier and would pursue war against them as president, he thought that the Federalist naval remedy was far more dangerous than the depredations against American shipping. With an army and naval establishment in place, Federalists could follow the British model of securing power indefinitely through patronage and placemen made possible by a continuous supply of war contracts.[31]

The Federalist Anglicizing project culminated in a series of policies connected to the Quasi-War with France between 1798 and 1800. Although less an immediate threat than the buildup of the so-called New Army or the Alien and Sedition Acts, the Federalist expansion of the navy raised the most direct fears that America was becoming Britain. In April 1798 President Adams signed an act establishing the Department of the Navy. The service had been located in the War Department, while the Treasury handled the navy's contracting and disbursing. Now, like the Royal Navy, the U.S. Navy had its own government department for the first time. Benjamin Stoddert, a Maryland merchant who served as secretary to the Continental Board of War during the American Revolution, became the first secretary of the navy. When Stoddert assumed the position in June 1798, only one naval vessel was deployed. By the end of the war, the United States had upward of thirty naval vessels commanded by about seven hundred officers and manned by approximately five thousand seamen. The ships patrolled the southern coast of the United States and the Caribbean, where they engaged primarily with French privateers.[32]

The Republican press responded to the navy's rapid growth with outrage. Benjamin Franklin Bache's *Philadelphia Aurora* led the charge. In June 1798 Bache published a letter that he claimed was from a Virginian in Congress to his constituents. The letter argued that all the country would accomplish with its naval expansion was an increase in debt and taxes without any promise of defeating France. To illustrate the point, the writer anticipated Murrin's approach in "The Great Inversion" by comparing America's position after the Revolution to that of Britain in 1688. Even though Britain's revolution at first appeared promising, the government soon became consumed with "levying standing armies or of building navies, of declaring war, of making distant conquests, and of maintaining distant dependencies." These were all "certain and deficient instruments to work the depression and misery of the mass of a nation, and the irresistible patronage and power of the executive." The United States was following the same path. Worse, the government risked duplicating Britain's cruel mistreatment of its sailors through impressment. The same conditions that made impressment necessary in Britain, high merchant seamen wages compared to much lower pay in the navy, were taking hold in America.[33]

Republicans in Congress used similar arguments to contest the Federalist shipbuilding program. In July 1798 Congress appropriated funds to build and equip the three remaining frigates that had never been completed under the act of 1794. More controversial was Stoddert's proposal in December 1798 to build twelve ships of the line, twelve frigates, and twenty ships of up to twenty-four guns. By February 1799, when the bill was debated in Congress, the total number of ships had been reduced by about half, including six instead of twelve ships of the line. The proposed expansion still horrified Republicans, especially Congressman Albert Gallatin of Pennsylvania, who opposed navies even more than did the two presidents, Jefferson and Madison, for whom he would serve as secretary of the treasury. Gallatin based his position almost entirely on the experience of Britain, arguing that the Royal Navy's costs had nearly ruined the country. The service was a burden to the British taxpayer and an endless source of political corruption and intrigue. For Gallatin, history had shown that "navies were used more as engines of power, than as a protection of commerce." He predicted a grim fate for the United States should it imitate Britain's naval establishment: ruinous debts and taxes, imperiled liberties, and sailors abused by press gangs.[34]

At the height of their power, Federalists in Congress quickly challenged Gallatin's characterization of the Royal Navy's impact on Britain. According to Robert Harper of South Carolina, "Britain is indebted to her navy, not for her commerce only, but for her independence; not only for the dominion of the seas, but for her existence as a nation." Without its navy, Harper continued, Britain "must long since have been a province of France." With the country at war with France, Republicans faced the politically impossible task of convincing a Federalist congressional majority that America's greatest risk was imitating the world's strongest navy. By mid-February 1799 the measure authorizing the construction of six ships of the line, expanding and upgrading smaller vessels in the navy's fleet, and building new naval dockyards became law.[35]

Jefferson and Madison, who was now out of the House of Representatives, watched helplessly as the naval legislation progressed in Congress. In early 1799 Jefferson turned to gallows humor, suggesting that to pay for the expansion of the army and navy, "a tax on air and light is meditated, but

I suppose not till the next session." Less charitably, he blamed Madison for leaving Congress and not doing more to prevent the passage of the Federalist statist agenda. Jefferson implored Madison to publish his notes from the Constitutional Convention, believing that "these measures of the army, navy and direct tax will bring about a revulsion of public sentiment is thought certain, and that the constitution will then receive a different explanation." As a final jab to his junior partner, Jefferson wrote, "[S]omething is required from you as set-off against the sin of your retirement."[36]

Fortunately for Jefferson and Madison, the Republican press more than compensated for the party's weakness in Congress. Newspapers and pamphlets treated the navy's expansion as the clearest signal yet of the Federalist design to rule as a British-style court party through placemen and other dependents. The debt necessary to support the navy would overwhelm the nation's finances and corrupt its political system. Writing to his fellow American citizens from France in March 1799, the poet and diplomat Joel Barlow was typical in identifying the navy as a dangerous "system": "They [the Federalists] have created a new ministerial department adorned with all the pomp of patronage, and ready to contribute its part to the splendor of the Executive and the growth of the public debt." Barlow had no doubt that the Federalists' naval program was "calculated for the destruction of liberty in the United States."[37] By late 1799 Republican critics of the military buildup connected to the Quasi-War had found an unlikely ally, President Adams. He sought to diminish Hamilton's growing influence on the government through his control of the army by acting on intelligence indicating a French willingness to talk; a peace was concluded by September 1800. The negotiations deeply divided the Federalist Party, aiding Jefferson's victory over Adams in the 1800 presidential election.[38]

As for the war, the Republicans' worst fears never came to pass. Contrary to Republican predictions, the American navy suffered only light losses to the French. The service also never resorted to impressment to man its growing number of vessels. In fact a commitment to avoiding compulsory naval service signified the one common precept of de-Anglicization across the American political spectrum. The Federalists continued the British practices of using ship captains and houses of rendezvous to recruit navy seamen but emphasized that the service would accept only volunteers. By the summer of 1798, once the Department of the Navy was in place, Stoddert stressed in recruiting instructions that "no indirect or forcible Measures be used to induce them [sailors] to enter the service."[39] Even amid later recruiting challenges, instructions emphasized, "It being important that those who enlist should feel an Inclination for the service—no indirect means are to be used in inveigle them, and therefore no Individual must be enlisted while in a state of intoxication, nor must he be sworn until 24 hours after signing the enlistment."[40]

The commitment to voluntary service, accomplished with the added challenge of one-year enlistments, was no small achievement. It made the U.S. Navy the only service in the western world, aside from the Dutch, that did not use some form of conscription in naval recruiting. The early American navy was less progressive than other navies, including the British, on matters of race. Stoddert, a slaveholder, tried to bar African Americans from the service, but individual captains ignored the directive, and it disappeared when Stoddert left the navy at the end of the Adams administration.[41]

Jeffersonian Retrenchment

Jefferson began his presidency devoted to undoing, in effect de-Anglicizing, Federalist state-building efforts of the previous twelve years. In early 1800, ticking off parts of the Federalist agenda, Jefferson lamented that "we are running navigation mad, and commerce mad, and navy mad, which is worst of all."[42] By the end of the Quasi-War, the navy indeed had the largest budget in the federal government. As one of his last duties as president and anticipating the coming Republican retrenchment, John Adams in March 1801 signed an act that reduced the navy officer corps and stopped construction of the six ships of the line called for in the naval bill of February 1799. Adams reasoned that the Jeffersonian Republicans would pursue even deeper cuts, and he sought to at least protect the navy's building of smaller frigates. Although Adams read Jefferson's intentions correctly, he vastly underestimated his rival's ambitions. By the end of Jefferson's presidency, the American navy was building no new warships, nor would it until a year *after* the United States declared war on Britain in 1812.[43]

Jefferson's views on naval affairs have long been misunderstood, despite multiple attempts to clarify them. Critics have accused him of everything from naive idealism to shameless hypocrisy. In truth, Jefferson adhered to a consistent republican vision of a navy that departed sharply from the imperial British naval tradition. In seeing the navy as an extension of republicanism, Jefferson's approach paralleled his army policy of drastically downsizing the national force, relying heavily on state militias, and creating a republican officer corps at the new military academy at West Point.[44] He most clearly presented his views on navies in *Notes on the State of Virginia* (1785). Given the association between navies and war, Jefferson stressed the need to break from the European tradition. "To aim at such a navy as the greater nations of Europe possess," according to Jefferson, "would be a foolish and wicked waste of the energies of our countrymen. It would be to pull on our own heads that load of military expense, which makes the European labourer go supperless to bed, and moistens his bread with the sweat of his brows." He concluded that only a small navy could avoid these problems; moreover a smaller force was sufficient given America's geographic isolation from Europe.[45] During his presidency, he would come to define the acceptable range of activities for his small navy. The primary objective was always defense, particularly of the nation's coastline. Jefferson's republicanism also allowed for a handful of larger vessels to defend commerce on the high seas, but not just any commerce. While the president and Treasury Secretary Gallatin supported the naval defense of agricultural exports, they frowned on expending national resources to support the carrying trade and other merchant activity that they deemed unhelpful—and even harmful—to the country's development.[46]

Outside events prevented Jefferson from initially cutting the navy's size as much as he would have liked. In 1801 renewed problems with the Barbary States led him to dispatch a small squadron to the Mediterranean. Tripoli soon declared war on the United States, compelling Jefferson to wage a prolonged overseas war that lasted until 1805. The conflict forced the president to send four consecutive squadrons to the Mediterranean to fight the Tripolitans and later the Moroccans. As a result, he never dismantled the six frigates protected by the legislation at the end of the Adams administration. As in so many areas, Henry Adams accused Jefferson of violating his supposed principles for keeping the navy "maintained and energetically employed." It was true, to Gallatin's constant despair, that Jefferson's two administrations spent far more on the navy than on the army. In promoting agricultural exports, though, the Barbary Wars aligned with his overall republican vision and ideology.[47]

Once the wars wound down, the main features of Jefferson's de-Anglicizing naval policy took shape. In 1805 he started advocating a shift in the navy's resources from frigates and more traditional warships to small gunboats. Each about fifty feet in length, fitted out with oars as well as sails, and armed with one or two medium-sized cannons, the gunboats were suited solely for coastal defense. Jefferson made his strongest case for the gunboats in his February 1807 message to Congress. He fully acknowledged that "this species of naval armament is proposed merely for defensive operations; that it can have but little effect towards protecting our commerce in the open seas, even on our own coast; and still less can it become an excitement to engage in offensive maritime war, towards which it would furnish no means." These apparent shortcomings of gunboats were exactly the point. The vessels' lack of offensive capability ensured that the American service would never be confused as a miniature Royal Navy.[48]

In addition the gunboats had the advantage of being cheap to build. Whereas a medium-sized frigate cost tens of thousands of dollars and a ship of the line hundreds of thousands, a gunboat could be built and outfitted for a few thousand. Congress authorized 25 in 1805, an additional 50 in 1806, and 188 in 1807. Even so, Jefferson's presidency ultimately slashed the annual $3 million naval budget that it inherited from the Adams administration by more than two-thirds. In the "Great Inversion," Murrin put Jeffersonian naval policy in typically memorable terms: "To take a guess, the American navy may not have exceeded the strength of the Tudor fleet of three centuries earlier, despite the fantastic growth of commercial shipping after 1790." It was a strong guess. Although the gunboat initiative made the total number of vessels in the U.S. Navy during the Jefferson and Madison administrations greater than that in the Tudor navy, the total tonnage of the American service was much lower.[49]

Jefferson encountered little resistance to his gunboat policy in the Republican Congress. The only true debate among Republicans was over whether the navy should return to building a small number of warships to deter the Royal Navy from impressing American sailors and interfering with the nation's commercial shipping. Hence, Anglophobia drove both sides of the issue. In the spring of 1806 Jefferson left open the possibility of adding a handful of seventy-four-gun ships of the line to the navy's fleet. Despite receiving support from the influential Republican Matthew Lyon of Kentucky, Congress overwhelmingly rejected the idea. Lyon argued that building just two large warships would not reproduce the worst features of the Royal Navy, particularly impressment. He asked, "Because Britain is obliged to make use of a press-gang to man her fleet, which goes abroad in pursuit of conquests, in which the lives of poor fellows are sported away, who have no interest in the issue, shall it be said that we shall be obliged to press our gallant, our patriotic seamen?" To this question he answered, "No, sir, we can never have occasion to press sailors."[50]

Ironies abounded in the Republican position. By rejecting Lyon's modest proposal, his fellow Republicans essentially chose to continue leaving American sailors unprotected from British impressments rather than risk even the remotest possibility that the U.S. Navy would need to conscript seamen. Moreover, by paring expenses during the Barbary Wars, the Jefferson administration had to reduce seamen's wages, use two-year naval enlistments (instead of one-year enlistments), and resort to greater measures of economic coercion in recruiting, including working directly with landlords in seaport communities, than ever used in the Quasi-War. Over time recruiting sailors to serve on gunboats became especially difficult because of the low wages and tedious work involved in coastal defense. The United States might not have had the men necessary to keep its navy afloat were it not for foreigners. Until the *Chesapeake-Leopard* Affair of June 1807, foreign seamen comprised between 35 and 40 percent of all crew members on American naval vessels, with some ships topping 50 percent. The foreigners came almost exclusively from the British Isles, resulting in a different form of Anglicization of the American service.[51]

Jefferson's Anglophobic naval policy carried over to the Madison administration. When Madison became president in 1809, no new warships had been built since 1806. The U.S. Navy consisted of ten frigates, many rotting from disuse and poor maintenance; two sloops; six brigs; and an assortment of gunboats and schooners. The Republican approach did not change, even as tensions with Britain increased in the years leading up to the War of 1812. The navy did not build a single new warship in preparation for the war.[52]

By comparison, the Royal Navy affirmed its supremacy in the French Revolution and the Napoleonic Wars. Contemporaries often cited the navy's one thousand warships in describing its superiority. The figure was misleading, for nearly a third of the ships were out of service, either in ordinary (being repaired) or still on the stocks (under construction). But the navy's global reach was still impressive. The service stationed fleets at home and in the Mediterranean, blockaded Europe, and patrolled sea lanes to North America, the West Indies, Africa, and the East. The one consolation for Americans was that the British navy could not concentrate all of its might in a single time and place.[53]

One of the longest debates in the War Hawk Congress leading to the War of 1812 concerned the building of new ships. In December 1811 and January

1812 the House of Representatives debated a bill introduced by Langdon Cheves of South Carolina, the new chairman of the House Naval Affairs Committee. Cheves prepared his proposal based on the recommendations of Madison's secretary of the navy, Paul Hamilton, to build twelve seventy-four-gunships of the line, twenty medium-sized frigates, and a variety of smaller vessels in preparation for war with Britain. As Congress debated the naval bill, it also approved and President Madison signed a measure to expand the U.S. Army by twenty-five thousand men, ostensibly to conquer Canada and force Britain to compromise on the maritime issues of impressment and seizing American merchant ships. The most extraordinary feature of the naval debate was that a large number of Republican War Hawks, who enthusiastically supported the expansion of the army, argued against the naval expansion. Their opposition was fueled by the old Jeffersonian fear of a British-style naval establishment taking hold in America. The spirit of de-Anglicization reversed the long-dominant pattern of Anglo-American political thought about military affairs: rather than fear a standing army, which they believed would be temporary, Jeffersonian Republicans opposed a navy because it would likely become permanent.[54]

In introducing his bill in December 1811, Cheves had to overcome several biases among his fellow Republicans. He first had to stress that the U.S. naval expansion would not incur the same costs required to maintain the Royal Navy. "The British Government has never been distinguished, at least not in modern times, for great economy," Cheves acknowledged. Repeating arguments made by Paine and Adams before the Revolution, he emphasized that America's natural resources meant that "ship-building is actually and practically cheaper with us than with them." In addition Cheves dismissed the possibility that the American navy would ever impress seamen. He had to address the ghosts of the Federalist naval expansion of 1798–99. He argued that the navy "was then objected to, not because it was anti-republican in itself, but because the Republicans of that time believed it was to be employed for improper objects." Cheves assured his colleagues that a new Republican navy would not have the same design of continuous war, crippling debt, and ever-increasing taxes.[55]

Opponents of the naval expansion disputed each of Cheves's claims. Adam Seybert of Pennsylvania summarized the opposition in his statement: "Sir, if we follow the British in the principle, we must look for the same results." The results included enormous government expenses and press gangs that would turn American seaports into "constant theatres of riot and debauchery." Most remarkably Seybert contended that the worst outcome would be if the United States proved *successful* in naval warfare: "Naval victories in the end would prove fatal to the United States . . . the public debt will become permanent; direct taxes will be perpetual; the paupers of the country will be increased; the nation will be bankrupt; and, I fear, the tragedy will end in a revolution." Samuel McKee of Kentucky reinforced the point, deeming navies "the vile offspring of those nations where the power and grandeur of the Government is everything, and the people are nothing but slaves!"[56]

By January 1812 supporters of a new shipbuilding program scaled back their ambitions. Cheves modified his original proposal by dropping the ships of the line and reducing the number of new frigates from twenty to ten. The proposed frigates attracted support from a handful of War Hawks, including Henry Clay, on the grounds that American shipping needed some defense against British aggression. Clay urged moderation, observing that "the source of alarm is in ourselves." Maintaining a small navy for defensive purposes would not overturn the Constitution or plunge the country into intractable debt. Other advocates of naval expansion made clear that they detested everything related to Britain. Congressman Robert Wright of Maryland characterized the British as "a band of perjured piratical plunderers, murderers, and sea-robbers" whom he wished "very soon to see chastised by the strong arm of avenging justice." Such anti-British epithets were not enough to convince the majority of Republicans in Congress that expanding the navy would not lead to the re-Anglicization of the American state. As a result Cheves continued to reduce the number of new frigates in the bill, from ten to six and then to five, four, and finally three. Still, the measure did not attract majority support. Exasperated, William Widgery, a Massachusetts Republican, accused the bill's opponents of "*hydrophobia*." "We seem to be like sheep, afraid of the water," he lamented.[57]

The same Congress that would declare war on Britain rejected every proposal to build new ships. Ultimately the body approved only limited naval expenses before the war related to purchasing timber and other raw materials and for repairing the navy's existing frigates, six of which descended from Congress's legislation establishing the navy in 1794. Two of the original forty-four-gun frigates, USS *Constitution* and USS *United States*, won stunning victories in single-ship actions against the British in 1812. In this case America's naval weakness proved to be a strength. The large American frigates, so built in part because of the difficulty of constructing true ships of the line, overwhelmed smaller British counterparts.[58]

America's naval victories in 1812 helped to calm Republican fears of a permanent naval establishment. Congress passed the Naval Act of 1813, which at last provided for the building of new warships: four seventy-four-guns and six forty-fours, at a cost of $2.5 million. Not all Republicans approved. In May 1813 Jefferson wrote to Madison from Monticello to lobby instead for the continued use of gunboats. "No one has been more gratified than myself by the brilliant atchievements of our little navy," Jefferson professed. But, he argued, larger naval vessels "contribute nothing to our defence." For coastal areas, Jefferson still supported "the humble, the ridiculed, but the formidable gun boats."[59]

His argument had merit, as none of the warships approved in 1813 saw service against Britain in the war. Moreover the navy struggled, as Republicans had predicted, to man all its vessels on a voluntary basis. The primary reason was competition from privateers and the army, which lured recruits with large bonuses and land bounties that the navy was not authorized to offer. In the last years of the war, building and manning vessels on the Great Lakes added to the difficulties. In October 1814 the new secretary of the navy, William Jones, implored Madison to cease the building of ships on Lake Ontario. "It must not be forgotten," Jones reminded the president, "that the services of our seamen are entirely voluntary and for which there is no substitute upon any pressing emergency as of militia for regulars." The Republicans' long commitment to de-Anglicizing the U.S. Navy proved detrimental by the end of the War of 1812. The service, with its short-term enlistments and motley assortment of vessels, won victories on the Great Lakes but never matched its early successes on the high seas.[60]

Legacies

The U.S. Navy's victories in the War of 1812 continued to provide the political cover necessary to expand the service in the years immediately following the war. In early February 1815, with rumors of a peace with Britain circulating throughout Washington, Congress passed legislation adding a board of commissioners to help administer the Department of the Navy. The immediate motivation was Secretary Hamilton's inefficient management of the navy, which had contributed to the British ease in burning Washington in August 1814. The measure also reflected abating concern about an Anglicized American state. For the first time since the American Revolution, the

U.S. Navy had an administrative structure that resembled the British Lords of Admiralty.

In April 1816 President Madison signed the "Act for the Gradual Increase of the Navy of the United States." The act authorized the construction of nine ships of the line, twelve heavy frigates, and three steam-driven "batteries." To fund the construction, the law provided $1 million per year for eight years. In creating the permanent naval establishment that they had so long opposed, Republicans finally accepted America's need for naval defense in a dangerous, unpredictable world. In the spring of 1815, following the formal end to the War of 1812, the United States plunged into another conflict with the Barbary States. The Second Barbary War ended by the summer, but not before reminding Americans that Britain was not their only potential global foe. The Republicans' new willingness to accept a naval establishment also contributed to a larger break from their de-Anglicizing agenda. Among other measures after the war, the Fourteenth Congress approved the Second Bank of the United States, maintenance of the army, and a system of internal improvements. The War of 1812 proved a cautionary event for Republicans. They recognized that America might have to be more like Britain, if only to guard its independence from the British and other European powers.[61]

Traditional narratives of the founding of the U.S. Navy often end on the high notes of the War of 1812 and its immediate aftermath. This approach misses the return to naval austerity that soon followed the war. By 1821 Congress had determined that the country's military establishment had become bloated and cut its appropriations. The navy's $1 million annual budget for ship construction shrank to $500,000.[62] Amid the debate on the navy's future, Albert Gallatin, now the U.S. minister to France, reminded his countrymen of why the original Jeffersonian Republicans had so opposed a naval establishment:

> The old republican party . . . of which I had the honor to be a zealous member, generally was . . . opposed to a large naval establishment. The chief grounds of objection [were]
> 1. The mighty patronage given thereby to the executive power, and the raising up of an interest that does not enter into the *common feelings* of the people at large. . . .
> 2. The disposition, created by power, to enter on war. . . .
> 3. The great expense of building and maintaining a navy, and supporting the officers and men.[63]

As in so many areas, Andrew Jackson adopted these Jeffersonian naval principles. In his first inaugural address in 1829, Jackson stated that the United
States had "need of no more ships of war than are requisite to the protection of commerce" and then followed through by further downsizing the service. The size of the U.S. Navy remained trivial by European standards until
the late nineteenth century. Policies that had once been motivated by fear of
becoming Albion became accepted simply as American.[64]

CHAPTER TEN

Anglicization and the American Taxpayer, c. 1763–1815

Anthony M. Joseph

Venturing to find Anglicization in the story of early American taxation might appear a fool's errand. The colonies were lightly taxed, and revolutionary America moved away from any recognizably English model of public finance, as it embraced "Country" ideas over "Court" ones, in John Murrin's "great inversion."[1] America's clear trajectory by 1815 was to establish a low-tax regime that did not replicate England's extensive system of exactions. The present essay affirms this basic narrative but proposes that significant Anglicizing forces were at work in American taxation from the late colonial years through the War of 1812. American taxation before the Revolution had begun to involve the structures and political debates common in England, and during the Revolution the American states experienced an intense fiscal Anglicization as they scrambled to finance a costly war. From 1789 to 1791, however, a new federal Constitution and a new federal fiscal program relieved the Anglicizing pressure hitherto felt in the states. The states "de-Anglicized" as the locus of Anglicization shifted from the "periphery" to a new "center," the federal government. At key moments thereafter, Congress considered implementing direct taxation and on two occasions actually did so. Especially in light of the support that "Country" Jeffersonian Republicans gave to direct taxation, it becomes clear that the tax regime of the United States came closer to being Anglicized in the early years of the young nation than has generally been recognized.

However much the colonial assemblies of British North America would have liked to have been viewed as "little Parliaments," their fiscal policies did not replicate the burgeoning tax regime of the British state. In England three basic types of levies—customs, excise, and land taxes—provided some 90 percent of revenues in the eighteenth century. After 1713 customs and excise generated an increasing portion of revenues as the percentage drawn from the land tax diminished. Warfare repeatedly amplified this fiscal regime. The Seven Years' War nearly doubled England's national debt and more than doubled its annual expenses. The land tax rate, which typically rose in wartime, doubled to four shillings per pound value and after 1763 never returned to its prewar level.[2] No American colony was as burdened by war as the mother country was.

Even so, the American colonies by the eve of the Revolution had introduced taxes in ways strongly suggestive of the fiscal regime in place in England. The case of Massachusetts is probably most telling. The colony had introduced paper money as legal tender in 1690 but abandoned the currency for a specie economy in 1750. The collapse of paper money in Massachusetts aggravated tensions between Boston and rural farmers, and a proposed liquor excise (1754) generated arguments in opposition that echoed those made in England against Walpole's excise two decades earlier. The Seven Years' War left the colony with a debt in excess of £800,000, despite its having levied almost £650,000 in land taxes. The fiscal pressure did not immediately abate at the conclusion of the war. Between 1762 and 1774 Massachusetts levied £449,184 in general taxes. Unlike in England, however, where taxes rose during the Seven Years' War and remained high after, Massachusetts's annual postwar taxes peaked at £50,000 in 1764 and 1765 and declined thereafter, falling to £10,312 in 1774. This divergence does not obscure the fact that Massachusetts had made itself a tax-levying and tax-paying colony along English lines by the eve of the Revolution. As late as 1773 only some £61,723 in taxes remained outstanding from Massachusetts towns—about 14 percent of the total levied. The tax burden was undeniable. "Collecting taxes has laid the foundation for the ruin of many great families," John Adams noted in 1766. He probably referred to the personal liability that tax collectors bore for tax monies, but that liability would not have seemed so hazardous in a lightly taxed society.[3]

Massachusetts's tax regime might seem exceptionally Anglicized, but war had brought similar developments to other colonies. Pennsylvania made effective use of paper money by ensuring that its currency was retired through taxation. From 1755 to 1775 the Pennsylvania Assembly enacted five emissions of paper money backed by a provincial property tax.[4] Pennsylvania's "eighteen-penny" tax on land—eighteen pence per pound assessed value—generated annual revenues ranging from roughly £18,000 to £28,000. The province also collected excise taxes, imposts, and fees for marriage and tavern licenses, but the eighteen-penny tax was Pennsylvania's most substantial levy on the people. By contemporary British standards, of course, Pennsylvania's tax system was small and rudimentary. The eighteen-penny tax amounted to only 7.5 percent of assessed value—as compared to the contemporaneous four-shilling tax (20 percent) on land in England. But the smoothness of tax collection in Pennsylvania suggested room for expansion. Despite complaints about valuations and assessments, compliance was high. By September 1775 only some £2,000 remained in arrears on all the property taxes levied since 1758.[5] Pennsylvania's tax system was operating without fundamental opposition during the twenty years preceding the Revolutionary War. The regularity of tax collection provided a strong cultural and political precedent for a taxpaying citizenry once the Revolutionary War began.

The heavy reliance on land taxes in Massachusetts and Pennsylvania ran counter to the trend in some other colonies, but throughout colonial America there were very English debates and decisions over which kind of levies to enact. New York's great landed families resisted property taxes and, as in England, viewed the land tax as a wartime-only measure. New York relied on import duties to a greater extent than any other colony, especially after its property tax was terminated in 1768. Virginia's House of Burgesses levied in 1755 the colony's first land tax in more than a century. As in New York, however, the tax did not endure—lasting in this case until 1769. Virginia relied most on a tobacco export tax.[6]

Tax regimes varied from colony to colony, with one or more Anglicizing themes present in each, including diversification of tax sources, land-versus-customs/excise debates, and tax increases in wartime. Britain's shouldering of so much of the burdens of war meant that no colony could replicate the recent history of British public finance. Massachusetts probably came closest. Even so, on the eve of the Revolutionary War it would not have been difficult to imagine a rapid fiscal Anglicization if the very source forestalling Anglicization—ironically, the British state itself—were suddenly removed and each colony was made to stand on its own as a sovereign state. The rudiments of English taxation—the basic options, the arguments, the traditions of payment and protest—were all in place by 1776.

The fiscal pressures of the Revolutionary War did indeed rapidly Anglicize state tax regimes. The Patriots could not and would not have fought the

Revolutionary War had it been otherwise. The money simply could not have been generated. The familiar English categories of land taxes, customs, and excises came to dominate the revenue structures of the states.[7] In one respect, moreover, the states became more English than the English, as they were more dependent on direct taxes than England had become. Whereas Virginia, for example, generated 70 percent of its revenue from direct taxes in the mid-1780s, England yielded perhaps only 20 percent from land taxes at that time. Not since the early eighteenth century had England depended as heavily on direct taxes as the American states did as late as 1787.[8]

The extent of tax payment was even more compelling evidence of Anglicization. The familiar story of a war funded with cheap continental paper money on behalf of tax-averse colonists can all too easily obscure the enormous financial contributions Americans made to the revolutionary cause— contributions that have been more fully appreciated in recent scholarship. In state after state, tax levies rose dramatically during the war. In Rhode Island direct taxes rose nearly 300 percent. New Jersey's property tax tripled by the mid-1780s. New York, which had done without direct taxes since 1767, levied $310,000 in direct taxes between 1785 and 1788. By 1781 Massachusetts's state taxes were ten times higher than its provincial taxes had been before the war began.[9]

The introduction of specie taxation during the early 1780s revealed fiscal Anglicization in yet another way. Congress requisitioned from the states taxes in coin to finance its foreign loans, and most states managed to contribute a significant portion of the funds Congress sought. By March 1788 Congress had received from the states more than $3 million in specie—nearly half (48 percent) of the total amount of congressional requisitions since 1781. The case of Pennsylvania is illustrative. By August 1784 Pennsylvanians had contributed $718,385 in coin. Although this was only some 43 percent of the total amount of specie requested, it was an unprecedented contribution from a population accustomed to supplying less than £30,000 annually—and that in paper money—during the last years of the colonial era.[10]

It is true, as Roger H. Brown has shown, that specie taxation was widely resisted and after a few years state taxes once more became payable in paper. Shays's Rebellion (1786–87) brought an abrupt halt to specie taxation in Massachusetts. In Pennsylvania resistance was not concentrated in a single, massive act of violence but scattered among various forms of noncompliance: taxpayers blocking assessments, assessors failing to submit returns, collectors declining to sue delinquents, communities arranging not to bid at sheriffs' auctions. In 1784 state treasurer David Rittenhouse reported "almost a total stop in the Collecting of Taxes." "We have miscalculated the abilities of the country," acknowledged Joseph Reed, president of the Supreme Executive Council, "and entirely the disposition of the people to bear taxes in the necessary extent." In 1785 Pennsylvania returned to paper money taxation, levying an annual "funding tax." Immediately tempers cooled and compliance rose. The funding tax continued to be levied through 1789, and by the end of 1792 roughly 85 percent of the entire amount, £384,729, had been paid in. Other states had similar experiences.[11]

Nonetheless, the rise and fall of state specie taxation should be considered part of more than one story. This is certainly a case where we must see the glass as half full. Specie was scarce in eighteenth-century America. Congress requisitioned specie taxes more according to its own need for coin than according to the citizens' ability to pay. That there should have arisen such a large gap between the one and the other should not surprise us. One must keep in view the 48 percent collected at least long enough to recognize a political culture pushing itself, from one state to the next, to be what it as yet lacked the financial wherewithal to be. By the mid-1780s the states were still taxing heavily in paper money and remained well positioned to pursue aggressive tax regimes. They could have paid off their own war debts and proportionate shares of the national debt using the tax practices they had become familiar with before 1776 and after.

Only the coming of the new Constitution and the establishment of the federal government truly de-Anglicized state tax regimes. During the debate on ratification of the Constitution, the Pennsylvania Federalist James Wilson had predicted that Pennsylvania's funding tax "must naturally expire" when a "competent and energetic foederal system shall be substituted."[12] Anti-Federalists feared that such a substitution would "annihilate" the state governments. They argued that Congress could levy taxes so high as to leave the state governments with no practicable objects of taxation for themselves. Federalists did not accept the notion that one taxing sovereign necessarily dislodged another in this way. But in 1790 the Anti-Federalists' fears did begin to be realized. Congress enacted Secretary of the Treasury Alexander Hamilton's fiscal program, whereby the federal government refinanced its war debt and assumed the war debts of the states. The Pennsylvania Assembly promptly repealed its annual funding tax, over the objections of its Anti-Federalist minority.[13] The state would remain without a tax on real or personal property for the next four decades.

Pennsylvania was far from alone. Federal assumption of state debts had a huge impact on state tax regimes. The Anglicizing pressure on state finance that had grown so intense in the Revolutionary War years was now suddenly, dramatically relieved. The tax regimes of the states shrank to pre–Revolutionary War—even pre–Seven Years' War—size and became, when viewed as policies of supposedly sovereign states, almost unrecognizably *un-English*. In state after state, direct taxes were either eliminated or greatly reduced. New York and Pennsylvania eliminated direct taxes altogether. New York resumed taxing property briefly from 1799 to 1801, intermittently between 1814 and 1826, and then not at all again until 1842. In New Hampshire, Rhode Island, Connecticut, New Jersey, and Delaware, state legislatures reduced direct taxes precipitously and in some years did not levy them at all. Massachusetts remained the most Anglicized fiscal state in the new Union. Its direct taxes were higher in 1795 than they had been when the national government had gone into operation in 1789. From the available evidence, we cannot say this about any other state. Even so, Massachusetts's state tax on property and polls settled at roughly $133,000 in 1795 and remained at that level until 1820. From 1794 to 1825 the state's total government expenditures were also more or less constant. Taken together, the northern states experienced a 77 percent reduction in their per capita tax burden. In the South the same phenomena can be observed. Every southern state abolished or very nearly abolished the poll tax for whites. Taxes on slaves declined precipitously, as did land taxes.[14]

Were the states simply reverting to type? As colonies their taxes had risen during the Seven Years' War and then diminished in the years that followed. Were they behaving the same way after the Revolutionary War? Not exactly. In some states legislatures introduced lighter tax regimes than had been in place in the colonial period. Pennsylvania had levied state property taxes from 1755 to 1775. Its elimination of direct taxes in 1790 constituted rather more than a return to a status quo antebellum. Moreover reversion-to-type historical explanations can obscure the actual history that took place while the supposed reversion was in progress. After all, the road back to a default setting, or to some "square one," can be long and winding. The newly sovereign states' contraction of their fiscal regimes down to colonial size involved a massive ideological concession. In the colonial era, the assemblies had claimed to be "little Parliaments." In the post–Revolutionary War era, the state legislatures abandoned not simply the words but also the substance of that claim. The states passed off fiscal responsibility to the United

States Congress. Henceforth Congress would be the only potential American equivalent to Parliament. Congress would become the locus of fiscal Anglicization, if any was to occur after 1789.

After 1789 the story would seem to be a familiar one: the Federalists of the 1790s favored taxation as part of an "energetic" national government, but then their agenda was undone by the electoral victory of the Jeffersonian Republicans in 1800–1801. What actually transpired, however, was rather different. The Federalists were less favorable toward taxation than has been supposed, and the Republicans were more so. By the early nineteenth century it was clear that the federal government would not introduce a tax regime along British lines. On the contrary, it would support a low-tax regime unknown to Britain. But the United States did not get to this "Country" outcome by a clean, direct route. At times American policy seemed poised for a fiscal Anglicization that would pick up where the states had left off.

Perhaps there was no greater force for Anglicization at the national level than Alexander Hamilton. Hamilton preferred a tax regime that downplayed direct taxation, just as Britain did, leaving land taxes for times of war.[15] Hence his fiscal program was heavily weighted toward customs duties, and by the mid-1790s customs duties would generate some 94 percent of federal revenues. A set of excise taxes supplied the remainder. Neither Hamilton nor the Federalist legislators who approved the program appear to have greatly overstepped public opinion. Taxpayer compliance was high. In the Anglo-American tradition, customs duties were viewed as the mildest form of tax because their ultimate payers in effect self-selected by choosing whether to purchase the items taxed. Not surprisingly, the customs duties were collected with little friction. But even the more intrusive excise taxes faired surprisingly well in a country lately in revolt against parliamentary taxation. The "whiskey" excise of 1791 was resisted in western Pennsylvania and in other frontier communities, but elsewhere the excises appear to have been accepted. Receipts on all the internal taxes rose steadily during the 1790s, from roughly $209,000 in 1792 to some $779,000 in 1799. Perhaps 80 percent of the taxes were being paid by the end of the decade.[16]

Hamilton's program, though far from a full replication of the British practice, should not be viewed in isolation from another Anglicizing tendency that became evident soon after the program was implemented. By the mid-1790s, as direct taxation was collapsing in the states, Congress readily considered it at the federal level. In 1796 Congress proposed a direct tax to make up for an expected shortfall in the federal budget. The debate that ensued showed that English understandings of taxation had permeated the entire American political spectrum. From the first a number of Federalists stated their preference for indirect taxation and insisted that direct taxes ought to be levied only in case of war or extreme necessity. The Republican Albert Gallatin, by contrast, became an early spokesman for the view that, as America's wealth lay chiefly in land, land ought to be taxed. Neither viewpoint was far from the English experience. Both Gallatin and the Federalists gave a role for direct taxation in a healthy tax regime.[17]

That role seemed even more pronounced the following year. Faced with another projected budget shortfall, Congress considered a permanent annual direct tax on land and slaves amounting to $1,484,000. In the debate on the measure, Republicans were among the strongest advocates of the tax. They argued, among other points, that the United States was dangerously dependent on customs revenues that could be cut short in the event of war; that equity required landowners to bear a share of the burden of government expenses; and that direct taxation had to be resorted to because there were no further objects of indirect taxation available. In addition to Albert Gallatin, Republicans such as William Findley, who represented Pennsylvania counties involved in the Whiskey Rebellion, stated their support of the direct tax on principle. Although his own property and that of his constituents was in land, Findley noted, "[W]e think [a direct tax] preferable to an indirect tax"; a direct tax was necessary "to equalize the taxes." Republican John Swanwick of Philadelphia lamented that the United States had not adopted a direct tax sooner. New England Federalists, meanwhile, formed the strongest bloc of opposition to the direct tax. Fisher Ames believed that a land tax was a government's "only safe resource" in time of war and preferred to see the collection of the existing taxes improved and the number of taxed objects extended. He also wished to see "the public mind . . . prepared for a land tax before it is imposed." The greatest objection New England Federalists made to the tax, however, was that the apportionment of the states' quotas according to the population figures of the 1790 census would leave their states overtaxed. Allowing for a new enumeration, Zephaniah Swift of Connecticut argued, would make the tax "more agreeable to a great many members who would object to vote for it in its present form."[18] The resolution for the direct tax passed with strong Republican support and with Federalists about evenly divided. The measure languished because federal revenues for 1796 proved greater than expected.

For congressional consideration of a direct tax, the third year proved the charm. In 1798, as conflict with France escalated into war, Federalists unanimously supported a one-year direct tax on houses, slaves, and lands. Republicans now were about evenly divided. Albert Gallatin, accused of inconsistency for his opposition to the measure, argued that the tax was not fiscally necessary and that the Federalist case for it—"invasion, the fate of Venice, divisions at home, weakness, &c."—would apply to "everything and nothing."[19] Republicans associated the direct tax with the Federalist-led war against France, Federalists' plans for military expansion, and the hated Alien and Sedition Acts. Already criticized for the whiskey excise, the Federalists thus became pegged as the party of oppressive taxation. Jefferson, as vice president, had proposed a land tax for 1798, but once the direct tax of 1798 passed, he relished the prospect that it would excite "the public mind" against the whole Federalist program of that year.[20]

The direct tax of 1798 had that political effect, but it was collected about as efficiently as the excise taxes had been. Levied on lands, houses, and slaves, the tax amounted to $2 million, apportioned in quotas among the states. Assessment was resisted in Fries's Rebellion (1799), but that opposition was not representative of the general response. Over the next two years, receipts flowed into the federal treasury. The hardships of direct taxation during the Revolutionary War seemed to fade like a meaningless dream as Americans ponied up. By November 1803 some 83 percent of the levy had been satisfied—a collection rate comparable to rates on federal income taxes today. When Treasury Secretary Oliver Wolcott noted in 1799 that the direct tax had received "as little opposition as I expected," he reflected more than the limited reach of Fries's Rebellion.[21] He pointed to a hitherto untapped reserve of tax revenue whose existence most Americans acknowledged and accepted.

Among politicians the tax debates of the 1790s revealed the ideological proximity of both parties to direct taxation and placed both within an English spectrum of political values. The debates also showed how readily the perception of a tax changed according to its context. Republicans' regard for equity compelled them to support the direct tax of 1797; their objections to Federalist foreign policy compelled them to reject the direct tax of 1798. Indeed in the fallout from the Federalist legislation of 1798, petitions and congressional debate focused much more on the Alien and Sedition Acts than on the direct tax. In the political equations of the early Republic, taxation was not always—perhaps not even usually—an independent variable. It took on the value, the meaning, the hue of other contextualizing issues that carried greater ideological force. The Jeffersonian Republican "Country" tradition proved to be not unalterably antitax. If the circumstances were ideologically appropriate, the Republicans could favor taxation even when Federalists did not.

The same pattern manifested itself after the Republicans gained control of the federal government in 1800–1801. Republicans did not again propose a direct tax in peacetime, as they had in the mid-1790s, but when war with Britain broke out in 1812, they acted like Anglicizers. Initially, Republicans hesitated to tax on account of the war. Distrust of Albert Gallatin, now secretary of the treasury, was one cause of the delay. Many Republicans suspected him of trying to derail the movement for a war against Britain by exaggerating its probable cost. And the government's books actually balanced out for 1812. But when in early 1813 it became unmistakably clear that fresh taxes were necessary, Republicans enacted them. The new taxes amounted to $5.5 million and included a duty on imported salt, a variety of excise taxes, and a direct tax on land, houses, and slaves. The direct tax alone amounted to $3 million. Employing a modified requisition system, the act permitted each state to raise its quota of the direct tax as it saw fit and promised reductions for states that made their deposits early. Only in those states that did not supply their own quotas would the federal government itself collect the tax.[22]

The modified requisition system went a great way toward resolving one of the central problems of American federalism that stretched back to the colonial period. How could a central government insure sufficient revenues without greatly weakening the powers of local governments? During the Seven Years' War, the British had settled on a requisition system that offered colonies partial reimbursement in specie for the war expenses they incurred.[23] After that war Parliament precipitated the pre–Revolutionary War crisis by abandoning the requisition principle and attempting to tax the colonists directly. During the Revolution the Continental Congress, powerless to tax directly, worked the other extreme by relying entirely on requisitions from the states. Despite the fiscal shortcomings of that method, Anti-Federalists arguing against ratification of the United States Constitution defended the requisition system as an alternative to the power of direct taxation the Constitution granted to Congress. Several of the ratifying conventions, in fact, had proposed an amendment to the Constitution requiring the system.[24] Their argument failed, and the first federal direct tax under the new regime, the tax of 1798, gave state governments no role in assessment or collection. Only in 1813 did Americans become subject to direct taxation that did not fully conform to either a requisition or traditional direct tax model. The modified requisition system employed during the War of 1812 effectively satisfied both state and federal interests. By all appearances the system performed superbly. It resolved the problem of federalism by giving the states an important role in determining how and even whether their citizens would be subject to federal tax collection.

Quite apart from the efficacy of the system, of course, many Republicans had supported taxation since the war's beginning and believed that Americans were both willing and able to bear a heavy tax burden for the cause. In a letter to Jefferson, James Monroe insisted that America's resources were abundant and her people "patriotic & virtuous, & willing to support the war." Some legislators from western states claimed that their constituents were *"eager* to be taxed." The results of the congressional elections of 1814, which followed enactment of the new taxes, did not prove anything different. The Republicans preserved their majorities in both chambers, increasing their presence slightly in the House of Representatives and suffering only a modest loss in the Senate.[25]

Collection rates also supported the protax Republican position. By the end of 1815 some 98 percent of the direct tax had been collected. Meanwhile, Congress levied another direct tax in the amount of $6 million. To be collected annually, this was the first permanent direct tax in the history of the United States government. But the American taxpayer hardly skipped a beat. Only four states supplied their own quotas, but within two years over 90 percent of the levy for 1815 had been paid in. In 1816 a third and final direct tax, a one-year levy of $3 million, replaced the annual levy of the preceding year. By November 1818 over 92 percent of the tax of 1816 had been paid in. "Almost everything is taxed which can be thought of," reported Daniel Webster in 1815. And with good reason President James Madison encouraged Congress to trust that the people would "cheerfully and proudly bear every burden of every kind which the safety and honor of the nation demand. We have seen them every where paying their taxes, direct and indirect, with the greatest promptness and alacrity."[26]

Direct taxation came to an end soon after the War of 1812 did. The direct tax of 1816 had no successor, and the numerous indirect taxes introduced during the war were repealed at one swipe in 1817.[27] But the war levies proved that Americans were willing to tax and be taxed if the cause was politically correct. There was a familiar Englishness to America's war taxation, both in 1798 and from 1812 to 1816. America had become a nation capable of sustaining significant taxation. After the intense Anglicization of the Revolutionary War years and then the rapid de-Anglicization of state finance, the federal government showed that it could employ the full range of tools available to British public finance.

Even so, the United States did not re-create the British fiscal regime. Its comparatively light federal taxes supported comparatively modest federal expenditures. The young United States was not burdened, as Britain was, with a massive civil list and a war debt accumulated over the course of a century. American legislators could afford to choose which elements of the British system to adopt and which to leave on the other side of the Atlantic. In addition American voters, though not reflexively antitax, knew that their legislators had that freedom, and they expected them to exercise it. The outcome was a federal tax regime that transferred the burden of military defense from the periphery to the center but did not greatly add to that burden. Indeed the federal tax regime substantially released state governments from the need to tax their own residents.

The British state, as things turned out, was capable of similar flexibility under similar circumstances. This becomes clear when we note what the British undertook in Canada after the Revolutionary War. Parliament established for Canada a tax regime that resembled the one Congress adopted for the United States: a low-tax periphery sustained by a central treasury.

From the constitutional point of view, British rule in Canada in the aftermath of the Revolutionary War was a massive exercise in Anglicization. Under the Canada Constitutional Act of 1791, Parliament divided the province of Quebec into Lower Canada, predominantly inhabited by French-speaking inhabitants, and Upper Canada, largely occupied by English speakers. A governor general based in Quebec City exercised military authority over both provinces, while a lieutenant governor acted as executive in Upper Canada alone. To preempt republican and revolutionary sentiments, Parliament granted an elective assembly and appointive council to each province; French-speaking Canadians would have legislative representation for the first time. In Upper Canada, however, the lieutenant governor effectively controlled the assembly (initially boasting only sixteen members) through patronage. Plural officeholding extended beyond militia officers and justices of the peace to executive and judicial positions at the highest levels. Over the next half-century, not surprisingly, only two Upper Canadian assemblies would take a course in opposition to the government.[28] In these essentials Parliament consciously replicated Britain's vaunted "mixed constitution" in a colonial setting.

But Canada's Anglicized constitutional order was not accompanied by an Anglicized system of public finance. The act of 1791 included Parliament's 1778 statutory commitment not to tax Britain's North American colonies except for the regulation of trade. Instead of taxing Canada, Parliament subsidized it. The British fiscal regime—that old, debt-burdened workhorse—made this possible. In the mid-1790s the Crown spent more than £57,000 sterling per year on Upper Canada's military defense, Indian relations, and judicial and executive salaries. These expenditures echoed the intentions of the Stamp Act (1765) and Townshend Duties (1767): to support Britain's military and diplomatic goals in North America; and to wean royal officers from dependence on local assemblies for their salaries. As late as 1808 Upper Canada's local revenue amounted to only £3,000.[29]

Canadians lauded the liberty and light taxation of their regime. An Upper Canadian legislative report of 1838 remarked that the 1791 act created a constitution "modelled on that of Great Britain" and praised British rule for its "love of liberty" and "generous policy"—the noblest "ever exhibited by a nation towards any of its Colonies." The many natural blessings of Canada could be "enjoyed without taxation—that deserves the name of a burthen—and which, trifling as it is, is applied exclusively to the necessary support of the Government, and the improvement of internal communication." Canada was "protected from foreign invasion without cost, by the fleets and armies of the United Kingdom."[30]

Canada, as much as the United States, revealed the limits of fiscal Anglicization in the North American setting. Parliament never made any North American colony a "little England" with respect to taxation. Nor did any colonial or state government do so. The periphery, in short, never became a long-term locus of fiscal Anglicization—neither when a colony remained a colony (as in Canada) nor when it became a state (as in the United States). In each case the costs of the periphery were borne by the center. We can point to various factors that contributed to this outcome, but perhaps most important was the participation of a center that was willing and able to foot the bill. The states of the revolutionary era are a clear example of how rapidly a periphery could be fiscally Anglicized when it has rejected one center without immediately being buttressed by another. Only the establishment in 1789 of a new central government for the United States permitted the restoration and fuller elaboration of the low-tax, lightly Anglicized regimes the states had enjoyed as colonies under British rule.

Anglicization Reconsidered

Ignacio Gallup-Diaz

Anglicization wields its explanatory power through an attention to both the general and the specific, incorporating an analysis of macrolevel themes and structures while at the same time exploring action on the microlevel, the arena of contingent events and face-to-face interactions. This essay explores how it balances structural mechanisms with the unpredictable motivations of individuals and the manner in which it is both relativistic and naturally transatlantic. Anglicization, a concept most often associated with the realms of political history and political economy, is placed beside recent philosophical and anthropological examinations of empire that place personal enactments of identity at the core of their interpretations, and the juxtaposition is found to be both apt and evocative for continued interdisciplinary research.

Initial Conditions and Regional Diversity

Although concerned with the integrating power of a centralizing state, Anglicization is structurally predicated upon the fact that Britons migrating to the Americas were leaving an England that had yet to attain the status of a strong, centralizing, bureaucratic state. In what might appear to be a paradox, centralization at the core *followed* activity by Britons on the periphery rather than preceding it. In peopling the Americas, the English traced out a spectrum of settlement, with migrants coming to occupy a series of diverse environments in separate climatic zones. In addition, the differing backgrounds of the settlers, coupled with variation of peoples and polities within Great

Britain, resulted in the formation of new societies displaying varied levels of regional, economic, and social distinctiveness. Rather than serving as an explanatory cudgel that effaces these differences, Anglicization explores and sets out to explain mechanisms that undergirded the broad diversity of the colonial experience in the Americas.

This attention to regions, and the differences that followed from their distinct economic and social systems, enables scholars of early American history to explain developments in the eighteenth-century British Empire in all of their particularity while also articulating the presence and importance of deep structural elements. For example, actions taken by imperial planners at the center, such as the imposition of rules designed to establish a regulated imperial market, were received with variation throughout the colonies. However, over time, pressure radiating out from the center led the colonies into closer line with one another: one empire, under the Navigation Acts.

Simon Newman's chapter in this book, "'In Great Slavery and Bondage': White Labor and the Development of Plantation Slavery in British America," provides a careful examination of the power exerted by initial conditions, exploring how the slave labor system that emerged in the Caribbean and the southern colonies drew upon long-standing forms of bonded labor practiced within England. Attuned to how the system emerged through an interplay of these initial conditions, Newman further explains how the labor system spread throughout the southern zone of the English empire. The empire was the reason for the labor regime's existence and refinement, while also serving as the vehicle through which it was propagated.

Anglicization explains how a multiplicity of colonial policies, local economic processes, and individual motives interacted and reinforced one another. The concept is powerful not because of any ability to predict or foretell; it does not set out to codify any iron laws of historical development. In privileging an analysis that explores local conditions and developments, it displays the links between central planners, elites in the colonies, and people on the peripheries. Anglicization's power rests in its ability to encompass and embrace diverse developments across the continent and, rather than homogenize these experiences, explain how the varied colonies were influenced by common administrative, political, and social processes while still retaining distinctive elements that set them apart.

As William Howard Carter's chapter, "Anglicizing the League: The Writing of Cadwallader Colden's *History of the Five Indian Nations*," shows, some of the local distinctions embedded within the British Empire could be quite dramatic. Carter displays the tensions that developed between the imperial center, colonial societies, and their agents in the Americas. On the frontiers indigenous communities were accepted as necessary allies against common enemies, and the need for alliances forced Englishmen to come to grips with the reality that shared goals and coordination of effort might occur with indigenous peoples who refused to accept or adopt British norms of governance and behavior. In what might be termed an *apparent* paradox, the Anglicizing empire could incorporate structural relationships with indigenous communities that rejected or parried moves to force their Europeanization.

The imperial center crafted, imposed, and refined a set of policies enabled by the emergence of a strong central government in the United Kingdom after 1707 (a process facilitated by the harnessing of colonial wealth). These policies aimed to exclude foreign merchants from colonial trade and establish London as market center and entrepôt. Anglicization itself was not a conscious policy; nor was it a directive that had the result of compelling individual settlers or colonies toward a specific cultural ideal. Rather it *emerged* as a result of the process through which colonial policies enacted by the centralizing state created lines of force that counteracted the above-mentioned trends toward continuing local diversification.

The colonies in the Americas might have experienced increasing social, economic, and cultural differentiation were it not for a nexus of developments at the core: the colonies were brought into the orbit of an expanding centralizing state. However, although powerful, this state was not a totalizing monolith: elites and political actors in places as disparate as Massachusetts and Virginia expressed and retained a measure of economic, political, and social autonomy. Virginians were not encouraged to adopt New England forms of land tenure or local government after the Glorious Revolution, nor were New Englanders encouraged to grow tobacco.

Andrew Shankman's chapter, "A Synthesis Useful and Compelling: Anglicization and the Achievement of John M. Murrin," makes clear that the Navigation Acts, refined and strengthened over time, emerged as one of the state's prime mechanisms for regulating the colonial economy. However, although the acts enumerated staple products from across the spectrum of agricultural, maritime, and commercial activity in the Americas, they steered income to the Crown by exacting duties on existing economic activity rather than encouraging or coercing the colonists to change their activities or follow new paths.[1] The imperial planners of post-Union Britain were forced to recognize that the problem they needed to solve so that they might most advantageously

manage the empire was how to strike a proper balance between local autonomy and central power. As a framework for historical analysis, Anglicization
derives its explanatory strength from its own ability to keep the macro- and
microlevels of analysis in conversation with one another.

Multiple Perspectives, Disruptions, and Continuities

Although Anglicization is centered on understanding the British experience
in the eighteenth century, it does so by asking scholars to embrace multiple
perspectives. In another apparent paradox, Anglicization derives its power
through a keen awareness of other empires, other histories, and other experiences rather than through a narrow focus on the English world. Writing
histories that encompass these connections can be effected through a variety
of forms, with narrative being one of them. Although the discipline of history has rejected *master narratives*, those problematic overarching descriptions of the actions of peoples thought so all-encompassing that all known or
knowable facts could be made to fit into them, we have not rejected narrative
forms altogether. In fact, narrative might be one of the best forms that can be
deployed to analyze and describe processes of such extensive scope.[2]

For example, from one perspective the eighteenth-century British Empire
might look like chaos: a welter of competing self-interested local elites. From
another, it could be described as undergoing a process of centralization, with
a bureaucracy and military tightening the state's hold on power. Although
either interpretation could be made to fit, this does not mean that historians are powerless to judge between them. Anglicization guides us to analyze
events and processes within a relativistic framework, to find a meaningful
way in which both interpretations might hold true. By positing multiple
sites of social, economic, and political power, the concept explores how they
might overlap, contend with, or reinforce one another. The vehicle of narrative enables context and analysis to be brought to bear upon the complex
way in which power was accrued and wielded in the empire. Most important,
narrative allows scholars to bring into the frame multiple points of vantage,
avoiding the myopia or tunnel vision that can sometimes be expressed by
contemporary figures making observations in the primary sources.

In his essay "Political Development," John M. Murrin charted a scholarly
path between Bernard Bailyn (ideologies of resistance to the state) and Jack
P. Greene (legislative languages of obstruction and the accretion of rights

and privileges). Murrin argued that taking into account the scholar's primary source perspective—the way in which particular bodies of sources can direct researchers almost inexorably to certain kinds of answers to the questions at hand—was the key to bringing into harmony a set of discordant interpretations that had emerged out of the study of political contestation between local elites and the imperial center in London.[3]

The empire was *both* orderly and chaotic, and Anglicization allows scholars to understand that the settlement that followed the Glorious Revolution allowed for both tendencies to flourish. The emergence of institutional spaces for a loyal opposition in British politics allowed mechanisms for opposition to government policies to be expressed in Parliament (ministerial review, impeachment) and in the popular press. In addition, the emergence of party politics provided the opportunity for elites in individual colonies to interact with London-based factions.

Whether pleased with affairs or upset by them, one could find a natural group in Parliament with which to align. Colonial elites, merchants, families, and factors representing specific economic pursuits and interests found ways to use these mechanisms to their advantage. In this they were not unique; merchants, families, and factors without colonial connections were doing the same kinds of things in the mother country. Most importantly, developments in England, and, after 1707, in Great Britain, made possible the growth of transatlantic institutions that were inhabited by and made use of by a transoceanic elite. These connections and institutions became the sinews of Anglicization. It becomes clear that, rather than being relegated to the colonies, the process was driven by changes experienced by the British world as a whole, in London as well as in New York or Boston.

The concept of Anglicization relies on, and draws attention to, the presence of mixed initial conditions, competing motives, and divergent outcomes. It allows scholars to explain the manner in which quite unpredictable (and unwelcome) results emanated from a set of initial processes and decisions. Although it posits a dynamic system that produced remarkable stability, it also encompasses the tensions created by increasing central engagement in colonial affairs and the series of crises that characterized the close of the first imperial age after 1750. Nancy Rhoden's chapter, "Anglicanism, Dissent, and Toleration in Eighteenth-Century British Colonies," and Jeremy Stern's, "Anglicization Against the Empire: Revolutionary Ideas and Identity in Townshend Crisis Massachusetts," illustrate the levels and kinds of counterpressure that could be exerted by local elites from varied backgrounds and colonies as they came to feel confined by the structures (and dictates) of the empire that had fostered their development.

Denver Brunsman's "De-Anglicization: The Jeffersonian Attack on an American Naval Establishment" and Anthony Joseph's "Anglicization and the American Taxpayer, c. 1763–1815" make clear that the continuing legacies of Anglicization were strongly felt in the early American Republic, as the leaders of the new nation both managed international relations with Great Britain and worked to channel and mitigate the effects of (what appeared to some to be) lingering relics of the imperial system. As Shankman's essay makes evident, fiscal arrangements, customs duties, and taxation were major structural levers deployed by the centralizing state in managing the empire; the Anglicizing state was a fiscal-military entity. Therefore it should be no surprise that the transition from empire to nation-state would be attended by ideological conflict and redefinition around these specific elements.

David Silverman's "Racial Walls: Race and the Emergence of American White Nationalism" and Geoffrey Plank's "A Medieval Response to a Wilderness Need: Anglicizing Warfare in Colonial America" explore deep continuities that were fostered in colonial spaces. In the midst of the divisive effects that development of distinct local economies and divergent social systems might have exerted, Silverman sees the imperial system fostering a unitary racial ideology among those varied communities in the Americas. Plank shows how the demands of war making compelled the imperial state to work to replicate innovations in the realms of military organization and strategy, deploying them throughout the colonies in as uniform a way as they were able. Imperial conflict would make planners at the center see that the goal of bringing the far corners of the realm into too-close alignment with the center might be easier to plan than it would be to bring into effect, something experienced by prior empires, from Rome to the Spanish.

The Empire as a Multinodal Network

Anglicization explains the biggest of big-picture questions: how a geographically dispersed collection of colonies exploiting different staple goods and labor regimes were more closely knit together to generate wealth for the mother country. Due to competition with the Dutch and later the French monarchy, the English state after 1688 developed and deployed powerful levers of centralization: a national bank, a funded debt, cabinet government, political parties, and the elements of legislative government that we call parliamentary supremacy. At the same time, the state balanced local interests and devolved a modicum of power to local institutions and figures of importance in the county communities.

In acknowledging that the center was itself undergoing radical change as it in turn effected change in the colonies, Anglicization is transatlantic at its heart. The concept emerged through John Murrin's engagement with the work of George Louis Beer, Viola Florence Barnes, Herbert Levi Osgood, and Charles McLean Andrews.[4] Andrews's scholarship has been especially influential in the field of colonial American studies; he argued for a turn to the sources and resources of the center in London in order to illuminate the study of the American colonies.

Andrews's work and approach are necessary precursors to the concept of Anglicization. However, as Richard R. Johnson has made clear, Andrews clearly thought that the center of gravity for understanding the development of American colonial history firmly resided in London.[5] In addition he thought and wrote in terms of what might be termed impersonal institutional developments. For example, he never published an essay about an individual, and Bacon's Rebellion and King Philip's War receive single-page treatments in his multivolume history of the colonial period.

Andrews avoided personal(ized) narratives because he desired to free the history of the colonial period from narratives steeped in problematic hero worship and partial truth that described the period as predicated upon the actions of a few great men. In order to avoid these problems, Andrews focused on deep structural elements that had taken time to evolve and that he assumed were not the purview of individuals. Individuals were shaped by them, rather than directing or shaping them. In contrast to Andrews's work, Murrin's essays and lectures display a delight in finding and telling the stories of individuals—with all of their foibles, vanities, peculiarities, and motivations.[6]

In telling these stories, Murrin illustrates how studying the past on the level of individual actions can overturn scholarly preconceptions about period, place, or religion, and his work directs us to understand the big picture at the same time that we scrupulously engage in site-specific research and analysis. Understanding the general frame is important not because it predicts all behaviors or allows us to explain all according to a specific model. Rather, Anglicization allows researchers to understand the range of reactions and motivations that individuals were free to explore, engage in, and express.

While Andrews's work and approach were necessary preconditions for the development of Anglicization, John Murrin went further in two ways: he placed London under the same forces of change that the colonies were experiencing; and he brought the periphery more squarely into the frame of analysis. Whereas Andrews established a dualistic "core-dependency" model of the English world, in Murrin's work it emerges as a multinodal network.

Empire Requires Daily Practice(s)

Anglicization, strongly associated with the fields of political history and political economy, can effectively be linked to several powerful strands of thought that have emerged through the study of the anthropology of empire. Several scholars have written about how the acquisition of certain trade goods, everyday items, and luxury goods enforced or reinforced a sense of common Englishness.[7] The consumption of a set of commonly available items allowed for peoples separated by space to share and express a common identity. While consumption and trade goods are indeed a part of the process of Anglicization, the concept also encompasses processes of daily action, regularized behavior, and the mundane structured interactions that became part of how subjects in the Americas made adjustments to empire, to use Johnson's term.[8] Anglicization shares intellectual kinship with the study of religious ceremony in early modern England, slave experiences in the Spanish world, and the integration of allied indigenous leaders and communities on imperial frontiers.

In their studies of seventeenth-century religion, Peter Lake, Kenneth Fincham, and Michael Questier have described the importance that certain churchmen placed on establishing a set of regularized, structured behaviors they considered crucially important to the faith they upheld.[9] What some saw as the trappings of popish ceremony were in the eyes of these churchmen elements well suited to guide the behavior of the faithful. Ritualized action ensured that people worshiped and embodied the faith in ways that were proper and guided and trained those who followed them to act in the manner that true believers did. By being steered to simulate the actions of faithful believers, the worshipers would in effect be(come) bona fide true believers.

Similarly, in his studies of slaves in Spanish colonial society, Herman Bennett explores the manner in which slaves were forced to engage in regulated, patterned, and guided behaviors in their communities.[10] In addition elements of local custom and practice might allow for the expression of a range of unregulated behaviors in particular communities and localities. The combination of these forced/unforced elements set the parameters for local behavior, and in their totality they reflected the character of a particular slave community. Consequently local particularities make broad generalizations about a (single) slave experience in the Americas impossible to sustain. Although slavery might have possessed a unitary legal definition that circumscribed the lives of the enslaved, local practices of enslavement—the enforcement of rules and norms, the severity of punishment, and the allowance or disallowance of manumission—also influenced what life in a particular slave society could be like for the enslaved. The force of local realities, the cultural, legal, and economic conditions, provided the contours of slave existence within these complex societies.

Anthropologists have enriched the ethnohistorical study of frontier interactions through the development of the term "tribalization" to express the manner in which indigenous leaders—accepted by colonial officials as representatives of their communities—took on particular roles and identities that embedded them within specific colonial structures.[11] Since warfare between competing Europeans was endemic on these frontiers, indigenous leaders and their communities were valued by Europeans for the military force they could bring to bear in these conflict zones. Leaders and peoples became "tribalized": they entered into a formal relationship with the colonial state that enumerated them as separate peoples. The problematic relationships that fall under the term "tribalization" had the power to create, guide, and reinforce certain kinds of structured behaviors. Alliances established a habitus of treaty-making peoples, a set of face-to-face interactions that at once reinforced and were subsumed under the colonial system. Indigenous leaders could learn how to become tribal figures in this milieu (by acting as "tribal figures") at the same time that European officials were doing the same.[12]

Having emerged out of a process of careful analysis of the manner in which individuals expressed complex identities within (and through) larger structural systems, Anglicization displays a kinship with philosophically and anthropologically derived concepts through which scholars interpret how communities and individuals make adjustments to empire. It allows us to perceive the full range of mechanisms the imperial state had at its disposal to structure the behavior of its subjects, while recognizing that local conditions introduced the potential for considerable variability. To these can be added the additional insight that the state recognized that its aim (increased revenue from colonial economic activity) might be achieved through modifying, or even muting, the state's coercive power. As was discussed earlier in the essay, in *The Passions and the Interests*, Albert O. Hirschman explores how the eighteenth-century state developed policies aimed at deriving profit from the control of preexisting practices, appetites, inclinations, and behaviors rather than the punishment of transgressions (although, of course, it never eschewed its hard-won monopoly on violence).

Economic planners used mechanisms other than coercion to effect changes in economic behavior, and to reenforce what they took to be acceptable forms through which individuals might embody colonial economic agency. At the same time, in communities throughout the empire, economic and political agents had their behavior guided and were urged to conform to a set of externally devised norms. They enacted and reinforced their identities as colonial subjects in local environments that were quite distinct from one another; in this way the nature of the empire was different in South Carolina than it was in Massachusetts. However, what was held in common across the continent was a shared situation in which subjects were directed to make personal and political adjustments to the empire through their daily actions and activities.

Anglicization directs us to discern the various ways in which the centralizing British state ultimately counteracted the processes that could have resulted in a collection of societies that dotted the continent and continually diverged from one another. On the one hand, the empire's rules and practices aimed to standardize economic activity, guide consumption, and enforce the laws. Although English subjects continued to differentiate themselves from one another (especially when the frontiers are compared to the coasts), their engagement with the state on this level introduced a strong regularizing element. On the other hand, day-to-day interactions also carried out under the aegis of the empire, quotidian engagements that involved monotonous practices, adjustment to norms, rejection of unwanted elements, and embrace of desired ones, themselves comprised a structural element in the British Empire, taking on an importance no less influential than those activities regulated under the Navigation Acts or the High Courts of Admiralty.

NOTES

Chapter 1

First published in *Princeton Alumni Weekly*, November 19, 1974.

Chapter 2

1. Edmund S. Morgan, *The Gentle Puritan: A Life of Ezra Stiles, 1727–1795* (New York: W. W. Norton, 1962), 134.

2. John M. Murrin, "The Irrelevance and Relevance of Colonial New England," *Reviews in American History* 18 (1990): 177–84, 180.

3. Stephen Foster, *The Long Argument: English Puritanism and the Shaping of New England Culture, 1570–1700* (Chapel Hill: University of North Carolina Press, 1991); Edmund S. Morgan, *Visible Saints: The History of a Puritan Idea* (Ithaca, NY: Cornell University Press, 1963), 126, 138.

4. John M. Murrin, "Magistrates, Sinners, and a Precarious Liberty: Trial by Jury in Seventeenth-Century New England," in David Hall, John M. Murrin, and Thad W. Tate, eds., *Saints and Revolutionaries: Essays on Early American History* (New York: W. W. Norton, 1984), 152–206, 193.

5. John M. Murrin, "Colonial Government," in Jack P. Greene, ed., *Encyclopedia of American Political History*, 3 vols. (New York: Scribner's, 1984), 1:293–315, 295.

6. This discussion draws on John M. Murrin, "English Rights as Ethnic Aggression: The English Conquest, the Charter of Liberties of 1683, and Leisler's Rebellion in New York," in William Pencak and Conrad Edick Wright, eds., *Authority and Resistance in Early New York* (New York: New-York Historical Society, 1988), 56–94; Murrin, "The Menacing Shadow of Louis XIV and the Rage of Jacob Leisler: The Constitutional Ordeal of Seventeenth-Century New York," in Stephen L. Schechter and Richard B. Bernstein, eds., *New York and the Union: Contributions to the American Constitutional Experience* (Albany: New York State Commission on the Bicentennial of the United States Constitution, 1990), 29–71; Murrin, "The New York Charter of Liberties, 1683 and 1691," in Stephen L. Schechter, Richard B. Bernstein, and Donald S. Lutz, eds., *Roots of the Republic: American Founding Documents Interpreted* (Madison, WI: Madison House Publications, 1990), 47–82; "Pluralism and Predatory Power: Early New York as a Social Failure," *Reviews in American History* 6 (1978): 473–79.

7. David Wootton, ed., *Divine Right and Democracy: An Anthology of Political Writing in Stuart England* (Indianapolis: Hackett, 2003), 124, 126; John M. Murrin, "Essay Review: The Papers of William Penn, Volume I, 1644–1679," *Pennsylvania Magazine of History and Biography* 105 (1981): 483–87, 483.

8. Murrin, "Colonial Government," 301–2.

9. Ibid., 299.

10. J. G. A. Pocock, "Machiavelli, Harrington, and English Political Ideologies in the Eighteenth Century," *William and Mary Quarterly*, 3rd ser., 22 (1965): 549–83.

11. Murrin, "Colonial Government," 299.

12. Edmund S. Morgan, *American Slavery, American Freedom: The Ordeal of Colonial Virginia* (New York: W. W. Norton, 1975); Kathleen Brown, *Good Wives, Nasty Wenches, and Anxious Patriarchs: Gender, Race, and Power in Colonial Virginia* (Chapel Hill: University of North Carolina Press, 1996).

13. John M. Murrin, "The Infernal Conspiracy of Indians and Grandmothers," *Reviews in American History* 31 (2003): 485–94.

14. John M. Murrin, Paul E. Johnson, James M. McPherson, Gary Gerstle, Emily S. Rosenberg, and Norman L. Rosenberg, *Liberty, Equality, Power: A History of the American People*, 4th ed. (New York: Thompson Gale, 2005), 101.

15. W. A. Speck, *Reluctant Revolutionaries: Englishmen and the Revolution of 1688* (Oxford: Oxford University Press, 1998); Steve Pincus, *1688: The First Modern Revolution* (New Haven, CT: Yale University Press, 2009); Lionel K. Glassey, ed., *The Reigns of Charles II and James VII and II* (London: Macmillan, 1997); Richard Ashcraft, "Revolutionary Politics and Locke's Two Treatises of Government: Radicalism and Lockean Political Theory," *Political Theory* 8 (1980): 429–86.

16. John M. Murrin and David J. Silverman, "The Quest for America: Reflections on Distinctiveness, Pluralism, and Public Life," *Journal of Interdisciplinary History* 33 (2002): 235–46.

17. J. P. Sommerville, *Royalists and Patriots: Politics and Ideology in England, 1603–1640* (London: Longman, 1999); Richard Cust and Ann Hughes, eds., *Conflict in Early Stuart England: Studies in Religion and Politics* (London: Longman, 1989); Robert Ashton, *The Crown and the Money Market* (Oxford: Clarendon Press, 1960); P. G. Lake, "Calvinism and the English Church, 1570–1635," *Past and Present* 114 (1987): 32–76; Kenneth Fincham and Peter Lake, "The Ecclesiastical Policy of King James I," *Journal of British Studies* 24 (1985): 169–207; Conrad Russell, *The Fall of the British Monarchies* (Oxford: Clarendon Press, 1991).

18. Linda Colley, *Britons: Forging the Nation, 1707–1837* (New Haven, CT: Yale University Press, 1992), chap. 1; Peter Lake, "Anti-Popery: The Structure of a Prejudice," in Cust and Hughes, eds., *Conflict in Early Stuart England*, 72–106.

19. John Brewer, *The Sinews of Power: War, Money, and the English State, 1688–1783* (New York: Alfred A. Knopf, 1989); A. L. Beir, David Cannadine, and James M. Rosenheim, eds., *The First Modern Society: Essays in English History in Honour of Lawrence Stone* (Cambridge: Cambridge University Press, 1989); Lawrence Stone, ed., *An Imperial*

State at War: Britain from 1689 to 1815 (London: Routledge, 1994); P. J. Marshall, ed., *The Oxford History of the British Empire: The Eighteenth Century* (Oxford: Oxford University Press, 1998).

20. Brewer, *Sinews of Power*; P. G. M. Dickson, *The Financial Revolution in England: A Study in the Development of Public Credit, 1688–1756* (London: Macmillan, 1967); J. H. Plumb, *The Growth of Political Stability in England, 1675–1725* (London: Macmillan, 1967); Patrick O'Brien, "The Political Economy of British Taxation, 1660–1815," *Economic History Review* 41 (1988): 1–32; Patrick O'Brien, "Inseparable Connections: Trade, Economy, Fiscal State, and the Expansion of Empire, 1688–1815," in Marshall, ed., *Oxford History of the British Empire*, 53–77.

21. John M. Murrin, "The Great Inversion, or Court Versus Country: A Comparison of the Revolution Settlements in England (1688–1721) and America (1776–1816)," in J. G. A. Pocock, ed., *Three British Revolutions: 1641, 1688, 1776* (Princeton, NJ: Princeton University Press, 1980), 368–453.

22. Isaac Kramnick, *Bolingbroke and His Circle: The Politics of Nostalgia in the Age of Walpole* (Ithaca, NY: Cornell University Press, 1968).

23. Paul Langford, *A Polite and Commercial People: England 1727–1783* (New York: Oxford University Press, 1989); Paul Langford, *Public Life and the Propertied Englishman, 1689–1798* (New York: Oxford University Press, 1991); H. T. Dickinson, *Liberty and Property: Political Ideology in Eighteenth-Century Britain* (London: Methuen, 1977); Neil McKendrick, John Brewer, and J. H. Plumb, eds., *The Birth of a Consumer Society: The Commercialization of Eighteenth Century England* (Bloomington: Indiana University Press, 1982).

24. John M. Murrin, "Beneficiaries of Catastrophe: The English Colonies in America," in Eric Foner, ed., *The New American History* (Philadelphia: Temple University Press, 1990), 3–23, 19–20.

25. John M. Murrin, "Review Essay," *History and Theory* 11 (1972): 226–75.

26. John M. Murrin, "The Legal Transformation: The Bench and Bar of Eighteenth-Century Massachusetts," in Stanley N. Katz and John M. Murrin, eds., *Colonial America: Essays in Politics and Social Development*, 3rd ed. (New York: Alfred A. Knopf, 1983), 540–72.

27. Jere R. Daniell, "Politics in New Hampshire Under Governor Benning Wentworth," *William and Mary Quarterly*, 3rd ser., 23 (1966): 76–105.

28. Pauline Maier, *From Resistance to Revolution: Colonial Radicals and the Development of American Opposition to Britain, 1765–1776* (New York: W. W. Norton, 1972), 6, 9.

29. Murrin, *Liberty, Equality, and Power*, 107.

30. Jack P. Greene, *Peripheries and Center: Constitutional Development in the Extended Polities of the British Empire and the United States, 1607–1788* (New York: W. W. Norton, 1986); Mary Sarah Bilder, *The Transatlantic Constitution: Colonial Legal Culture and the Empire* (Cambridge, MA: Harvard University Press, 2004); Alison LaCroix, *The Ideological Origins of American Federalism* (Cambridge, MA: Harvard University Press, 2010).

31. Stanley N. Katz, "Between Scylla and Charybdis: James DeLancey and Anglo-American Politics in Early Eighteenth-Century New York," in Katz and Murrin, eds., *Colonial America*, 394–409.

32. James H. Hutson, *Pennsylvania Politics, 1746–1770: The Movement for Royal Government and Its Consequences* (Princeton, NJ: Princeton University Press, 1972).

33. Gordon S. Wood, *The Americanization of Benjamin Franklin* (New York: Penguin Press, 2004).

34. Ira Berlin, *Many Thousands Gone: The First Two Centuries of Slavery in North America* (Cambridge, MA: Harvard University Press, 1998); Philip Morgan, *Slave Counterpoint: Black Culture in the Eighteenth-Century Chesapeake and Low Country* (Chapel Hill: University of North Carolina Press, 1998).

35. Carville Earle and Ronald Hoffman, "Staple Crops and Urban Development in the Eighteenth-Century South," *Perspectives in American History* 10 (1976): 7–78.

36. T. H. Breen, *Tobacco Culture: The Mentality of the Great Tidewater Planters on the Eve of Revolution* (Princeton, NJ: Princeton University Press, 1985).

37. Bernard Bailyn, *The Origins of American Politics* (New York: Vintage, 1967).

38. Murrin, *Liberty, Equality, Power*, 137–40.

39. John M. Murrin, "Political Development," in Jack P. Greene and J. R. Pole, eds., *Colonial British America: Essays in the New History of the Early Modern Era* (Baltimore: Johns Hopkins University Press, 1984), 408–56, 436; John M. Murrin, "The Myths of Colonial Democracy and Royal Decline in Eighteenth-Century America: A Review Essay," *Cithara* 5 (1965–66): 53–69.

40. For a general discussion, see Maier, *From Resistance to Revolution*, chap. 2.

41. James A. Henretta, "Wealth and Social Structure," in Greene and Pole, eds., *Colonial British America*, 262–89; Gary B. Nash, *The Urban Crucible: Social Change, Political Consciousness, and the Origins of the American Revolution* (Cambridge, MA: Harvard University Press, 1979); Toby Ditz, "Ownership and Obligation: Inheritance and Patriarchal Households in Connecticut, 1750–1820," *William and Mary Quarterly*, 3rd ser., 47 (1990): 235–65; Lucy Simler, "Tenancy in Colonial Pennsylvania," *William and Mary Quarterly*, 3rd ser., 43 (1986): 542–69.

42. Gordon S. Wood, *The Radicalism of the American Revolution* (New York: Vintage, 1991).

43. Gary J. Kornblith and John M. Murrin, "The Making and Unmaking of an American Ruling Class," in Alfred F. Young, ed., *Beyond the American Revolution: Explorations in the History of American Radicalism* (DeKalb: Northern Illinois University Press, 1993), 27–79, 36–44.

44. Rowland Berthoff and John M. Murrin, "Feudalism, Communalism, and the Yeoman Freeholder: The American Revolution Considered as a Social Accident," in Stephen G. Kurtz and James H. Hutson, eds., *Essays on the American Revolution* (Chapel Hill: University of North Carolina Press, 1973), 256–88.

45. Ibid., 264.

46. Ibid., 265–67.

47. Alfred F. Young, *The Democratic Republicans of New York: The Origins* (Chapel Hill: University of North Carolina Press, 1967); Edward Countryman, *A People in Revolution: The American Revolution and Political Society in New York, 1760–1790* (Baltimore: Johns Hopkins University Press, 1981); Thomas J. Humphrey, *Land and Liberty: Hudson Valley Riots in the Age of Revolution* (DeKalb: Northern Illinois University Press, 2004); Kevin Kenny, *Peaceable Kingdom Lost: The Paxton Boys and the Destruction of William Penn's Holy Experiment* (Oxford: Oxford University Press, 2009); Marvin L. Michael Kay, "The North Carolina Regulation, 1766–1776: A Class Conflict," in Alfred F. Young, ed., *The American Revolution: Explorations in the History of American Radicalism* (DeKalb: Northern Illinois University Press, 1976), 71–124; Marjolene Kars, *Breaking Loose Together: The Regulator Rebellion in Pre-Revolutionary North Carolina* (Chapel Hill: University of North Carolina Press, 2002).

48. E. P. Thompson, *Whigs and Hunters: The Origin of the Black Act* (New York: Pantheon, 1975); E. P. Thompson, *Customs in Common: Studies in Traditional Popular Culture* (New York: New Press, 1993).

49. Young, *American Revolution*; Nash, *Urban Crucible*; Woody Holton, *Forced Founders: Indians, Debtors, Slaves, and the Making of the American Revolution in Virginia* (Chapel Hill: University of North Carolina Press, 1999); Michael A. McDonnell, *The Politics of War: Race, Class, and Conflict in Revolutionary Virginia* (Chapel Hill: University of North Carolina Press, 2007); Terry Bouton, *Taming Democracy: The People, the Founders, and the Troubled Ending of the American Revolution* (Oxford: Oxford University Press, 2007); T. H. Breen, *American Insurgents, American Patriots: The Revolution of the People* (New York: Hill & Wang, 2010).

50. Murrin, "Political Development," 433.

51. John M. Murrin, "The French and Indian War, the American Revolution, and the Counterfactual Hypothesis: Reflections on Lawrence Henry Gibson and John Shy," *Reviews in American History* 11 (1983): 161–71.

52. Fred Anderson, *A People's Army: Massachusetts Soldiers and Society in the Seven Years' War* (Chapel Hill: University of North Carolina Press, 1984), 14.

53. Murrin, "French and Indian War," 314.

54. John Shy, "The American Colonies in War and Revolution, 1748–1783," in Marshall, ed., *Oxford History of the British Empire,* 300–324, 308.

55. John M. Murrin, "1776: The Countercyclical Revolution," in Michael A. Morrison and Melinda Zook, eds., *Revolutionary Currents: Nation Building in the Transatlantic World* (New York: Rowman & Littlefield, 2004), 65–90, 67.

56. Andrew Jackson O'Shaughnessy, *An Empire Divided: The American Revolution and the British Caribbean* (Philadelphia: University of Pennsylvania Press, 2000).

57. Jack P. Greene, "Empire and Identity from the Glorious Revolution to the American Revolution," in Marshall, ed., *Oxford History of the British Empire,* 208–30; Julie Flavell, *When London Was Capital of America* (New Haven, CT: Yale University Press, 2010).

58. Nicole Eustace, *Passion Is the Gale: Emotion, Power, and the Coming of the American Revolution* (Chapel Hill: University of North Carolina Press, 2008); Sarah

Nott, *Sensibility and the American Revolution* (Chapel Hill: University of North Carolina Press, 2009); Richard Bushman, *The Refinement of America: Persons, Houses, Cities* (New York: Alfred A. Knopf, 1992).

59. Young, *Democratic Republicans of New York*; Holton, *Forced Founders*; Benjamin Carp, *Defiance of the Patriots: The Boston Tea Party and the Making of America* (New Haven, CT: Yale University Press, 2010); Lawrence Henry Gipson, *The Coming of the Revolution, 1763–1775* (New York: Harper, 1954), in which Gipson provides a helpful introduction to his treatment in his fifteen-volume study *The British Empire Before the American Revolution*; George Louis Beer, *The Old Colonial System, 1660–1754*, 2 vols. (New York: P. Smith, 1933); Edmund S. Morgan and Helen Morgan, *The Stamp Act Crisis: Prologue to Revolution* (Chapel Hill: University of North Carolina Press, 1953); Bernard Bailyn, *The Ideological Origins of the American Revolution* (Cambridge, MA: Harvard University Press, 1967).

60. Murrin, "1776: The Countercyclical Revolution," 73; John M. Murrin to Andrew Shankman, e-mail exchange, August 28, 2012.

61. J. M. Bumsted, "'Things in the Womb of Time': Ideas of American Independence, 1633–1763," *William and Mary Quarterly*, 3rd ser., 31 (1974): 534–64; John Shy, "The Spectrum of Imperial Possibilities: Henry Ellis and Thomas Pownall, 1763–1775," in Shy, *A People Numerous and Armed: Reflections on the Military Struggle for the American Revolution* (Ann Arbor: University of Michigan Press, 1990), 43–80; LaCroix, *Ideological Origins of American Federalism*, chap. 2.

62. Murrin, "French and Indian War," 313–15.

63. Ibid., 316.

64. Murrin, *Liberty, Equality, Power*, 167–68.

65. Morgan and Morgan, *Stamp Act Crisis*; John L. Bullion, "British Ministers and American Resistance to the Stamp Act, October–December 1765," *William and Mary Quarterly*, 3rd ser., 49 (1992): 89–107; Wood, *Americanization of Benjamin Franklin*.

66. A good portion of Franklin's session is reprinted in Jack P. Greene, ed., *Colonies to Nation: A Documentary History of the American Revolution* (New York: W. W. Norton, 1975), 72–78.

67. For the Sons of Liberty, see Maier, *From Resistance to Revolution*, 112.

68. Murrin, "1776: The Countercyclical Revolution," esp. 76–78.

69. For a complete narrative of events in Massachusetts, see Jeremy A. Stern, "The Overflowings of Liberty: Massachusetts, the Townshend Acts Crisis, and the Reconception of Freedom, 1766–1770" (Ph.D. diss., Princeton University, 2010).

70. See also Richard S. Dunn, "The Glorious Revolution in America," in Nicholas Canny, ed., *The Oxford History of the British Empire: The Origins of Empire* (Oxford: Oxford University Press, 1998), 445–66.

71. John M. Murrin, "In the Land of the Free and the Home of the Slave, Maybe There Was Room Even for Deference," *Journal of American History* 85 (1998): 86–91.

72. See Jackson Turner Main, "Government by the People: The American Revolution and the Democratization of the Legislatures," *William and Mary Quarterly*, 3rd

ser., 23 (1966): 391–407; Wood, *Radicalism of the American Revolution*; Jay Fliegelman, *Prodigals and Pilgrims: The American Revolution Against Patriarchal Authority, 1750–1800* (Cambridge: Cambridge University Press, 1992); W. J. Rorbaugh, "'I Thought I Should Liberate Myself from the Thraldom of Others': Apprentices, Masters, and the Revolution," in Young, ed., *Beyond the American Revolution*, 185–217; Allan Kulikoff, "The American Revolution, Capitalism, and the Formation of the Yeoman Classes," in Young, ed., *Beyond the American Revolution*, 80–119; Mary Beth Norton, *Liberty's Daughters: The Revolutionary Experience of American Women, 1750–1800* (Boston: Little, Brown, 1980); and David Brion Davis, *The Problem of Slavery in the Age of Revolution, 1770–1823* (Oxford: Oxford University Press, 1975), for the merest sampling of a vast literature.

73. Douglas R. Egerton, *Death or Liberty: African Americans and Revolutionary America* (Oxford: Oxford University Press, 2009); Eva Sheppard Wolf, *Race and Liberty in the New Nation: Emancipation in Virginia from the Revolution to Nat Turner's Rebellion* (Baton Rouge: Louisiana State University Press, 2006); George William Van Cleve, *A Slaveholders' Union: Slavery, Politics, and the Construction of the Early American Republic* (Chicago: University of Chicago Press, 2010); Trevor Burnard, "Freedom, Migration, and the American Revolution," in Eliga H. Gould and Peter S. Onuf, eds., *Empire and Nation: The American Revolution in the Atlantic World* (Baltimore: Johns Hopkins University Press, 2005), 295–314; Gregory Evans Dowd, *A Spirited Resistance: The North American Indian Struggle for Unity, 1745–1815* (Baltimore: Johns Hopkins University Press, 1992); James H. Merrell, "Declarations of Independence: Indian-White Relations in the New Nation," in Jack P. Greene, ed., *The American Revolution: Its Character and Limits* (New York: New York University Press, 1987), 197–223; Rosemarie Zagarri, *Revolutionary Backlash: Women and Politics in the Early American Republic* (Philadelphia: University of Pennsylvania Press, 2007); Linda K. Kerber, *Women of the Republic: Intellect and Ideology in Revolutionary America* (Chapel Hill: University of North Carolina Press, 1980).

74. Gordon S. Wood, *Creation of the American Republic* (Chapel Hill: University of North Carolina Press, 1969); Woody Holton, *Unruly Americans and the Origins of the Constitution* (New York: Hill & Wang, 2007).

75. John M. Murrin to Andrew Shankman, e-mail correspondence, August 28, 2012.

76. Murrin, "Great Inversion," 403.

77. John M. Murrin, "Gordon S. Wood and the Search for Liberal America," *William and Mary Quarterly*, 3rd ser., 44 (1987): 597–601, 597, 599.

78. The Madison administration briefly revived internal taxation at the lowest point of the War of 1812, but the Jeffersonians abandoned the taxes after the war. See John M. Murrin, "1787: The Invention of American Federalism," in J. M. Murrin, David E. Narrett, Ronald L. Hatzenbuehler, and Michael Kammen, eds., *Essays on Liberty and Federalism: The Shaping of the U.S. Constitution* (College Station: Texas A&M University Press, 1988), 20–47; Thomas Slaughter, *The Whiskey Rebellion: Frontier Epilogue to the Revolution* (Oxford: Oxford University Press, 1986); Paul Douglas Newman, *Fries*

Rebellion: The Enduring Struggle for the American Revolution (Philadelphia: University of Pennsylvania Press, 2004).

79. Murrin, "1787: The Invention of American Federalism," 36.

80. Alfred F. Young, "The Framers of the Constitution and the 'Genius' of the People," *Radical History Review* 42 (1988): 8–18.

81. David J. Siemers, *Ratifying the Republic: Antifederalists and Federalists in Constitutional Time* (Stanford, CA: Stanford University Press, 2002).

82. John M. Murrin, "Fundamental Values, The Founding Fathers, and the Constitution," in Herman Belz, Ronald Hoffman, and Peter J. Albert, eds., *To Form a More Perfect Union: The Critical Ideas of the Constitution* (Charlottesville: University Press of Virginia, 1992), 1–37.

83. John M. Murrin, "A Roof Without Walls: The Dilemma of American National Identity," in Richard Beeman, Stephen Botein, and Edward C. Carter II, eds., *Beyond Confederation: Origins of the Constitution and American National Identity* (Chapel Hill: University of North Carolina Press, 1987), 333–48.

84. James Roger Sharp, *American Politics in the Early Republic: The New Nation in Crisis* (New Haven, CT: Yale University Press, 1993); John Ferling, *Adams vs. Jefferson: The Tumultuous Election of 1800* (Oxford: Oxford University Press, 2004).

85. Richard Bonney, ed., *The Rise of the Fiscal State in Europe, c. 1200–1815* (Oxford: Oxford University Press, 1999); Richard Bonney, ed., *Economic Systems and State Finance* (Oxford: Oxford University Press, 1995); Mark Ormrod, Margaret Bonney, and Richard Bonney, eds., *Crises, Revolutions, and Self-Sustained Growth: Essays in European Fiscal History, 1130–1830* (Lincolnshire, UK: Alden Group, 1999); Philip T. Hoffman and Kathryn Norberg, eds., *Fiscal Crises and Representative Government, 1450–1789* (Stanford, CA: Stanford University Press, 1994).

86. John M. Murrin, "The Jeffersonian Triumph and American Exceptionalism," *Journal of the Early Republic* 20 (2000): 1–25, 2.

87. Murrin, "Great Inversion," 425; Murrin, "Jeffersonian Triumph and American Exceptionalism," 3.

88. Robert E. Gallman, "Economic Growth and Structural Change in the Long Nineteenth Century," and Stuart Blumin, "The Social Implications of U.S. Economic Development," in Stanley L. Engerman and Robert E. Gallman, eds., *The Cambridge Economic History of the United States, Volume II: The Long Nineteenth Century* (Cambridge: Cambridge University Press, 2000), 1–55 and 813–63 respectively; Murrin, "Great Inversion," 428–29; Kornblith and Murrin, "Making and Unmaking of an American Ruling Class," 62–65.

89. John M. Murrin, "Can Liberals Be Patriots? Natural Right, Virtue, and Moral Sense in the America of George Mason and Thomas Jefferson," in Robert P. Davidow, ed., *Natural Rights and Natural Law: The Legacy of George Mason* (Fairfax, VA: George Mason University Press, 1986), 35–65; John M. Murrin, "Escaping Perfidious Albion: Federalism, Fear of Aristocracy, and the Democratization of Corruption in Postrevolutionary America," in Richard K. Matthews, ed., *Virtue, Corruption, and Self-Interest:*

Political Values in the Eighteenth Century (Bethlehem, PA: Lehigh University Press, 1994), 103–47.

90. Berthoff and Murrin, "Feudalism, Communalism, and the Yeoman Freeholder," 282. See also James L. Huston, "The American Revolutionaries, the Political Economy of Aristocracy, and the American Concept of the Distribution of Wealth, 1765–1900," *American Historical Review* 98 (1993): 1079–105.

91. For a discussion of many of these themes to the start of the Civil War, see Andrew Shankman, "Conflict for a Continent: Land, Labor, and the State in the First American Republic," in Shankman, ed., *The World of the Revolutionary American Republic: Land, Labor, and the Conflict for a Continent* (London: Routledge, 2014), 1–24.

Chapter 3

1. Some of the ideas in this essay have been developed in Simon P. Newman, *A New World of Labor: The Development of Plantation Slavery in the British Atlantic* (Philadelphia: University of Pennsylvania Press, 2013).

2. John M. Murrin, "Anglicizing an American Colony: The Transformation of Provincial Massachusetts" (Ph.D. diss., Yale University, 1966), 20. See also John M. Murrin, "A Roof Without Walls: The Dilemma of American National Identity," in Richard Beeman, Stephen Botein, and Edward C. Carter II, eds., *Beyond Confederation: Origins of the Constitution and American National Identity* (Chapel Hill: University of North Carolina Press, 1987), 344, 346.

3. T. H. Breen, "An Empire of Goods: The Anglicization of Colonial Virginia, 1690–1776," *Journal of British Studies* 25 (1986): 467–99; Jack P. Greene, *Pursuits of Happiness: The Social Development of Early Modern British Colonies and the Formation of American Culture* (Chapel Hill: University of North Carolina Press, 1988), 150–51; Robert Olwell, *Masters, Slaves, and Subjects: The Culture of Power in the South Carolina Low Country, 1740–1790* (Ithaca, NY: Cornell University Press, 1998), 40, 41–42.

4. Murrin, "Anglicizing an American Colony," 259–60.

5. Ibid., 14.

6. Samuel Cohn, "After the Black Death: Labour Legislation and Attitudes Towards Labour in Late-Medieval Western Europe," *Economic History Review* 60 (2007): 457–85; Christopher Tomlins, *Freedom Bound: Law, Labor, and Civic Identity in Colonizing English America, 1580–1865* (Cambridge: Cambridge University Press, 2010), 234–35; Robert J. Steinfeld, *The Invention of Free Labor: The Employment Relation in English and American Law and Culture, 1350–1870* (Chapel Hill: University of North Carolina Press, 1991), 22–23.

7. Jane Whittle, "Servants in Rural England c. 1450–1650: Hired Work as a Means of Accumulating Wealth and Skills Before Marriage," in Maria Ågren and Amy Louise Erickson, eds., *The Marital Economy in Scandinavia and Britain, 1400–1900* (Aldershot: Ashgate, 2005), 91–92; Keith Wrightson, *Earthly Necessities: Economic Lives in Early Modern Britain* (New Haven, CT: Yale University Press, 2000), 32–33; Ann Kussmaul, *Servants in Husbandry in Early Modern England* (Cambridge: Cambridge University

Press, 1981), 3, 34. See also Donald Woodward, "Early Modern Servants in Husbandry Revisited," *Agricultural History Review* 48 (2000): 141–50; Ilana Krausman Ben-Amos, "Service and the Coming of Age of Young Men in Seventeenth Century England," *Continuity and Change* 3 (1988): 41–64; Carolyn Steedman, "Service and Servitude in the World of Labour: Service in England, 1750–1820," in Colin Jones and Dror Wahrman, eds., *The Age of Culture Revolutions: Britain and France, 1750–1820* (Berkeley: University of California Press, 2002), 124–36; E. A. Wrigley, R. S. Davies, J. E. Oppen, and R. S. Schofield, *English Population History from Family Reconstitution, 1580–1837* (Cambridge: Cambridge University Press, 1997), 130; Jane Whittle, *The Development of Agrarian Capitalism: Land and Labour in Norfolk, 1440–1580* (Oxford: Clarendon Press, 2000), 255.

8. Susan Dwyer Amussen, *An Ordered Society: Gender and Class in Early Modern England* (New York: Columbia University Press, 1988), 160–61.

9. Kussmaul, *Servants in Husbandry*, 9, 34–49, 32–33, 44–47, 70–75; Wrightson, *Earthly Necessities*, 35; Amussen, *Ordered Society*, 40.

10. Margaret Spufford, *Contrasting Communities: English Villagers in the Sixteenth and Seventeenth Centuries* (Cambridge: Cambridge University Press, 1974), 13; E. A. Wrigley, "A Simple Model of London's Importance in Changing English Society and Economy, 1650–1750," *Past & Present* 37 (1967): 49.

11. "An Homyly against Idlenesse," in *The seconde tome of homilies of such matters as were promised and intituled in the former part of Homylyes, set out by the aucthoritie of the Queenes Maiestie. And to be read in euery paryshe churche agreablye* (London, 1563), 264, 265.

12. A. L. Beier, *Masterless Men: The Vagrancy Problem in England, 1560–1640* (New York: Methuen, 1985).

13. Sir Thomas Smith cited in Tomlins, *Freedom Bound*, 228–31; William Gouge, *Of Domesticall Duties: Eight Treatises* (London, 1622), 18. See also Amussen, *Ordered Society*, 31–38; John Donoghue, "Unfree Labor, Imperialism, and Radical Republicanism in the Atlantic World, 1630–1661," *Labor: Studies in Working Class History of the Americas* 1 (2004): 47–68; Tomlins, *Freedom Bound*, 236–45; Steinfeld, *Invention of Free Labor*, 23–24; Kussmaul, *Servants in Husbandry*, 33–34.

14. Sir Thomas Smith, *De republica Anglorum The maner of gouernement or policie of the realme of England* (London, 1583), 113; Steve Hindle, *On the Parish: The Micro-Politics of Poor Relief in Rural England, c. 1550–1750* (Oxford: Clarendon Press, 2004), 205–7.

15. C. S. L. Davies, "Slavery and Protector Somerset: The Vagrancy Act of 1547," *Economic History Review*, 2nd ser., 19 (1966): 534, 533–49. See also Paul Slack, *The English Poor Law, 1531–1782* (Cambridge: Cambridge University Press, 1990), 10.

16. Davies, "Slavery and Protector Somerset," 541, 545; A. L. Beier, "'A New Serfdom': Labor Laws, Vagrancy Statutes, and Labor Discipline in England, 1350–1800," in L. Beier and Paul Ocobock, eds., *Cast Out: Vagrancy and Homelessness in Global and Historical Perspective* (Athens: Ohio University Press, 2008), 35–38.

17. Steinfeld, *Invention of Free Labor*, 3–6.

18. Tomlins, *Freedom Bound*, 31–66. See also David W. Galenson, *White Servitude in Colonial America: An Economic Analysis* (Cambridge: Cambridge University Press, 1981), 15–19; Richard S. Dunn, "Servants and Slaves: The Recruitment and Employment of Labor," in Jack P. Greene and J. R. Pole, eds., *Colonial British America: Essays in the New History of the Early Modern Era* (Baltimore: Johns Hopkins University Press, 1984), 157–94.

19. Galenson, *White Servitude*, 125; Richard S. Dunn, *Sugar and Slaves: The Rise of the Planter Class in the English West Indies, 1624–1713* (Chapel Hill: University of North Carolina Press, 1972), 58, 91, 96–98; Richard S. Dunn, "The Barbados Census of 1680: Profile of the Richest Colony in English America," *William and Mary Quarterly,* 3rd ser., 26 (1969): 7–8.

20. An intercepted letter from William George to anonymous, May 1655, in *A Collection of the State Papers of John Thurloe, Esq; Secretary, First, to the Council of State, And afterwards to The Two Protectors, Oliver and Richard Cromwell,* vol. 3 (London, 1742), 495. This is an early use of the term "Barbadosed," referring to the transportation of white Britons—usually without their consent—to labor on Barbados plantations. See also Mark S. Quintanilla, "Late Seventeenth-Century Indentured Servants in Barbados," *Journal of Caribbean History* 27 (1993): 114–28; John Donoghue, "'Out of the Land of Bondage': The English Revolution and the Atlantic Origins of Abolition," *American Historical Review* 115 (2010): 960; Hilary McD. Beckles, *White Servitude and Black Slavery in Barbados, 1627–1715* (Knoxville: University of Tennessee Press, 1989), 68.

21. Trevor Burnard, "Thomas Thistlewood Becomes a Creole," in Bruce Clayton and John A. Salmond, eds., *Varieties of Southern History: New Essays on a Region and Its People* (Westport, CT: Greenwood Press, 1996), 100; "Certaine Propositions for the better accommodating ye Foreigne Plantations with Servants reported from the Committee to the Councell of Foreign Plantations" (1664), Papers Relating to English Colonies in America and the West Indies, 1627–1699, Egerton 2395, British Library Manuscripts Collection, 277; Hilary McD. Beckles, "Land Distribution and Class Formation in Barbados, 1630–1700: The Rise of a Wage Proletariat," *Journal of the Barbados Museum and Historical Society* 36 (1980): 137, 139–40; Hilary McD. Beckles, *A History of Barbados: From Amerindian Settlement to Nation-State* (Cambridge: Cambridge University Press, 1989), 15.

22. John Oldmixon, *The British Empire in America, Containing the History of the Discovery, Settlement, Progress and present State of all the British Colonies, on the Continent and Islands of America,* vol. 2 (London, 1708), 116; Henry Whistler, "A Journall of a voyadg from Stokes Bay and Intended by Gods assistance for the West Inga: and performed by the Right Honorable Generall penn: Admirall: As folowes. Taken by Mr. Henry Whistler, 1654," Sloane Ms. 3926, British Library Manuscripts Collection, 9; anonymous letter from Barbados dated March 20, 1676, in P. Hume Brown, ed., *The Register of the Privy Council of Scotland,* 3rd ser., 16 vols. (Glasgow: James Hedderwick and Sons, 1911), 4:675; Edmund Burk, will, dated January 7, 1661, and entered March 7, 1661, Will Record Books, RB6, Barbados Department of Archives, 15:10.

23. "Certaine Propositions," 277–78. The Council of Foreign Plantations existed between 1660 and 1672, at which point it was supplanted by the Council of Trade and Foreign Plantations, allowing us to date this document. See G. E. Aylmer, *The Crown's Servants: Government and the Civil Service Under Charles II, 1660–1685* (Oxford: Oxford University Press, 2002), 50–55; Beckles, *White Servitude and Black Slavery*, 48; Oldmixon, *British Empire in America*, 113; Whistler, "Journall of a voyadg from Stokes Bay," 9.

24. Richard Ligon, *A True & Exact History of the Island of Barbados* (London: for Humphrey Moseley, 1657), 40. This argument has been developed by Hilary Beckles, who disagrees with previous historians by concluding that relatively few former servants were able to join the ranks of the planters; see Beckles, "Land Distribution and Class Formation," 136–37.

25. Beckles, *White Servitude and Black Slavery*, 5; Beckles, *History of Barbados*, 17, 24–25.

26. Beckles, *White Servitude and Black Slavery*, 80–90, 119; Ligon, *True & Exact History*, 43.

27. Beckles, *White Servitude and Black Slavery*, 48–49; Brown, *Register of the Privy Council of Scotland*, 3rd ser., 1:181, 2:101, 195.

28. William Fulbecke, *The Pandectes of the Law of Nations, Contayning Severall Discourses of the questions, points, and matters of law, wherein the nations of the world doe consent and accord* (London, 1602), 46v. See also Geoffrey Parker, "Early Modern Europe," in Michael Howard, George J. Andreopoulos, and Mark R. Shuman, eds., *The Laws of War: Constraints on Warfare in the Western World* (New Haven, CT: Yale University Press, 1994), 40–58; Alexander Gunkel and Jerome S. Handler, eds. and trans., "A German Indentured Servant in Barbados in 1652: The Account of Heinrich Von Uchteritz," *Journal of the Barbados Museum and Historical Society* 33 (1970): 92, 93.

29. Brown, *Register of the Privy Council of Scotland*, 3rd ser., 1:266.

30. Marcellus Rivers and Oxenbridge Foyle, *England's slavery, or Barbados merchandize; represented in a petition to the high court of Parliament* (London, 1659), 5, 6, 8.

31. Nicholas Canny, *Kingdom and Colony: Ireland in the Atlantic World, 1560–1800* (Baltimore: Johns Hopkins University Press, 1988); Oliver Cromwell to William Lenthall, Dublin, September 17, 1649, quoted in Sean O'Callaghan, *To Hell or Barbados: The Ethnic Cleansing of Ireland* (Dingle: Brandon, 2000), 25; Sir William Petty's estimate cited in Peter Linebaugh and Marcus Rediker, *The Many-Headed Hydra: Sailors, Slaves, Commoners and the Hidden History of the Revolutionary Atlantic* (Boston: Beacon Press, 2000), 123; "The Clonmacnoise Decrees," December 4, 1649, reprinted in Denis Murphy, *Cromwell in Ireland: A History of Cromwell's Irish Campaign* (Dublin: M. H. Gill & Son, 1897), 406–8; petition quoted in O'Callaghan, *To Hell or Barbados*, 80.

32. Aubrey Gwynn, "Indentured Servants and Negro Slaves in Barbados (1642–1650)," *Studies: An Irish Quarterly Review* 19 (1930): 279–94; O'Callaghan, *To Hell or*

Barbados, 85–86; Hilary McD. Beckles, "A 'Riotous and Unruly Lot': Irish Indentured Servants and Freemen in the English West Indies, 1644–1713," in Verene A. Shepherd and Hilary McD. Beckles, eds., *Caribbean Slavery in the Atlantic World* (Kingston, Jamaica: Ian Randle, 2000), 231.

33. Oldmixon, *British Empire in America*, 116; Sir Thomas Montgomery to the Lords of Trade and Plantations, Barbados, 1688, quoted in Beckles, *White Servitude and Black Slavery*, 92; Anonymous manuscript entitled "Some Observations on the Island of Barbadoes," Privy Council and Related Bodies: America and West Indies, Colonial Papers, National Archives, CO 1/21, no. 170, 120.

34. "An Act for the good Governing of Servants, and ordaining the Rights between Masters and Servants," in *Acts, Passed in the Island of Barbados: From 1643 to 1762, inclusive* (London, 1764), 35, 40, 41, 42, 36, 37, 39.

35. Ligon, *True & Exact History*, 44; Hilary McD. Beckles, "Rebels and Reactionaries: The Political Response of White Labourers to Planter-Class Hegemony in Seventeenth Century Barbados," *Journal of Caribbean History* 15 (1981): 11; "An ACT for the encouragement of White Servants," 158, 159.

36. Beckles, "Rebels and Reactionaries," 8, 9–10; Beckles, "Riotous and Unruly Lot," 226–38.

37. Ligon, *True & Exact History*, 45, 46; Beckles, "Rebels and Reactionaries," 8, 10; Barbados Council quoted in Shona Johnston, "'Being None of Any Account': Religion and Economic Status in Seventeenth Century Barbados," unpublished paper presented at the annual conference of the Omohundro Institute of Early American History and Culture, 2009, 4; Board of Trade, Barbados, January 20, 1692, CO 28/1, National Archives. I am grateful to Dr. Johnston for sharing her paper.

38. Dunn, *Sugar and Slaves*, 64; Beckles, *White Servitude and Black Slavery*, 132–38, 168; Quintanilla, "Late Seventeenth-Century Indentured Servants," 114–17.

39. Tomlins, *Freedom Bound*, 2–27, 9–10, 78–81, 231, 411, 429.

40. Dunn, *Sugar and Slaves*, 68.

41. William Dickson, *Mitigation of Slavery, in Two Parts* . . . (London: R. and A. Taylor, 1814), 275; William Dickson, *Letters on Slavery* (London: J. Phillips, 1789), 23; George Pinckard, *Notes on the West Indies* . . . (London: Baldwin, Craddock and Joy, 1816), 1:140. See also Justin Roberts, "Working Between the Lines: Labor and Agriculture on Two Barbadian Sugar Plantations, 1796–1797," *William and Mary Quarterly*, 3rd ser., 63 (2006): 551–86; David Watts, "The Origins of Barbadian Cane Hole Agriculture," *Journal of the Barbados Museum and Historical Society* 32 (1968): 143–51.

42. Winthrop Jordan, *White Over Black: American Attitudes Towards the Negro, 1550–1812* (Chapel Hill: University of North Carolina Press, 1968). Justin Roberts is a leading young scholar of slavery as, first and foremost, a labor system; see Roberts, *Slavery and the Enlightenment in the British Atlantic, 1750–1807* (Cambridge: Cambridge University Press, 2013). Scholars who have explored commonalities between the labor of enslaved Africans and that of other subjugated working people include Seth Rockman,

Scraping By: Wage Labor, Slavery, and Survival in Early Baltimore (2009), and Linebaugh and Rediker, *Many-Headed Hydra*.

Chapter 4

1. For an overview of the various editions of Colden's *History*, see John Gilmary Shea's introduction to Cadwallader Colden, *The History of the Five Indian Nations Depending on the Province of New York*, ed. John Gilmary Shea (New York, 1866); Cadwallader Colden, *The Letters and Papers of Cadwallader Colden*, 9 vols. (New York, 1918), 9:359n1 [hereafter cited as *Colden Papers*]; and Alfred R. Hoermann, *Cadwallader Colden: A Figure of the American Enlightenment* (Westport, CT: Greenwood Press, 2002), 164–69.

2. Peter Wraxall, *An Abridgment of the Indian Affairs Contained in Four Folio Volumes, Transacted in the Colony of New York, from the Year 1678 to the Year 1751*, ed. Charles Howard McIlwain (Cambridge, MA: Harvard University Press, 1915), 219.

3. For the imperial interest in Anglicizing the League in this period, see Timothy J. Shannon, *Indians and Colonists at the Crossroads of Empire: The Albany Congress of 1754* (Ithaca, NY: Cornell University Press, 2000); Timothy J. Shannon, "Dressing for Success on the Mohawk Frontier: Hendrick, William Johnson, and the Indian Fashion," *William and Mary Quarterly*, 3rd ser., 31 (1996): 13–42; Timothy J. Shannon, *Iroquois Diplomacy on the Early American Frontier* (New York: Viking, 2008); Eric Hinderaker, "The 'Four Indian Kings' and the Imaginative Construction of the First British Empire," *William and Mary Quarterly*, 3rd ser., 53 (1996): 487–526; and Eric Hinderaker, *The Two Hendricks: Unraveling a Mohawk Mystery* (Cambridge, MA: Harvard University Press, 2010), 72–104.

4. For a brief analysis of Colden's *History* through the lens of postcolonialism, see Ed White, "Early American Nations as Imagined Communities," *American Quarterly* 56 (2004): 49–81. In forming this argument, I have drawn more generally on the following: Michel de Certeau, *The Writing of History*, trans. Tom Conley (New York: Columbia University Press, 1988); Michel de Certeau, *Heterologies: Discourse on the Other*, trans. Brian Massumi (Minneapolis: University of Minnesota Press, 1986); Gyan Prakash, "Writing Post-Orientalist Histories of the Third World," *Comparative Studies in Society and History* 32 (1990): 383–408; Peter Nabokov, *A Forest of Time: American Indian Ways of History* (New York: Cambridge University Press, 2002); Calvin Martin, ed., *The American Indian and the Problem of History* (New York: Oxford University Press, 1987); and the essays in the forum "Colonial Historians and American Indians," *William and Mary Quarterly* 69 (2012): 451–540.

5. *Colden Papers*, 1:128.

6. Ibid., 1:128–30. Francis Jennings speculated about this incident, "It may be wondered whether Decanisora [Teganissorens] lost all influence back in Onondaga, out of Burnet's sight, but he does not appear again in the treaty records." This is, however, incorrect, because his mark appeared on a treaty the following year (in 1722), according to William Fenton, and then again in 1724. See Francis Jennings, *The Ambiguous Iroquois*

Empire: The Covenant Chain Confederation of Indian Tribes with the English Colonies (New York: W. W. Norton, 1984), 188; William N. Fenton, *The Great Law and the Longhouse: A Political History of the Iroquois Confederacy* (Norman: University of Oklahoma Press, 1998), 395; Daniel K. Richter, *The Ordeal of the Longhouse: The Peoples of the Iroquois League in the Era of European Colonization* (Chapel Hill: University of North Carolina Press for the Institute of Early American History and Culture, 1992), 273.

7. *Colden Papers*, 1:128–30. For Teganissorens's first public appearance, see Richter, *Ordeal of the Longhouse*, 153.

8. E. B. O'Callaghan and Berthold Fernow, eds., *Documents Relative to the Colonial History of the State of New York,* 15 vols. (Albany, 1853–87), 5:721.

9. Cadwallader Colden, *The History of the Five Indian Nations Depending on the Province of New-York in America* (1727, 1747; Ithaca, NY: Cornell University Press, 1958), 140–41. Unless otherwise noted, all further citations will be to this edition of the text.

10. John Locke, *Second Treatise of Civil Government*, ed. and intro. C. B. McPherson (Cambridge: Cambridge University Press, 1980), chap. 5, "On Property," sec. 49.

11. Pierre Clastres, *Society Against the State: Essays in Political Anthropology* (New York: Zone Books, 1987), 197, 206. For other classificatory schemes, see Elmer R. Service, *Primitive Social Organization* (New York: Random House, 1962); and the criticism of Morton Fried, "On the Evolution of Social Stratification and the State," in Stanley Diamond, ed., *Culture in History* (New York: Columbia University Press, 1960), 713–31. Currently, North American archaeologists prefer to use a more flexible concept of cultural complexity; see Timothy R. Pauketat and Diana DiPaolo Loren, eds., *North American Archaeology* (Oxford: Blackwell, 2005). For the exercise of coercive power in states, see the work of Michel Foucault, particularly *Discipline and Punish: The Birth of the Prison* (New York: Pantheon Books, 1977).

12. Colden, *History,* "living images" of the remote past, x; other quotations, xxi.

13. Ibid., xx.

14. Clastres, *Society Against the State*, 207. For gift economies, see Maurice Godelier, *The Enigma of the Gift*, trans. Nora Scott (Chicago: University of Chicago Press, 1999), and the important works of Marcel Mauss, Claude Levi-Strauss, and Annette Weiner discussed therein.

15. Colden, *History,* xxi. For the spatial mobility of Haudenosaunee in this period, which is demonstrative of the extent of these networks, see Jon Parmenter, *The Edge of the Woods: Iroquoia 1534–1701* (East Lansing: Michigan State University Press, 2010).

16. Colden, *History*, ix.

17. Ibid.

18. On the authority of firsthand experience, see Anthony Pagden, *European Encounters with the New World: From Renaissance to Romanticism* (New Haven, CT: Yale University Press, 1993), chap. 2; and Anthony Pagden, *The Fall of Natural Man: The American Indian and the Origins of Comparative Ethnology* (Cambridge: Cambridge University Press, 1992). For Lahontan, see W. J. Eccles, *The French in North America, 1500–1783,* rev. ed. (East Lansing: Michigan State University Press, 1998), 29. For La

Potherie, see Gilles Havard, *The Great Peace of Montreal of 1701: French-Native Diplomacy in the Seventeenth Century*, trans. Phyllis Aronoff and Howard Scott (Montreal and Kingston: McGill-Queen's University Press, 2001), 202–3. On Spanish histories and ethnographies, see Jorge Cañizares-Esguerra, *How to Write the History of the New World: Histories, Epistemologies, and Identities in the Eighteenth-Century Atlantic World* (Stanford, CA: Stanford University Press, 2001), esp. 1, 8, 133. For French and English literature, see Gordon M. Sayre, *Les Sauvages Américains: Representations of Native Americans in French and English Colonial Literature* (Chapel Hill: University of North Carolina Press, 1997). For a general overview, see Wilcomb E. Washburn and Bruce G. Trigger, "Native Peoples in Euro-American Historiography," in Bruce G. Trigger and Wilcomb E. Washburn, eds., *The Cambridge History of the Native Peoples of the Americas, Vol. 1: North America* (New York: Cambridge University Press, 1996), 61–124.

19. Colden, *History*, xii. For earlier English textual precedents and Colden's cocreation of a new genre, see Lawrence C. Wroth, "The Indian Treaty as Literature," *Yale Review* 17 (1928): 749–66; and William N. Fenton, "Structure, Continuity, and Change in the Process of Iroquois Treaty Making," in Francis Jennings, William N. Fenton, Mary A. Druke, and David R. Miller, eds., *The History and Culture of Iroquois Diplomacy: An Interdisciplinary Guide to the Treaties of the Six Nations and Their League* (Syracuse, NY: Syracuse University Press, 1985), 3–36, esp. 5–7. The original manuscript records used by Colden were bound in four folio volumes in the eighteenth century and were taken to Canada during the Revolutionary War, but the first two volumes are now lost. See Wraxall,, *Abridgment of the Indian Affairs*, ed. McIlwain, chap. 3, intro. Luckily a great deal of the lost material survived in copies made by Robert Livingston, secretary for Indian affairs. See Lawrence H. Leder, *The Livingston Indian Records, 1666–1723* (Gettysburg: Pennsylvania Historical Association, 1956), intro.

20. Colden, *History*, xii, xvii.

21. Ibid., x–xii.

22. Ibid., ix. On the problem of translation, see also James H. Merrell, "'I Desire All That I Have Said . . . May Be Taken Down Aright': Revisiting Teedyuscung's 1756 Treaty Council Speeches," *William and Mary Quarterly*, 3rd ser., 63 (2006): 777–826; and Andrew Newman, *On Records: Delaware Indians, Colonists, and the Media of History and Memory* (Lincoln: University of Nebraska Press, 2012).

23. All quotations in this paragraph are from Cadwallader Colden, *History of the Five Indian Nations . . . Third Edition* (London, 1755), "Part II the Preface," 94–96. See also "A Memorial Concerning the Furr-Trade of the Province of New York, Presented to . . . William Burnet . . . the 10th of November 1724," reprinted therein. For Colden's vilification of the Albany Dutch, see the above edition, 100–101. See also Colden to Peter Collinson, May 1742, *Colden Papers*, 2:259. For Colden's role in these efforts, see Shannon, *Indians and Colonists at the Crossroads of Empire*.

24. Colden, *History*, 6.

25. Ibid., 18.

26. Ibid., 19; Richard White, *The Middle Ground: Indians, Empires, and Republics in the Great Lakes Region, 1650–1815, Twentieth Anniversary Edition* (New York: Cambridge University Press, 2011), xxvi.

27. Colden, *History,* xxi.

28. Ibid., 21.

29. Leder, "Livingston Indian Records, 1666–1723," 46; and for similar statements by the other four nations, see 44, 45, 48.

30. *An Account of the Treaty Between His Excellency Benjamin Fletcher Captain General and Governour in Chief of the Province of New-York, &c. and the Indians of the Five Nations* (New York, 1694), 26–27.

31. Seth Newhouse, "Mohawk Cosmogony of De-ka-na-wi-da's Government, 1885," Newhouse Collection, American Philosophical Society, Philadelphia, p. 11

32. "Deganawi:dah Epic, Fenton's Complete Version, Dictated by John Arthur Gibson to A. A. Goldenweiser, June 30, 1912," trans. William N. Fenton and Simeon Gibson, October 14, 1943, William Fenton Papers, American Philosophical Society, Philadelphia, ms. coll. 20, ser. 3, works by Fenton, box Deganawidah #8, folder #8, ¶221.

33. On the problem of vengeance in states and nonstates, see Jared Diamond, "Vengeance Is Ours: What Can Tribal Societies Tell Us About Our Need to Get Even?" *New Yorker,* April 21, 2008, 74–87.

34. Colden, *History,* 28–29.

35. Ibid., 33.

36. Ibid., 34–35.

37. Ibid., 36–37.

38. See Richter, *Ordeal of the Longhouse*, ch. 8–10 for fuller discussion of neutralist diplomacy.

39. Colden, *History*, 39–40.

40. Ibid., 51.

41. Ibid., 52–53.

42. Quotation is from Lahontan, *New Voyages*, 71. For the spies, see ibid., 75; and Colden, *History*, 53.

43. Colden, *History*, 55.

44. Ibid.; "Chair of State," Lahontan, *New Voyages,* 80.

45. Colden, *History,* 57; Lahontan, *New Voyages,* 86–87.

46. Colden, *History*, 159.

47. Ibid., 41–42.

48. As cited in Jennings, *Ambiguous Iroquois Empire*, 194.

49. Colden, *History,* 60.

50. Ibid., 62.

51. Ibid., 63–65.

52. Ibid., 66.

53. Ibid., 66–69.

54. For a biography of Kondiaronk, see Havard, *Great Peace of Montreal of 1701*, 199–202; Washburn and Trigger, "Native Peoples in Euro-American Historiography," 71–72.

55. Colden, *History*, 70–72.

56. Ibid., 73–74.

57. Wilbur R. Jacobs, "Cadwallader Colden's Noble Iroquois Savages," in Lawrence H. Leder, ed., *The Colonial Legacy: Volume III, Historians of Nature and Man's Nature; Volume IV, Early Nationalist Historians* (New York, Harper & Row,1973), 43; Jennings, *Ambiguous Iroquois Empire*, 11, 13.

Chapter 5

1. Frederick Jackson Turner, "The First Official Frontier of the Massachusetts Bay," in Turner, ed., *The Frontier in American History* (New York: Henry Holt, 1920), 39–66, 40.

2. See Frederick Jackson Turner, "The Significance of the Frontier in American History," in Turner, *Frontier*, 1–38.

3. John M. Murrin, "Anglicizing an American Colony: The Transformation of Provincial Massachusetts" (Ph.D. diss., Yale University, 1966), 118–19.

4. Ibid., 13–14.

5. Ibid., 1.

6. On the importance of recognizing the commonalities between colonists and Indians generally, see Nancy Shoemaker, *A Strange Likeness: Becoming Red and White in Eighteenth-Century North America* (Oxford: Oxford University Press, 2004).

7. Fred Anderson, *A People's Army: Massachusetts Soldiers and Society in the Seven Years' War* (New York: W. W. Norton, 1984).

8. See in particular Douglas Edward Leach, *Roots of Conflict: British Armed Forces and Colonial Americans* (Chapel Hill: University of North Carolina Press, 1986). See generally Don Higginbotham, "The Early American Way of War: Reconnaissance and Appraisal," *William and Mary Quarterly*, 3rd ser., 44 (1987): 230–33, 246–49.

9. John Grenier, *The First Way of War: American War Making on the Frontier* (Cambridge: Cambridge University Press, 2007), 42–43.

10. Murrin, "Anglicizing an American Colony," 95.

11. Guy Chet, *Conquering the American Wilderness: The Triumph of European Warfare in the Colonial Northeast* (Amherst: University of Massachusetts Press, 2003).

12. John M. Murrin, "Beneficiaries of Catastrophe: The English Colonies in America," in Eric Foner, ed., *The New American History*, rev. ed. (Philadelphia: Temple University Press, 1997), 3–30.

13. David J. Silverman, *Faith and Boundaries: Colonists, Christianity, and Community Among the Wampanoag Indians of Martha's Vineyard* (Cambridge: Cambridge University Press, 2005), contains a persuasive analysis of the impact of disease on the outlook of Martha's Vineyard's Indians.

14. Murrin, "Anglicizing an American Colony," 129–36.

15. Philip D. Curtin, "Epidemiology and the Slave Trade," *Political Science Quarterly* 83 (1968): 190–216; William H. McNeil, *Plagues and Peoples* (Garden City, NY: Anchor Press, 1976); Alfred Crosby, "Virgin Soil Epidemics as a Factor in the Aboriginal Depopulation in America," *William and Mary Quarterly*, 3rd ser., 33 (1976): 289–99. For an incisive review of the impact and implications of the literature on "virgin soil epidemics," see David S. Jones, "Virgin Soils Revisited," *William and Mary Quarterly*, 3rd ser., 40 (2003): 703–42.

16. Murrin, "Anglicizing an American Colony," 91.

17. This is from my conversation with John Murrin at the McNeil Center for Early American Studies in Philadelphia on April 20, 2013.

18. Works by Murrin's students on Native American history include Gregory Evans Dowd, *A Spirited Resistance: The North American Indian Struggle for Unity, 1745–1815* (Baltimore: Johns Hopkins University Press, 1992); Gregory Evans Dowd, *War Under Heaven: Pontiac, the Indians Nations, and the British Empire* (Baltimore: Johns Hopkins University Press, 2002); Evan Haefeli and Kevin Sweeney, *Captors and Captives: The 1704 French and Indian Raid on Deerfield* (Amherst: University of Massachusetts Press, 2003); Silverman, *Faith and Boundaries;* David J. Silverman, *Red Brethren: The Brothertown and Stockbridge Indians and the Problem of Race in Early America* (Ithaca, NY: Cornell University Press, 2010); and Ignacio Gallup-Diaz, *The Door of the Seas and the Key to the Universe: Indian Politics and Imperial Rivalry in the Darien, 1640–1750* (New York: Columbia University Press, 2004).

19. Patrick M. Malone, *The Skulking Way of War: Technology and Tactics Among New England Indians* (Lanham, MD: Madison Books, 1991). See also Ian K. Steele, *Warpaths: Invasions of North America* (Oxford: Oxford University Press, 1994); Armstrong Stuckey, *Europeans and Native American Warfare, 1675–1815* (Norman: University of Oklahoma Press, 1998).

20. Craig S. Keener, "An Ethnohistorical Analysis of Iroquois Assault Tactics Used Against Fortified Settlements of the Northeast in the Seventeenth Century," *Ethnohistory* 46 (1999): 777–807. See also Wayne E. Lee, "Fortify, Fight, or Flee: Tuscarora and Cherokee Defensive Warfare and Military Culture Adaptation," *Journal of Military History* 68 (2004): 713–70.

21. See James H. Merrell, "The Indians' New World: The Catawba Experience," *William and Mary Quarterly*, 3rd ser., 41 (1984): 537–65.

22. The most influential proponent of this kind of research, concentrating on the postcontact, "historical" era, is Richard White. See White, *The Roots of Dependency: Subsistence, Environment and Social Change Among the Choctaws, Pawnees, and Navajos* (Lincoln: University of Nebraska Press, 1983); White, *The Middle Ground: Indians, Empires, and Republics in the Great Lakes Region, 1650–1815* (New York: Cambridge University Press, 1993).

23. For a recent analysis of this problem, and an evocative demonstration of how it might be overcome, see James F. Brooks, "Women, Men, and Cycles of Evangelism in the Southwest Borderlands, A.D. 750 to 1750," *American Historical Review* 118 (2013):

738–64. Daniel K. Richter, *Before the American Revolution: America's Ancient Pasts* (Cambridge, MA: Harvard University Press, 2011), takes a similar approach to the history of eastern North America on a grand scale.

24. Francis Jennings, *The Invasion of America: Indians, Colonialism, and the Cant of Conquest* (New York: W. W. Norton, 1975), 220–25; Chet, *Conquering the American Wilderness*, 24–27, 34–36. See also Ronald Dale Karr, "'Why Should You Be So Furious': The Violence of the Pequot War," *Journal of American History* 85 (1998): 876–909, citing many earlier works.

25. For a starting point, and an indication of how a better analysis might proceed, see Wayne Lee, *Barbarians and Brothers: Anglo-American Warfare, 1500–1865* (Oxford: Oxford University Press, 2011), 130–41, esp. 139.

26. See Andrew Lipman, "'A Meanes to Knitt Them Togeather': The Exchange of Body Parts in the Pequot War," *William and Mary Quarterly*, 3rd ser., 45 (2008): 3–28.

27. See Richard R. Johnson, "The Search for a Usable Indian: An Aspect of the Defense of Colonial New England," *Journal of American History* 64 (1977): 623–51.

28. See generally Wayne Lee, ed., *Empires and Indigenes: Intercultural Alliance, Imperial Expansion, and Warfare in the Early Modern World* (New York: New York University Press, 2012).

29. Jeffers Lennox, "An Empire on Paper: The Founding of Halifax and Conceptions of Imperial Space, 1744–1755," *Canadian Historical Review* 88 (2007): 373–412.

30. A. J. B. Johnson, *Endgame 1758: The Promise, the Glory, and the Despair of Louisbourg's Last Decade* (Lincoln: University of Nebraska Press, 2008), 161.

31. Brian D. Carroll, "'Savages' in the Service of Empire: Native American Soldiers in Gorham's Rangers, 1744–1762," *New England Quarterly* 85 (2012): 383–429.

32. Geoffrey Plank, *An Unsettled Conquest: The British Campaign Against the Peoples of Acadia* (Philadelphia: University of Pennsylvania Press, 2000), 129; Geoffrey Plank, *Rebellion and Savagery: The Jacobite Rising of 1745 and the British Empire* (Philadelphia: University of Pennsylvania Press, 2006), 161.

33. William Thynne to John Campbell, 4th Earl of Loudon, February 12, 1756, LO (NA) 823, Huntington Library, San Marino, California. See also William Thynne to John Campbell, 4th Earl of Loudon, February 27, 1756, LO 861, Huntington Library.

34. James Wolfe to Charles, 3d Duke of Richmond, July 28, 1758, in R. H. Whitworth, ed., "Some Unpublished Wolfe Letters, 1755–58," *Journal of the Society for Army Historical Research* 53 (1975): 65–86, 83.

35. Charles Lawrence, orders for attacking Louisbourg, May 1758, AB 303, Huntington Library.

36. Jeffery, 1st Baron Amherst, "Address to the Officers and Men of the Army before Attacking Louisbourg", June 3, 1758, LO (NA) 5847, Huntington Library.

37. Olaudah Equiano, *The Interesting Narrative of the Life of Olaudah Equiano, Written by Himself* (New York: Bedford Books, 1995), 69.

38. See generally Geoffrey Plank, "Deploying Tribes and Clans: Mohawks in Nova Scotia and Scottish Highlanders in Georgia," in Lee, ed., *Empires and Indigenes*, 221–49.

39. John Shy, "The American Military Experience: History and Learning," *Journal of Interdisciplinary History* 1 (1971): 205–28, 212, 213.

40. Russell F. Weigley, *The American Way of War* (Bloomington: Indiana University Press, 1973). See also Brian M. Linn, "*The American Way of War* Revisited," *Journal of Military History* 66 (2002): 501–33.

41. Grenier, *First Way of War*, 21.

42. Lee, *Barbarians and Brothers*.

43. See John G. Reid, "*Pax Britannica* or *Pax Indigena*? Planter Nova Scotia (1760–1782) and Competing Strategies of Pacification," *Canadian Historical Review* 85 (2004): 669–92. Also see John G. Reid, "Imperial-Aboriginal Friendship in Eighteenth-Century Mi'kma'ki/Wulstukwik," in Jerry Bannister and Liam Riordan, eds., *The Loyal Atlantic: Remaking the British Atlantic in the Revolutionary Era* (Toronto: University of Toronto Press, 2012), 75–102.

44. See *Pennsylvania Gazette*, June 26 and November 17, 1755.

45. Peter Silver, *Our Savage Neighbors: How Indian War Transformed Early America* (New York: W. W. Norton, 2008), 161–63; Geoffrey Plank, *John Woolman's Path to the Peaceable Kingdom: A Quaker in the British Empire* (Philadelphia: University of Pennsylvania Press, 2012), 127–29.

46. Silver, *Our Savage Neighbors*.

47. T. H. Breen, *American Insurgents, American Patriots: The Revolution of the People* (New York: Hill & Wang, 2010), 21–24, 42, 84, 268, 298.

48. Ibid., 218, 268, 275.

49. See Lawrence Delbert Cress, *Citizens in Arms: The Army and Militia in American Society to the War of 1812* (Chapel Hill: University of North Carolina Press, 1982).

50. Joyce Lee Malcolm, *To Keep and Bear Arms: The Origins of an Anglo-American Right* (Cambridge, MA: Harvard University Press, 1994).

51. J. R. Western, *The English Militia in the Eighteenth Century: The Story of a Political Issue, 1660–1802* (London: Routledge, 1965), 85.

52. See Plank, *Rebellion and Savagery*, 83–84; Western, *English Militia*, 112–13.

53. Eliga H. Gould, "To Strengthen the King's Hands: Dynastic Legitimacy, Militia Reform and Ideas of National Unity in England 1745–1760," *Historical Journal* 34 (1991): 329–48.

54. David Thomas Konig, "The Second Amendment: A Missing Transatlantic Context for the Historical Meaning of 'the Right of the People to Keep and Bear Arms,'" *Law and History Review* 22 (2004): 119–59.

55. Michael A. Bellesiles, *Arming America: The Origins of a National Gun Culture* (New York: Alfred A. Knopf, 2000).

56. See James T. Lindgren, "Fall from Grace: *Arming America* and the Bellesiles Scandal," *Yale Law Journal* 111 (2002): 2195–249; Stanley N. Katz, Hanna H. Gray, and Laurel Thatcher Ulrich, "Report of the Investigative Committee in the Matter of Professor Michael Bellesiles," Emory University, 2002, http://www.emory.edu/news/Releases/Final_Report.pdf.

57. Patricia Cohen, "Scholar Emerges from Doghouse," *New York Times*, August 3, 2010, C1.

58. On the making of the print, see David Hackett Fisher, *Paul Revere's Ride* (New York: Oxford University Press, 1994), 24.

59. See generally Hiller B. Zobel, *The Boston Massacre* (New York: W. W. Norton, 1970).

60. See particularly essays by A. Roger Ekirch, Jeffrey J. Crow, Emory G. Evans, and Edward J. Cashin in Ronald Hoffman, Thad W. Tate, and Peter J. K. Albert, eds., *An Uncivil War: The Southern Backcountry during the American Revolution* (Charlottesville: University Press of Virginia, 1985); Jim Piecuch, *Three Peoples, One King: Loyalists, Indians, and Slaves in the Revolutionary South, 1775–1782* (Columbia: University of South Carolina Press, 2008), 228–337; Wayne Lee, *Crowds and Soldiers in Revolutionary North Carolina: The Culture of Violence in Riot and War* (Gainesville: University Press of Florida, 2001). The classic study highlighting the role of militia forces in the Revolution is John Shy, *A People Numerous and Armed: Reflections on the Military Struggle for American Independence*, rev. ed. (Ann Arbor: University of Michigan Press, 1990). Recent, important works on the Loyalists include Maya Jasanoff, *Liberty's Exiles: American Loyalists in the Revolutionary World* (New York: Alfred A. Knopf, 2011); and Bannister and Riordan, eds., *Loyal Atlantic*.

61. For a revealing episode, see Report of the General Officers, May 23, 1778, Loudon Papers, North America 6577, Huntington Library; Plank, *Rebellion and Savagery*, 187–88.

62. Eliga Gould, *Among the Powers of the Earth: The American Revolution and the Making of a New World Empire* (Cambridge, MA: Harvard University Press, 2012), emphasizes the leverage individual combatants and civilians gained from belonging to internationally recognized, powerful, and respected polities. For a discussion of the rules of war in another revolutionary context, see Barbara Donagan, "Atrocity, War Crime and Treason in the English Civil War," *American Historical Review* 99 (1994): 1137–66.

63. Adam J. Hirsch, "The Collision of Military Cultures in Seventeenth-Century New England," *Journal of American History* 74 (1988): 1187–212.

64. See for example Hal Langfur, *The Forbidden Lands: Colonial Identity, Frontier Violence, and the Persistence of Brazil's Eastern Indians* (Stanford, CA: Stanford University Press, 2006).

65. Richter, *Before the American Revolution*.

Chapter 6

1. John M. Murrin, "Anglicizing an American Colony: The Transformation of Provincial Massachusetts" (Ph.D. diss., Yale University, 1966). On prism producing spectrum of settlement, see John M. Murrin et al., *Liberty, Equality, Power: A History of the American People Volume 1: To 1877*, 2nd ed. (Fort Worth, TX: Harcourt-Brace, 1999), 87–92, esp. 87–88.

2. Murrin, "Anglicizing an American Colony," 290.

3. Jon Butler, *New World Faiths: Religion in Colonial America* (2000; Oxford: Oxford University Press, 2008), 110. The argument that various religious transformations of 1680 to 1770 were "special, sometimes unique, American choices" is elaborated in Jon Butler, *Becoming America: The Revolution Before 1776* (Cambridge, MA: Harvard University Press, 2000), 185–224, esp. 224. Cf. John M. Murrin and David S. Silverman, "The Quest for America: Reflections on Distinctiveness, Pluralism, and Public Life," *Journal of Interdisciplinary History* 33 (2002): 235–46.

4. Two such helpful examples on Virginia are Jewel L. Spangler, *Virginians Reborn: Anglican Monopoly, Evangelical Dissent, and the Rise of the Baptists in the Late Eighteenth Century* (Charlottesville: University Press of Virginia, 2008); and John A. Ragosta, *Wellspring of Liberty: How Virginia's Religious Dissenters Helped Win the American Revolution and Secured Religious Liberty* (New York: Oxford University Press, 2010).

5. Ned Landsman argues that the union (1707) decentralized lines of authority and meant that colonial Anglicans had to reestablish "the place of an English national church in a British American empire"; see Ned C. Landsman, "The Episcopate, the British Union, and the Failure of Religious Settlement in Colonial British America," in Chris Beneke and Christopher S. Grenda, eds., *The First Prejudice: Religious Toleration and Intolerance in Early America* (Philadelphia: University of Pennsylvania Press, 2011), 75–97, esp. 77–78.

6. On the Church of England's expansion, see Patricia Bonomi, *Under the Cope of Heaven: Religion, Society, and Politics in Colonial America* (New York: Oxford University Press, 1986), 41–61.

7. On British Atlantic integration as both unifying and divisive, see Nancy L. Rhoden, "The American Revolution (I): The Paradox of Atlantic Integration," in Stephen Foster, ed., *British North America in the Seventeenth and Eighteenth Centuries,* Oxford History of the British Empire Companion Series (Oxford: Oxford University Press, 2013), 255–88.

8. Edward L. Bond, "Colonial Origins and Growth: The Church of England Adapts to North America, 1607–1760," chap. 1 of Edward L. Bond and Joan R. Gundersen, "The Episcopal Church in Virginia, 1607–2007," *Virginia Magazine of History and Biography* 115 (2007): 165–99, esp. 172–81.

9. Maryland's 1696 legislation was approved in 1702; South Carolina's establishment dates from 1706; and North Carolina's establishment passed in 1765.

10. James B. Bell, *The Imperial Origins of the King's Church in Early America, 1607–1783* (Basingstoke: Palgrave, 2004), 26–40; and on royal governors' ecclesiastical duties, see 43–57, esp. 46–47, 56.

11. Ned C. Landsman, *Crossroads of Empire: The Middle Colonies in British North America* (Baltimore: Johns Hopkins University Press, 2010), 122–24. On toleration and tolerance/intolerance in the Netherlands and New Netherland, see Ned C. Landsman, "Roots, Routes, and Rootedness: Diversity, Migration, and Toleration in Mid-Atlantic Pluralism," *Early American Studies* 2 (2004): 267–309, esp. 281–82; Evan Haefeli, *New*

Netherland and the Dutch Origins of American Religious Liberty (Philadelphia: University of Pennsylvania Press, 2012).

12. Rowan Strong, *Anglicanism and the British Empire, c. 1700–1850* (Oxford: Oxford University Press, 2007), 37.

13. Ibid., 6, 108–9.

14. Bell, *Imperial Origins of the King's Church*, 75.

15. Butler, *New World Faiths*, 111, 112–13, estimates that Congregationalists in New England created sixty new congregations between 1680 and 1710.

16. On relative strength of Anglicanism on the coast rather than the frontier, see Nancy L. Rhoden, *Revolutionary Anglicanism: The Colonial Church of England Clergy During the American Revolution* (Basingstoke: Macmillan, 1999), 24–26.

17. Travis Glasson, *Mastering Christianity: Missionary Anglicanism and Slavery in the Atlantic World* (New York: Oxford University Press, 2012).

18. Jon Butler, *Awash in a Sea of Faith: Christianizing the American People* (Cambridge, MA: Harvard University Press, 1990), 108–16.

19. Dell Upton, *Holy Things and Profane: Anglican Parish Churches in Colonial Virginia* (1986; New Haven, CT: Yale University Press, 1997).

20. Lauren Winner, *A Cheerful and Comfortable Faith: Anglican Religious Practice in the Elite Households of Eighteenth-Century Virginia* (New Haven, CT: Yale University Press, 2010).

21. Rhoden, *Revolutionary Anglicanism*, 11–12; John K. Nelson, *A Blessed Company: Parishes, Parsons, and Parishioners in Anglican Virginia, 1690–1776* (Chapel Hill: University of North Carolina Press, 2001), 187–210.

22. Edward L. Bond, "Anglican Theology and Devotion in James Blair's Virginia, 1685–1743: Private Piety in the Public Church," *Virginia Magazine of History and Biography* 104 (1996): 313–40, esp. 324.

23. On Anglican conventions of clergy, see Bell, *Imperial Origins of the King's Church*, 107–24.

24. Gerald J. Goodwin, "The Anglican Reaction to the Great Awakening," *Historical Magazine of the Protestant Episcopal Church* 35 (1966): 343–71.

25. Carla Gardina Pestana, *Protestant Empire: Religion and the Making of the British Atlantic World* (Philadelphia: University of Pennsylvania Press, 2009), 195.

26. On Whitefield and Garden, see Bell, *Imperial Origins of the King's Church*, 66–69.

27. Bell, *Imperial Origins of the King's Church*, 43–57, esp. 43, 125–41. There were seventeen commissaries in the colonial period. Governors granted licenses for marriage, proved wills, and conferred benefices, duties which fell to prelates in England.

28. For the suggestion that commissaries and clergy conventions fit in the "emerging Americanization process of the King's church," see Bell, *Imperial Origins of the King's Church*, 73; and on conventions of the clergy, see 107, 123.

29. Peter M. Doll, *Revolution, Religion, and National Identity: Imperial Anglicanism in British North America, 1745–1795* (Cranbury, NJ: Associated University Presses, 2000), 178.

30. On southern Anglican opposition to bishops, see Frederick V. Mills, Sr., *Bishops by Ballot: An Eighteenth Century Ecclesiastical Revolution* (New York: Oxford University Press, 1978); and John F. Woolverton, *Colonial Anglicanism in North America* (Detroit: Wayne State University Press, 1984).

31. Doll, *Revolution, Religion, and National Identity*, 160.

32. Ibid., 163; and on Yale apostates' work to end legal disabilities of New England Anglicans, see 161–63.

33. On Harvard, see Bell, *Imperial Origins of the King's Church*, 144–45. Bell notes that over one hundred native-born men from Massachusetts became Anglican clergy in the colonial era. See also Doll, *Revolution, Religion, and National Identity*, 160, which claims that between 1724 and 1765 Yale graduated four hundred ministers and that 10 percent of those became Anglican clergymen.

34. Bell, *Imperial Origins of the King's Church*, 158–62.

35. Julie Flavell, *When London Was Capital of America* (New Haven, CT: Yale University Press, 2010).

36. Strong, *Anglicanism and the British Empire*, 115, argues that the failure to secure colonial bishops proved the "de facto subservience of church to Parliament" and demonstrated that the SPG was not merely "British imperialism in ecclesiastical guise," as Carl Bridenbaugh claimed. Cf. Carl Bridenbaugh, *Mitre and Sceptre: Transatlantic Faiths, Ideas, Personalities, and Politics, 1689–1775* (New York: Oxford University Press, 1965).

37. Jonathan Mayhew, *Observations on the Charter and Conduct of the Society for the Propagation of the Gospel in Foreign Parts: Designed to Shew Their Non-Conformity to Each Other* (Boston, 1763); Charles Chauncy, *A Letter to a Friend, Containing Remarks on Certain Passages in a Sermon Preached by the Right Reverend Father in God, John Lord Bishop of Landaff, Before the Incorporated Society for the Propagation of the Gospel in Foreign Parts, at Their Anniversary Meeting in the Parish Church of St. Mary-le-Bow, February 20, 1767* (Boston, 1767).

38. Thomas Bradbury Chandler, *An Appeal to the Public* (New York: James Parker, [1767]), 90. For an argument about Chandler's own insensitivities, including his language of national establishment and his use of the term "dissenters," see Landsman, "The Episcopate, the British Union," 89–91.

39. Doll, *Revolution, Religion, and National Identity*, 157, 175, claims that in "private writings and less discrete public utterances" English and American advocates of episcopacy did reveal their hope for regular bishops. This is a reasonable argument, although in the case of colonial missionaries writing to the SPG secretary, the content was naturally also shaped by the author's impression of the society's goals.

40. Doll, *Revolution, Religion, and National Identity*, 164, notes that Bishop Gibson knew he legally could consecrate suffragan bishops, with only the king's consent, but that he also knew it would not be politically prudent to do so.

41. Bell, *Imperial Origins of the King's Church*, 193.

42. Pestana, *Protestant Empire*, 159–82, esp. 169.

43. Henry Melchior Mühlenberg to Joachim Oporin, August 12, 1743, in John W. Kleiner and Helmut T. Lehmann, eds. and trans., *The Correspondence of Heinrich Melchior Mühlenberg*, 4 vols. (Camden, ME: Picton Press, 1993–2010), 1:116.

44. This is not to suggest English churchmen did not find the Toleration Act and bills for occasional conformity unsettling. Cf. Norman Sykes, *Church and State in England in the Eighteenth Century* (Hamden, CT: Archon Books, 1962), 315–16.

45. SPG missionary George Craig estimated that Anglican parishioners made up less than 1/50 of the population of Pennsylvania. See George Craig to SPG, September 3, 1764, in *Historical Collections Relating to the American Colonial Church*, 5 vols. (New York: AMS Press, 1969), 2:361 [henceforth *Hist. Coll.*].

46. Nancy L. Rhoden, "Is God American or English: The English Clergy as Political Agents of Loyalism and Revolutionary Order," in Hermann Wellenreuther, Thomas Müller-Bahlke, and A. Gregg Roeber, eds., *The Transatlantic World of Heinrich Melchior Mühlenberg in the Eighteenth Century*, Hallesche Forschungen [Halle Researches] 35 (Halle, Germany: Franckesche Stiftungen, 2013), 317–46; William Pencak, "Out of Many, One: Pennsylvania's Anglican Loyalist Clergy in the American Revolution," in William Pencak, ed., *Pennsylvania's Revolution* (University Park: Pennsylvania State University Press, 2010), 97–120.

47. Case of the Protestant Episcopal Missionaries of Pennsylvania to Assembly, May 20, 1778, in *Hist. Coll.*, 2:491–92.

48. Richard Peters to Bishop of London, August 30, 1768, in *Hist. Coll.*, 2:433; Thomas Barton and Episcopal Clergy of Pennsylvania to SPG, May 2, 1760, in *Hist. Coll.*, 2:315.

49. For a more detailed discussion of Anglican-German union, see Rhoden, "Is God American or English," 321–30.

50. William Smith to SPG, October 2, 1768, in *Hist. Coll.*, 2:434; Richard Peters, William Smith, and Jacob Duché to SPG, October 14, 1772, in *Hist. Coll.*, 2:460.

51. William Smith to Earl of Shaftsbury and others, March 12, 1759, in *Hist. Coll.*, 2:541; Archbishop of Canterbury (Herring) to William Smith, undated, in *Hist. Coll.*, 2:548.

52. [Gotthilf August Francke] to Mühlenberg, June 24, 1756, in Kleiner and Lehmann, eds. and trans., *Correspondence of Heinrich Melchior Mühlenberg*, 3:344.

53. Hugh Neill's opinions are described in Archbishop of Canterbury to Jacob Duché, September 16, 1763, in *Hist. Coll.*, 2:389–90; Richard Peters to Archbishop of Canterbury, October 17, 1763, in *Hist. Coll.*, 2:391; William Smith to SPG, March 3, 1763, in *Hist. Coll.*, 2:403.

54. Nelson, *Blessed Company*, 286.

55. On the House of Burgesses' persecution of Quakers in 1660s, see Monica Najar, "Sectarians and Strategies of Dissent in Colonial Virginia," in Paul Rasor and Richard E. Bond, eds., *From Jamestown to Jefferson: The Evolution of Religious Freedom in Virginia* (Charlottesville: University Press of Virginia, 2011), 117–18.

56. Bonomi, *Under the Cope of Heaven*, 42–44, esp. 42

57. Bell, *Imperial Origins of the King's Church*, 141.

58. Governors had largely compelled vestries to offer clergy permanent positions, rather than their previous practice of hiring a minister on a yearly basis.

59. Warren M. Billings, John E. Selby, and Thad W. Tate, *Colonial Virginia: A History* (White Plains, NY: KTO Press, 1986), 139–46.

60. On ecclesiastical courts losing effectiveness after 1660, see Norman Sykes, *From Sheldon to Secker: Aspects of English Church History, 1660–1768* (Cambridge: Cambridge University Press, 1959), 19. A more recent summary indicates that the pace of decline was different for each diocese, and their work did persist through the eighteenth century. See John Walsh and Stephen Taylor, "The Church and Anglicanism in the 'Long' Eighteenth Century," in John Walsh, Colin Haydon, and Stephen Taylor, eds., *The Church of England, c. 1689–c. 1833: From Toleration to Tractarianism* (Cambridge: Cambridge University Press), 6.

61. Bell, *Imperial Origins of the King's Church*, 66.

62. Billings et al., *Colonial Virginia*, 141.

63. Walsh and Taylor, "Church and Anglicanism," 16–17; Sykes, *Church and State*, 32–33. Sykes argues that while the Toleration Act may seem to have offered lukewarm terms for dissenters, given the persistence of the Test and Corporation Acts, "the situation of the Church of England was vitally affected" (33).

64. Monica Najar, *Evangelizing the South: A Social History of Church and State in Early America* (New York: Oxford University Press, 2008), 37–38; and on the role of Baptist petitions in the early 1770s to clarify the applicability of the English Toleration Act, see 118–19, 211–12n7.

65. Walsh and Taylor, "Church and Anglicanism," 54–57, argues that by the 1730s it looked like English dissent was "decaying" and "marginalized" and was no longer a threat to Anglican hegemony.

66. Nelson, *Blessed Company*, 282–85.

67. Spangler, *Virginians Reborn*, 77, 97, 104.

68. Bishop of London to Rev. Dr. Doddridge, May 11, 1751, in *Hist. Coll.*, 1:371–74, quotation 372.

69. For a list of arrests and prosecutions for religion in Virginia, 1763–83, see Ragosta, *Wellspring of Liberty*, 171–83.

70. Address to the Burgesses [1751], in *Hist. Coll.*, 1:381–83.

71. Najar, "Sectarians and Strategies," 120–22, 124.

72. Ibid., 125–26, 129.

73. Ragosta, *Wellspring of Liberty*; Spangler, *Virginians Reborn*.

Chapter 7

1. See, for example, "Britannus Americanus," *Boston Gazette*, March 17, 1766; and "A British Subject," *Boston Evening Post*, April 28, 1766.

2. For a narrative analysis of Massachusetts politics and political ideas during the Townshend crisis, see Jeremy A. Stern, "The Overflowings of Liberty: Massachusetts,

the Townshend Crisis and the Reconception of Freedom, 1766–1770" (Ph.D. diss., Princeton University, 2010).

3. For the origins and early history of the sermons, see Timothy Breen, *The Character of the Good Ruler: Puritan Political Ideas in New England, 1630–1730* (New Haven, CT: Yale University Press, 1970), 282–85. For a general overview of their history, see Lindsay Swift, "The Massachusetts Election Sermons," *Publications of the Colonial Society of Massachusetts*, vol. 1: *Transactions, 1892–94* (Boston, 1895), 388–449. Election sermons, according to contemporary newspaper accounts, were delivered in the late morning, followed by the election dinner attended by the governor, the council, the election preacher, and assorted guests. In the 1760s and 1770s sermons were delivered in Boston's Old Brick meetinghouse, near the town house where the General Court met; when the assembly was removed to Harvard College (for the 1770–72 sermons), the venue was described as "the meeting house," presumably the college's own.

4. The only accessible biographical source for the 1766–73 election preachers—all Harvard graduates—is Clifford Shipton, *Sibley's Harvard Graduates*, vols. 9–13 (Boston: Harvard University Press, 1956–65). Although Shipton's research is invaluable, his well-known bias against the revolutionaries must always be kept firmly in mind, as it often distorted his analysis and even his presentation of fact. Indeed, Shipton severely distorted several of the sermons discussed in this paper, ripping selected quotes from context and falsely claiming that the preachers shared the governors' jaundiced view of the opposition "faction."

5. The sermons have received remarkably little historiographical attention, rating, at best, passing mentions by Bernard Bailyn, Donald Weber, Harry Stout, Nathan Hatch, and others. Swift, in "Massachusetts Election Sermons," surveys the sermons from their start in the 1630s to their finish in 1885, but his treatment of the prerevolutionary period is necessarily brief; he also exaggerates the conservatism of the sermons prior to 1770 and the uniformity of those after. Alice M. Baldwin, *The New England Clergy and the American Revolution* (Durham, NC: Duke University Press, 1928), deemphasizes change in political attitudes over time, seeing an almost consistent revolutionary fervor throughout the period; but Baldwin's well-researched discussion of the sermons' wide-ranging impact is valuable. A. W. Plumstead, *The Wall and the Garden: Selected Massachusetts Election Sermons, 1670–1775* (Minneapolis: University of Minnesota Press, 1968), prints nine sermons, including that of 1770, largely on the strength of literary style; Plumstead's general introduction offers a useful overview of the history, form, and content of seventeenth- and eighteenth-century Massachusetts election sermons but largely neglects the political importance of those discussed here, sharply underplaying the emerging disaffection and even protorepublicanism of the sermons before 1775. John Wingate Thornton, *The Pulpit of the American Revolution, or the Political Sermons of the Period of 1776* (Boston, 1860), also considers the election sermons in general terms and reprints the 1770 sermon; but Thornton, a Massachusetts minister, was mainly interested in celebrating his ancestors' Puritan piety.

6. Harbottle Dorr, annotated newspaper collection, Massachusetts Historical Society, vol. 1, 372, noted that the list of targeted representatives, which appeared in the March 31, 1766, *Boston Gazette*, was "Call'd the Black List," the "Tools to the Governor."

7. Edward Barnard, 1720–74, minister of the First Church of Haverhill, graduated from Harvard in 1736 at age sixteen. Open-minded toward other Christian sects, he was a strong opponent of Great Awakening enthusiasm; his father had preached the election sermon twenty years earlier. See Shipton, *Sibley's Harvard Graduates*, 10:4–11.

8. Edward Barnard, *A Sermon preached before his Excellency . . . May 28, 1766* (Boston, 1766), Evans no. 10235; Barnard's text, Nehemiah 5:19, emphasized the debt the people owed to their political guardians and God's support of wise rulers: "Think upon me, my God, for good, according to all that I have done for this people."

9. Ebenezer Bridge, 1715/6–92, was minister of the First Congregational Society of Chelmsford. Though the son of a blacksmith, he graduated from Harvard in 1736 and returned later for his M.A. A Calvinist traditionalist, he was a strong opponent of the New Lights. See Shipton, *Sibley's Harvard Graduates*, 10:17–26. Bridge eventually became a firm revolutionary; see below.

10. Ebenezer Bridge, *A Sermon preached before his Excellency . . . May 27, 1767* (Boston, 1767), Evans no. 10569. Bridge's text, Deuteronomy 33:29, plainly reflects his view of the present political situation: "Happy art thou O Israel: who is like unto thee, O people saved by the Lord, the shield of thy help, and who is the sword of thy excellency."

11. Daniel Shute, 1722–1802, minister of the Third Church of Hingham, graduated from Harvard in the class of 1743 and returned later for his M.A. (Shipton, *Sibley's Harvard Graduates*, 11:304–9). John Adams noted in 1765 that Shute "is for sinking every person who either favors the stamps or trims about them, into private station" and that he—accurately—predicted "a great mortality" in the May 1766 council election (L. H. Butterfield, ed., *Diary and Autobiography of John Adams*, vol. 1 [1961; repr., New York: Atheneum Press, 1964], 278; Shipton, *Sibley's Harvard Graduates*, 11:306, unfortunately renders the phrase as a "great morality," which makes nonsense of the passage).

12. Daniel Shute, *A Sermon preached before his Excellency . . . May 25, 1768* (Boston, 1768), Evans no. 11071; Shute preached from Ezra 10:4: "Arise; for this matter belongeth unto thee; we also will be with thee; be of good courage, and do it." The text invoked Ezra's charge to the people of Jerusalem to aid him in restoring the city: its meaning, Shute explained, was the need for united exertions by people and rulers. All Shute quotes in following paragraphs are from this sermon.

13. For the furor over Bernard letters, including a larger batch published later in the fall, see Stern, "Overflowings," chaps. 14, 17, 18; and Francis G. Wallett, "Governor Bernard's Undoing: An Earlier Hutchinson Letters Affair," *New England Quarterly* 38 (1965): 217–26. The letters drew fire in other colonies as well; see Pauline Maier, *From Resistance to Revolution: Colonial Radicals and the Development of American Opposition to Britain, 1765–1776*, rev. ed. (New York: W. W. Norton, 1991), 152–57.

14. Bernard first nominated the "Rev. Mr. Jackson" of Brookline, who was approved by the council but declined the invitation. The governor then nominated Haven, who

was approved by the council. See Massachusetts Archives, Council Records, vol. 16, 399–401, March 29 and April 5, 1769, Massachusetts State Archives, Boston. Jason Haven, 1733–1803, minister of the First Congregational Church of Dedham, graduated from Harvard in 1754. Haven was a determinedly orthodox Congregationalist and was reputed to be an affecting speaker. At thirty-six, he was the youngest election preacher of the eight considered here. See Shipton, *Sibley's Harvard Graduates*, 13:447–55.

15. Jason Haven, *A Sermon preached before his Excellency . . . May 31, 1769* (Boston, 1769), Evans no. 11289; Haven preached from Psalm 75:6–7: "For promotion cometh neither from the east, nor from the west, nor from the south: But God is the Judge; He putteth down one, and setteth up another." All Haven quotes in following paragraphs are from this sermon.

16. *A Report of the Record Commissioners of the City of Boston*, vol. 18, Boston Town Records, 1770–77 (Boston, 1887), 26–32, May 15, 1770.

17. In 1770 it would, in the normal rotation, have been the council's turn to choose the preacher. But due to the dissolution of the 1768–69 assembly, the council had made the choice for the past two years. The choice reverted to the House for 1770. Samuel Cooke, 1709–83, minister of the Second Church of Cambridge (in the district then called Menotomy, now Arlington) graduated from Harvard in 1735, having entered somewhat late. Cooke was sixty-one years old in May 1770, the oldest preacher called in the years before the Revolution. Cooke apparently had a reputation for dullness; Shipton describes him as "a dull and staid Old-Light," acknowledging, however, that his election sermon was probably the high point of his career (Shipton, *Sibley's Harvard Graduates*, 9:500–508).

18. Thomas Hutchinson to Israel Mauduit, January 7, 1770, Massachusetts Archives Series, 26:427, Massachusetts State Archives, Boston.

19. Samuel Cooke, *A Sermon preached at Cambridge . . . May 30, 1770* (Boston, 1770), Evans no. 11613; Cooke took as his text 2 Samuel 23:3–4: "He that ruleth over Men must be just, ruling in the fear of God. And he shall be as the light of the morning when the sun riseth, even as a morning without clouds: as the tender grass springing out of the earth by clear shining after rain"—the last words of King David. All Cooke quotes in following paragraphs are from this sermon.

20. The habitual use of the word "reserved" shows that Cooke had not yet fully divested himself of the still-reflexive older notion of charters as royal grants, in which the king granted privileges and reserved the remainder of his inherent sovereignty to himself—even though his argument explicitly said the opposite.

21. The assembly had in fact launched several antislavery bills in recent years and would attempt more before the Revolution; all either stalled or were vetoed by the governor. By contrast, Moses Parsons, the 1772 election preacher, was accused in 1780 of violating his own principles by continuing to hold slaves. With the matter brought before his local parish, Parsons argued that slavery was one of the providences of God. Parsons successfully fought off the charges, by which time slavery's constitutional status

in Massachusetts was coming into question; he then voluntarily freed his slaves. See Shipton, *Sibley's Harvard Graduates*, 10:56–57.

22. John Tucker, 1719–92, minister of the First Church of Newbury, graduated from Harvard in 1741 and returned for his M.A. Like several of his peers in the election pulpit, Tucker was a religious liberal; he had spent difficult years in Newbury trying to reunite a church broken by the revivalists, of whom he heartily disapproved. He had a reputation as a restrained but skillful orator. See Shipton, *Sibley's Harvard Graduates*, 11:78–91.

23. John Tucker, *A Sermon preached at Cambridge . . . May 29, 1771* (Boston, 1771), Evans no. 12256. All Tucker quotes in following paragraphs are from this sermon.

24. Moses Parsons, 1716–83, minister of Newbury Falls, or Byfield, graduated from Harvard in 1736 and returned for his M.A. Despite his sympathy for Great Awakening revivalism—unique among the recent election preachers—the full-blown New Lights rejected him violently. Parsons's interest in revivalism may have influenced his reputedly powerful preaching style. He was known to be highly politicized. See Shipton, *Sibley's Harvard Graduates*, 10:52–59.

25. Moses Parsons, *A Sermon preached at Cambridge . . . May 27, 1772* (Boston, 1772), Evans no. 12502. All Parsons quotes in following paragraphs are from this sermon.

26. Charles Turner, 1732–1818, minister of Duxbury, graduated from Harvard in 1752. Interestingly, until shortly before his ordination, Turner had seriously considered leaving the ministry for the law. He may even have practiced for a short time before the call from Duxbury settled his vocation. A popular religious liberal and reputedly powerful preacher, Turner rejected much of Calvinism outright. See Shipton, *Sibley's Harvard Graduates*, 13:293–99.

27. Shipton, *Sibley's Harvard Graduates*, 13:295.

28. Charles Turner, *A Sermon preached before his Excellency . . . May 26, 1773* (Boston, 1773), Evans no. 13053. All Turner quotes in following paragraphs are from this sermon.

29. "Z.T.," *Boston Evening Post*, May 15, 1769, supplement.

30. *A Report of the Record Commissioners of the City of Boston*, vol. 18, Boston Town Records, 1770–77 (Boston, 1887), 26–32, May 15, 1770.

31. The passage is Revelation 18:4–5, warning the godly to escape the fall of Babylon.

32. Shipton, *Sibley's Harvard Graduates*, 13:295. Turner maintained an active involvement with politics for the rest of his life. He served in the Massachusetts House of Representatives in 1780 and in the state Senate from 1783 to 1788; he was elected to the Federal Ratifying Convention, in which he reluctantly supported ratification with the proviso of a bill of rights; and he served as a Jeffersonian presidential elector in 1804 (Shipton, *Sibley's Harvard Graduates*, 13:296–97).

33. Baldwin, *New England Clergy*, 119n43.

34. L. H. Butterfield, ed., *Diary and Autobiography of John Adams*, vol. 2 (1961; repr., New York: Atheneum Press, 1964), 83.

35. *Massachusetts Spy*, May 27, 1773; *Boston Gazette*, May 31, 1773; *Massachusetts Gazette and Boston Weekly News-Letter*, May 27, 1773. The *News-Letter*'s wording was

reprinted by the *Massachusetts Gazette and Boston Post-Boy* (May 31, 1773), whose new owners would soon take a staunchly progovernment stance, and—perhaps inadvertently—by the *Boston Evening Post* (May 31, 1773), whose editors, though officially neutral, in fact inclined strongly to the liberty camp.

36. Bridge seems to have remained neutral into the 1770s, continuing to associate politely with Governor Hutchinson. But, apparently influenced by his son, a prominent local liberty leader, he became increasingly alienated. According to "local traditions" reported by Shipton, it was the 1773 publication of Hutchinson's letters that proved decisive. By 1775 Bridge was an active supporter of the revolutionary cause. See Shipton, *Sibley's Harvard Graduates*, 10:24–25.

37. Samuel Adams to Joseph Hawley, October 4, 1773, in Harry Alonzo Cushing, *Writings of Samuel Adams*, vol. 3 (Boston, 1907), 52–58.

Chapter 8

1. John M. Murrin, "1776: The Countercyclical Revolution," in Michael A. Morrison and Melinda Zook, eds., *Revolutionary Currents: Nation Building in the Transatlantic World* (Lanham, MD: Rowman and Littlefield, 2004), 65–90.

2. John M. Murrin, "A Roof Without Walls: The Dilemma of American National Identity," in Richard Beeman, Stephen Botein, and Edward C. Carter, eds., *Beyond Confederation: Origins of the Constitution and American National Identity* (Chapel Hill: University of North Carolina Press, 1987), 333–48.

3. John M. Murrin, "Anglicizing an American Colony: The Transformation of Provincial Massachusetts" (Ph.D. diss., Yale University, 1966), 20.

4. Jon Butler, *Becoming America: The Revolution Before 1776* (Cambridge, MA: Harvard University Press, 2000); Michael Zuckerman, "Authority in Early America: The Decay of Deference on the Provincial Periphery," *Early American Studies* 1 (Fall 2003): 1–29. See also the exchange, Michael Zuckerman, "Tocqueville, Turner, and Turds: Four Stories of Manners in Early America," and John M. Murrin, "In the Land of the Free and the Home of the Slave Maybe There Was Room Even for Deference," in "Deference or Defiance in Eighteenth-Century America? A Round Table," *Journal of American History* 85, no. 1 (June 1998): 13–42, 86–91.

5. Rebecca Anne Goetz, *The Baptism of Early Virginia: How Christianity Created Race* (Baltimore: Johns Hopkins University Press, 2012), 65–70.

6. *Early American Indian Documents: Treaties and Laws, 1607–1789*, gen. ed. Alden T. Vaughan, vol. 17: *New England and Middle Atlantic Laws*, vol. eds., Alden T. Vaughan and Deborah Rosen (Bethesda, MD: University Publications of America, 2004), 105–6.

7. Michael Leroy Oberg, *Dominion and Civility: English Imperialism and Native America, 1585–1685* (Ithaca, NY: Cornell University Press, 1999).

8. On Virginia's later missionary work, see James Axtell, *The Invasion Within: The Contest of Cultures in Colonial North America* (New York: Oxford University Press, 1985), 190–96.

9. Helen C. Rountree, *Pocahontas's People: The Powhatan Indians of Virginia Through Four Centuries* (Norman: University of Oklahoma Press, 1990).

10. Jenny Hale Pulsipher, *Subjects unto the Same King: Indians, English, and the Contest for Authority in Colonial New England* (Philadelphia: University of Pennsylvania Press, 2005), 134–59.

11. Quoted in Alden T. Vaughan, "From White Man to Redskin: Changing Anglo-American Perceptions of the American Indian," in Vaughan, *Roots of American Racism: Essays on the Colonial Experience* (New York: Oxford University Press, 1995), 21.

12. On race and Christianity, see Colin Kidd, *The Forging of Races: Race and Scripture in the Atlantic World 1600–2000* (Cambridge: Cambridge University Press, 2006); David J. Silverman, *Red Brethren: The Brothertown and Stockbridge Indians and the Problem of Race in Early America* (Ithaca, NY: Cornell University Press, 2010); Richard A. Bailey, *Race and Redemption in Puritan New England* (New York: Oxford University Press, 2011); Goetz, *Baptism of Early Virginia*.

13. Guy Chet, *Conquering the American Wilderness: The Triumph of European Warfare in the Colonial Northeast* (Amherst: University of Massachusetts Press, 2003).

14. Hilary McD. Beckles, "A 'Riotous and Unruly Lot': Irish Indentured Servants and Freemen in the English West Indies, 1644–1713," *William and Mary Quarterly*, 3rd ser., 47, no. 4 (October 1990): 503–22; Margaret Ellen Newell, "Indian Slavery in Colonial New England," and C. S. Everett, "'They Shalbe Slaves for Their Lives': Indian Slavery in Colonial Virginia," in Allan Gallay, ed., *Indian Slavery in Colonial America* (Lincoln: University of Nebraska Press, 2010), 33–66, 67–108.

15. A recent examination is Robin Blackburn, "The Old World Background to European Colonial Slavery," *William and Mary Quarterly*, 3rd ser., 3 (1997): 65–102.

16. Alan Gallay, *The Indian Slave Trade: The Rise of the English Empire in the American South, 1670–1717* (New Haven, CT: Yale University Press, 2002); Melissa Cioffi, "The Indian Slave Trade and the Development of Race in the Colonial Southeast" (M.A. thesis, George Washington University, 2008).

17. Richard Slotkin, *Regeneration Through Violence: The Mythology of the American Frontier, 1600–1860* (Middletown, CT: Wesleyan University Press, 1973); Richard Drinnon, *Facing West: The Metaphysics of Indian Hating and Empire Building* (Norman: University of Oklahoma Press, 1997); Jill Lepore, *King Philip's War and the Origins of American Identity* (New York: Alfred A. Knopf, 1998); Peter Silver, *Our Savage Neighbors: How Indian War Transformed Early America* (New York: W. W. Norton, 2008); Carroll Smith-Rosenberg, *This Violent Empire: The Birth of an American National Identity* (Chapel Hill: University of North Carolina Press for the Omohundro Institute of Early American History and Culture, 2012).

18. *Boston News-Letter*, November 26, 1711, 2, col. 1.

19. Ibid., June 2, 1712, 2, col. 2. See also the issues from May 26 (2, col. 2), June 23 (2, col. 2), and September 1 (2, col. 2).

20. Silver, *Our Savage Neighbors*; Daniel K. Richter, *Facing East from Indian Country: A Native History of Early America* (Cambridge, MA: Harvard University Press, 2001), 191–216.

21. *Boston Evening-Post*, April 1, 1754, 1, col. 1.

22. Quoted in Richter, *Facing East from Indian Country*, 108.

23. Silver, *Our Savage Neighbors*, 161–226; Alden T. Vaughan, "Frontier Banditti and the Indians: The Paxton Boys' Legacy, 1763–1775," *Pennsylvania History* 51 (1984): 1–23; Kevin Kenny, *Peaceable Kingdom Lost: The Paxton Boys and the Destruction of William Penn's Holy Experiment* (New York: Oxford University Press, 2011); Krista Camezind, "Violence, Race, and the Paxton Boys," in William A. Pencak and Daniel K. Richter, eds., *Friends and Enemies in Penn's Woods: Indians, Colonists, and the Racial Construction of Pennsylvania* (University Park: Penn State University Press, 2004), 201–20; Daniel K. Richter, "Onas the Long Knife: Pennsylvanians and Indians," in Frederick E. Hoxie, Ronald Hoffman, and Peter J. Albert, *Native Americans and the Early Republic* (Charlottesville: University Press of Virginia, 1999), 125–61.

24. Christopher Tomlins, *Freedom Bound: Law, Labor, and Civic Identity in Colonizing English America, 1580–1865* (New York: Cambridge University Press, 2010), 417; Ira Berlin, "Time, Space, and the Evolution of Afro-American Society on British Mainland North America," *American Historical Review* 85 (1980): 44–78.

25. Kathleen M. Brown, *Good Wives, Nasty Wenches, and Anxious Patriarchs: Gender, Race, and Power in Colonial Virginia* (Chapel Hill: University of North Carolina Press for the Institute of Early American History and Culture, 1996); Kirsten Fischer, *Suspect Relations: Sex, Race, and Resistance in North Carolina* (Ithaca, NY: Cornell University Press, 2002); John Wood Sweet, *Bodies Politic: Negotiating Race in the American North, 1730–1830* (Baltimore: Johns Hopkins University Press, 2003).

26. Sweet, *Bodies Politic*; Mary Beth Norton, *Founding Mothers and Fathers: Gendered Power and the Forming of American Society* (New York: Alfred A. Knopf, 1996); Ann M. Little, "Men on Top: The Farmer, the Minister, and Marriage in Early New England," *Pennsylvania History* 64 (1997): 123–50.

27. A. Leon Higginbotham, *In the Matter of Color: Race and the American Legal Process: The Colonial Period* (Oxford: Oxford University Press, 1978); David Waldstreicher, *Runaway America: Benjamin Franklin, Slavery, and the American Revolution* (New York: Hill & Wang, 2005).

28. Zachary Rice, "Bodies for Display in Gotham: Dutch-English Usages of Racialized Torture, Violence and Execution in Public Spaces in Colonial New York, 1640–1741" (senior honor's thesis, George Washington University, 2012).

29. Brown, *Good Wives*, 113–14; Anthony S. Parent, Jr., *Foul Means: The Formation of a Slave Society in Virginia, 1660–1740* (Chapel Hill: University of North Carolina Press for the Omohundro Institute of Early American History and Culture, 2004), 111–14; Goetz, *Baptism of Early Virginia*, 86–111.

30. Richard J. Boles, "Dividing the Faith: The Rise of Racially Segregated Northern Churches, 1730–1850" (Ph.D. diss., George Washington University, 2013).

31. Alden T. Vaughan, "Slaveholders' 'Hellish Principles': A Seventeenth-Century Critique," in Vaughan, *Roots of American Racism*, 55–81.

32. April Lee Hatfield, *Atlantic Virginia: Intercolonial Relations in the Seventeenth Century* (Philadelphia: University of Pennsylvania Press, 2003), 137–68; Edward B.

Rugemer, "The Development of Mastery and Race in the Comprehensive Slave Codes of the Greater Caribbean During the Seventeenth Century," *William and Mary Quarterly*, 3rd ser., 70 (2013): 429–58.

33. Tomlins, *Freedom Bound*, 437–38.

34. Brown, *Good Wives*, 197–98; Parent, *Foul Means*, 117.

35. M. Halsey Thomas, *The Diary of Samuel Sewall, 1674–1729* (New York: Farrar, Straus, and Giroux, 1973), 532.

36. *Early American Indian Documents*, vol. 17: *New England and Middle Atlantic Laws*, 371.

37. Nicholas P. Canny, "The Ideology of English Colonization: From Ireland to America," *William and Mary Quarterly*, 3rd ser., 30 (1973): 575–98; Colin G. Calloway, *White People, Indians, and Highlanders: Tribal Peoples and Colonial Encounters in Scotland and America* (New York: Oxford University Press, 2008), 60–87, 230–31.

38. Alden T. Vaughan, *Transatlantic Encounters: American Indians in Britain, 1500–1776* (New York: Oxford University Press, 2006).

39. Figures from John J. McCusker and Russell R. Menard, *The Economy of British North America, 1607–1789* (Chapel Hill: University of North Carolina Press for the Omohundro Institute of Early American History and Culture, 1991), 221.

40. Catherine Molineux, *Faces of Perfect Ebony: Encountering Atlantic Slavery in Imperial Britain* (Cambridge, MA: Harvard University Press, 2012).

41. Roxan Wheeler, *The Complexion of Race: Categories of Difference in Eighteenth-Century British Culture* (Philadelphia: University of Pennsylvania Press, 2000); Nicholas Hudson, "From 'Nation' to 'Race': The Origin of Racial Classification in Eighteenth-Century Thought," *Eighteenth-Century Studies* 29 (1996): 247–64; George Boulukos, *The Grateful Slave: The Emergence of Race in Eighteenth-Century British and American Culture* (Cambridge: Cambridge University Press, 2008); Kathleen Wilson, *The Island Race: Englishness, Empire, and Gender in the Eighteenth Century* (New York: Routledge, 2003); Philip D. Morgan, "British Encounters with Africans and African-Americans, circa 1600–1780," in Bernard Bailyn and Philip D. Morgan, eds., *Strangers Within the Realm: Margins of the First British Empire* (Chapel Hill: University of North Carolina Press for the Institute of Early American History and Culture, 1991), 159, 166, 213.

42. The following discussion draws on Owen Stanwood, *An Empire Reformed: English America in the Age of the Glorious Revolution* (Philadelphia: University of Pennsylvania Press, 2011), esp. 54–81.

43. "The Boston Declaration of Grievances, April 18, 1689," in Michael G. Hall, Lawrence H. Leder, and Michael G. Kammen, eds., *The Glorious Revolution in America* (Chapel Hill: University of North Carolina Press for the Institute of Early American History and Culture, 1964), 42.

44. Mary Beth Norton, *In the Devil's Snare: The Salem Witchcraft Crisis of 1692* (New York: Vintage, 2002); John M. Murrin, "Coming to Terms with the Salem Witch Trials," *Proceedings of the American Antiquarian Society* 110 (2000): 309–47.

45. John Murrin, "English Rights as Ethnic Aggression: The English Conquest, the Charter of Liberties of 1683, and Leisler's Rebellion in New York," in William Pencak and Conrad Edick Wright, eds., *Authority and Resistance in Early New York* (New York: New-York Historical Society, 1988), 56–94.

46. John D. Krugler, *English and Catholic: The Lords Baltimore in the Seventeenth Century* (Baltimore: Johns Hopkins University Press, 2004), 233–50; Stanwood, *Empire Reformed*, 106–14, 133–35.

47. The following discussion draws on Justin Pope, "Dangerous Spirit of Liberty: Slave Rebellion, Conspiracy, and the First Great Awakening, 1729–1746" (Ph.D. diss., George Washington University, 2014); Mark M. Smith, *Stono: Documenting and Interpreting a Southern Slave Revolt* (Columbia: University of South Carolina Press, 2005); Serena R. Zabin, ed., *The New York Conspiracy Trials of 1741: Daniel Horsmanden's Journal of the Proceedings, with Related Documents* (Boston: Bedford/St. Martin's, 2004); Jill Lepore, *New York Burning: Liberty, Slavery, and Conspiracy in Eighteenth-Century Manhattan* (New York: Alfred A. Knopf, 2005); Peter Charles Hoffer, *The Great New York Conspiracy of 1741: Slavery, Crime, and Colonial Law* (Lawrence: University Press of Kansas, 2003); John Thornton, "African Dimensions of the Stono Rebellion," *American Historical Review* 96 (1991): 1101–13; and John M. Murrin et al., *Liberty, Equality, Power: A History of the American People* (Orlando, FL: Harcourt, Brace, 1996), 150–52.

48. Murrin et al., *Liberty, Equality, Power*, 51.

49. Lepore, *New York Burning*, 13.

50. Zabin, *New York Conspiracy Trials*, 103.

51. Ibid., 83–84.

52. Ibid., 136.

53. Ibid., 130.

54. Reginald Horsman, *Expansion and American Indian Policy, 1783–1812* (Lansing: Michigan State University Press, 1967).

55. The following discussion draws on Gary B. Nash, *The Unknown American Revolution: The Unruly Birth of Democracy and the Struggle to Create America* (New York: Penguin, 2005), 114–28; Benjamin Quarles, *The Negro in the American Revolution* (Chapel Hill: University of North Carolina Press for the Institute of Early American History and Culture, 1961).

56. Quoted in Nash, *Unknown American Revolution*, 117.

57. Ibid., 119.

58. Woody Holton, "'Rebel Against Rebel': Enslaved Virginians and the Coming of the American Revolution," *Virginia Magazine of History and Biography* 105 (1997): 157–92.

59. Alan Taylor, *The Divided Ground: Indians, Settlers, and the Northern Borderland of the American Revolution* (New York: Vintage, 2006), 81–93; Isabel Thompson Kelsay, *Joseph Brant, 1743–1807: Man of Two Worlds* (Syracuse, NY: Syracuse University Press, 1984), 160–84.

60. Pauline Maier, *American Scripture: Making the Declaration of Independence* (New York: Alfred A. Knopf, 1997), 105–23; Robert G. Parkinson, "Twenty-Seven

Reasons for Independence," in Christian Y. Dupont and Peter S. Onuf, eds., *Declaring Independence: The Origin and Influence of America's Founding Document* (Charlottesville: University Press of Virginia, 2008), 11–18.

61. Sylvia Frey, *Water from the Rock: Black Resistance in a Revolutionary Age* (Princeton, NJ: Princeton University Press, 1991).

62. Colin Calloway, *The American Revolution in Indian Country: Crisis and Diversity in Native American Communities* (New York: Cambridge University Press, 1995); Barbara Graymont, *The Iroquois in the America Revolution* (Syracuse, NY: Syracuse University Press, 1972); Taylor, *Divided Ground*, 93–94; Richard White, *The Middle Ground: Indians, Empires, and Republics in the Great Lakes Region, 1650–1815* (New York: Cambridge University Press, 1991), 389–91; Richter, *Facing East from Indian Country*, 216–23.

63. White, *Middle Ground*, 384.

64. James H. Merrell, "Declarations of Independence: Indian-White Relations in the New Nation," in Jack P. Greene, ed., *The American Revolution: Its Character and Its Limits* (New York: New York University Press, 1987), 197–223; Horsman, *Expansion and American Indian Policy*, 53–103; Wiley Sword, *President Washington's Indian War: The Struggle for the Old Northwest, 1790–1795* (Norman: University of Oklahoma Press, 1985), esp. 160–95; Richter, *Facing East from Indian Country*, 223–35. The figure comes from Thomas P. Slaughter, *The Whiskey Rebellion: Frontier Epilogue to the American Revolution* (New York: Oxford University Press, 1986), 94.

65. Quoted in Calloway, *American Revolution in Indian Country*, 297.

66. Adam Rothman, *Slave Country: American Expansion and the Origins of the Deep South* (Cambridge, MA: Harvard University Press, 2005).

67. Arthur Zilversmit, *The First Emancipation: The Abolition of Slavery in the North* (Chicago: University of Chicago Press, 1967); Leon F. Litwack, *North of Slavery: The Negro in the Free States, 1790–1860* (Chicago: University of Chicago Press, 1965); Gary B. Nash and Jean R. Soderlund, *Freedom by Degrees: Emancipation in Pennsylvania and Its Aftermath* (New York: Oxford University Press, 1991); Joanne Pope Melish, *Disowning Slavery: Gradual Emancipation and "Race" in New England, 1780–1860* (Ithaca, NY: Cornell University Press, 1998).

68. Nicholas Guyatt, "'The Outskirts of Our Happiness': Race and the Lure of Colonization in the Early Republic," *Journal of American History* 95, no. 4 (2009): 986–1011.

69. In addition to Rothman, *Slave Country*, see Sweet, *Bodies Politic*; Robert J. Cottrol, *The Afro-Yankees: Providence's Black Community in the Antebellum Era* (Westport, CT: Greenwood Press, 1982); James Oliver Horton and Lois E. Horton, *Black Bostonians: Family Life and Community Struggle in the Antebellum North* (New York: Holmes and Meir, 1979); Douglas Bradburn, *The Citizenship Revolution: Politics and the Creation of the American Union, 1774–1804* (Charlottesville: University Press of Virginia, 2009), 262–71; Laurence M. Hauptman, *Conspiracy of Interests: Iroquois Dispossession and the Rise of New York State* (Syracuse, NY: Syracuse University Press, 1999); Daniel R. Mandell, *Tribe, Race, History: Native Americans in Southern New England, 1780–1880* (Baltimore: Johns Hopkins University Press, 2008); Peggy Pascoe, *What Comes Naturally:*

Miscegenation Law and the Making of Race in America (New York: Oxford University Press, 2009), 19–22.

70. Matthew Frye Jacobson, *Whiteness of a Different Color: European Immigrants and the Alchemy of Race* (Cambridge, MA: Harvard University Press, 1998), 7 (quote), 22–23. See also Bradburn, *Citizenship Revolution*, 260.

71. Jacobson, *Whiteness of a Different Color*, 25–26.

72. John M. Murrin and David J. Silverman, "The Quest for America: Reflections on Distinctiveness, Pluralism, and Public Life," *Journal of Interdisciplinary History* 33 (2002): 237.

Chapter 9

1. John M. Murrin, "The Jeffersonian Triumph and American Exceptionalism," *Journal of the Early Republic* 20 (2000): 13.

2. I have drawn primarily from the following four essays: John M. Murrin, "The Great Inversion, or Court Versus Country: A Comparison of the Revolution Settlements in England (1688–1721) and America (1776–1816)," in J. G. A. Pocock, ed., *Three British Revolutions: 1641, 1688, 1776* (Princeton, NJ: Princeton University Press, 1980), 368–453, 407 (quote); Gary J. Kornblith and John M. Murrin, "The Making and Unmaking of an American Ruling Class," in Alfred F. Young, ed., *Beyond the American Revolution: Explorations in the History of American Radicalism* (DeKalb: Northern Illinois University Press, 1993), 27–79; John M. Murrin, "Escaping Perfidious Albion: Federalism, Fear of Aristocracy, and the Democratization of Corruption in Postrevolutionary America," in Richard K. Matthews, ed., *Virtue, Corruption, and Self-Interest: Political Values in the Eighteenth Century* (Bethlehem, PA: Lehigh University Press, 1994), 103–47; and Murrin, "Jeffersonian Triumph," 1–25.

3. For the British fiscal-military state, see John Brewer, *Sinews of Power: War, Money and the English State, 1688–1783* (Cambridge, MA: Harvard University Press, 1988); Lawrence Stone, ed., *An Imperial State at War: Britain from 1689 to 1815* (London: Routledge, 1994); and N. A. M. Rodger, "From the 'Military Revolution' to the 'Fiscal-Naval State,'" *Journal for Maritime Research* 13 (2011): 119–28. Rodger favors describing the British government by the eighteenth century as a "fiscal-naval state," a term coined by the historian Patrick O'Brien. For the singularity of the British case, see also Raphael Torres Sánchez, "The Triumph of the Fiscal-Military State in the Eighteenth Century: War and Mercantilism," in Raphael Torres Sánchez, ed., *War, State and Development: Fiscal Military States in the Eighteenth Century* (Pamplona: Eunsa, 2007), 16. I thank Katherine Epstein of Rutgers University, Camden, for sharing these and other sources with me.

4. Lawrence A. Peskin, "Conspiratorial Anglophobia and the War of 1812," *Journal of American History* 98 (2011): 647–69. For additional studies of continuing British influence on the early United States, particularly in the cultural realm, see Kariann Akemi Yokota, *Unbecoming British: How Revolutionary America Became a Postcolonial Nation* (New York: Oxford University Press, 2011); and Elisa Tamarkin, *Anglophilia: Deference, Devotion, and Antebellum America* (Chicago: University of Chicago Press, 2008).

5. Jefferson quoted in Murrin, "Jeffersonian Triumph," 18.

6. Thomas Jefferson to Philip Mazzei, Monticello, April 24, 1796, in *The Papers of Thomas Jefferson, Volume 29: 1 March 1796 to 31 December 1797*, ed. Barbara B. Oberg (Princeton, NJ: Princeton University Press, 2002), 81–83.

7. Jefferson quoted in Murrin, "Jeffersonian Triumph," 18.

8. For the military within the British opposition tradition, see Lois G. Schwoerer, *"No Standing Armies!" The Antiarmy Ideology in Seventeenth-Century England* (Baltimore: Johns Hopkins University Press, 1974); and David Armitage, *The Ideological Origins of the British Empire* (Cambridge: Cambridge University Press, 2000), 143–44, 185–86. For the influence of the Country Party tradition on the Jeffersonians, see Murrin, "Great Inversion"; Lance Banning, *The Jeffersonian Persuasion: Evolution of a Party Ideology* (Ithaca, NY: Cornell University Press, 1978); Drew R. McCoy, *The Elusive Republic: Political Economy in Jeffersonian America* (Chapel Hill: University of North Carolina Press, 1980); and Robert W. Smith, *Keeping the Republic: Ideology and Early American Diplomacy* (DeKalb: Northern Illinois University Press, 2004).

9. Isaac Land, *War, Nationalism, and the British Sailor, 1750–1850* (New York: Palgrave Macmillan, 2009), 20. For classic scholarly treatments of the founding of the U.S. Navy, see Harold Sprout and Margaret Sprout, *The Rise of American Naval Power, 1776–1918* (Princeton, NJ: Princeton University Press, 1939); Marshall Smelser, *The Congress Founds the Navy, 1787–1798* (Notre Dame, IN: University of Notre Dame Press, 1959); William M. Fowler, Jr., *Rebels Under Sail: The American Navy During the Revolution* (New York: Scribner's, 1976); Craig L. Symonds, *Navalists and Antinavalists: The Naval Policy Debate in the United States, 1785–1827* (Newark: University of Delaware Press, 1980); and Kenneth J. Hagan, *This People's Navy: The Making of American Sea Power* (New York: Free Press, 1991). There is no equivalent for the Jeffersonian navy of Theodore J. Crackel's scholarly work placing Jefferson's army policy into a republican ideological context; see Crackel, *Mr. Jefferson's Army: Political and Social Reform of the Military Establishment, 1801–1809* (New York: New York University Press, 1987). The best attempt is Jeffrey J. Seiken, "American Naval Policy in an Age of Atlantic Warfare: A Consensus Broken and Reforged, 1783–1816" (Ph.D. diss., Ohio State University, 2007). See also Julia H. Macleod, "Jefferson and the Navy: A Defense," *Huntington Library Quarterly* 8 (1945): 153–84. Useful, yet still overly triumphal, recent popular accounts of the early U.S. Navy include Ian W. Toll, *Six Frigates: The Epic History of the Founding of the U.S. Navy* (New York: W. W. Norton, 2006); and George C. Daughan, *If by Sea: The Forging of the American Navy—From the American Revolution to the War of 1812* (New York: Basic Books, 2008).

10. Benjamin Franklin to Joseph Galloway, London, April 7, 1759, in *The Papers of Benjamin Franklin, Volume 8: April 1, 1758 through December 31, 1759*, ed. Leonard W. Labaree (New Haven, CT: Yale University Press, 1965), 316.

11. Adams quoted in Murrin, "Jeffersonian Triumph," 7; Thomas Paine, *Common Sense* (1776; repr., Mineola, NY: Dover Publications, 1997), 36.

12. Fowler, *Rebels Under Sail*, 56–57, 65, 81.

13. Ibid., 212–55; Toll, *Six Frigates*, 15–17; James C. Bradford, "The Navies of the American Revolution," in Kenneth J. Hagan, ed., *In Peace and War: Interpretations of American Naval History, 1775–1978* (Westport, CT: Greenwood Press, 1978), 3–26.

14. Christopher McKee, *Edward Preble: A Naval Biography, 1761–1807* (Annapolis, MD: Naval Institute Press, 1972), 71–72, 219–20.

15. William M. Fowler, Jr., "The Non-Volunteer Navy," United States Naval Institute, *Proceedings* 100 (1974): 74–78; Fowler, *Rebels Under Sail*, 279–89; Elizabeth Cometti, "Impressment During the American Revolution," in Vera Largent, ed., *The Walter Jackson Essays in the Social Sciences* (Chapel Hill: University of North Carolina Press, 1942), 97–109; John W. Jackson, *The Pennsylvania Navy, 1775–1781: The Defense of the Delaware* (New Brunswick, NJ: Rutgers University Press, 1974), 82–83, 311.

16. Winthrop D. Jordan, *White over Black: American Attitudes Toward the Negro, 1550–1812* (Chapel Hill: University of North Carolina Press for the Institute of Early American History and Culture, 1968). For the American colonial experience with impressment, see Denver Brunsman, *The Evil Necessity: British Naval Impressment in the Eighteenth-Century Atlantic World* (Charlottesville: University Press of Virginia, 2013). For impressment and American national identity, see Denver Brunsman, "Subjects vs. Citizens: Impressment and Identity in the Anglo-American Atlantic," *Journal of the Early Republic* 30 (2010): 557–86.

17. November 2, 1776, in *Journals of the Continental Congress, 1774–1789*, 34 vols., ed. Worthington C. Ford et al. (Washington, DC: U.S. Government Printing Office, 1904–37), 16:919 (quote); *Naval Documents of the American Revolution*, 11 vols., ed. William Bell Clark et al. (Washington, DC: U.S. Government Printing Office, 1964–2005), 7:220–21, 229; *New-Jersey Gazette* (Trenton), May 9, 1781.

18. Jackson, *Pennsylvania Navy*, 82–83; Fowler, *Rebels Under Sail*, 251.

19. Joseph Reed to Congress, October 21, 1779, in *Pennsylvania Archives*, 12 vols., ed. Samuel Hazard (Philadelphia: Joseph Severns, 1852–56), 7:761–62.

20. Fowler, "Non-Volunteer Navy," 78.

21. Joseph Reed to Congress, [December 1780?], in *Pennsylvania Archives*, ed. Hazard, 8:643.

22. Pauline Maier, *Ratification: The People Debate the Constitution, 1787–1788* (New York: Simon and Schuster, 2010), 12; William M. Fowler, Jr., *Jack Tars and Commodores: The American Navy, 1783–1815* (Boston: Houghton Mifflin, 1984), 4–9.

23. U.S. Constitution, in *The Constitutional Convention and the Formation of the Union*, ed. Winton U. Solberg (Urbana: University of Illinois Press, 1990), 352, 355.

24. "The Federal Convention: Madison's Notes of Debates," in *Constitutional Convention*, ed. Solberg, 144.

25. Smelser, *Congress Founds the Navy*, 16–17.

26. Patrick Henry, June 5, 1788, in *The Anti-Federalist Papers and the Constitutional Convention Debates*, ed. Ralph Ketcham (New York: Mentor Books, 1986), 207–8. For Anti-Federalist concerns, see Kenneth R. Bowling, "'A Tub to the Whale': The Founding Fathers and the Adoption of the Federal Bill of Rights," *Journal of the Early Republic* 8

(1988): 223–51; and Saul Cornell, "Aristocracy Assailed: The Ideology of Backcountry Anti-Federalism," *Journal of American History* 76 (1990): 1148–72.

27. Peskin, "Conspiratorial Anglophobia," 650–51; Richard H. Kohn, *Eagle and Sword: The Federalists and the Creation of the Military Establishment in America, 1783–1802* (New York: Free Press, 1975), 174.

28. Fowler, *Jack Tars and Commodores*, 18–19.

29. *Annals of Congress*, 3rd Cong., 1st sess., 490; Symonds, *Navalists and Antinavalists*, 30–37.

30. John Adams to Thomas Jefferson, October 15, 1822, in *The Writings of Thomas Jefferson*, 20 vols., ed. Albert Ellery Bergh (Washington, DC: Thomas Jefferson Memorial Association, 1903–7), 15:397–99; Macleod, "Jefferson and the Navy," 157.

31. Thomas Jefferson to James Madison, Monticello, April 3, 1794, in *The Papers of Thomas Jefferson, Volume 28: 1 January 1794 to 29 February 1796*, ed. John Catanzariti (Princeton, NJ: Princeton University Press, 2000), 49–50.

32. Michael J. Crawford and Christine F. Hughes, *The Reestablishment of the Navy, 1787–1801: Historical Overview and Select Bibliography* (Washington, DC: Naval Historical Center, 1995), 9; Stanley Elkins and Eric McKitrick, *The Age of Federalism: The Early American Republic, 1788–1800* (New York: Oxford University Press, 1993), 589–90, 643–62; Alexander DeConde, *The Quasi-War: The Politics and Diplomacy of the Undeclared War with France, 1797–1801* (New York: Scribner's, 1966), 109–41.

33. "Interesting Letter from a Member of Congress from Virginia, to His Constituents," *Aurora* (Philadelphia), June 30, 1798. See also *Aurora*, May 22, 1798, and June 28, 1798.

34. *Annals of Congress*, 5th Cong., 3rd sess., 2823–32, 2831 (quote); Crawford and Hughes, *Reestablishment of the Navy*, 10. For Gallatin's opposition to navies, see Alexander S. Balinky, "Albert Gallatin, Naval Foe," *Pennsylvania Magazine of History and Biography* 82 (1958): 293–304; and Alexander S. Balinky, "Gallatin's Theory of War Finance," *William and Mary Quarterly*, 3rd ser., 16 (1959): 73–82.

35. *Annals of Congress*, 5th Cong., 3rd sess., 2837; Symonds, *Navalists and Antinavalists*, 72–80.

36. Thomas Jefferson to James Madison, Philadelphia, January 16, 1799, in *The Republic of Letters: The Correspondence Between Thomas Jefferson and James Madison, 1776–1826*, 3 vols., ed. James Morton Smith (New York: W. W. Norton, 1995), 2:1088–89.

37. Joel Barlow, *To His Fellow Citizens of the United States of America* (London, 1800), 26–27; Banning, *Jeffersonian Persuasion*, 259–62.

38. Elkins and McKitrick, *Age of Federalism*, 726–43; James Roger Sharp, *American Politics in the Early Republic: The New Nation in Crisis* (New Haven, CT: Yale University Press, 1993), 235–49.

39. Benjamin Stoddert to Lieutenant Henry Kenyon, Philadelphia, August 8, 1798, in *Naval Documents Related to the Quasi-War Between the United States and France*, 7 vols., ed. Dudley W. Knox (Washington, DC: Government Printing Office, 1935–38), 1:281.

40. Benjamin Stoddert to Commanders of Gallies, Navy Department [Trenton], September 11, 1798, in *Naval Documents Related to the Quasi-War*, ed. Knox, 1:388. For the U.S. Navy's recruiting difficulties, see Michael A. Palmer, *Stoddert's War: Naval Operations During the Quasi-War with France, 1798–1801* (Columbia: University of South Carolina Press, 1987), 122, 138.

41. For Stoddert's policy, see Daughan, *If by Sea,* 320. For black sailors in the British navy, see Brunsman, *Evil Necessity,* 120–22. For the unique status of the U.S. Navy among western navies, see Jan Glete, *Navies and Nations: Warships, Navies and State Building in Europe and America, 1500–1860,* 2 vols. (Stockholm: Almqvist and Wiksell International, 1993), 1:173–74; and Paul C. van Royan et al., eds., *"Those Emblems of Hell"? European Sailors and the Maritime Labour Market, 1570–1870* (St. John's, Newfoundland: International Maritime Economic History Association, 1997), 8, 17.

42. Thomas Jefferson to Joseph Priestley, January 18, 1800, in *Writings of Thomas Jefferson,* ed. Bergh, 10:139.

43. Leonard D. White, *The Jeffersonians: A Study in Administrative History, 1801–1829* (New York: Free Press, 1951), 142–44, 265–98.

44. Crackel, *Mr. Jefferson's Army.*

45. Thomas Jefferson, *Notes on the State of Virginia,* ed. William Peden (Chapel Hill: University of North Carolina Press, 1954), 175.

46. Macleod, "Jefferson and the Navy"; McCoy, *Elusive Republic,* 174–78.

47. Henry Adams, *History of the United States During the Administrations of Thomas Jefferson and James Madison,* 9 vols. (New York: Scribner's, 1889–91), 2:205; Symonds, *Navalists and Antinavalists,* 86–87. For the place of trade in Jefferson's republican political economy, see McCoy, *Elusive Republic,* esp. 209–35. For the Barbary Wars, see Frank Lambert, *The Barbary Wars: American Independence in the Atlantic World* (New York: Hill & Wang, 2005); and Lawrence A. Peskin, *Captives and Countrymen: Barbary Slavery and the American Public, 1785–1816* (Baltimore: Johns Hopkins University Press, 2009).

48. Thomas Jefferson, Message to Congress, February 10, 1807, in *American State Papers,* class 6, *Naval Affairs,* vol. 1 (Washington, DC: Gales and Seaton, 1834), 163. For Jefferson's gunboat policy, see Gene A. Smith, *"For the Purposes of Defense": The Politics of the Jeffersonian Gunboat Program* (Newark: University of Delaware Press, 1995); and Spencer C. Tucker, *The Jeffersonian Gunboat Navy* (Columbia: University of South Carolina Press, 1993).

49. Murrin, "Great Inversion," 425; White, *Jeffersonians,* 267–68. For the Tudor and Jeffersonian navies, compare the tables in N. A. M. Rodger, *The Safeguard of the Sea: A Naval History of Britain* (London: HarperCollins, 1997), 475–80; and in James Madison, "Condition of the Naval Force . . . Communicated to Congress, December 5, 1809," in *American State Papers,* class 6, *Naval Affairs,* 1:202.

50. *Annals of Congress,* 9th Cong., 1st sess., 1047; Symonds, *Navalists and Antinavalists,* 112–14.

51. For recruiting challenges during the Barbary Wars, see *Naval Documents Related to the United States Wars with the Barbary Powers,* 7 vols., ed. Dudley W. Knox

(Washington, DC: Government Printing Office, 1939–44), 2:496; 3:548; 4:2–3, 136, 241. For foreigners in the early U.S. Navy, see Christopher McKee, "Foreign Seamen in the United States Navy: A Census of 1808," *William and Mary Quarterly*, 3rd ser., 42 (1985): 383–93. The *Chesapeake-Leopard* Affair, followed by the U.S. embargo on trade in 1808, led to a decline of foreigners in the navy, although they continued to serve in smaller numbers through the War of 1812.

52. Fowler, *Jack Tars and Commodores*, 162; Donald R. Hickey, *Don't Give Up the Ship! Myths of the War of 1812* (Urbana: University of Illinois Press, 2006), 93–96.

53. N. A. M. Rodger, *The Command of the Ocean: A Naval History of Britain, 1649–1815* (New York: W. W. Norton, 2004), 606–9, 615–17; Fowler, *Jack Tars and Commodores*, 167.

54. The fullest narrative of the debate is Symonds, *Navalists and Antinavalists*, 148–68.

55. *Annals of Congress*, 12th Cong., 1st sess., 803–22, 812 ("great economy" and "ship-building"), 819 ("anti-republican").

56. *Annals of Congress*, 12th Cong., 1st sess., 828 ("same results"), 831 ("riot and debauchery"), 833 ("Naval victories"), 841 ("vile offspring").

57. *Annals of Congress*, 12th Cong., 1st sess., 912 ("source of alarm"), 949 ("band of perjured"), 998 ("*hydrophobia*").

58. Toll, *Six Frigates*, 337–69.

59. Thomas Jefferson to James Madison, Monticello, May 21, 1813, in *Republic of Letters*, ed. Smith, 3:1720. For the Naval Act of 1813, see Fowler, *Jack Tars and Commodores*, 185–86; and Symonds, *Navalists and Antinavalists*, 174–84.

60. William Jones to James Madison, October 26, 1814, in *The Naval War of 1812: A Documentary History*, 3 vols., ed. William S. Dudley and Michael J. Crawford (Washington, DC: Naval Historical Center, 1985–2004), 3:632; Linda Maloney, "The War of 1812: What Role for Sea Power?," in Hagan, ed., *Peace and War*, 57.

61. Symonds, *Navalists and Antinavalists*, 196–99, 213–16. For the Second Barbary War, see Lambert, *Barbary Wars*, 179–202.

62. White, *Jeffersonians*, 120–21.

63. "The Naval Establishment of the United States," *Niles Register* (Washington, DC), October 20, 1821.

64. Jackson quoted in Symonds, *Navalists and Antinavalists*, 235. Outside of the Mexican War (1846–48), America's long peace with foreign states until the Spanish-American War in 1898 also helped to shape its defensive naval force. See Kenneth J. Hagan, *American Gunboat Diplomacy and the Old Navy, 1877–1889* (Westport, CT: Greenwood Press, 1973).

Chapter 10

1. John M. Murrin, "The Great Inversion, or Court Versus Country: A Comparison of the Revolution Settlements in England (1688–1721) and America (1776–1816)," in J. G. A. Pocock, ed., *Three British Revolutions: 1641, 1688, 1776* (Princeton, NJ: Princeton University Press, 1980), 368–453.

2. John Brewer, *The Sinews of Power: War, Money and the English State, 1688–1783* (New York: Alfred A. Knopf, 1989), 95–99; Robert A. Becker, *Revolution, Reform, and the Politics of American Taxation, 1763–1783* (Baton Rouge: Louisiana State University Press, 1980), 34.

3. John M. Murrin, "Anglicizing an American Colony: The Transformation of Provincial Massachusetts" (Ph.D. diss., Yale University, 1966), 118, 263–64, 269–70; Becker, *Politics of American Taxation*, 34–35, 38, 236.

4. James T. Mitchell and Henry Flanders, eds., *The Statutes at Large of Pennsylvania, from 1682 to 1801*, 18 vols. (Harrisburg: State of Pennsylvania, 1896–1911), 5:201, 294, 303, 337; 6:7, 344.

5. See Anthony M. Joseph, *From Liberty to Liberality: The Transformation of the Pennsylvania Legislature, 1776–1820* (Lanham, MD: Lexington Books, 2012), 80–81.

6. Becker, *Politics of American Taxation*, 43, 78–79.

7. Max M. Edling and Mark D. Kaplanoff, "Alexander Hamilton's Fiscal Reform: Transforming the Structure of Taxation in the Early Republic," *William and Mary Quarterly*, 3rd ser., 61 (October 2004): 720.

8. Ibid. 719–21; Brewer, *Sinews of Power*, 95.

9. Edling and Kaplanoff, "Hamilton's Fiscal Reform," 729–30, 733; Becker, *Politics of American Taxation*, 121–22.

10. Roger H. Brown, *Redeeming the Republic: Federalists, Taxation, and the Origins of the Constitution* (Baltimore: Johns Hopkins University Press, 1993), 12–13, 14, 58; Lemuel Molovinsky, "Pennsylvania's Legislative Efforts to Finance the War for Independence: A Study of the Continuity of Colonial Finance, 1775–83" (Ph.D. diss., Temple University, 1975), 267.

11. Brown, *Redeeming the Republic*, 60–63; Terry Bouton, "A Road Closed: Rural Insurgency in Post-Independence Pennsylvania," *Journal of American History* 87 (December 2000): 855–87; Becker, *Politics of American Taxation*, 188; *Report of the Register-General of the State of the Finances of Pennsylvania, for 1792* (Philadelphia, 1793), no. 26.

12. Bernard Bailyn, ed., *The Debate on the Constitution: Federalist and Antifederalist Speeches, Articles, and Letters During the Struggle over Ratification*, 2 vols. (New York: Library of America, 1993), 1:68.

13. *Journal of the First House of Representatives of the Commonwealth of Pennsylvania* [1790–91] (Philadelphia, 1791), 230–31, 335; *Journal of the Senate of the Commonwealth of Pennsylvania* [1790–91] (Philadelphia, 1791), 195, 199.

14. Edling and Kaplanoff, "Hamilton's Fiscal Reform," 729–32; L. Ray Gunn, *The Decline of Authority: Public Economic Policy and Political Development in New York State, 1800–1860* (Ithaca, NY: Cornell University Press, 1988), 138–41, 166; H. James Henderson, "Taxation and Political Culture: Massachusetts and Virginia, 1760–1800," *William and Mary Quarterly*, 3rd ser., 47 (January 1990): 111–12; Charles J. Bullock, *Historical Sketch of the Finances and Financial Policy of Massachusetts from 1780 to 1905* (New York: American Economic Association, 1907), 24–29.

15. Alexander Hamilton, Harold Coffin Syrett, and Jacob Ernest Cooke, *The Papers of Alexander Hamilton,* vol. 21 (New York: Columbia University Press, 1974).

16. Stanley Elkins and Eric McKitrick, *The Age of Federalism* (New York: Oxford University Press, 1993), 470; U.S. Congress, *American State Papers: Documents, Legislative and Executive, of the Congress of the United States,* 38 vols. (1832–61), "Finance," 1:621, 668; Edling and Kaplanoff, "Hamilton's Fiscal Reform," 738.

17. *Annals of Congress,* House of Representatives, 4th Cong., 1st sess., 841–56; Mark Cachia-Riedl, "Albert Gallatin and the Politics of the New Nation" (Ph.D. diss., University of California, Berkeley, 1998), 76.

18. *Annals of Congress,* House of Representatives, 4th Cong., 2nd sess., 1843–44, 1850, 1909; *Annals of Congress,* House of Representatives, 4th Cong., 2nd sess., 1909, 1917, 1920; W. B. Allen, ed., *Works of Fisher Ames, as Published by Seth Ames,* vol. 2 (Indianapolis: Liberty Classics, 1983), 1213, 1219.

19. *Annals of Congress,* House of Representatives, 4th Cong., 2nd sess., 1920, 1941; *Annals of Congress,* House of Representatives, 4th Cong., 2nd sess., 1933, 1941–42; *Journal of the House of Representatives of the United States, 1789–1873,* July 2, 1798, 362–63; *Annals of Congress,* House of Representatives, 5th Cong., 2nd sess., May 7, 1798, 1617, 1619. As late as June 1798 Jefferson reported that New Englanders' objections to the apportionment of the tax quotas might yet prevent a direct tax from passing Congress. See Thomas Jefferson to James Madison, June 7, 1798, in *The Works of Thomas Jefferson in Twelve Volumes,* ed. Paul Leicester Ford (Library of Congress, American Memory Online Edition).

20. Thomas Jefferson to Peregrine Fitzhugh, June 4, 1797, Thomas Jefferson to John Taylor, November 26, 1798, Thomas Jefferson to James Madison, January 3, 1799, Thomas Jefferson to James Madison, January 16, 1799, Thomas Jefferson to James Monroe, January 23, 1799, Thomas Jefferson to Elbridge Gerry, January 26, 1799, in *Works of Thomas Jefferson,* ed. Ford; Herbert E. Sloan, "Hamilton's Second Thoughts: Federalist Finance Revisited," in Doron Ben-Atar and Barbara Oberg, eds., *Federalists Reconsidered* (Charlottesville.: University Press of Virginia, 1998), 74, 75.

21. *Annals of Congress,* House of Representatives, 5th Cong., 3rd sess., 2985–3016; U.S. Congress, *American State Papers,* "Finance," 2:66–67, 919; Allen, *Works of Fisher Ames,* 1341. In the mid-1980s the Internal Revenue Service estimated that close to 20 percent of federal personal income taxes went unpaid; see Jeffrey A. Roth et al., eds., *Taxpayer Compliance,* vol. 1 (Philadelphia: University of Pennsylvania Press, 1989), 1, 47–48.

22. Donald R. Hickey, *The War of 1812: A Forgotten Conflict* (Urbana: University of Illinois Press, 1989), 122; *Statutes at Large,* 3:22, 53, 164, 255.

23. John M. Murrin, "The French and Indian War, the American Revolution, and the Counterfactual Hypothesis: Reflections on Lawrence Henry Gipson and John Shy," *Reviews in American History* 1 (September 1973): 314.

24. Merrill Jensen, Gaspare J. Saladino, and John P. Kaminski, *The Documentary History of the Ratification of the Constitution,* vol. 3 (Madison: State Historical Society of Wisconsin, 1976), 352, 526; Bailyn, *Debate on the Constitution,* 1:723; 2:105.

25. James Monroe quoted in Steven Watts, *The Republic Reborn: War and the Making of Liberal America, 1790–1820* (Baltimore: Johns Hopkins University Press, 1987), 278; Charles M. Wiltsie and David G. Allen, eds., *The Papers of Daniel Webster,* ser. 1, vol. 1: *Correspondence, 1798–1824* (Hanover, NH: University Press of New England, 1974), 139; Hickey, *War of 1812,* 232.

26. U.S. Congress, *American State Papers,* "Finance," 2:856; 3:43, 190, 301; *Statutes at Large,* 3:22, 53, 164, 255; Wiltsie and Allen, *Papers of Daniel Webster,* ser. 1, vol. 1, 181; U.S. Congress, *American State Papers,* Finance, 2:856; 3:43, 190, 301; *Statutes at Large,* 3:22, 53, 164, 255; *Journal of the House of Representatives of the Commonwealth of Pennsylvania* [1810–11] (Lancaster, PA, 1811), 16; *Journal of the House of Representatives of the State of Georgia* (October–November 1814 session) [1815], 6 (Early State Records microfilm); *Journal of the Senate of the United States of America, 1789–1873,* vol. 5 (Washington, DC: Gales & Seaton, 1821), 526–27.

27. *Statutes at Large,* 3:401.

28. Alan Taylor, "The Late Loyalists: Northern Reflections of the Early American Republic," *Journal of the Early Republic* 27 (Spring 2007): 2–3, 7–11; *Report of a Select Committee, of the House of Assembly, on the Political State of the Provinces of Upper and Lower Canada* (1838), 21.

29. Taylor, "Late Loyalists," 7.

30. *Report of a Select Committee,* 5.

Conclusion

1. The early modern state's shift from punishment/coercion to perception/guidance is explored in Albert O. Hirschman, *The Passions and the Interests: Political Arguments for Capitalism Before Its Triumph* (Princeton, NJ: Princeton University Press, 1977).

2. For a discussion of the passing of the master narrative, see Peter Novick, "*That Noble Dream*": *The Objectivity Question and the American Historical Profession* (New York: Cambridge University Press, 1988), esp. pt. 4. Alan Taylor, *American Colonies: The Settling of North America* (New York: Penguin, 2001), provides an exemplar of an expanded narrative of early American history that includes New France, the Dutch state, and the Spanish Empire, as does J. H. Elliott in his magisterial *Empires of the Atlantic World: Britain and Spain in America, 1492–1830* (New Haven, CT: Yale University Press, 2007).

3. John M. Murrin, "Political Development," in Jack P. Greene and J. R. Pole, eds., *Colonial British America: Essays in the New History of the Early Modern Era* (Baltimore: Johns Hopkins University Press, 1984), 408–56; Jack P. Greene, "Political Mimesis: A Consideration of the Historical and Cultural Roots of Legislative Behavior in the British Colonies in the Eighteenth Century," with a reply by Bernard Bailyn, *American Historical Review* 75 (1969): 337–67.

4. George Louis Beer, *British Colonial Policy 1754–1765* (Cambridge: Cambridge University Press, 1907); Beer, *The Origins of the British Colonial System 1578–1660* (New York: Macmillan, 1908); Beer, *The Old Colonial System 1660–1754* (Cambridge:

Cambridge University Press, 1912); Charles McLean Andrews, *The Colonial Period in American History*, 4 vols. (New Haven, CT: Yale University Press, 1934–37); Viola F. Barnes, *The Dominion of New England: A Study in British Colonial Policy* (New Haven, CT: Yale University Press, 1923); Herbert L. Osgood, *The American Colonies in the Seventeenth Century*, 3 vols. (New York: Macmillan, 1904–7); Osgood, *The American Colonies in the Eighteenth Century*, 4 vols. (New York: Macmillan, 1924–25). For a recent biography of Barnes, see John G. Reid, *Viola Florence Barnes 1885–1979: A Historian's Biography* (Toronto: Toronto University Press, 2005). For a study of Andrews's historical practices, see Abraham Seldin Eisenstadt, *Charles McLean Andrews: A Study in American Historical Writing* (New York: Columbia University Press, 1956). For an appreciation of Osgood's life, see H. J. Coppock, "Herbert L. Osgood," *Mississippi Valley Historical Review* 19 (1932): 394–403.

5. Richard R. Johnson, "Charles McLean Andrews and the Invention of American Colonial History," *William and Mary Quarterly*, 3rd ser., 43 (1986): 519–41.

6. Many personal narratives are embedded in John M. Murrin, "Review Essay," *History and Theory* 11 (1972): 226–75; Murrin, "English Rights as Ethnic Aggression: The English Conquest, the Charter of Liberties of 1683, and Leisler's Rebellion in New York," in William Pencak and Conrad E. Wright, eds., *Authority and Resistance in Early New York* (New York: New-York Historical Society, 1988), 56–94; Murrin, "The Menacing Shadow of Louis XIV and the Rage of Jacob Leisler: The Constitutional Ordeal of Seventeenth-Century New York," in Stephen L. Schechter and Richard B. Bernstein, eds., *New York and the Union* (Albany: NYS Commission on the Bi-Centennial of the U.S. Constitution, 1990), 29–71; and Murrin, "'Things Fearful to Name': Bestiality in Early America," *Pennsylvania History* 65 (1998): 8–43.

7. See Richard L. Bushman, *The Refinement of America: Persons, Houses, Cities* (New York: Vintage, 1993); John Brewer and Roy Porter, eds., *Consumption and the World of Goods* (New York: Routledge, 1994); and T. H. Breen, *The Marketplace of Revolution: How Consumer Politics Shaped the American Revolution* (New York: Oxford University Press, 2005).

8. Richard R. Johnson, *Adjustment to Empire: The New England Colonies, 1675–1715* (New Brunswick, NJ: Rutgers University Press, 1981).

9. See Peter G. Lake and Michael C. Questier, "Introduction," in Lake and Questier, eds., *Conformity and Orthodoxy in the English Church, c. 1560–1660* (Woodbridge, Suffolk, UK: Boydell Press, 2000); and Ken Fincham and Peter G. Lake, "The Ecclesiastical Policy of King James I," *Journal of British Studies* 24 (1985): 169–207.

10. Herman L. Bennett, "The Subject in the Plot: National Boundaries and the 'History' of the Black Atlantic," *African Studies Review* 43 (2000): 101–24; Bennett, "'Sons of Adam': Text, Context, and the Early Modern African Subject," *Representations* 92, no. 1 (2005): 16–41; Bennett, "Writing into a Void: Representing Slavery and Freedom in the Narrative of Colonial Spanish America," *Social Text* 93 (2007): 67–89.

11. For the definition of the term, see R. Brian Ferguson and Neil L. Whitehead, "The Violent Edge of Empire," in their collection of essays *War in the Tribal Zone: Expanding*

States and Indigenous Warfare (1992; repr., Santa Fe, NM: School of American Research Press, 1999), 1–30.

12. Revolutionary-era New York provides an example of bidirectional change, with figures such as the indigenous leader Joseph Brant *and* Sir William Johnson both being transformed; see Isabel Thompson Kelsay, *Joseph Brant, 1743–1807: Man of Two Worlds* (Syracuse, NY: Syracuse University Press, 1986); and Timothy J. Shannon, "Dressing for Success on the Mohawk Frontier: Hendrick, William Johnson, and the Indian Fashion," *William and Mary Quarterly*, 3rd ser., 53 (1996): 13–42.

CONTRIBUTORS

Denver Brunsman is Associate Professor of History at George Washington University. He is author of *The Evil Necessity: British Naval Impressment in the Eighteenth-Century Atlantic World* (2013) and an editor of *The American Revolution Reader* (2013), among other works.

William Howard Carter is Assistant Professor of History at the College of New Jersey. After studying under Gary Kornblith at Oberlin College, he had the immense good fortune to work with his mentor's mentor, John Murrin, at Princeton University. He is currently writing a book titled *The Hideous and the Beautiful: The Decorated Body in Iroquoia, 1550–1850*.

Ignacio Gallup-Diaz is Associate Professor of History and Chair of the Department of History at Bryn Mawr College. A specialist on the early modern Atlantic world, he is author of *The Door of the Seas and Key to the Universe: Indian Politics and Imperial Rivalry in the Darién, 1640–1750* (2005).

Anthony M. Joseph is Associate Professor of History at Houston Baptist University. He is author of *From Liberty to Liberality: The Transformation of the Pennsylvania Legislature, 1776–1820* (2012). He is currently editing the legal papers of the early Supreme Court justice James Iredell.

Simon P. Newman is Sir Denis Brogan Professor of American History at the University of Glasgow. His most recent book is *A New World of Labor: The Development of Plantation Slavery in the British Atlantic World* (2013), which was recognized by the British Association for American Studies as the best book of 2013.

Geoffrey Plank is Professor of History at the University of East Anglia. He is author of *John Woolman's Path to the Peaceable Kingdom: A Quaker in the*

British Empire (2012), *Rebellion and Savagery: The Jacobite Rising of 1745 and the British Empire* (2005), and *An Unsettled Conquest: The British Campaign Against the Peoples of Acadia* (2003).

Nancy L. Rhoden is Associate Professor of History at the University of Western Ontario. She is author of *Revolutionary Anglicanism: The Colonial Church of England Clergy During the American Revolution* (1999) and has edited and coedited several anthologies.

Andrew Shankman, Associate Professor of History at Rutgers University, Camden, is author of *Crucible of American Democracy: The Struggle to Fuse Egalitarianism and Capitalism in Jeffersonian Pennsylvania* (2004) and editor of *The World of the Revolutionary American Republic: Land, Labor, and the Conflict for a Continent* (2014).

David J. Silverman is Professor of History at George Washington University. He is author of *Faith and Boundaries: Colonists, Christianity, and Community Among the Wampanoag Indians of Martha's Vineyard, 1600–1871* (2005) and *Red Brethren: The Brothertown and Stockbridge Indians and the Problem of Race in Early America* (2010) and coauthor of *Ninigret, Sachem of the Niantics and Narragansetts: War, Diplomacy, and the Balance of Power in Seventeenth-Century New England and Indian Country* (2014).

Jeremy A. Stern is an independent historian and history education consultant. In addition to his work on scholarly articles, research, and lectures, he has written on history as presented by mass culture and in schools. He has consulted on state history standards for organizations including the Thomas B. Fordham Institute and the Southern Poverty Law Center, along with multiple state governments and officials, and has prepared extensive explanatory history content for teachers through the Washington, D.C.–based organization Common Core.

"Act for the Better Ordering of Slaves" (1690), 189

"Act for the General Increase of the Navy of the United States" (1816), 224

"Act for the Good Governing of Servants" (1661), 76

Adams, Henry, 205, 207, 218

Adams, John, 177, 206, 207, 208, 209, 213, 214, 216, 217, 218, 227

Adams, Samuel, 177

Adjustment to Empire, 1

Agariata, 96

Alabama, 201

Albany, N.Y., 85, 94, 100, 104, 186

Algiers, 212

Alien and Sedition Acts (1798), 234

American colonies: Anglicization of, 37–38; anti-Catholicism of, 33, 191–93; British identity of, 154–55; crises of, 25, 26; diversity of, 9–11, 22, 29, 126, 241; English identity of, 18–19; Episcopacy and, 128–29, 136–40; "feudal revival" of, 38; fiscal policies of, 228; founding of, 21; Indian relations of, 183–87; Indian wars of, 185–86; migration to, 147, 239; newspapers of, 185–86; political culture of, 29; politics of, 15; religious pluralism of, 125, 126; royal governors of, 31, 32, 35–36, 37, 40, 45; slavery in, 12, 185, 187, 188; trade of, 40; warfare of, 16, 30, 40; wealth distribution of, 38

Americanization, 1, 17, 35, 127, 183

American Revolution, 4, 42–49, 226; armies in, 120; causes of, 16; imperial crises of, 43; Indians' role in, 196, 198–99, 200; militias' role in, 120; navies' role in, 209–10; as racial watershed, 196–201; slaves' role in, 196, 197–98, 199–200; social history of, 49

Amherst, Jeffery, 116

Anderson, Fred, 111

Andrews, Charles McLean, 245

Andros, Edmund, 110, 191

Anglicanization, 125–26, 150–51

Anglicization, 1, 11–12, 20–21, 25, 26–27, 29, 37–38, 59, 110, 125–27, 181–82, 239–48; in American colonies, 37–38; and American Revolution, 42–43; and cultural history, 43; Jeffersonian policies against, 206; in Massachusetts, 30, 31, 33, 153; in Middle Colonies, 12, 14, 34; in New England, 12, 34; in New Hampshire, 31, 33; in Pennsylvania, 34; and slavery, 60; in southern colonies, 37

"Anglicizing an American Colony: The Transformation of Provincial Massachusetts," 109

Anglo-Dutch Wars, 40

Annapolis Royal, 115

Anne, 137

anthropology, 247

anti-Catholicism, 23, 24, 191–96

Anti-Federalists, 212, 230, 235
Antigua, 193
anti-popery. *See* anti-Catholicism
Archbishop of Canterbury, 130, 136, 139, 143, 152
Articles of Confederation, 50
Ashley, Anthony. *See* Shaftesbury, Anthony Ashley, Earl of
Atlantic world, 2

Bache, Benjamin Franklin, 214
"Back to Africa" movements, 202
Bacon's Rebellion (1676), 25, 187, 245
Bacqueville de La Potherie, Calude Charles Le Roy, 92, 105
Bailyn, Bernard, 35–36, 43, 242
Baltimore, Calvert, Charles, 3rd Lord, 192
Baptists, 126, 132, 134, 147–50, 151
Barbados: assembly of, 79; criminal laborers of, 79; demographics of, 70; diseases of, 72; distribution of wealth in, 68; Irish of, 75, 78; labor system of, 69, 78–79, 80, 81; laws of, 76–77, 79; migration to, 67–68; planter power in, 68, 77; race and, 189; servant rebellion in, 78; slavery in, 78–79, 80, 81; society in, 69; and southern North American colonies, 60; white labor force of, 68–77; work conditions in, 74, 76
Barbary States, 212, 214, 218
Barbary Wars, 212–13, 218, 220, 224
Barlow, Joel, 216
Barnard, Edward, 155, 161
Barnes, Viola Florence, 245
Battle of Halifax (1749), 114
Battle of Lexington and Concord (1775), 46, 118, 120, 181, 198
Battle of Louisbourg (1745), 114
Battle of Louisbourg (1758), 115
Battle of Yorktown, 209
Beard, Charles, 51
Beckles, Hilary, 79

Beer, George Louis, 245
Before the American Revolution, 122
Bell, James B., 145
Bellesiles, Michael A., 119
Bennett, Herman, 246
Bereton, William, 75
Berlin, Ira, 187
Bernard, Francis, 155, 158, 159, 162, 165, 166, 168, 177
Berthoff, Rowland, 38
Bill of Rights (1689; England), 119
Bishop of London, 129, 137, 148
Black Death, 61
Bland, Richard, 197
Board of Admiralty, 209
Board of Customs, 45
Board of Trade, 18, 46, 131
Bolingbroke, St. John, Henry, Viscount, 207
Bonhomme Richard, 209
Book of Common Prayer, 133
Boston, Mass., 16, 130, 156, 159, 162, 165, 172, 243
Boston Gazette, 177
Boston Massacre, 120, 162, 167, 176
Boston News-Letter, 177, 186
Boston Tea Party, 177
Brant, Joseph, 198
Brazil, 12
Breen, T. H., 1, 59, 118, 120
Bridge, Ebenezer, 156, 162, 177
British Empire: and American Revolution, 43–49; authority of, 243; governance of, 16, 17–18, 26, 40, 43, 240; Indian relations of, 241
Brown, Roger H., 229
Burnet, Richard, 85, 86, 95, 101
Burton, Mary, 194, 195–96
Burton, Thomas, 143
Bushman, Richard, 1
Butler, John, 1
Byfield, Mass., 169

Caesar, 193–95

Calvinism, 22, 133

Cambridge, Mass., 162, 169, 172

Cambridge Platform (1648), 22

Campbell, John, Earl of Loudon, 115

Canada, 41, 199, 221, 237

Canada Constitutional Act of 1791, 237

Caribbean. *See* West Indies

Cartaret, John, 39

Catawbas, 200

Cayugas, 104

Chandler, Thomas Bradbury, 138

Charles I, 22, 161

Charles II, 23, 24, 25, 174

Charleston. *See* Charles Town

Charles Town, S.C., 18, 189, 197

Chauncy, Charles, 138

Chelmsford, Mass., 156

Cherry Valley, N.Y., 200

Chesapeake: court system of, 12; economy of, 11; labor force of, 9–10; life expectancy in, 10; migration to, 9–10; social patterns of, 10, 12, 13. *See also* Maryland; Virginia

Chesapeake-Leopard Affair (1807), 220

Chet, Guy, 111–12, 114

Cheves, Langdon, 221

Church of England, 27; and American colonies, 125–52; anti-revivalism of, 134–35; architecture of, 132–33; church-state tradition of, 125, 128; in Maryland, 192; missionary work of, 131–32, 150; in Pennsylvania, 141–44, 150, 151; rituals of, 133; varieties of, 126; in Virginia, 144–52

Civil War (U.S.), 60

Clastres, Pierre, 88–89

Clay, Henry, 222

Clonmacnoise Decrees, 75

Coercive Acts (1774), 48

Coercive Acts crisis, 43

Colden, Cadwallader, 83–108

College of Philadelphia, 144, 197

College of William and Mary, 13, 145

Colonial America. *See* American colonies

Common Sense (1776), 208

Compton, Henry, 130

Conestoga Indians, 187

Congregationalism, 22, 63, 127, 133, 136

Congress (U.S.), 52, 210, 211, 213, 215, 219, 220, 222, 223, 224, 229, 230, 232–33

Connecticut: Church of England in, 137; fiscal policies of, 231; Indian relations of, 202; slavery in, 188; social stability of, 11; wars of, 114. *See also* New England

Constitution (U.S.), 53, 119, 202, 212, 226, 230

Constitutional Convention, 50, 181, 182, 212, 230

Continental Congress, 198, 199

Coode, John, 192

Cooke, Samuel, 162–66, 167

Cooper, Anthony Ashley, 24

Cornwallis, Edward, 115

Council of Foreign Plantations, 70

country ideology, 15, 18, 35, 37, 48, 49, 52, 53

Courtland Manor, 39

Covenant Chain Alliance, 83, 84, 88, 95, 100, 108

Coventry (Eng.), 62

Creation of the American Republic, 51

Crévecouer, J. Hector St. John de, 203

Cromwell, Oliver, 73, 74, 75

Crosby, Alfred, 112

Cuba, 195

Currency Act (1764), 17, 44, 45

Curtin, Philip D., 112

Cushing, Thomas, 177

Dartmouth, William Legge, Lord, 172, 177

Davies, Samuel, 147, 149

Declaration of Independence, 1988
Declaratory Act (1766), 154, 157
Dedham, Mass., 160
DeLancy, James, 34
Delaware, 10, 11, 35, 210, 231
Delaware Indians, 117, 200
Democratic Republicans, 52, 53–55, 205;
    fiscal policies of, 234–35, 236; naval
    policies of, 207, 213–14, 215, 220, 222,
    224; press of, 214, 216; taxation policies
    of, 226
Department of the Navy (U.S.), 214, 223
Department of the Treasury (U.S), 214
Derry (Ire.), 75
Dominion of New England, 11, 25, 29,
    110, 191
Dongan, Thomas, 100, 101, 102, 104, 106,
    130
Dublin, 75
Duke of York. See James II
Dunmore, John Murray, 4th Earl of, 18,
    198
Dunmore's Proclamation (1775), 18, 198
Dunn, Richard, 79
Dutch, 94, 95
Dutch Empire, 111
Dutch Reformed church, 131
Duxbury, Mass., 172

Earl of Granville. See Cartaret, John
East Jersey. See New Jersey
Edinburgh, 72, 73, 85, 88
election of 1800, 216, 235
England, 26, 27, 74; Bill of Rights of, 119;
    labor system of, 61; poor laws of, 61,
    63–64; servants in, 62; Toleration Act
    of, 128, 131, 140, 146–47, 149, 152. See
    also Great Britain
Enlightenment, 84, 85, 89
epidemic disease, 112
Episcopacy, 128–29
Episcopalians, 126

Essex County, Mass., 155
Exclusion Crisis (1679–81), 1, 25

Fairfax, Thomas, 38–39
Faquier, Fancis, 149
Fawkes, Guy, 193
Federalists, 52, 53, 55, 206, 211, 214, 215,
    216–17, 221, 232, 233–34
Fincham, Kenneth, 246
Findley, William, 233
Five Nations. See Haudenosaunee
Fletcher, Benjamin, 130
Florida, 185, 192, 193
Fort Frontenac, 105
France, 28, 207, 209
Franklin, Benjamin, 14, 34, 46–47, 177,
    208
French colonies, 2
French Empire, 111
French and Indian War. See Seven Years'
    War
French Revolution, 220
French wars. See Imperial Wars
Frey, Sylvia, 199
Fries's Rebellion (1799), 234

Gage, Thomas, 44
Gallatin, Albert, 215, 218, 224, 233, 234,
    235
Galloway, Joseph, 34
Garakontié, 104
Garden, Alexander, 135
George III, 161, 170, 181, 198, 199
Georgia, 14, 35, 187, 193, 195, 199
German Lutherans, 134, 187
German Reformed church, 134
Germans, 147
Giles, William Branch, 213
Glasgow, 190
Glorious Revolution (1688), 3, 11, 25,
    27, 28, 29, 33, 37, 41–42, 140, 166, 176,
    191–92, 214, 243

Gnadenhutten Massacre, 200
"God Save the King," 192
Gordon, Thomas, 207
Gorham, John, 115
Gorham, Joseph, 115
Gorham's Rangers, 115
Granville. *See* Cartaret, John
gradual emancipation, 181, 197, 201
Grayson, William, 212
Great Awakening, 16
Great Britain: Anglicization of, 29;
    Canada policies of, 237–38; constitu-
    tional monarchy of, 27; fiscal policies
    of, 27, 30, 31, 33, 229, 235; founding
    of, 26, 241; French relations of, 28, 33;
    Hanoverian succession of, 3, 26, 37;
    Parliament of, 153–78, 238, 243; politics
    of, 14–15; military of, 27, 30, 31, 33;
    navy of, 207, 208–10; slavery in, 190;
    tax policies of, 227; wars of, 27, 30, 40
Great Lakes, 212, 223
Greene, Jack P., 59, 242
Grenier, John, 111, 116–17
Grenville, George, 43, 46, 154
Gunpowder Plot (1605), 193
Gwin, John. *See* Caesar

Halifax, 114–15, 116
Hamilton, Alexander, 53, 212, 213, 216,
    223, 230, 232
Hamilton, Paul, 221
Hancock, John, 159
Hanoverian succession, 3, 26, 37
Harper, Robert, 215
Harrington, James, 24
Harvard College, 137
Haudenosaunee, 4, 83, 89–91; condolence
    ceremony of, 99; play-off politics of,
    87; relations of with British colonies,
    98, 102, 103–6; relations of with New
    France, 103–6; and Revolution, 200;
    values of, 99; wars of, 98

Haven, Jason, 160–62, 164
Haverhill, Mass., 155
Henry VIII, 66
Henry, Patrick, 212
High Courts of Admiralty, 248
Hillsborough, Wills Hill, Earl of, 172
Hingham, Mass., 157
Hirschman, Albert O., 248
Historie de l'Amérique Septentrionale, 92
History of the Five Indian Nations, 83–108
Hobbes, Thomas, 88
Holton, Woody, 43
Hopkins, Samuel, 198
Horsmanden, Daniel, 194–95
Howard of Effingham, Francis, Lord,
    100–101, 102
Hughson, John, 193–95
Huguenots, 127
Hurons, 106
Hutchinson, Thomas, 162, 165, 166, 169,
    172, 174, 176, 177, 185
Hyde, Edward, Lord Cornbury, 130

Imperial Wars, 16, 27
impressment, 210–10, 220
indentured servitude, 9–10
Indians, 1, 2, 3; and American territorial
    expansion, 54; Christianity of, 183;
    enslavement of, 185; imperial rela-
    tions of, 241; newspaper depictions of,
    186–86; racial violence against, 187;
    relations of with British colonies, 114;
    and Revolution, 196, 198–99, 200; visits
    of to London, 190; war ways of, 113;
    wars of against colonists, 183–84; and
    white racism, 184–85, 201
Intolerable Acts. *See* Coercive Acts
Ireland, 74, 134
Iroquois League. See Haudenosaunee

Jackson, Andrew, 225
Jacobite Rising (1745), 119

Jacobs, Wilbur, 107
Jamaica, 60, 73
James II, 23, 25, 48, 104, 191
Jay Treaty (1794), 53
Jefferson, Thomas, 197, 205, 209, 211,
    215–16, 236; Anglophobia of, 206–7,
    213; election of, president, 216; naval
    policies of, 207, 223; presidency of,
    217–20
Jeffersonians. *See*
    Democratic-Republicans
Jennings, Francis, 107, 114
jeremiads, 14, 25
Johnson, Guy, 198
Johnson, Richard R., 1, 245, 246
Johnson, Samuel, 137
Johnson, William, 107
Jones, John Paul, 209
Jones, William, 223
Jordon, Winthrop, 81, 210

Keithian schism, 25
Kerry, Peggy, 195–96
Ket's Rebellion, 66
*King and People in Provincial Massachu-
    setts*, 1
King George's War (1744–48), 191, 192
King Philip's War (1675–78), 25, 109, 115,
    184, 187, 245
King's Three Faces, 1
King William's War. *See* War of the
    League of Augsburg
Kondiaronk, 106, 107
Konig, David Thomas, 119

La Barre, Joseph-Antoine Le Febvre de,
    102, 103, 104
Lahontan, Louis Armand de Lom de
    l'Arce Baron de, 92, 103–4
Lake Ontario, 94, 102, 223
Lake, Peter, 246
Land, Isaac, 208

land tax of 1799, 53
latitudinarianism, 143
Laud, William, Archbishop, 136
Lawrence, Charles, 116
Lee, Arthur, 177, 197
Lee, Wayne, 117
Leeward Islands, 60
Leisler, Jacob, 192
Leisler's Rebellion (1689), 25
Le Rat. *See* Kondiaronk
Levelers, 24
Liberty, 159
Liberty, Equality, Power, 26
Ligon, Richard, 71, 72
Liverpool, 190
Livingston Manor, 39
Locke, John, 24, 88, 89, 157, 160, 167, 168
London, 15, 64, 190, 243
Louisbourg, 114–15
Louisiana, 201
Lower Canada, 237
Loyalists, 17, 19, 120, 210
Lutheran Ministerium of Pennsylvania,
    134
Lutherans, 134, 143, 187
Lyon, Matthew, 219

Madison, James, 212, 213, 215–16, 220,
    223, 224
Maier, Pauline, 199
Maine, 112, 186, 191
Malcom, Joyce Lee, 118
Malone, Patrick, 113
Marketplace of Revolution, 1
Mary II, 29, 192
Maryland: anti-Catholicism in, 191, 192;
    Church of England in, 130, 139, 192;
    Indian relations of, 191, 192; migration
    to, 10; relations of with Haudeno-
    saunee, 96; slavery in, 35, 188, 193. *See
    also* Chesapeake
Mashpee, 200

Massachusetts, 29, 182, 241, 248; 1629
    charter of, 29–30, 164, 174; 1691 charter
    of, 29–30, 153, 164; Anglicization of,
    30, 31, 33, 153; anti-Catholicism in, 191;
    Church of England in, 137; demograph-
    ics of, 30; economy of, 31; election
    sermons of, 154–78; fiscal policies of,
    227, 228, 229; General Court of, 14,
    40; House of Representatives of, 154,
    162, 169, 171, 172; Indian relations of,
    184; military system of, 110; missionary
    work in, 184; political culture of, 38;
    politics of, 15, 30–31, 34; racial laws of,
    189; relations of with Haudenosaunee,
    99–100; religion in, 22, 30; royal gover-
    nors of, 155, 158, 159, 162, 165, 166, 169,
    174; Shays's Rebellion in, 229; slavery in,
    188, 189, 197, 201; society in, 11; warfare
    of, 30, 44, 114. *See also* New England
Massachusetts Government Act (1774).
    See Coercive Acts
Mayhew, Jonathan, 138
Mazzei, Philip, 206
McConville, Brendan, 1
McKee, Samuel, 222
McNeil, William H., 112
Merrell, James, 113
Methodists, 126, 134
Michilimackinac, 106
middle colonies, 25; Anglicization of, 12,
    14, 34; diversity of, 11, 34; economy of,
    14; political culture of, 36, 38; politics
    of, 11; religion in, 14, 126; society in,
    10–11; utopian vision for, 24. *See also*
    Delaware; New Jersey; New York;
    Pennsylvania
Mi'kmaqs, 115, 116, 117
Militia Act (U.S., 1792), 203
Ministry Act (1691), 130
Mississippi, 201
Mohawks, 94, 98, 100–101, 132, 191, 198
Mohegans, 200

Mohicans, 200
Molasses Act (1764). *See* Sugar Act
Monmouth's Rebellion (1685), 25, 79
Monroe, James, 236
Monticello, 223
Montreal, 94
Moravians, 138, 187
Morgan, Edmund S., 20, 43
Morocco, 212, 218
Mühlenberg, Henry, 141, 143, 144
Murrin, John M., 1, 5, 20–21, 22, 30, 31,
    35, 36, 40, 44–45, 48, 56, 59, 84, 114,
    118, 119, 122, 126, 181–82, 203, 205, 241,
    242–43, 245; "beneficiaries of catas-
    trophe" thesis of, 112; "feudal revival"
    thesis of, 38; "Great Inversion" thesis
    of, 214, 219, 226; "radical, imperial,
    Whig" synthesis of, 43–49; "roof
    without walls" thesis of, 53. *See also*
    Anglicization
Mystic Massacre (1637), 114

Napoleonic Wars (1799–1815), 220
Narragansetts, 114, 200
Native Americans. *See* Indians
Naturalization Act (U.S., 1790), 203
Naval Act of 1813, 223
Naval Chronicle, 210
Navigation Acts, 31, 32, 40, 73, 248
Newbury, Mass., 167
New England: Anglicization of, 12, 34;
    Church of England in, 130; demog-
    raphy of, 10; economy of, 13; English
    heritage of, 11; Indians relations of, 184,
    191; legal culture of, 22; migration to, 10,
    21–22; militias of, 118; political culture
    of, 35; politics of, 15; religion in, 10, 14,
    22, 126; slavery in, 188, 197, 201; society
    in, 10, 12, 13; utopian vision for, 22, 24;
    wars of, 16, 25, 114, 184, 186–87. *See also*
    Connecticut; Maine; Massachusetts;
    New Hampshire; Rhode Island

New France, 30, 85, 87, 96–97, 106, 191

New Hampshire, 29; Anglicization of, 31, 33; politics of, 15, 34; society in, 18. *See also* New England

New Jersey, 11, 117; fiscal policies of, 229; slavery in, 188, 193, 201; wars of, 16. *See also* middle colonies

New Model Army, 74

New Netherland, 11, 84

Newport, R.I., 16, 197–98

New Sweden, 11

New Voyages to North America, 92

New York, 10, 11, 23, 46; Anglicization of, 34; Church of England in, 130–31; fiscal policies of, 228, 229, 231; Indian relations of, 191, 202; political culture of, 36; politics of, 23, 34; relations of with Haudenosaunee, 96, 102; and Revolution, 200; slavery in, 188, 193–96, 201; society in, 15, 39; warfare of, 16. *See also* middle colonies; Restoration colonies

New York City, 14, 16, 130, 131, 189, 193–96, 243

New York Slave Conspiracy Trials (1741), 193–96

Nicholson, Francis, 130

North Carolina: Church of England in, 130; migration to, 10; Regulator movement of, 39; wars of, 16, 186. *See also* southern colonies

northern states, 202

Notes on the State of Virginia (1785), 218

Nova Scotia, 115, 116, 117

Oglethorpe, James, 193, 195

Ohio Country, 200, 212

Olwell, Robert, 60

Oneidas, 99, 100, 200

Onondagas, 86, 103, 104

Ordinance of Laborers (1349), 61, 64

Osgood, Herbert Levi, 245

Oswego, 87, 94, 95

Otreouti, 102, 103, 104

Ottawas, 105

Oxford University, 23

Paine, Thomas, 208

Parkinson, Robert, 199

Parkman, Francis, 109

Parliament (Great Britain): colonial policies of, 18, 153–78, 181, 182, 238; crown relations of, 27; factions of, 15, 243

Parsons, Moses, 169

Passions and the Interests, 248

Paxton Boys, 39, 187

Peace of Paris. *See* Treaty of Paris

Penn, Thomas, 39

Penn, William, 23

Pennsylvania, 14, 23, 25, 182; Anglicization of, 34; assembly of, 143, 227–28; Church of England in, 141–44, 151; council of, 210; English heritage of, 11; fiscal policies of, 227–28, 229–30, 231; Fries's Rebellion of, 234; Indian relations of, 184, 187; political culture of, 36; politics of, 34, 37; religion in, 25, 128, 134, 141; and Revolution, 200; slavery in, 188, 201; wars of, 16, 117, 186. *See also* middle colonies

People's Army, 111

Pequots, 200

Pequot War (1636–37), 114

Peters, Richard, 142, 143, 144

Philadelphia, 14, 16, 34, 52, 134

Philadelphia Aurora, 214

Pickney, Thomas, 207

Pitt, William, 40, 41, 43, 45, 47

Pocahontas, 184

Pontiac's War (1763–64), 186

Popish Plot (1678), 23, 25

Potawatomies, 105

Powhatan Wars, 184

Pownall, Thomas, 44

praying Indians, 184–85

Preble, Edward, 201

Presbyterians, 126, 128, 132, 134, 141, 143, 147–50, 151, 187
Presbytery of Philadelphia, 134
Prince George's County, Md., 193
Prussia, 110
Puritanism. *See* Congregationalism

Quakers (Society of Friends), 24, 34, 134, 141, 145, 149, 189
Quartering Act (1765), 44
Quasi-War (1798–1800), 216, 220, 233–34
Québec City, 237
Queen Anne's War. *See* War of the Spanish Succession
Questier, Michael, 246

race, 4, 181–204
Randolph, Edward, 130
Randolph, Peyton, 147, 198
rationalism, 142
Reed, Joseph, 210, 230
Reformation (Protestant), 63
regulator movements, 39
Reid, John, 117
Rensselaerswyck, 39
Restoration colonies, 23, 25. *See also* New York; Pennsylvania; South Carolina
Revere, Paul, 120
Rhode Island, 188, 202, 229, 231. *See also* New England
Richter, Daniel K., 122
Rockingham, Charles Watson Wentworth, 2d Marquess of, 46, 47
Rolfe, John, 184
Roman Catholicism, 23, 133, 138, 143
Royal Navy, 207, 208–10
"Rule Britannia," 192
"Rules and Regulations for the Government of the Navy," 209

St. Mary's City, 192
Salem Witch Trials, 191

Schenectady, N.Y., 192
Schlesinger, Arthur, Sr., 17
Scotland, 29, 73, 74, 119, 134
Scots-Irish, 147, 187
Secker, Thomas, 139, 152
Second Amendment (U.S.), 119
Senecas, 98, 105, 192
Separate Baptists, 149–50
Seven Years' War (1754–63), 26, 40, 45, 110, 181, 186, 227, 231, 235
Seybert, Adam, 221–21
Shaftesbury, Anthony Ashley, Earl of, 24
Shawnees, 186
Shays's Rebellion (1786–87), 229
Shirley, William, 110, 117
Shute, Daniel, 157–58, 164
Shy, John, 42, 116, 117
"Significance of the Frontier in American History," 109
Silver, Peter, 118
slavery, 1, 3, 35, 60, 201, 246–47; development of in American colonies, 12; English influence on, 60–82; gradual emancipation laws against, 197, 201–2; and Indians, 185; and the law, 187–88; and Revolution, 196, 197–98, 199–200; spread of, 201; varieties of, 187–88
slaves, missionary work among, 132
Smith, William, 144
Society for the Propagation of the Gospel in Foreign Parts, 129, 131–32, 141, 150, 152
Society of Friends. *See* Quakers
Somerset v. Stewart (1772), 190
South Carolina, 23, 35, 60, 248; Barbadian influence on, 60; Church of England in, 130; Commons House of, 14; crises of, 25; English heritage of, 11; legal profession of, 13; political culture of, 36, 37; slavery in, 35, 185, 188, 189, 193, 199; society in, 12, 18; wars of, 25, 185, 195. *See also* Restoration colonies; southern colonies

southern colonies: Anglicization of, 37;
Barbadian influence on, 60; consumer
culture of, 59; economy of, 13; planter
culture of, 59; political culture of,
35, 36; politics of, 15; religion in, 126;
slavery in, 35, 60; society in, 13; utopian
vision for. *See also* Georgia; Mary-
land; North Carolina; South Carolina;
Virginia
Spain, 30
Spanish colonies, 2
Spanish Empire, 111
Spotswood, Alexander, 187
Stamp Act (1765), 18, 45, 46, 47, 53,
154–55, 156, 167
Stamp Act crisis, 34, 43, 153, 155, 157
Statute of Artificers, 65–67
Statute of Laborers (1351), 61, 64
Stiles, Ezra, 20
Stoddert, Benjamin, 214
Stono Rebellion (1739), 193
Strong, Rowan, 131
Sugar Act (1764), 43, 45, 46, 47, 53, 155
Susquehannocks, 98
Swanwick, John, 233
Swift, Zephaniah, 233

Tea Act (1773), 177
Teganissorens, 86–87, 101, 106
Tenison, Thomas, 130
Thirty Years' War, 117
Toleration Act (1689), 128, 131, 140,
146–47, 149, 152
Tomlins, Christopher, 67, 187
Tories (America). *See* Loyalists
Tories (Great Britain), 29
Townshend Acts (1767), 48, 154, 158, 166
Townshend Acts crisis, 18, 43
Townshend, Charles, 46
Treaty of Greenville (1794), 200
Treaty of Paris (1783), 200
Trenchard, John, 207

Tripoli, 212, 218
Tucker, John, 167–69
Tunis, 212
Turner, Charles, 172
Turner, Frederick Jackson, 84, 109, 110,
111, 113, 118, 119
Tuscarora War (1711–15), 186

United States, 4; anti-Anglicization of, 50;
Articles of Confederation of, 50; Congress of, 52, 210, 211, 213, 215, 219, 220,
222, 223, 224, 229, 230, 232–33; Constitution of, 53, 119, 202, 212, 226; Constitutional Convention of, 50; elections
of, 216, 235; fiscal policies of, 230, 231,
232–38; House of Representatives of,
215, 221; Indian relations of, 200–201;
national bank of, 206; national identity
of, 15–16, 17, 48, 54; navy of, 207–8,
211–15, 220; racial citizenship of, 196,
202–4; racial laws of, 202–3; regional-
ism of, 202; slavery in, 201; tax policies
of, 226; taxing power of, 52; wars of,
120, 200, 212–13, 217, 218, 220–21, 223
Upper Canada, 237
Ury, John, 194
USS *Constitution*, 209, 222
USS *United States*, 222

Vagrancy Act (1547), 66, 69
Virginia: architecture of, 133; Church of
England in, 130, 139, 144–52; clergy of,
13; English heritage of, 11; fiscal policies
of, 228, 229; founding of, 21; governors
of, 149; House of Burgesses of, 14, 145,
189, 197, 228; Indian policies of, 54, 55;
Indian relations of, 184; land policies
of, 55; legal profession of, 13; migration
to, 10; missionary work of, 184; political culture of, 35, 36, 37, 38; politics of,
14, 24, 241; racial laws of, 189; relations
of with Haudenosaunee, 96, 99–100;

religion in, 16, 126, 128, 141, 146–47; slavery in 188, 189, 201; society in, 15, 18, 25, 29, 54; territorial expansion of, 54; wars of, 16, 184, 186. *See also* Chesapeake; southern colonies
Virginia Gazette, 197
Virginia Plan, 51, 52
Viscount Bolingbroke, 28, 35

Wabenakis, 191
Wales, 74
Walpole, Robert, 26, 31, 35, 227
Wampanoags, 115, 200
wampum, 99
War for Independence. *See* American Revolution
War Hawks, 220, 222
War of 1812, 200, 212, 217, 220–21, 222, 223, 224, 226
War of Jenkin's Ear (1739–43), 191, 192
War of the League of Augsburg (1688–97), 27
War of the Spanish Succession (1702–13), 86
Wars of the Three Kingdoms, 69, 73, 74
Washington, D.C., 52
Washington, George, 52, 206, 213; presidential administration of, 200, 206

Weigley, Russell R., 116
Wentworth, Benning, 31, 32, 35
Wentworth, John, 31, 32
West Indies, 2, 3, 32, 41, 45, 47, 185, 212, 214, 220; development of slavery in, 12, 240
Whigs, 25, 27, 29
Whiskey Rebellion (1794), 232, 233
White, Richard, 85, 97
Whitefield, George, 134–35
whiteness, 54, 181, 189–90
White Pines Act, 31, 33, 40, 44
white racism, 181–85, 189–96, 201, 202–4
Widgery, William, 222
William III, 29, 170, 192
William of Orange. *See* William III
Wilson, James, 230
Winthrop, John, 23, 153
Wolcott, Oliver, 234
Wolfe, James, 116
Wood, Gordon S., 38, 51
Wren, Christopher, 137
Wright, Robert, 222

Yale College, 20, 137
Yale University, 109
Yamasee War (1715–17), 25
Young, Alfred, 43, 52

ACKNOWLEDGMENTS

A number of professional and personal considerations served as the seeds of this volume. On the professional side, the editors recognized the need to reconsider the Anglicization concept in light of trends that have reshaped early American history over the last few decades, particularly in terms of transatlantic, American Indian, and cultural history. Furthermore we sensed the need to familiarize a new generation of scholars with Anglicization, given that the articles in which John M. Murrin developed the idea lie scattered in volumes that are now generally out of print. Personally, we saw this as an opportunity to honor Murrin's scholarship and mentoring. All of the editors and contributors to this volume were fortunate to be students of Murrin's. To the extent that their work in this volume captures the breadth and depth of the early American field, it is largely because of Murrin's example.

The publication of this book was made possible by the generous support of the McNeil Center for Early American Studies, an institution with which Murrin has proudly been affiliated for many years. We are especially grateful to Daniel Richter and Amy Baxter Bellamy of the McNeil Center, who provided gracious support and invaluable assistance at every stage of the creation of this volume; to Evan Haefeli, Gary Kornblith, Elizabeth Lewis Pardoe, and Danny Vickers for their early involvement in the project; to Ned Landsman for his penetrating critique of the first draft of the manuscript; and to Robert Lockhart of the University of Pennsylvania Press for his encouragement and guidance along the way.

We dedicate this volume, of course, to John M. Murrin. Murrin always let his graduate students know that he considered them to be junior colleagues, that he expected them to succeed, and that he planned to learn from them just as they did from him. Collectively, we will never be able to balance the ledger, but we hope he will accept this book as evidence that his commitment to teaching and the example of his scholarly intellect and integrity continue to influence those proud to call themselves his students.